AF631662

SIAM & CHINA

Through the Lens of John Thomson

RIVER BOOKS

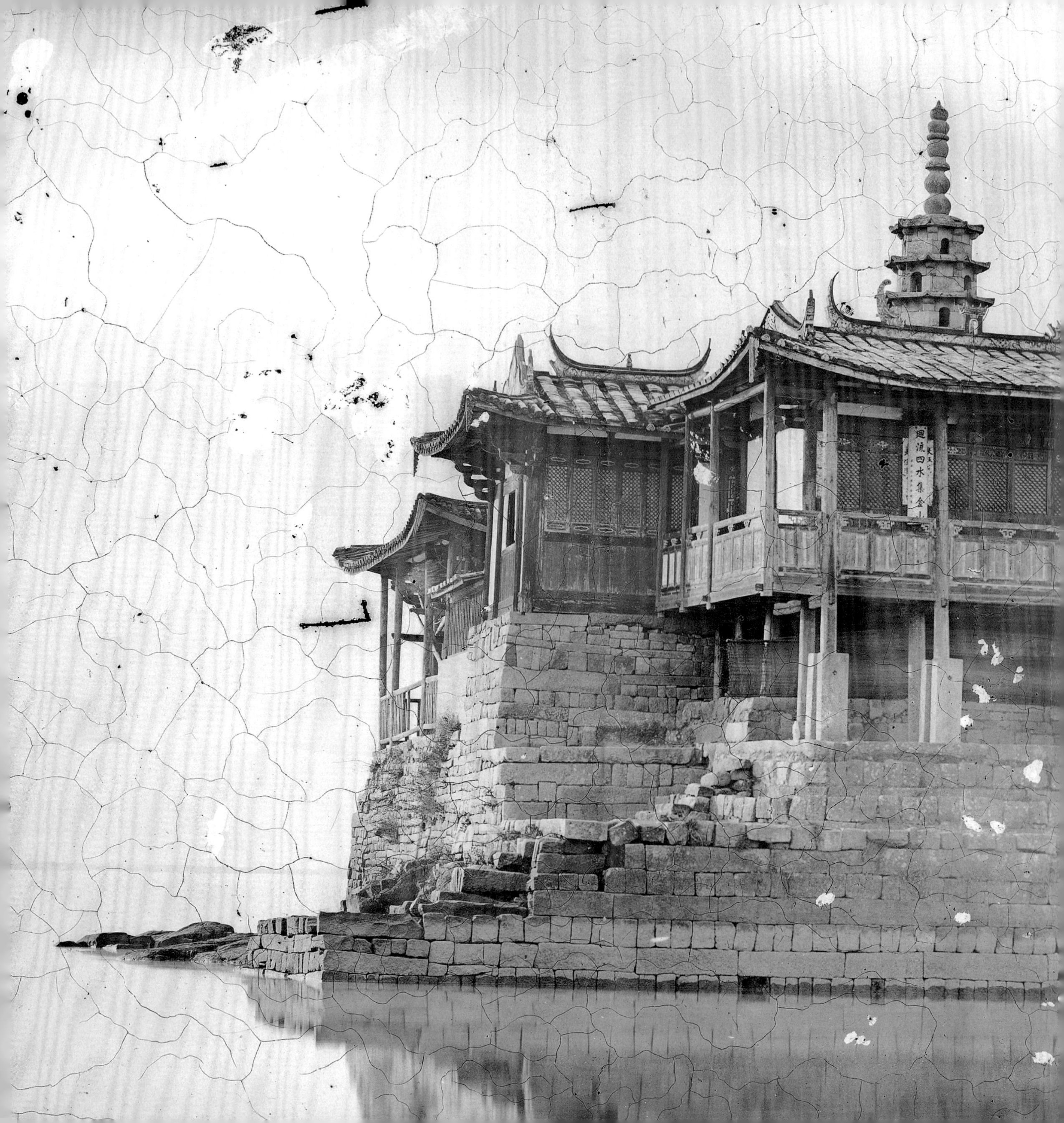

廻流四水集金

SIAM & CHINA

Through the Lens of John Thomson

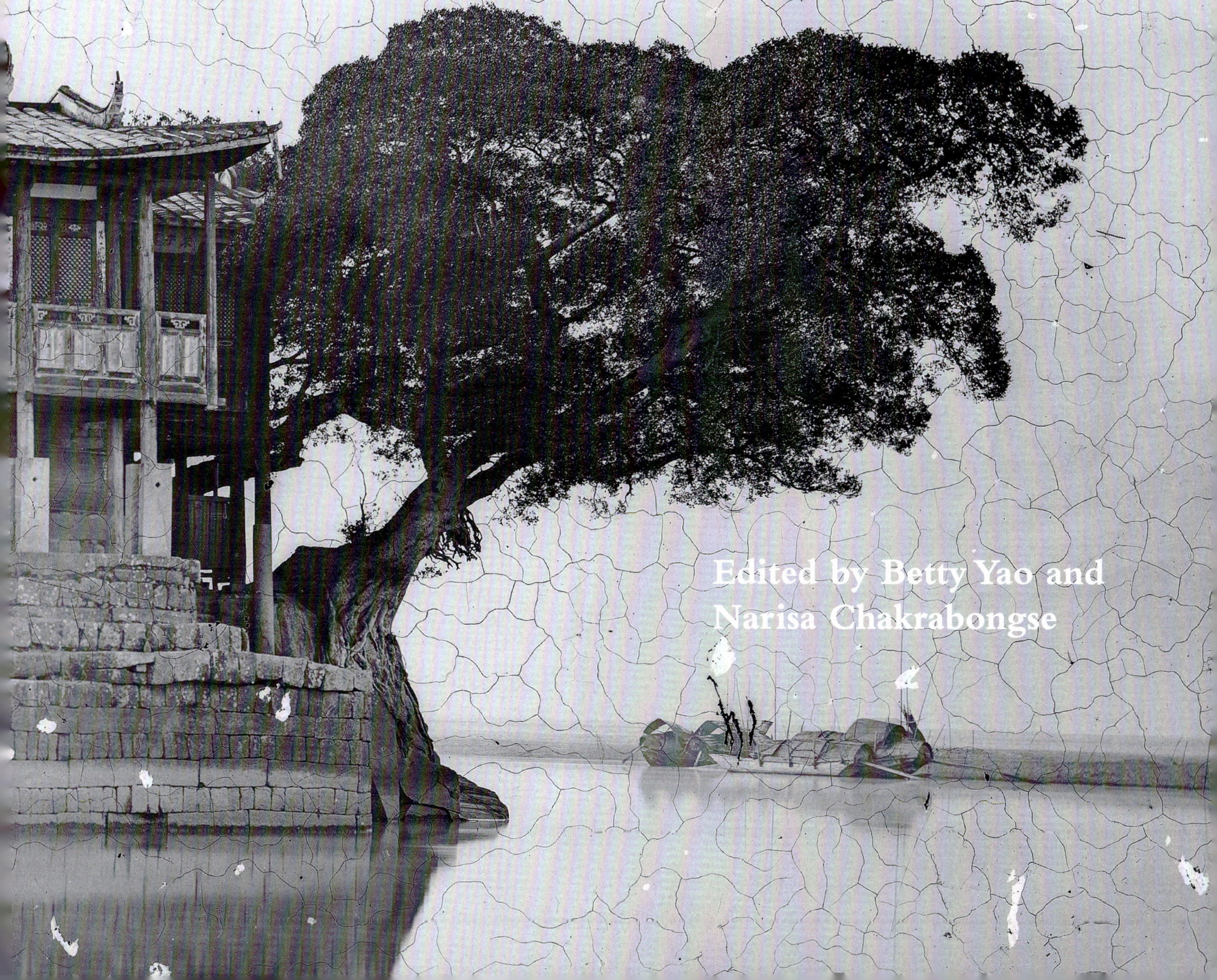

Edited by Betty Yao and Narisa Chakrabongse

First edition published in 2023 by
River Books Press Ltd.,
396/1 Maharaj Road, Phra Borommaharajawang,
Phra Nakorn, Bangkok Bangkok 10200 Thailand
T: (66 2) 225-0139, 225-9574
E: order@riverbooksbk.com
www.riverbooksbk.com

River Books   riverbooksbk   @riverbooks

Copyright collective work © River Books 2023
Copyright John Thomson photographs © Wellcome Collection, London
except where indicated otherwise

All rights reserved. No part of this publication may be reproduced, stored in a retrieval system, or transmitted, in any form, or by any means electronic, chemical, mechanical, photocopying, recording or otherwise, without the prior permission of the publisher.

Editor: Narisa Chakrabongse

Design: River Books Press

ISBN 978 616 451 069 2

Printed in Thailand by Sirivatana Interprint Co., Ltd.

Contents

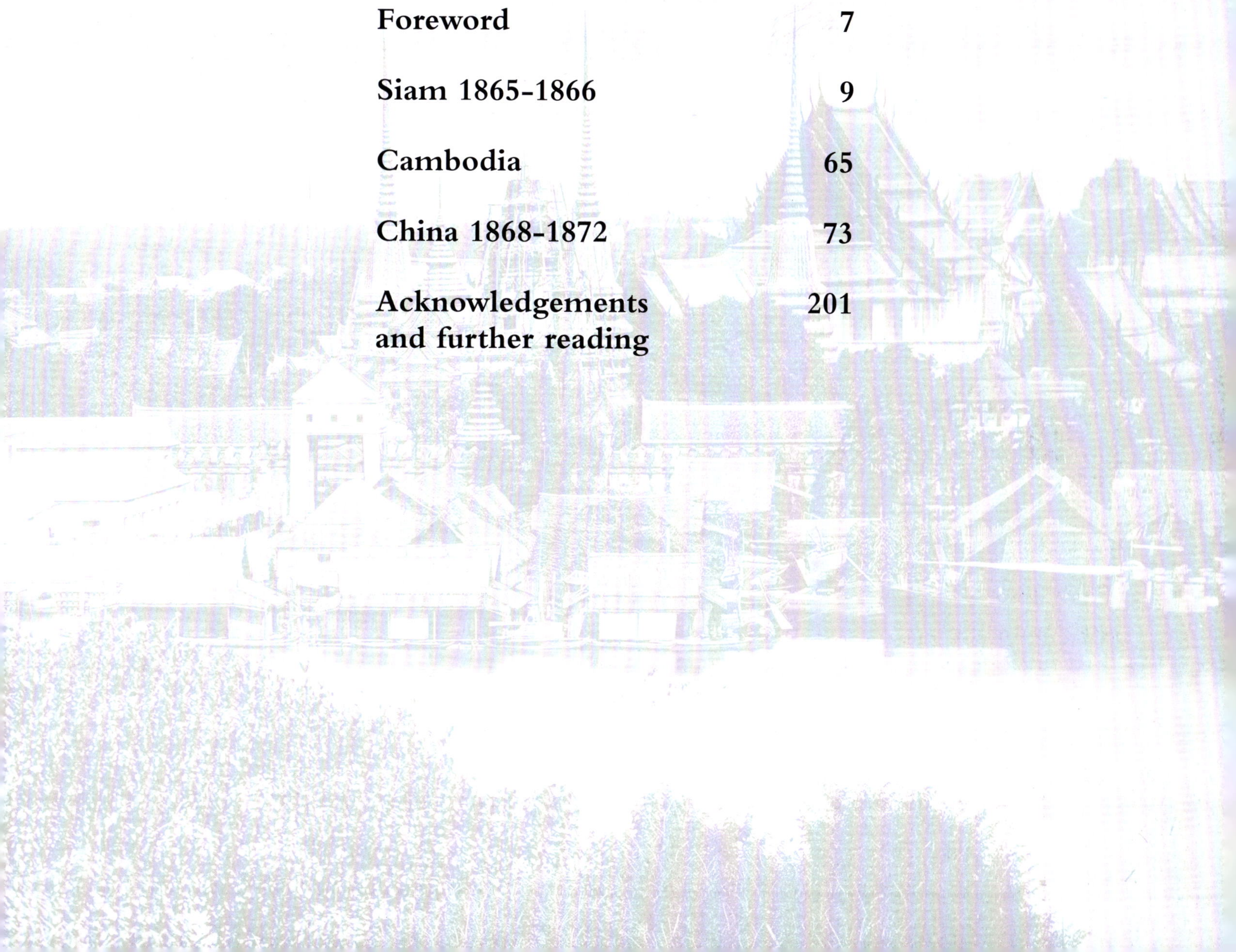

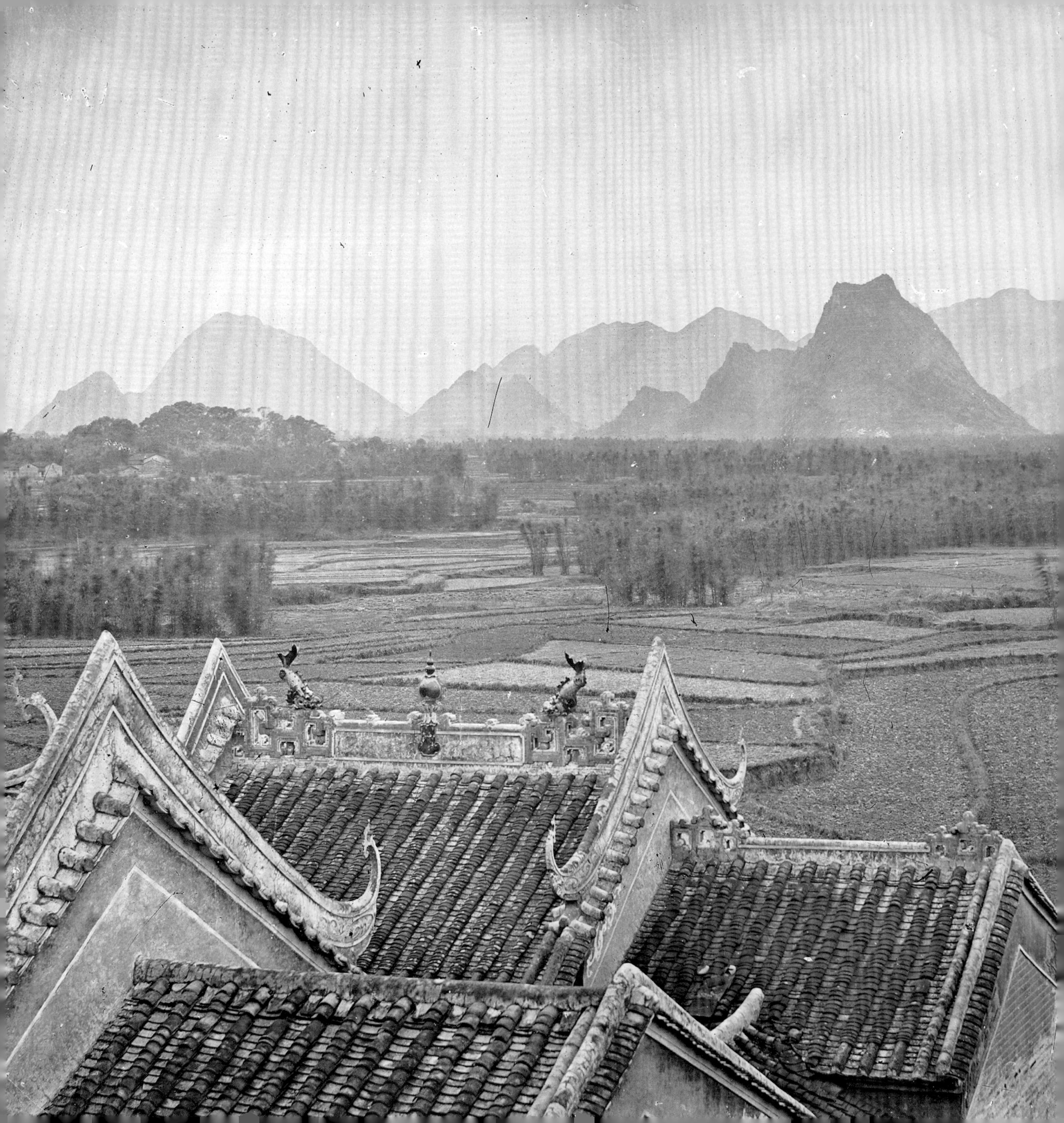

Foreword

My first introduction to the photographs of John Thomson was when I attended a talk by William Schupbach of the Wellcome Collection in London, on Thomson's life and work. As soon as I saw these images, I was immediately fascinated by them. Some months later, we met again at a reception. My husband Paul casually asked William whether Thomson's collection had ever been exhibited in China. We were both surprised when William said no and added that it would be wonderful if they could be seen by a wider public. That chance remark resulted in two international touring exhibitions, *China through the Lens of John Thomson* and *Siam through the Lens of John Thomson,* which have been seen by over one million visitors in over 30 cities across three continents. The *Siam* exhibition was a co-operation with my special friend and publisher Narisa Chakrabongse. We have been overwhelmed by the many enthusiastic comments by people of all backgrounds and age groups.

We hope today's audience and readers will enjoy and learn something new from these images and will be inspired to cherish Thailand and China's heritage and history. Photographic enthusiasts will marvel at the fine quality of his work, particularly given the arduous conditions that a 19th century photographer had to endure. Designers will admire the clothes, hairstyles, furniture, and architecture and be able to study them in fine detail. Historians will revel in the street and domestic scenes, observing the day-to-day lives of people from a time past. We were especially surprised by the large number of images of women, showing Thomson's remarkable ability to communicate across language and cultural barriers. To enhance the enjoyment of this book our contributors and research team have done excellent work in producing informative and engaging text and captions, setting these images in the context of their time.

This book and these exhibitions have been a labour of love and would never have been possible without the enthusiastic encouragement and support of my family, friends and of the many museums and institutions, especially the Wellcome Collection. It has been a joy to work with Narisa Chakrabongse and the publishing team at River Books.

Betty Yao MBE and Narisa Chakrabongse

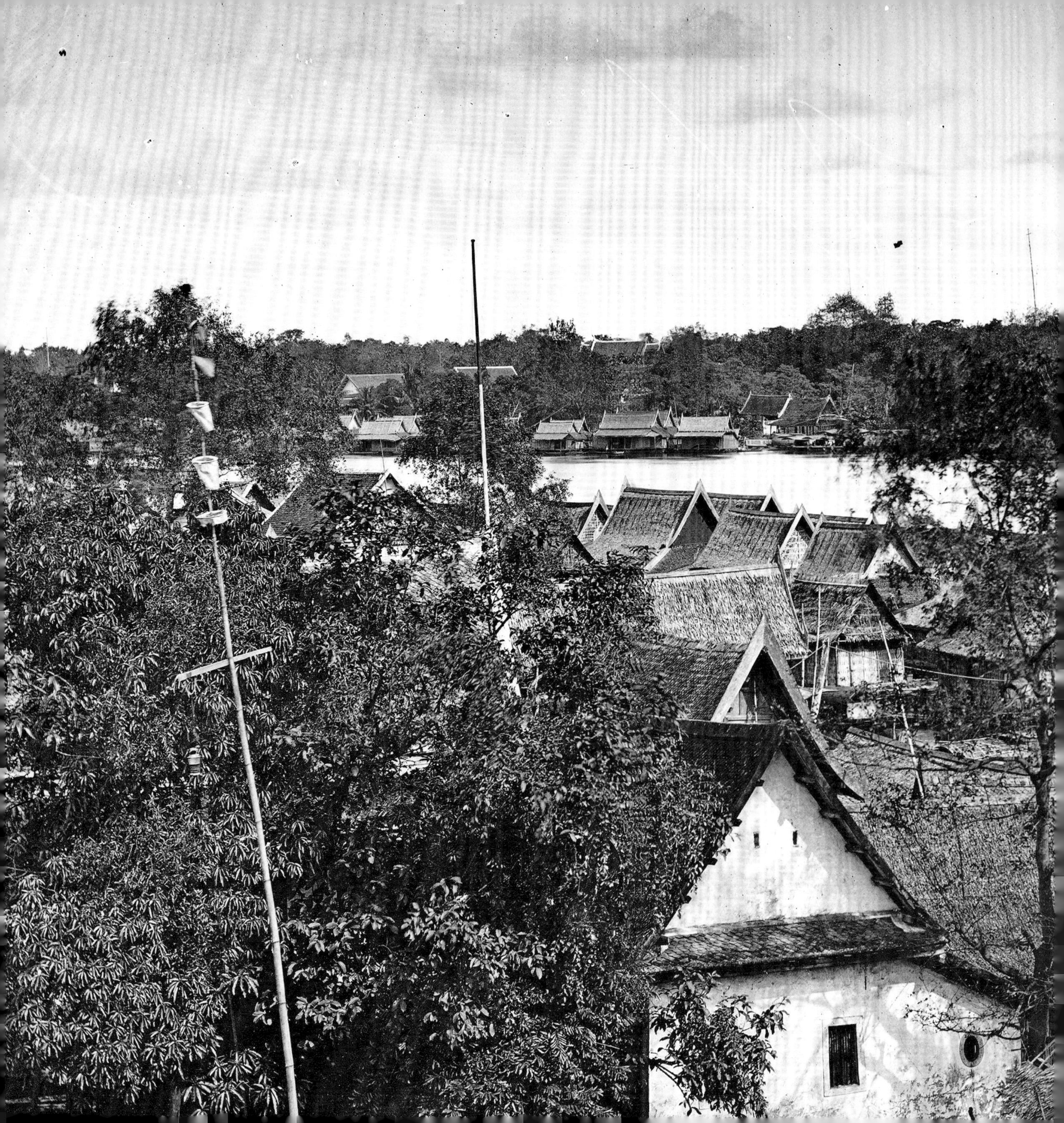

Siam 1865-1866

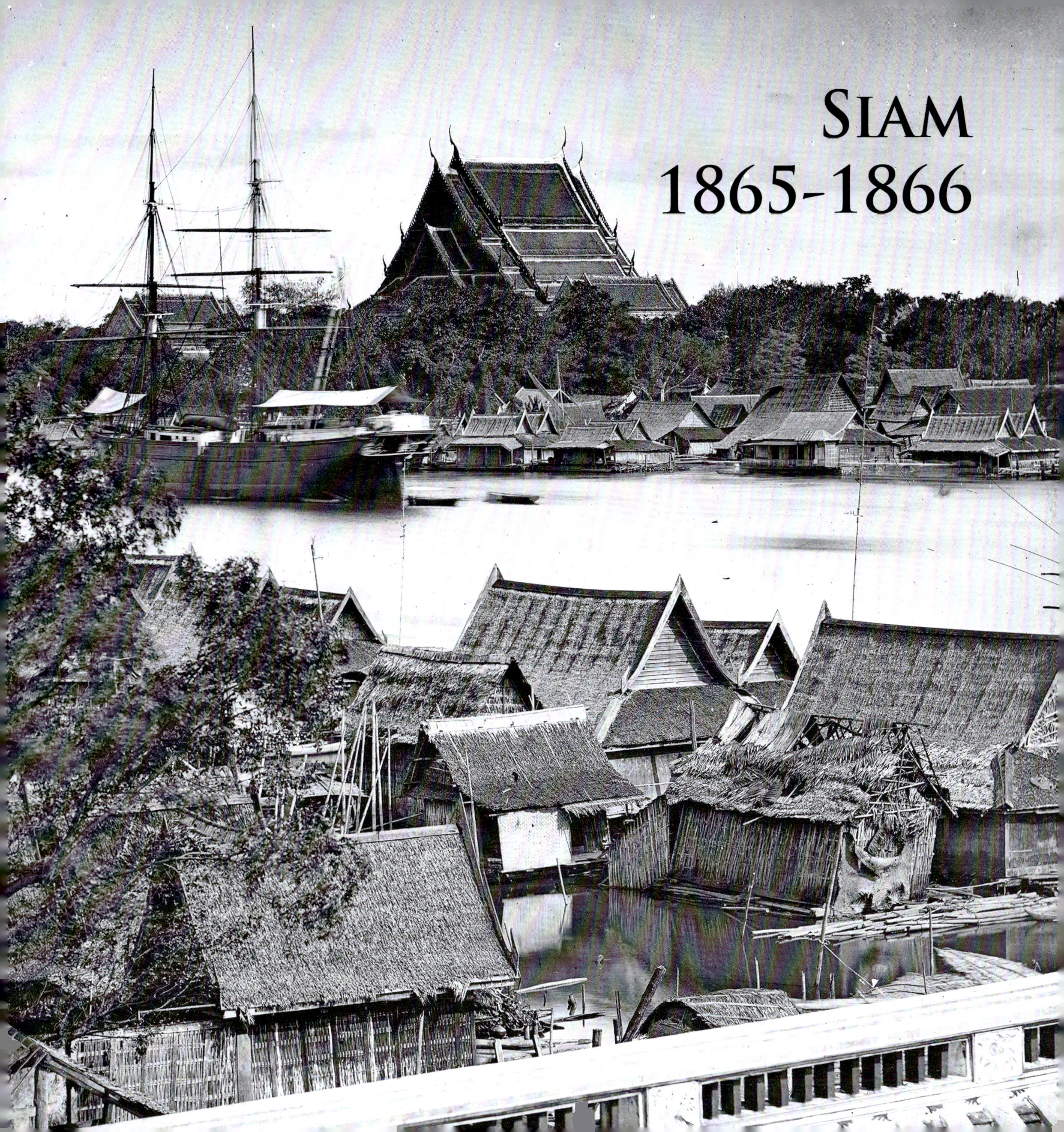

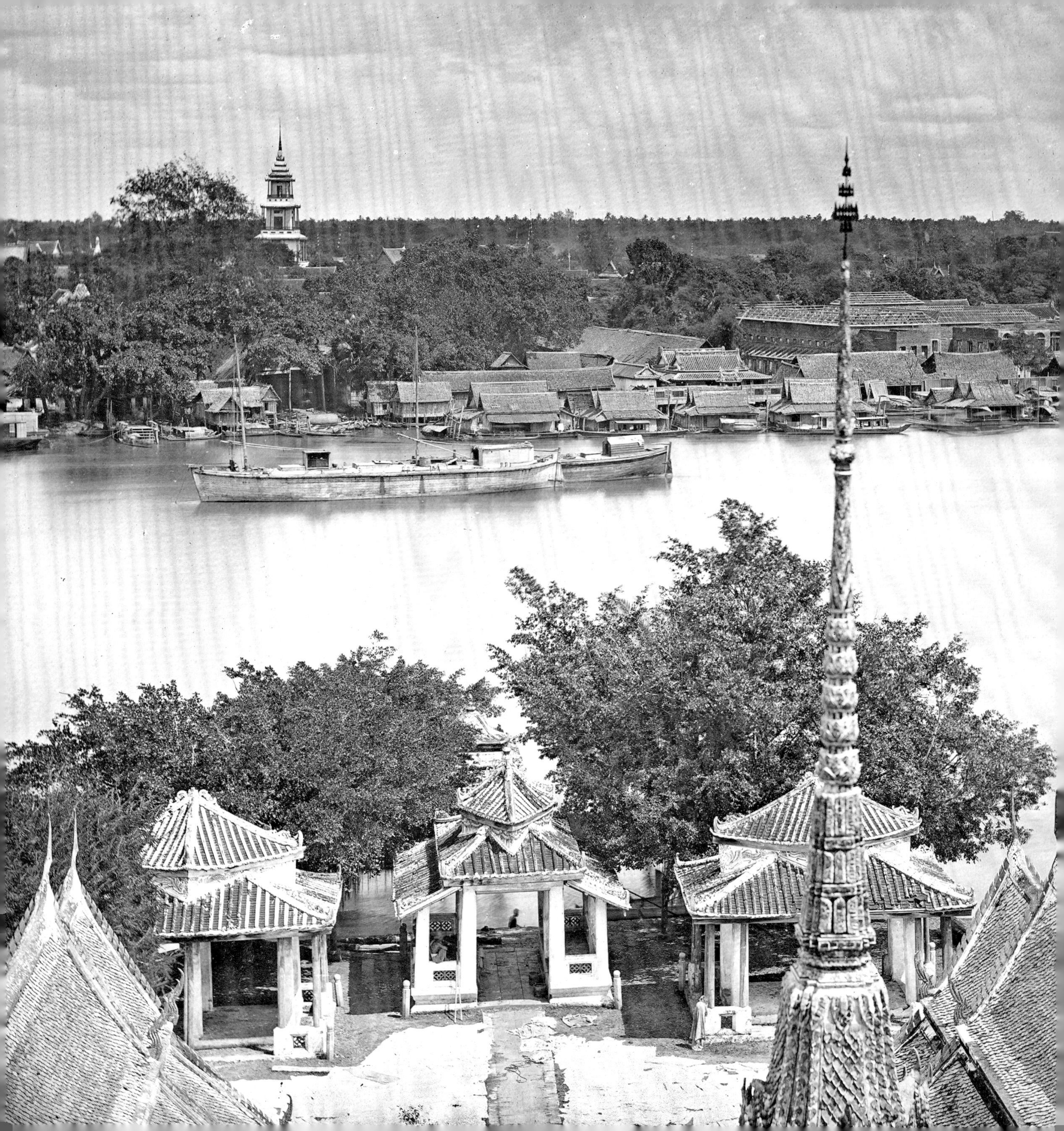

SIAM 1865-1866

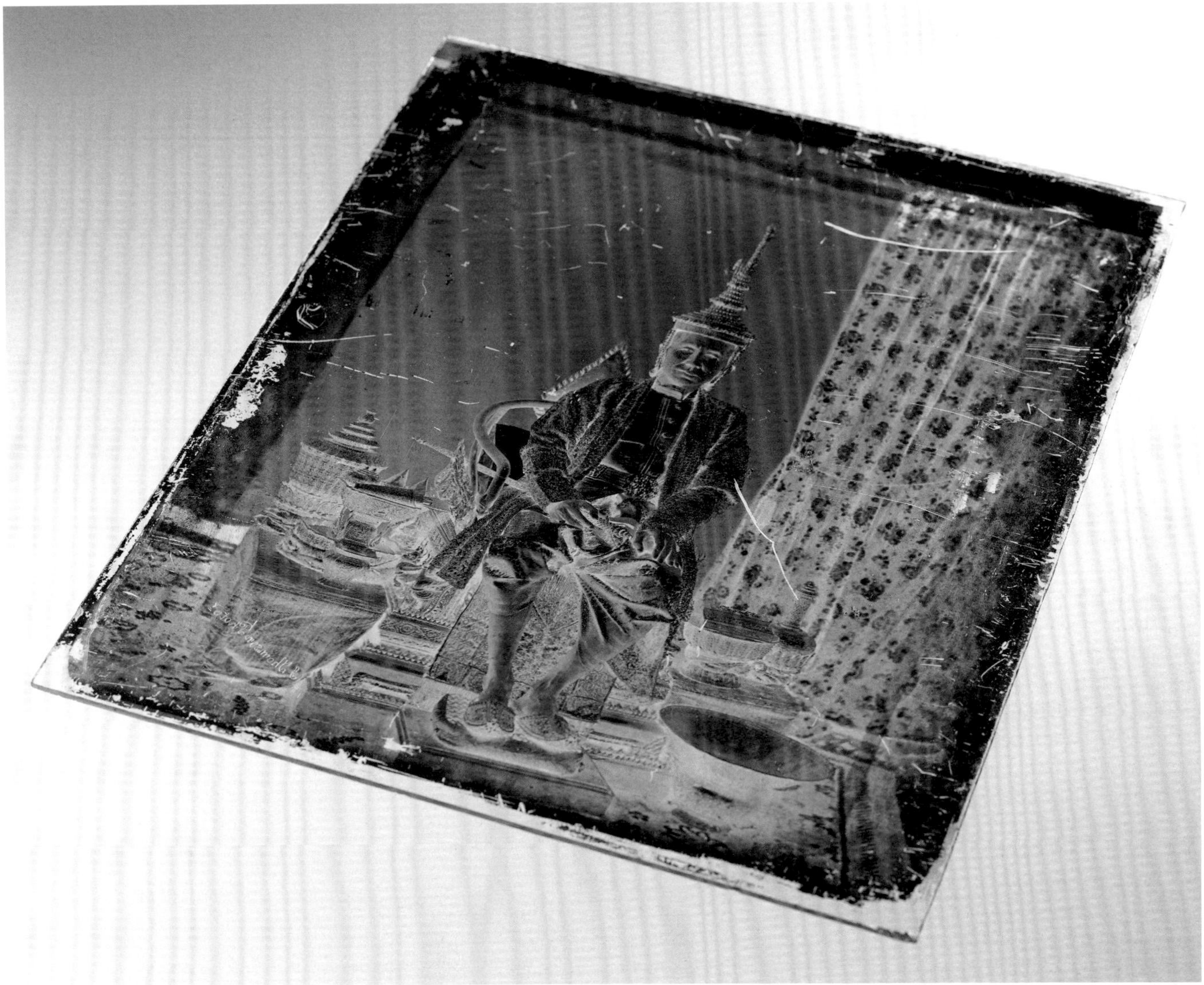

Original glass negative of the photograph of King Mongkut shown on page 38. These are stored in the Wellcome Collection, London.

John Thomson's photographs of Thailand in the Wellcome Collection

William Schupbach, Wellcome Collection, London

The photographs by John Thomson now in the Wellcome Collection in London were acquired by Henry S. Wellcome in 1921 and they form one of the Wellcome Collection's best known possessions. The collection consists of nearly 700 photographs, mostly in the form of glass sheets coated with the chemical collodion forming a negative image of the photograph. Digital copies of these, reversed to give a positive image, were made in the 1990s and then again at a much higher resolution in 2009. They include 59 photographs of Thailand, and 64 of Cambodia. The subjects were described by John Thomson in a letter to Wellcome on 12 May 1920 as:

> *"antiquities, arts, architecture, industries, and evidence of evolution. The regions include Siam, Cochin China, Cambodia, China and the islands of Formosa and Cyprus".*

Although Thomson achieved fame as the photographer of China, he listed "Siam, Cochin China, Cambodia" in that order and before China because that was the order of his travels in south Asia. The good start which he got in Siam (Thailand), Cambodia, Vietnam and the Lao region laid the groundwork for his later work in China, England and elsewhere. His classic photographs of Beijing, the Chinese Treaty Ports, and of street life in London could never have come into existence without his successful beginnings in Bangkok.

Siam was a good place to start because it was right at the beginning of its westernization boom. In bringing the new western chemical and optical techniques of photography to Bangkok, Thomson was in the right place at the right time. The boom was encouraged by the man who became his patron in Siam, none other than the King, H.M. King Mongkut.

H.M. King Mongkut ruled from 1851 to 1868. His character was in many respects similar to that of his contemporary, the Consort of Queen Victoria, Prince Albert (1819-1861). Mongkut learnt to speak good English, was a scholar of Latin and astronomy, was versed in Buddhist scriptures, and supported the introduction of western science and technology into Thailand. He was well-disposed to friendship with Great Britain and France, and openly supported the opponents of slavery in the American Civil War. He was very helpful to John Thomson when Thomson arrived in Bangkok, sitting for photographs and helping him to visit Angkor Wat. He dominates Thomson's photographs of Thailand in much the same way that Prince Gong anchored his photographs of China.

Thomson left his own written account of his visit to Thailand and Cambodia in his book The Straits of Malacca, Indo-China and China, which was published in 1875. From that account we learn that Thomson arrived in Thailand in September 1865. The port of Samut Prakan did not impress him, but as he neared Bangkok city, the scenery grew more promising to his artist's eye. "Palms, fruit-trees, and groves of feathery bamboo, diversify the plains; and the latter, when covered with half-grown crops of rice, present a vast surface of vivid and beautiful green." On 28th September he arrived in Bangkok and "steamed up through the floating city in the

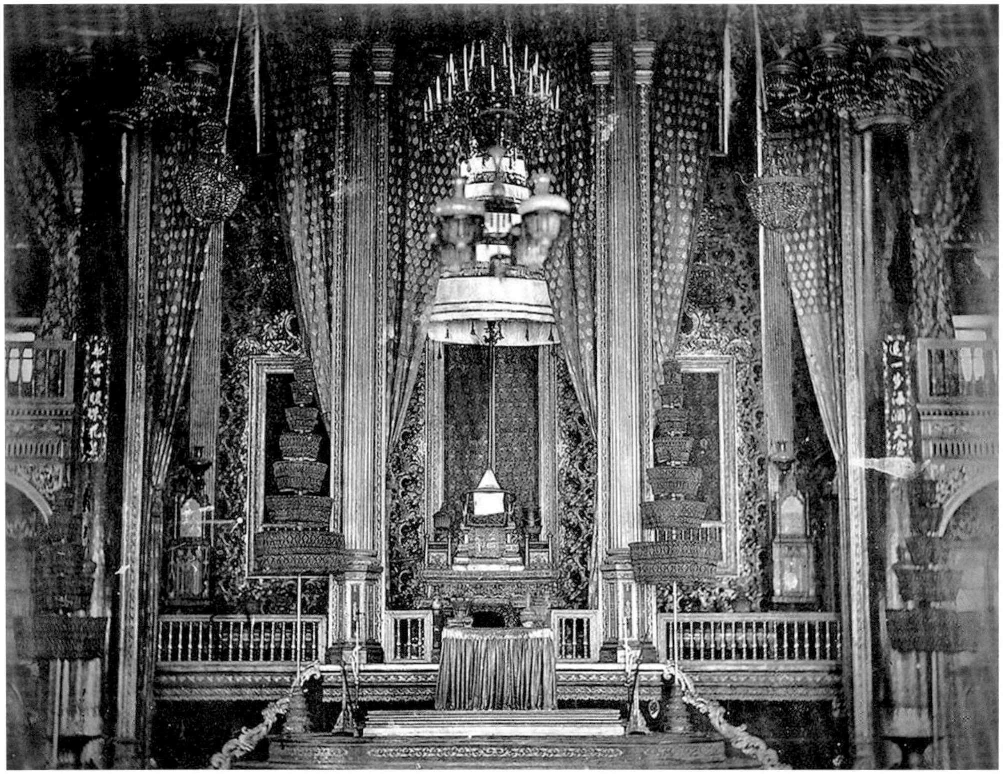

The interior of the Aphinao Niwet Throne Hall decorated in an impressive mix of Siamese and Western styles.

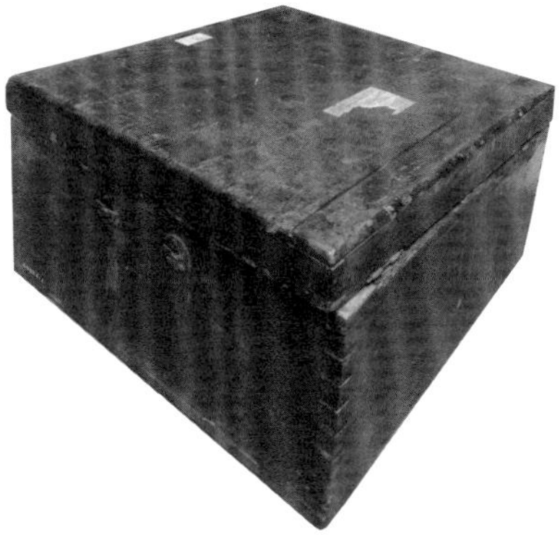

The sturdy wooden box in which Thomson stored his glass negatives, now preserved in the Wellcome Collection.

dimness of the early morning light". Naturally he was impressed by the temple spires, "decorated, most of them, with rich mosaics of glass, porcelain and enamel, and [which] present, as they shine in the sunlight, a dazzling coruscation which is difficult to describe."

Thomson's ambition was to photograph the King's palace, for which purpose he asked the British Consul if he could obtain permission. Not only was permission granted, but the King was pleased to appoint a day, Monday 6th October 1865, on which Thomson could take a portrait of him as well.

To introduce Thomson to the court, the King appointed his relative whom Thomson names as Krum-mun-alongkot (Prince Alongkot Pricha). The King wrote to Thomson that his royal brother "was well understanding of the work of taking photographs, and being with Mr Thomson will have a good opportunity to do according to his pleasure in and about this palace". This prince's duty at court was to advise the king on astrology and on technological questions. Thomson was struck and it seems amused by the prince's collection of western gadgets of all sorts, including a telegraph machine, an electroplated coffee pot, watch-tools, turning lathes, "a very fine sextant", telescopes, revolvers, brass wire and beer-bottles.

The prince and Thomson arrived at the palace, and a guard of soldiers presented arms as they passed through the entrance gates. They entered a courtyard and joined a group of nobles. All this was a very new experience for the young Scotsman, then aged 28. Thomson described what happened as follows:

"After a pleasant refreshment of fruit, cake, and wine, we were informed that his majesty was engaged in his morning devotions, and that in his absence we could amuse ourselves by examining the objects of interest in the audience hall. This palace has been constructed partially in a foreign style. A flight of broad marble steps conducts us within the audience hall, and facing us, as we enter, is the throne of state, ablaze with gold and jewels, and erected in the centre of the back wall of the apartment.

"The furniture in the room made up a miscellaneous collection of Chinese, Siamese and European wares; the pillars were covered with polished brass to the height of four feet above their bases. At one end of the hall were life-sized portraits of Napoleon III and the Empress of the French, while a well-executed picture of the late Siamese King adorned the opposite side of the apartment.

"A shrill blast of horns heralded the approach of the King and caused us hastily to descend into the court. His Majesty entered through a massive gateway, and I must confess that I felt much impressed by his appearance, as I had never been in the presence of an anointed sovereign before. He stood about five feet eight inches, and his figure was erect and commanding; but an expression of severe gravity was settled on his somewhat haggard face. His dress was a robe of spotless white, which reached right down to his feet; his head was bare.

"I was admiring the simplicity and purity of this attire, when His Majesty beckoned to me to approach him, and informed me that he wished to have his portrait taken as he knelt in an attitude of prayer. I accordingly adjusted my instrument, but not without a feeling of some surprise, for I had thought, incorrectly, as I afterwards discovered, that a Buddhist had no need of prayer. All was prepared beneath a space in the court, which had been canopied and carpeted for this special purpose; when, just as I was about to take the photograph, His Majesty changed his mind, and without a word to anyone, passed suddenly out of sight.

"I though this a strange proceeding, and fancied I must have given him some offence; but it was possibly only one of his practical jokes. I appealed to the Prince; but his reply was simply that 'the King does everything which is right, and if I were to accost him now, he might conclude his morning's work by cutting off my head.'

"As that would have been a result distasteful to His Royal Highness, we patiently waited, and at length the King reappeared, dressed this time in a sort of French Field Marshal's uniform. There was no cotton stuff visible about his person now, not even stockings. The portrait was a great success, and His Majesty afterwards sat in his court robes, requesting me to place him where and how I pleased. I consulted the Prince, who said, 'Yes, place him, but do not for the life of you lay hands on him, more especially on his thrice sacred head.'

"Here was a difficulty. How to pose an Oriental potentate who has ideas of his own as to propriety in attitude, and that too without touching a fold of his garments? I told the King in plain English what I wanted to do, and he said, 'Mr Town-shun, do what you require for the excellency of your photograph.' He enquired my nationality. 'Ah! You are Scotchman, and speak English I can understand; there are Englishmen here who have not understanding of their own language when I speak.'

"When all had been finished, His Majesty thanked me and retired, and then the Krum-mun-alongkot invited me to join him at a table spread with Siamese and foreign delicacies. The nobles also, at his highness's invitation, added their presence to the repast."

This is a precious account of Thomson's two photographs of King Mongkut, one in Western military costume and the other in his Thai robes. Unfortunately Thomson does not describe the circumstances in which he took the other portraits. One he describes as the Prime Minister, possibly the Phra Kralahom named by Moffatt (*Mongkut the King of Siam*, p. 75). The other he names as the King's brother: he resembles other portraits of Prince Wongsa Dhiraj Snid (1808-1871). Prince Wongsa was a physician who shared the King's

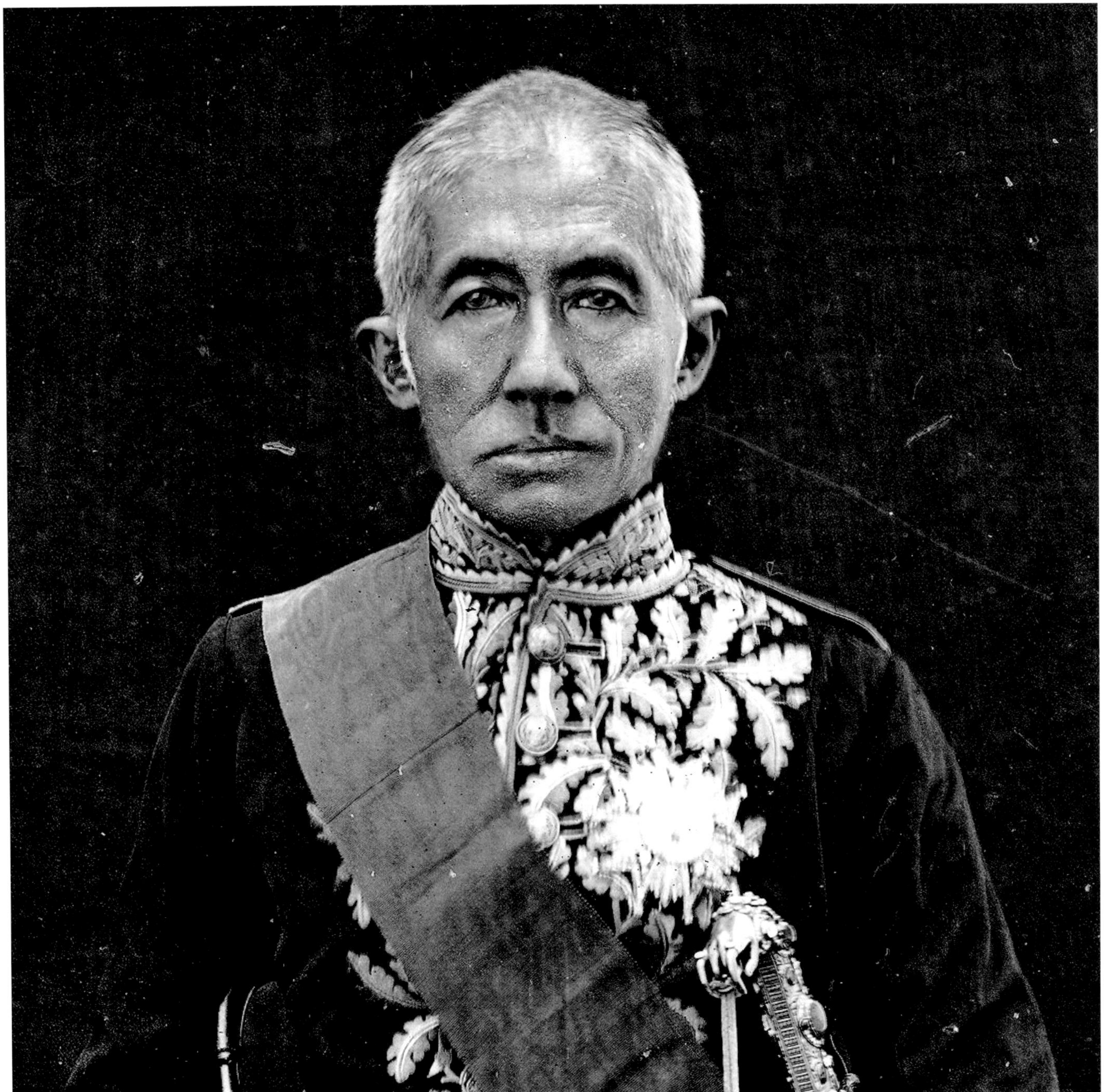

THE REIGN OF KING MONGKUT (r. 1851-1868)

Maj. Gen. M. R. Supbhawat Kasemsri and Rachanee Supvichit

The reign of King Mongkut was one of the most remarkable epochs in Siamese history. In a short period of only 17 years, when the country was feeling the pressure of Western expansionism for the first time, a series of treaties were signed with, among others, Britain (1855), France (1856), and the USA (1856). These ended the crown monopoly on trade and opened the country to western commerce. Prior to ascending the throne, the King had spent 27 years in the monkhood and he used the opportunity to reform the Buddhist Sangha, as well as studying Latin and English with missionaries, in particular Jean-Baptiste Pallegoix. In addition, the King was keenly interested in Western sciences such as geography and astronomy. Thus when John Thomson arrived in 1865, near the end of his reign, the King was well versed in Western ideas and was keen to exploit the relatively new science of photography. He granted the Scottish photographer unparalleled access to himself and several ceremonies in and near the Grand Palace.

Phra Bat Somdet Phra Poramenthra Maha Makut Phra Chom Klao Chao Yu Hua or King Rama IV, the fourth King of the Chakri Dynasty, formerly Prince Mongkut, was born on 18 October 1804, in Thonburi Palace, to King Rama II and Queen Srisuriyendra. He was one of the couple's three sons; his older brother died on the day he was born, and his younger sibling was called Prince Issaret Chuthamani (King Pinklao).

King Mongkut first learned to read and write about the Buddha's teachings with the then-Supreme Patriarch of Siam, and Somdej Phra Buddha Kosachan (Khun) of Wat Molee Lokayaram. Later, when he turned 9 years old, his father conferred on him an official name in a royal naming ceremony, and in 1816, when he was 13, a topknot cutting ceremony was held for him. The following year, after being ordained as a novice at the Temple of the Emerald Buddha, he spent seven months at Mahathat Temple before he left the monkhood to continue the education traditionally reserved for a Crown Prince. Among other skills, he was trained in the use of weaponry and the science of elephants. He was later appointed commander of the royal pages by his father.

At the age of 21, he returned to the monkhood. Again, he was ordained at the Temple of the Emerald Buddha, but after just 15 days at Wat Rajanivat, his father King Rama II died without officially appointing a successor. Other royal family members and some of the court ministers agreed to give the throne to the deceased sovereign's eldest son, Mongkut's half brother, Krom Muen Jessdabodin, who became the third King of Siam. Mongkut decided to remain in the monkhood throughout the 27 years of the new King's reign, during which time he studied and excelled in Pali and the canons from the Buddhist Scripture. He also created a new Buddhist sect called Thammayut, or Dhammayuttika Nikaya, which encouraged a more stringent observance of the Buddhist precepts among the monks. When the construction of Wat Bovorn Nivet, commissioned by King Rama III, was completed, the King invited Mongkut, then 32, to be the temple's first abbot. Under

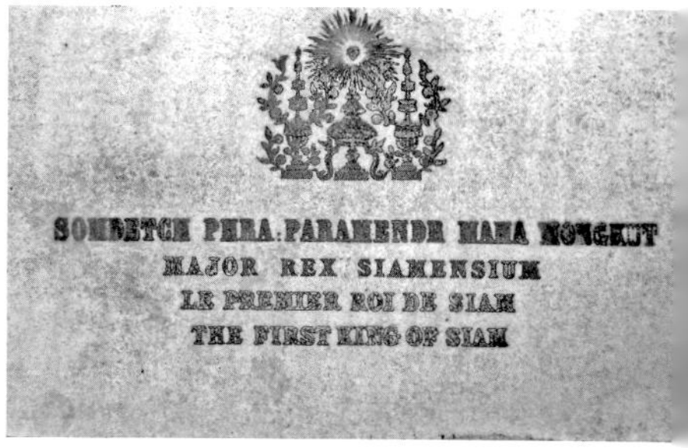

Name card of HM King Mongkut. Most likely it was printed at the Aksorn Pimpakarn publishing house within the Grand Palace. At the top is His Majesty's royal crest followed by his name in English and the title First King of Siam in Latin, French and English. (Private Collection)

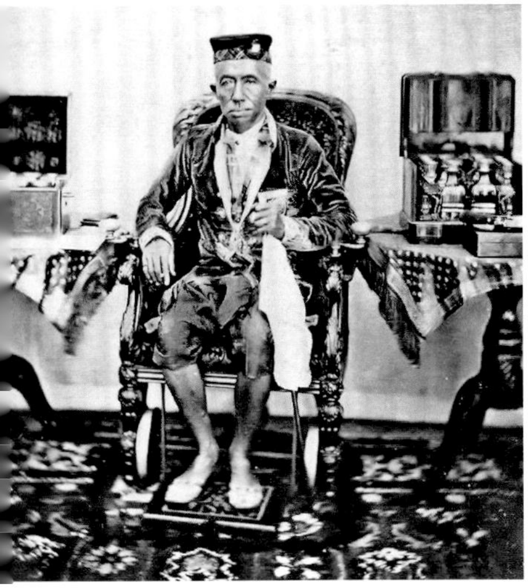

Hand-coloured photograph of His Majesty King Mongkut by Abbé Larnaudie. It was presented to Emperor Napoleon III on 27th June, 1861. (Fontainebleau Palace Museum)

his supervision, Mongkut brought about ecclesiastical reform and founded a Pali school in the temple. He sent a group of monks to Sri Lanka to study Buddhist discipline so that they could set an example for other monks when they returned. He invented Ariyaka characters both for typefaces and handwriting to be used in the publication of Pali textbooks. He founded the first Thai-run printing house at the temple and oversaw publication of several Buddhist books.

During his monkhood, Western influence began to spread throughout Southeast Asian. Mongkut recognized the strategic importance of befriending westerners and learning their languages. He studied Latin with the then-vicar apostolic of Siam, Jean-Baptiste Pallegoix of the Church of the Conception and learned English with missionaries, including Dr. Dan Beach Bradley, Dr. Reynold House and Mr. Jesse Caswell. His knowledge of English enabled him to explore Western academic disciplines such as geography, mathematics and astronomy which helped him to deal with the Europeans, and stay abreast of volatile situations in the world at that time.

Upon King Rama III's death, Mongkut, with the consent of other members of the royal family and court ministers, left the monkhood to ascend the throne on 3 April 1850. His coronation was held on 15 May 1851. He appointed his younger brother Prince Chutamani as Second King, and bestowed on him the name Phra Bat Somdet Phra Pinklao Chao Yu Hua.

King Mongkut and Foreign Affairs

Having ascended the throne at the age of 47, King Mongkut realized that as the Siamese monarch, his priority was to protect the kingdom's sovereignty and independence. Towards the end of the previous reign, Siam and its neighbors had experienced increasing threats from Western imperialist nations, especially England and France, which were competing fiercely to increase their colonial power in the region. While this imminent peril helped to mitigate Siam's conflicts with neighboring states, the Kingdom faced new, increasingly worrisome challenges from farther afield. Resenting Siam's monopolistic trade system, England and the United States of America sought to amend the treaty Britain had signed with Siam in 1753. However, the negotiations failed and when James Brook, England's representative, returned to his country, he urged his government to resort to military force. However, at the height of these tensions King Rama III died, and England decided to delay any further action.

In these circumstances, King Mongkut realized that if Siam remained recalcitrant, the Kingdom would be at grave risk of losing its independence or would be forced to cede territory as had happened to its neighbors. To safeguard the country from this possibility, he chose the path of diplomatic conciliation. In a personal letter addressed to the British Ambassador, Sir John Bowring, King Mongkut suggested that the diplomat make direct official contact with his Harbour Minister (the equivalent of today's Minister of Foreign Affairs), so that Siam could prepare for his public reception. This would help quell the fears of the local people, sparked by the arrival of British battleships carrying Her Majesty's diplomatic corps. In the meantime, in the hope of facilitating negotiations between the two countries, King Mongkut asked the British envoy to inform him in private of what England hoped to achieve so that he could respond to the objections he knew his ministers would have.

The signing of the Bowring Treaty with England in 1855 and several more subsequent pacts with other Western countries brought about the most significant changes in the Kingdom's long history of foreign trade. As free

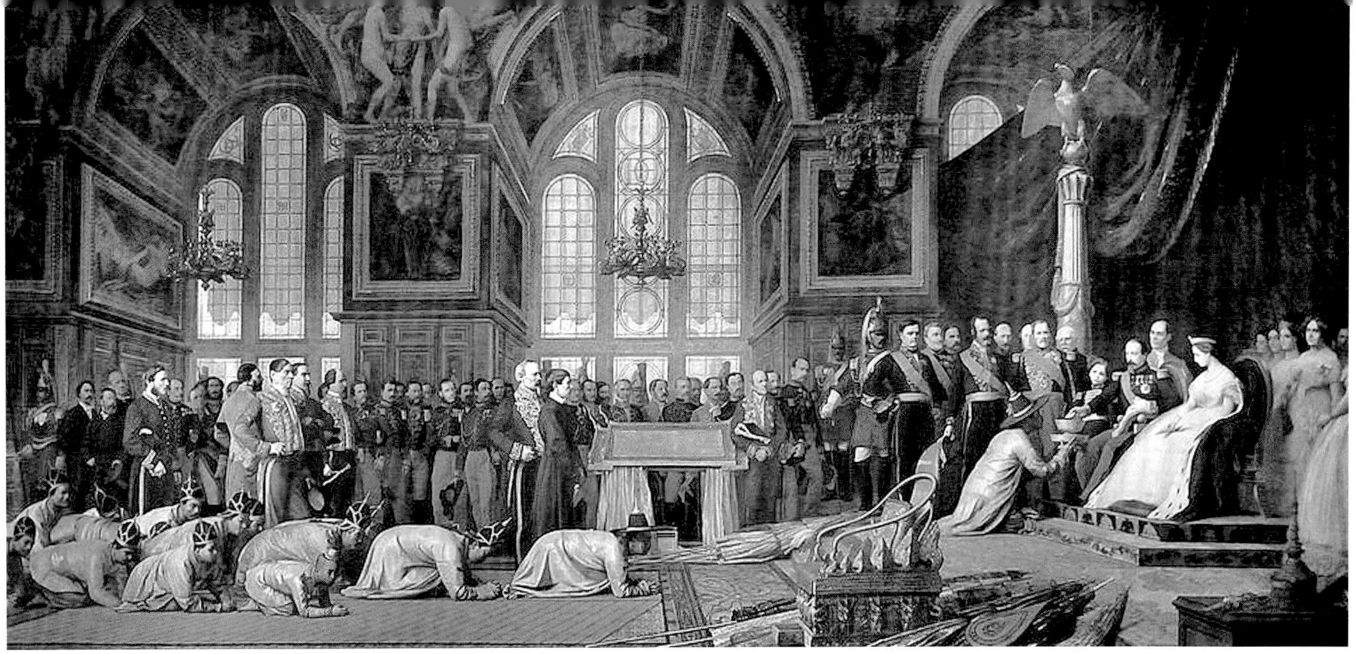

The Siamese embassy to France, led by Chao Phraya Sripipat Ratana Rajakosa (Pae Bunnag), presents His Majesty's royal message and tribute to Emperor Napoleon III in the ballroom of the Palace of Fontainebleau, 27th June, 1861. Painting by Jean-Léon Gérôme.

trade replaced the old system of monopolies, Siam saw its overseas commerce grow dramatically. The country started to impose duties on imports and exports according to international standards, and as a result, rice became and still remains its main export. To accommodate the economic expansion ushered in by these treaties, Siamese consulates were founded in many partner countries, which in turn led to further changes in the economic system and even greater growth in commerce.

King Mongkut was well aware of the value of diplomatic conciliation and handled international affairs with great sensitivity. He saw that a closed door policy toward foreign countries would imperil Siam's sovereignty. Following the Bowring Treaty, the king entered into trade agreements with eight Western countries: England, the USA, France, Denmark, Portugal, Holland, Germany and Italy.

Interestingly, Sir John Bowring, who had been given the title Phraya Siamanukulkij Siammitrmahayot, was appointed special envoy to represent Siam in talks in London, aimed at establishing trade relations with Italy. Thanks to King Mongkut's efforts to treat all the countries equally, Siam and her new trading partners enjoyed a stable relationship. The monarch's foreign policy proved successful as Siam managed to protect its independence and sovereignty from the Western superpowers, unlike its neighbours, who succumbed to colonization.

In addition to opening the country to foreign trade, King Mongkut was the first King of the Bangkok era to send diplomatic envoys to foster relations with European countries. In 1857, Phraya Montri Suriyawong (Chum Bunnag) was appointed ambassador to England, where he had an audience with Queen Victoria and presented her with King Mongkut's royal message and tribute. In 1861, the King sent Phraya Sripipat (Pae Bunnag) on a diplomatic mission to France to present Emperor Napoleon III with a royal message and tribute.

King Mongkut also sent letters to several other countries with whom Siam had established ties. In 1863, France's Emperor Napoleon III sent Admiral Bonard to present King Mongkut with the Légion d'Honneur. The King later commissioned the creation of

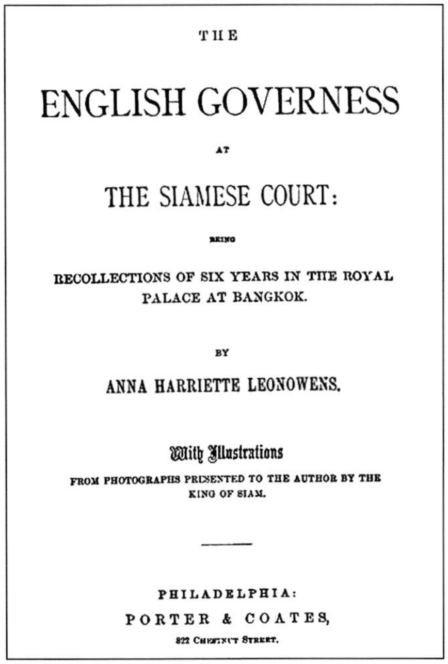

THE

ENGLISH GOVERNESS

AT

THE SIAMESE COURT:

BEING

RECOLLECTIONS OF SIX YEARS IN THE ROYAL PALACE AT BANGKOK.

BY

ANNA HARRIETTE LEONOWENS.

With Illustrations

FROM PHOTOGRAPHS PRESENTED TO THE AUTHOR BY THE KING OF SIAM.

PHILADELPHIA:
PORTER & COATES,
822 CHESTNUT STREET.

Cover of the book by Anna Leonowens describing her life in the Siamese court.

the Nine Gems royal decoration, which was given to his French counterpart in return. The international reputation of King

Mongkut among European monarchs, philosopher clubs and the public, both in his own right and as the representative of Siam, was further enhanced when he had his court officials oversee the shipment of objects for display at the Exposition Universelle in Paris.

Embracing western civilization and technology

With his modern mindset, King Mongkut showed great farsightedness in setting out to adapt Western customs and technology to the country's administration. During his reign Siam can be said to have entered a new era with many changes attributable to his initiatives. Notable areas where the King was active follow below.

Administrative Development

King Mongkut prepared his administrative officials, ladies of the court, and his people for the new political reality by reforming many outdated traditions and customs. Following the signing of the Bowring Treaty, he had roads built for horse-drawn carriages which served as commercial routes linking the centre of the capital with its outskirts. New canals were excavated, and footbridges built across them were raised so that boats could pass underneath. He realized that even though Siam had abundant labour and natural resources, it was still lacking in investments and technology; therefore, he encouraged increasing numbers of Westerners to enter the kingdom. As he once wrote, "French, British and American nationals have good knowledge about their jobs. If they come and settle in our country, they are certain to create exotic and useful products which are of higher quality than what we usually make in town or what has long been in existence. When these foreigners sell their products, they will be much less expensive than goods not produced locally. Seeing that, artisans in the capital city will want to learn the skills of the expatriates, which will raise the quality of our own craftsmanship. Besides, the French, British and Americans have textbooks that teach them how to farm the land..." His thinking showed him to be well ahead of his time.

In engineering and military matters, King Mongkut received tremendous help from his younger brother, Deputy King Phra Pin Klao Chao Yu Hua. He also employed the Englishman Captain Impey to train a group of conscripts to follow the military rules and discipline practiced in Europe. To strengthen his navy, he commissioned the construction of several steamboats for use in sea combat. Among these were the *Ran Rook Pairee, Siam Moo Phra Sadam,* and *Yongyot Ayochiay*. He purchased Armstrong and Needham's Patent rifles, and blunderbusses from England, and muskets from Holland and the USA. King Mongkut also showed special interest in other mechanical devices such as the rain purification equipment used in England, a gift presented to him by Queen Victoria.

Educational Development

King Mongkut had been a champion of education throughout his tenure as a monk in the previous reign. While he was at Wat Bovorn Nivet, he ordered a lithograph machine from overseas to publish Buddhist literature. After he ascended the throne, he founded a printing house in the grounds of the Grand Palace to publish official announcements and royal gazettes for public distribution.

He hired Anna Leonowens, from England, to teach his sons and daughters, realising that proficiency in English would benefit the

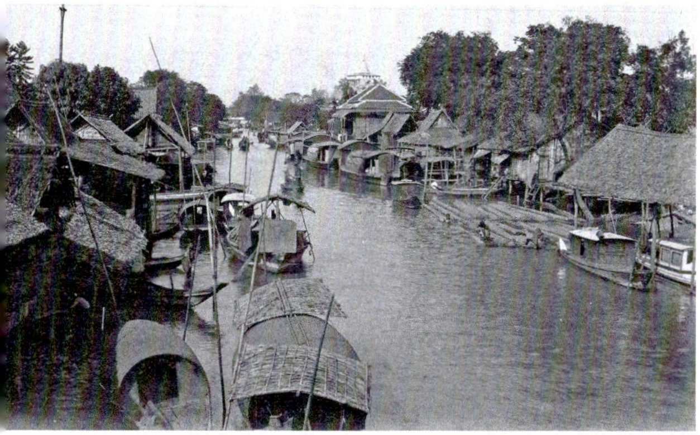

Many canals were dug during this reign and linked together to create a transport system.

country's development. He also took a direct role in teaching his children about royal customs and traditions, using modern pedagogical methods. He saw to it that they learned things first-hand to ensure that they would have accurate knowledge when the time came for them to perform rituals such as the naming of Prince Chulalongkorn and the topknot cutting of Princess Ying Yaowaluck.

Social Development

Thanks to his studies in the monkhood, King Mongkut was the first royal from an oriental country who was well-versed in written and spoken English. He also learned French, Pali, Sanskrit, Mon, Burmese, Singhalese, Vietnamese, and Khmer. Most importantly, he invented Ariyaka characters to be used for Buddhist purposes. When news of his ingenious invention became known abroad, foreign scholars, merchants and missionaries wrote letters expressing a desire to meet him. He handwrote responses to all these letters and signed them himself, in keeping with western conventions. After his coronation, he continued this practice, maintaining correspondence with his foreign acquaintances, as well as writing letters in Thai.

Traditionally, Thai monarchs would stamp their royal seal on top of their names. King Mongkut was the first to adopt the western convention of using a signature. He signed his letters using his initials in Roman characters: S.P.P.M.M. and S.P.P.M Mongkut. This is a custom still observed by Thai people today.

King Mongkut was also a supporter of monogamy as practiced in Europe. He took one new consort at a time, not several simultaneously as his predecessors had done. He also gave the ladies of the court permission to end their service to the throne and leave the palace without punishment. They were allowed to marry or become the concubine of any other royal. Only those consorts who had borne the King children were excluded from these new freedoms.

Miscellaneous

With regard to flags, the international symbols of king and country, King Mongkut had a national flag designed which was flown by Siamese ships and Siamese consuls overseas. He was the first to devise a flag for use specifically by the monarch, called the "Thong Jom Klao" flag. It was flown on the mast of his royal barge during journeys by water and on the pole inside the Grand Palace during his stay in the capital. If he was away, the flag would be flown at half-mast. Later, the King devised another flag known as the "Thong Phandin" to signify his absence from the capital.

Royal decorations or insignia, worn on the chest to indicate the wearer's order or social rank, date back to many hundreds of years in Europe. However, in Siam they were introduced by King Mongkut in 1857, and insignia began to be conferred on royal family members, government employees and foreigners who had made contributions to the country. Different insignia were designed to indicate the various ranks.

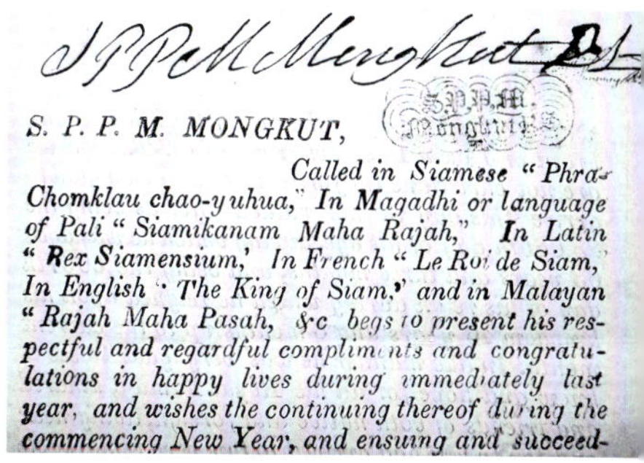

S. P. P. M. MONGKUT,

Called in Siamese "Phra-Chomklau chao-yuhua," In Magadhi or language of Pali "Siamikanam Maha Rajah," In Latin "Rex Siamensium,' In French "Le Roi de Siam, In English "The King of Siam," and in Malayan "Rajah Maha Pasah, &c begs to present his respectful and regardful compliments and congratulations in happy lives during immediately last year, and wishes the continuing thereof during the commencing New Year, and ensuing and succeed-

Signature of His Majesty King Mongkut on a letter sent to one of the foreigners with whom he corresponded. He signed the letter S.P.P.M. Mongkut RS followed by his royal seal. (Private Collection)

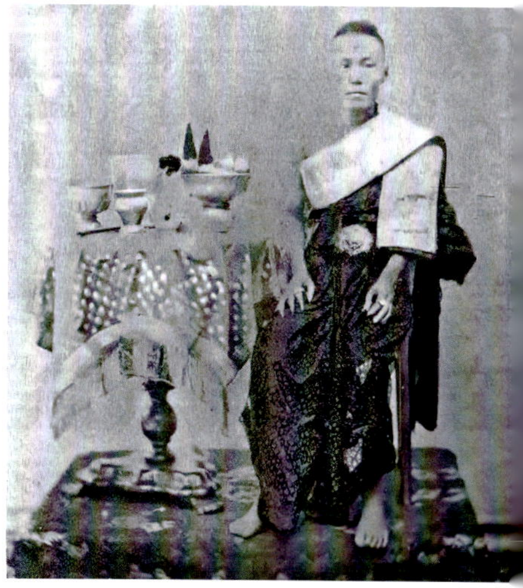

Photograph of HM Queen Debsirindra by Abbé Larnaudie. She is in formal attire with a pleated silk scarf. Items of regalia are on the table. (Fontainebleau Palace Museum)

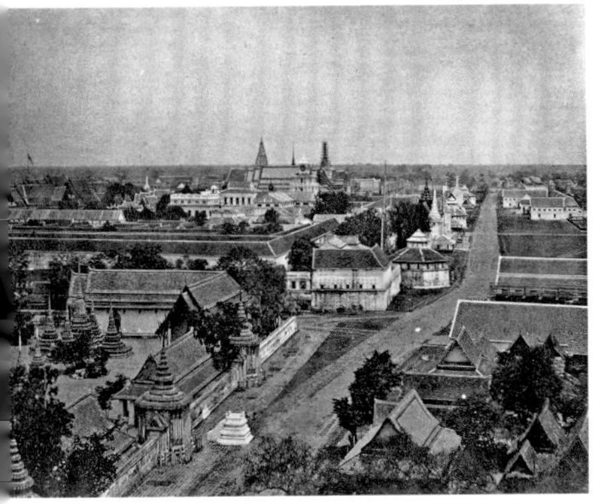

The Grand Palace seen from a high viewpoint looking along Sanam Chai road and showing the Aphinao Niwet group of throne halls built in this reign.

The money most widely used at the beginning of King Mongkut's reign was the Pod Duang and cowries. But both had drawbacks as currency. The former could be easily forged, while the latter was just a seashell, which was fragile and whose value varied. While the King sought a solution, the Kingdom's money supply began to prove inadequate for the rising foreign trade. In 1856, King Mongkut allowed the public and merchants to trade using foreign coins, widely referred to as *Rien Nok* (bird coins). However, they were never popular among the Siamese even after the King passed a law stipulating that they be used officially as Thai money. To solve the problem, the King ordered that Pod Duang and cowries be replaced with metal coins in keeping with international practice. In 1856, when the King sent a group of ambassadors on a mission to forge diplomatic ties with European countries, he ordered that they buy a minting machine. Upon hearing this, a British consul, who happened to be visiting Bangkok at the time, presented King Mongkut with a machine as a gift. The founding of the first mint enabled Siam to produce many other coins for circulation in the market. Thanks to the King's foresight, the currency reform he initiated proved an economic boon to the country.

King Mongkut also modernized several traditions and customs. With regards to dress, court officials were instructed to cover the upper part of their body when in audience with him, while in audiences foreigners were allowed to stand close to His Majesty. He also dressed in Western style, wearing a hat he ordered from France or Britain. As John Thomson wrote in his memoir, sometimes the King would dress in a French field marshal's uniform, with stockings and a cape, when giving a public audience to his court officials. At other times, he would put on French insignia, don a Scottish-style hat or wear a US naval officer's uniform. Family members and other people in the palace soon began to follow suit. For example, his son Prince Chulalongkorn, and his concubines Chao Chom Manda Piem and Chao Chom Manda Sangwal sported Western-style clothes at the reception held in 1862 to welcome Lord John Hay, British Royal Navy admiral of the Indian Ocean fleet. King Mongkut also ordered officials of the Department of "Klone" (female palace guards) to wear Scottish military uniforms. These guards were later dubbed "Kangaroo Soldiers". The new fashion was also adopted by King Pinklao and his children, as Sir John Bowring once remarked, "Today, His Highness is wearing a Western outfit."

King Mongkut ordered the construction of new palaces in Bangkok and other provinces. One, called Phra Apinao Niwet, was built in the Grand Palace compound and features in Thomson's photographs; one was built in Petchburi and another in Nakon Pathom. Repairs were ordered for the Narai Rajnivet Palace in Lopburi. Phra Aphinao Niwet was beautifully furnished and decorated with imported items from Europe such as lamps, candle holders, and lanterns made of crystal or German silver. Foreign visitors, such as French Ambassador Montigny, spoke of the palace with admiration when he had an audience with the King there. The palace of Siam's Second King was also redecorated in European style.

In front of Sutthai Sawan Throne Hall in the Grand Palace, King Mongkut had a row of large commercial buildings erected to house foreign government officials and local businesses. The King meant for the new structures to show Europeans that Siam was also a civilized country.

Because of his great interest in astronomy, King Mongkut asked Sir John Bowring to purchase for him a high-quality telescope, instruments of measurement and a book of astronomical symbols. His expertise in this field was exceptional, as was proven by his accurate prediction of the occurrence of a solar eclipse on 18th August 1868, in Tambon Wakor, Prachuab Kirikhan province.

Photography had already been introduced to Siam in the reign of King Rama III, when Father Larnaudie, on the orders of Pallegoix, had brought in the first photographic equipment. However, this new contraption was not met with much enthusiasm. It was not until the time of King Mongkut that interest in photography started to take root in the Kingdom. King Mongkut was the first Thai monarch to give permission for foreign photographers to take his picture. Most notable among these was John Thomson who took his picture in the French field marshal's uniform. The King also had his photograph taken during the Kathin ceremony at Wat Phra Chetupon in 1865. As part of his mission to forge relations with countries in Europe and with America, he saw to it that his correspondence with foreign rulers was customarily accompanied by his photo, using this clever diplomatic tactic to make a statement to his foreign counterparts that Siam was by no means a backward country. He also led by example because in supporting photography, he wanted to dissuade the Siamese from indulging in superstitious belief and urge them to embrace modern technology instead.

In the field of medicine, he welcomed Western methods and ordered various medications from abroad including cough lozenges, which he really liked. He had such trust in modern medicine that he allowed missionaries to collaborate with traditional Thai doctors in treating Krom Meun Mahesuan Siwawilas, his eldest son, and one of his royal consorts.

He advised government officials and his people to maintain cleanliness in and around their houses as well as within the city walls and around the city gates so that they would not become a breeding ground for germs or an eyesore to foreign visitors. Royal family members and senior government officials were also urged to stop eating with their hands and to use spoons and forks instead. As Sir John Bowring wrote in his memoir: "Four contract committee members came to have dinner with me. *Somdet* (prince) was very clumsy with spoon and fork."

Finally, in keeping with European and Chinese customs, which called for a grand celebration on a person's 60th birthday, King Mongkut followed suit in 1864. A religious ceremony was held to bestow merit on the King. Other activities included plays and the lighting of lanterns of various shapes. "Foreign customers and consuls enjoyed making European-style lanterns. Flags were flown. People from all walks of life hung brightly lit lamps in front of their houses both on land and on water. The entire land was filled with light." Another highlight of the celebration was that the King gave each royal family member and government official a gold coin with a crown design weighing one tamlung (38.11 grams) as a souvenir. He gave money to the handicapped and the elderly. More importantly, for the first time ever, the King bestowed blessings on participants and everyone who helped organize the celebration for him.

Sadly, while pursuing one of his scientific interests and setting up camp to observe the solar eclipse in Prachuap Kirikhun province in August 1868, King Monkut became infected with malaria and passed away six weeks later on 1 October 1868 at the age of 65. He had reigned for 18 years and had 82 children. He was succeeded by his son Prince Chulalongkorn, who as King Rama V was to reign for over 40 years and continue the reforms and great advancements of his father.

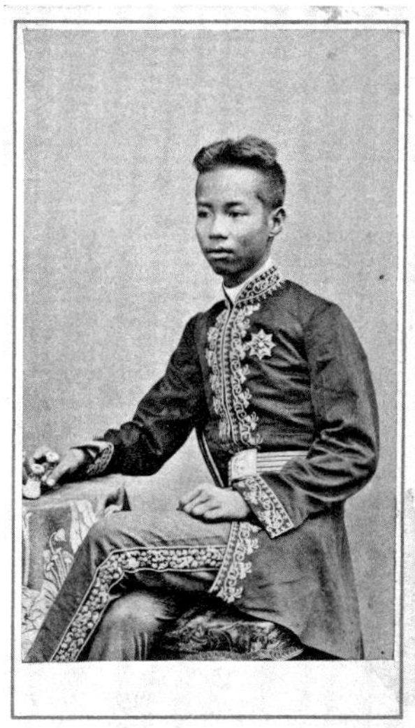

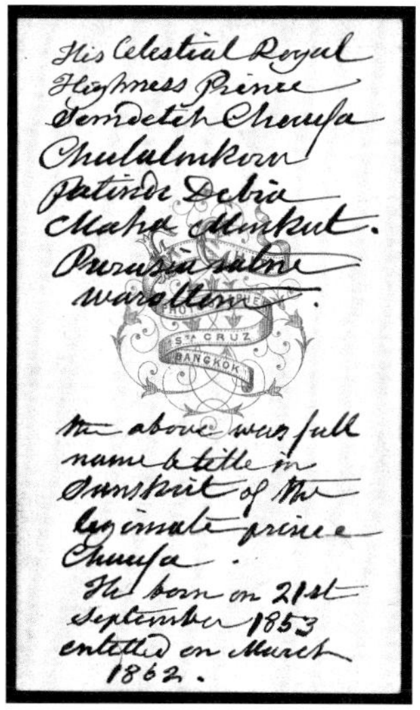

His Celestial Royal
Highness Prince
Somdetch Chowfa
Chulalonkorn
Patinda Debia
Maha Monkut.
Purusia ratna
warottom.
Sta CRUZ
BANGKOK
The above was full
name & title in
Sanskrit of the
legitimate prince
Chowfa.
He born on 21st
September 1853
entitled on March
1862.

Above and bottom: Crown Prince Chulalongkorn (who later reigned as King Rama V) photographed by Francis Chit. On the back HM King Mongkut has written the Crown Prince's name, as well as recording his date of birth and when he was elevated to the rank of Crown Prince.

H.M. King Mongkut, King Rama IV (r. 1851-1868)

Signed "J. Thomson Photo" on the tablecloth

This photograph of the king was exhibited at the Exposition Universelle in Paris in 1867. He is seated on the Kong throne, carved with garudas and nagas. He wears coronation robes and the Maha Kathin Crown, created in the reign of King Rama I. In his left hand he holds a walking stick; on his feet are curved gold and enamel slippers. On the right-hand table are items of ceremonial regalia – spittoon, water jug, betel box.

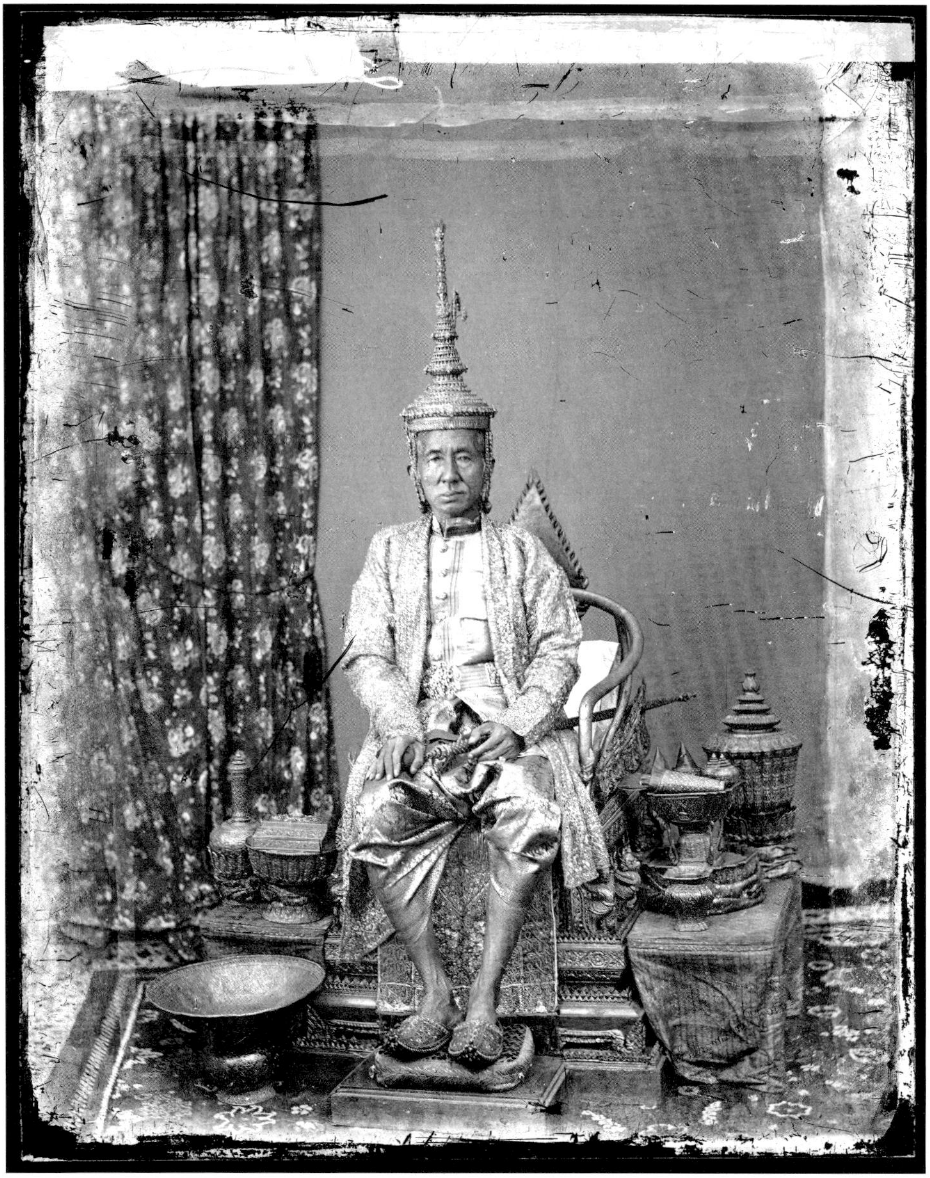

OPPOSITE: H.M. King Mongkut

One of three portraits taken outside the Aphinao Niwet Throne Hall in the Grand Palace on Monday, 6th October 1865.

The king wears the uniform of a French Field Marshall and the sash of the Légion d'Honneur and Star First Class, a decoration presented to him on behalf of Emperor Napoleon III by Admiral Bonard, Commander of the Fleet in Indochina, on 10th May 1863.

On the table are items of regalia in gold and enamel: an oval box with gemstones on a pedestal tray, a gold ewer on a pedestal tray, a spittoon and a wool cap embroidered with gold thread in the French style. The small telescope may refer to the king's interest in Western science and astronomy.

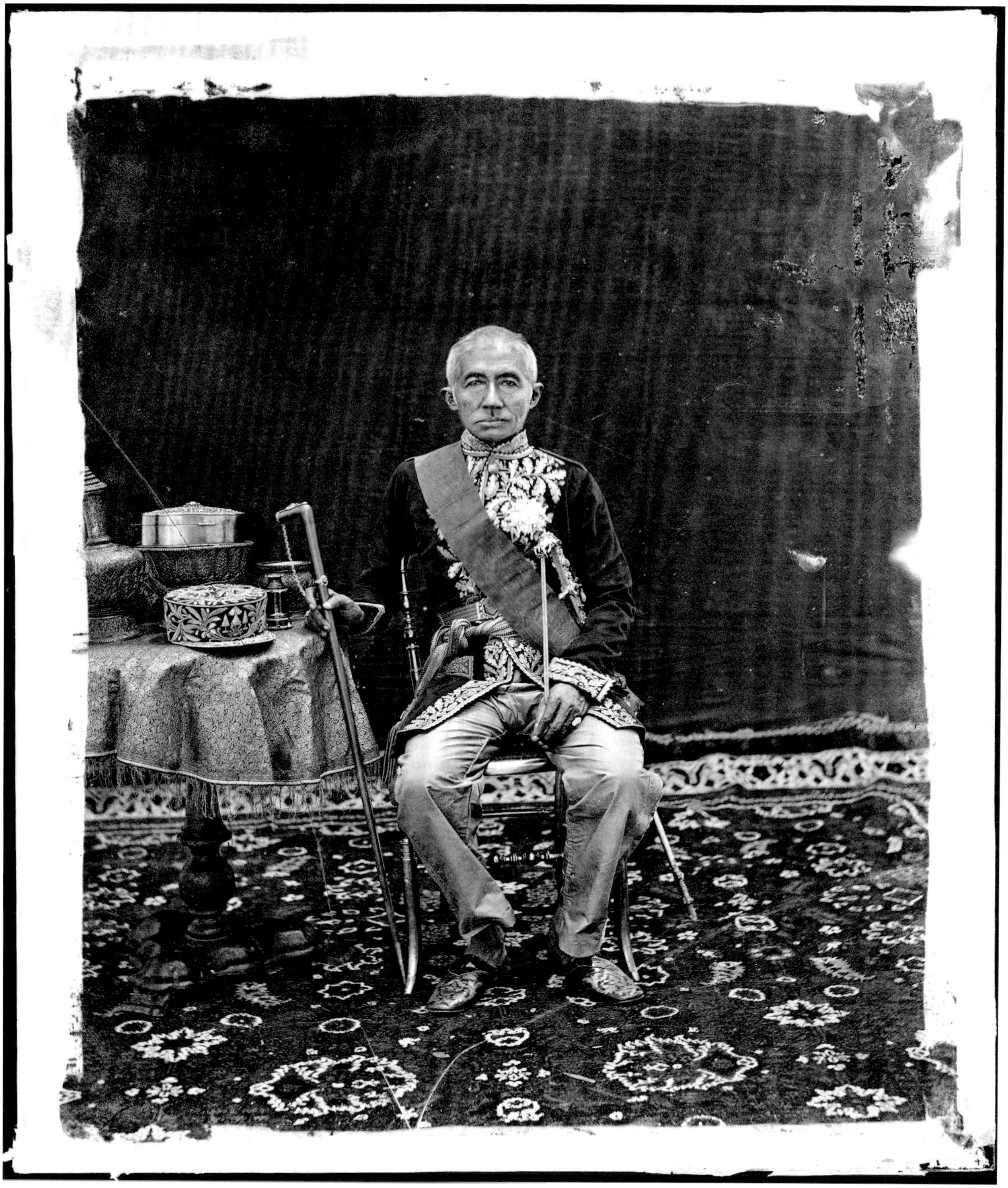

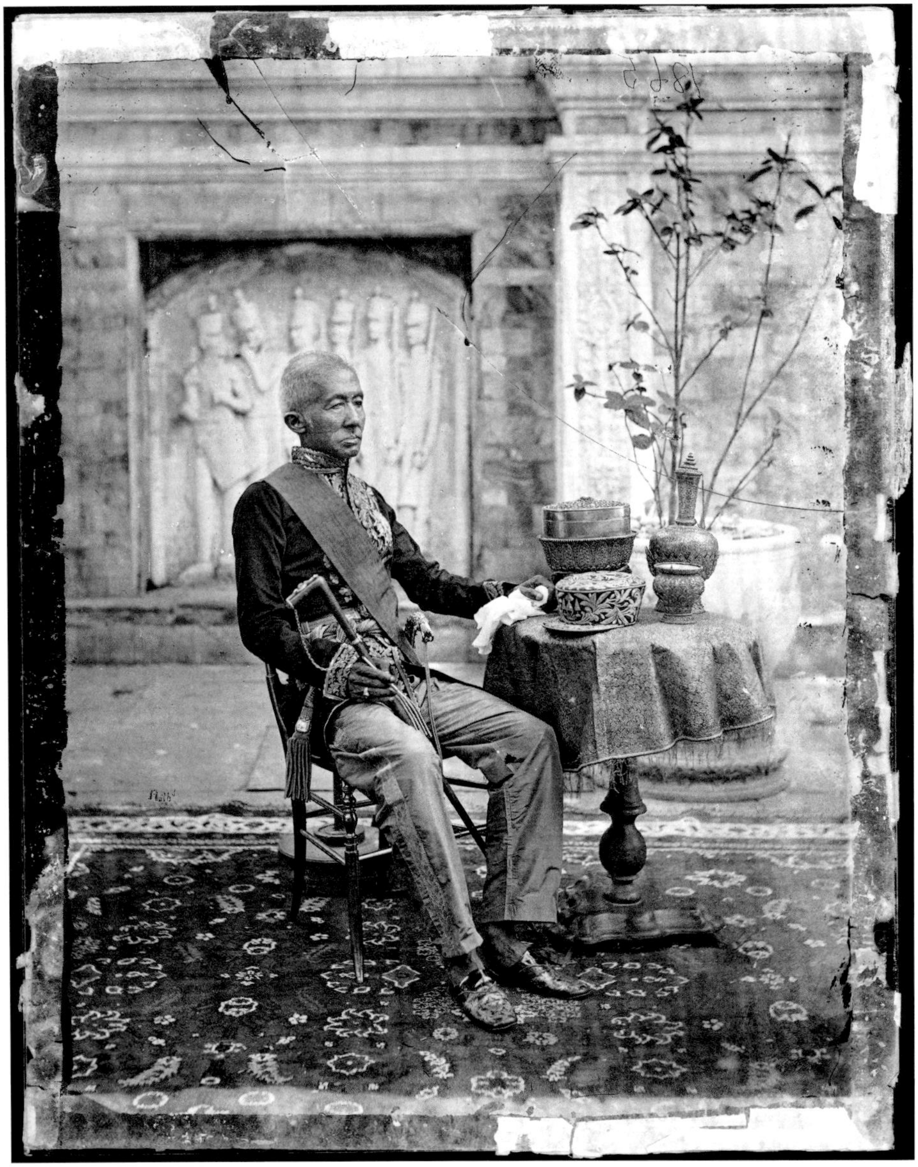

H.M. KING MONGKUT, KING RAMA IV (r. 1851-1868)

Thomson, aware of his good fortune in gaining privileged access to the king, described their first encounter most vividly:

"His Majesty entered through a massive gateway, and I must confess that I felt much impressed by his appearance, as I had never been in the presence of an anointed sovereign before. He stood about five feet eight inches, and his figure was erect and commanding; but an expression of severe gravity was settled on his face."

Portrait of a Princess (possibly one of the daughters of Prince Nilarat, Prince of Alongkot Kitpreecha)

Signed "J. Thomson Photo" below the leg of the left-hand stool

The setting is likely a corner of the Thai-style wooden palace of Prince Alongkot, who took Thomson to his audience and photographic session with the King.

The young girl, her hair still in a topknot, wears traditional dress with a gold belt, breast chains, a necklace and many bracelets, anklets and rings. A miniature potted garden has been created using blue and white Chinese jardinières among which two small European-style sculptures are visible. Such arrangements were extremely popular at this time.

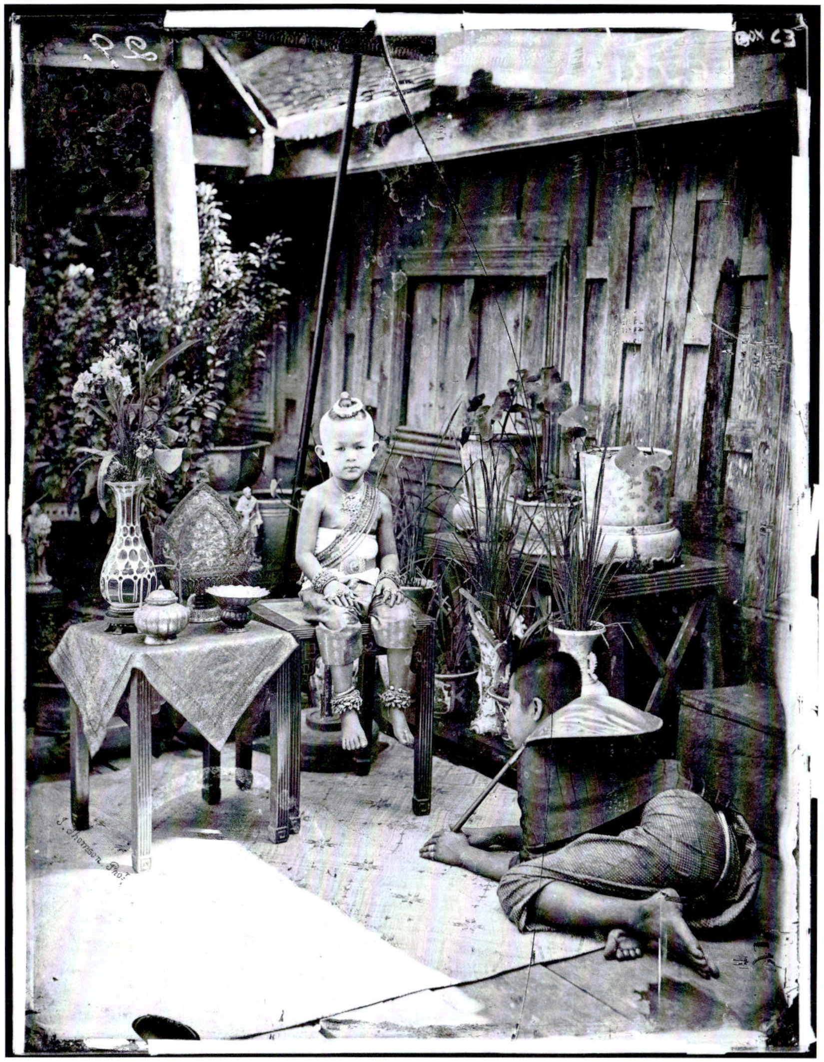

Prince Nilarat of Alongkot sits in the same spot as his daughter but has the elaborate regalia of a prince on the table and at his feet kneels a young male attendant with a sword. (Photograph: John Thomson)

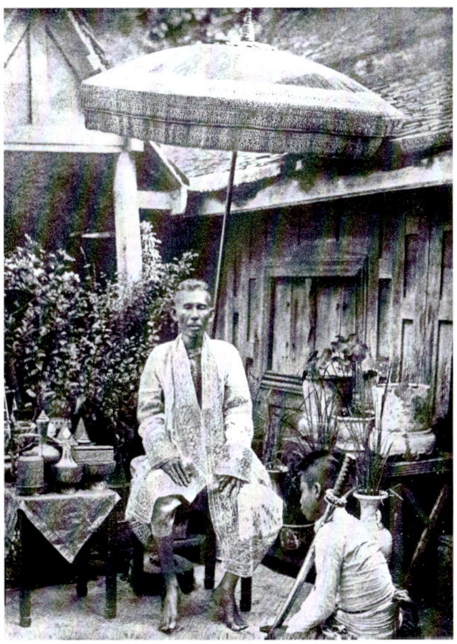

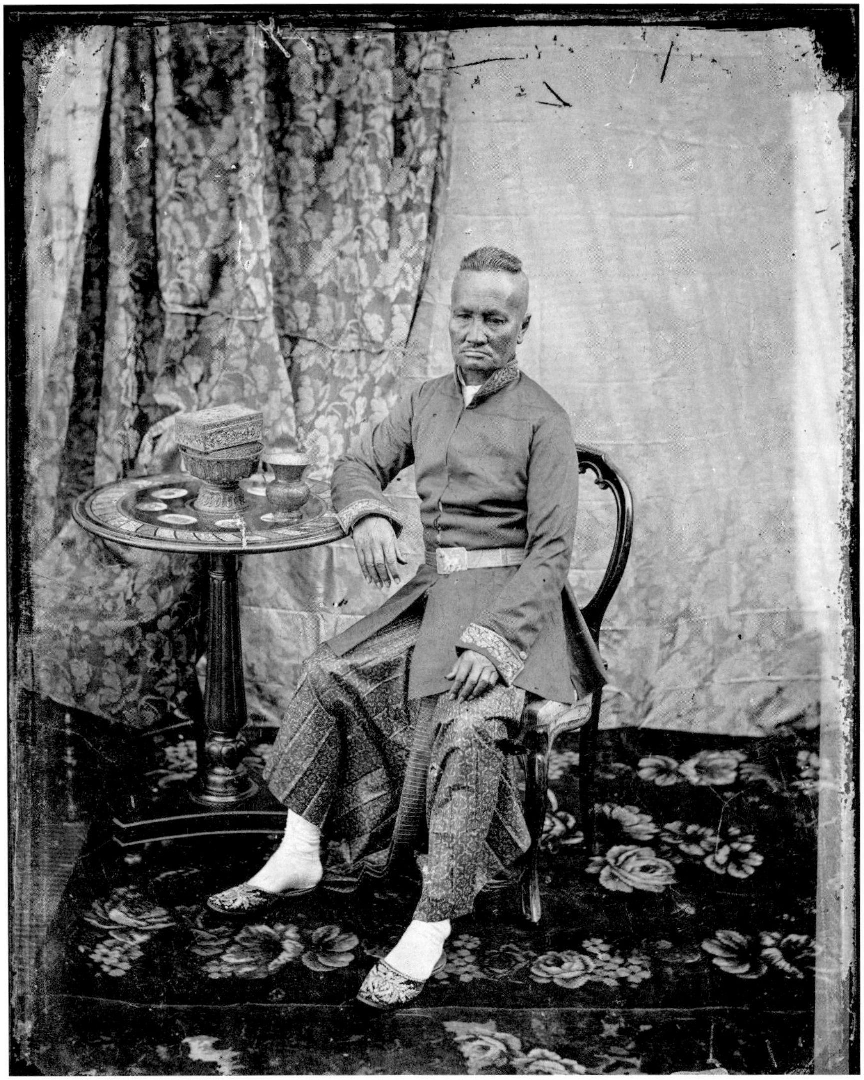

PRIME MINISTER IN 1865, THE KRALAHOM, BANGKOK

Somdet Chao Phraya Borom Maha Sri Suriyawongse (Chuang Bunnag), (1808-1882), was the most influential non-royal figure in the early Bangkok period. He began his career as a royal page during the Second Reign (1809-1824) and by the Fourth Reign was Prime Minister.

He wears the dress of a senior official – a brocade sarong with a front pleat, a long jacket with embroidered collar and cuffs, the ensemble held in place with a gold belt, the buckle adorned with a male lion, the emblem of the Prime Minister at that time.

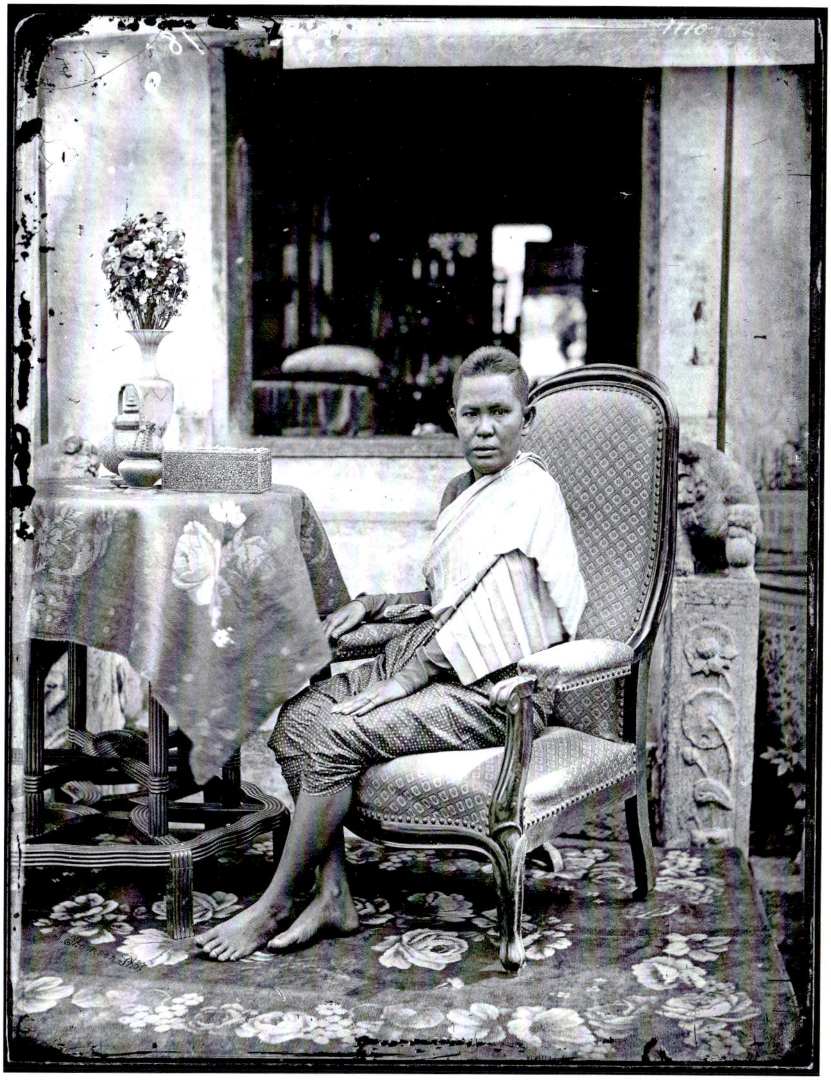

WIFE OF THE PRIME MINISTER

Signed "J. Thomson Photo" on the carpet

This is one of the Prime Minister's (opposite) three wives, either Lady Pun or Lady Yad. She sits outside her house on a European-style chair. Beside her is an elaborate Chinese-style rosewood table with a flowered cloth, a gold teapot and tray, a gold spittoon and betel nut box.

She is dressed in the style of a high-ranking lady of the Fourth Reign, namely silk *jonggraben* (baggy trousers) and a Chinese-style long-sleeved blouse and pleated silk shawl. Her hair is shaven at the sides, slightly longer on top and has two long sideburns, which have been tucked behind her ears. Her teeth are black from betel nut chewing.

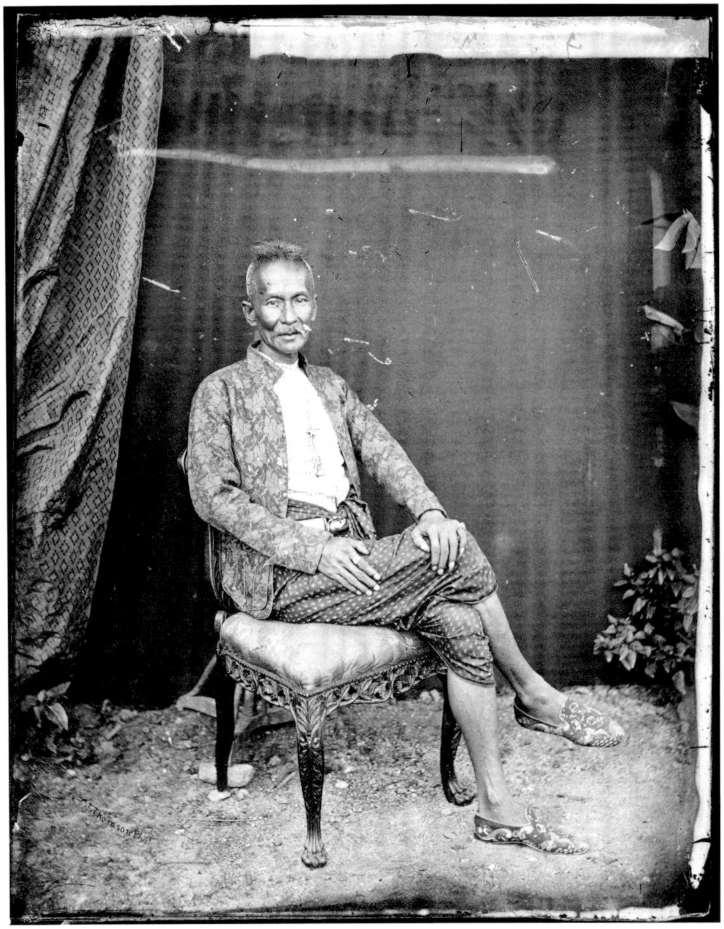

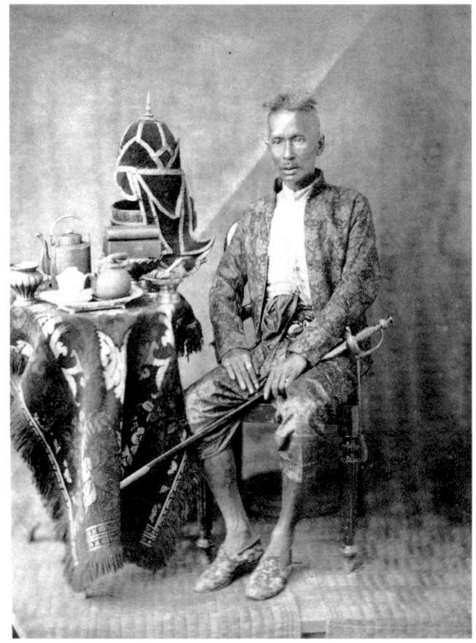

This photograph of Mom Rachothai shows him wearing the identical outfit as in the photograph by John Thomson, but a table with items of regalia has been added. It was probably taken by Francis Chit.

Mom Rachothai (Mom Rajawongse Kratai Issarangkul) (1820-1867)

Signed "J. Thomson photo"

His father, Prince Cha-um, presented M. R. Kratai as an attendant to Prince Mongkut when the latter was still a monk. He was a close companion and excelled in English. When Prince Mongkut became king, M. R. Kratai received the title of Mom Rachothai.

In 1857, he was interpreter on the ambassadorial mission of Phraya Montri Suriyawongse (Chum Bunnag) to Queen Victoria. On his return he wrote an account in verse of his travels and in 1861 sold the rights to Dr. Dan Beach Bradley for 400 baht (a large amount at the time), the first sale of publishing rights in Thailand.

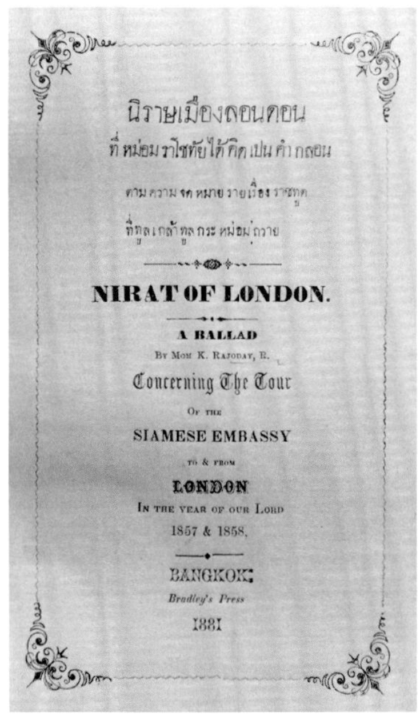

นิราษเมืองลอนดอน
ที่หม่อมราโชทัยได้คิดเปนคำกลอน
ตามความจดหมายรายเรื่องราชทูต
ที่ทูลเกล้าทูลกระหม่อมถวาย

NIRAT OF LONDON.

A BALLAD

By Mom K. Rajoday, R.

Concerning The Tour

Of the

SIAMESE EMBASSY

to & from

LONDON

In the year of our Lord

1857 & 1858,

BANGKOK:

Bradley's Press

1881

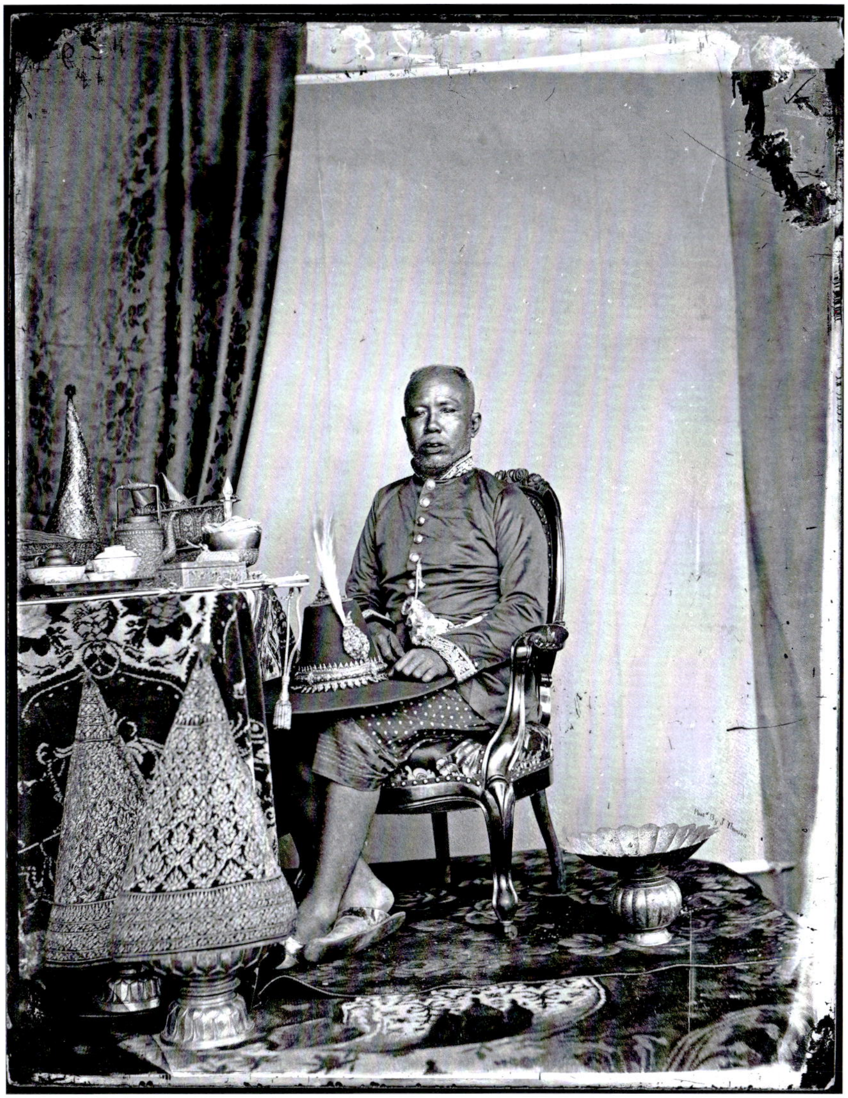

HRH Prince Mahamala (1819-1886)

Signed "John Thomson" at the edge of the plate

The prince, wearing formal attire, was a younger brother of King Mongkut by a different mother and the founder of the Malakul family. Only princes of the highest rank could have such items of gold regalia, which include a pedestal tray adorned with *garuda* and *naga*, a miniature tea set, a gold box and a gold Chinese-style teapot.

The Crown Prince of Siam, 1865

Inscribed "The Crown Prince of Thailand" at the top and signed "Photo by J. Thomson" just above the base of the table

This arresting portrait of HRH Prince Chulalongkorn, later King Chulalongkorn (1853-1910, r.1868-1910) was taken in the courtyard of the Aphinao Niwet Compound within the Grand Palace, Bangkok.

The prince is in traditional Thai dress with silk *jonggraben* and a fitted silk jacket, together with anklets and embroidered slippers. The only items of regalia are the conical gold teapot and tray and the betel-nut box adorned with diamonds on a gold pedestal tray in European style. Behind him the wooden stand used to limit any vibration during the long exposure time, is just visible.

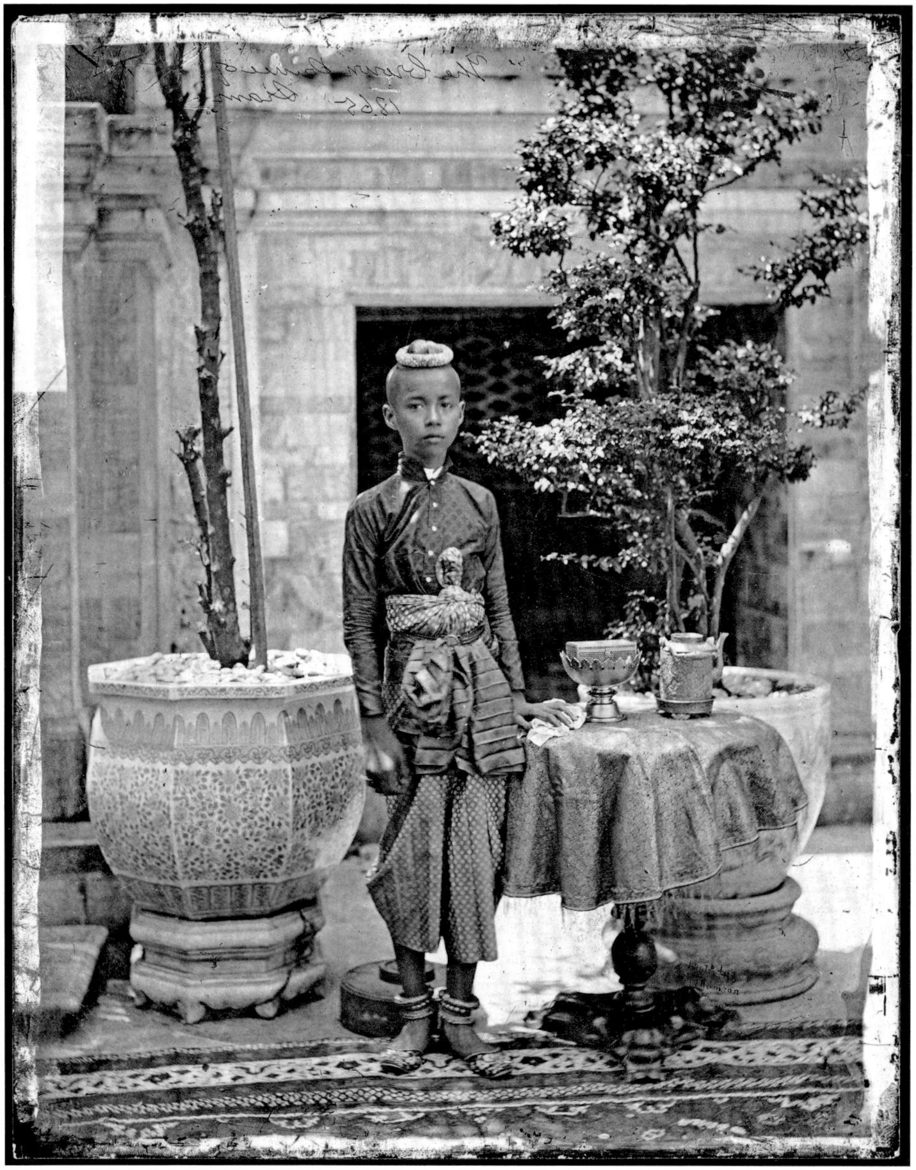

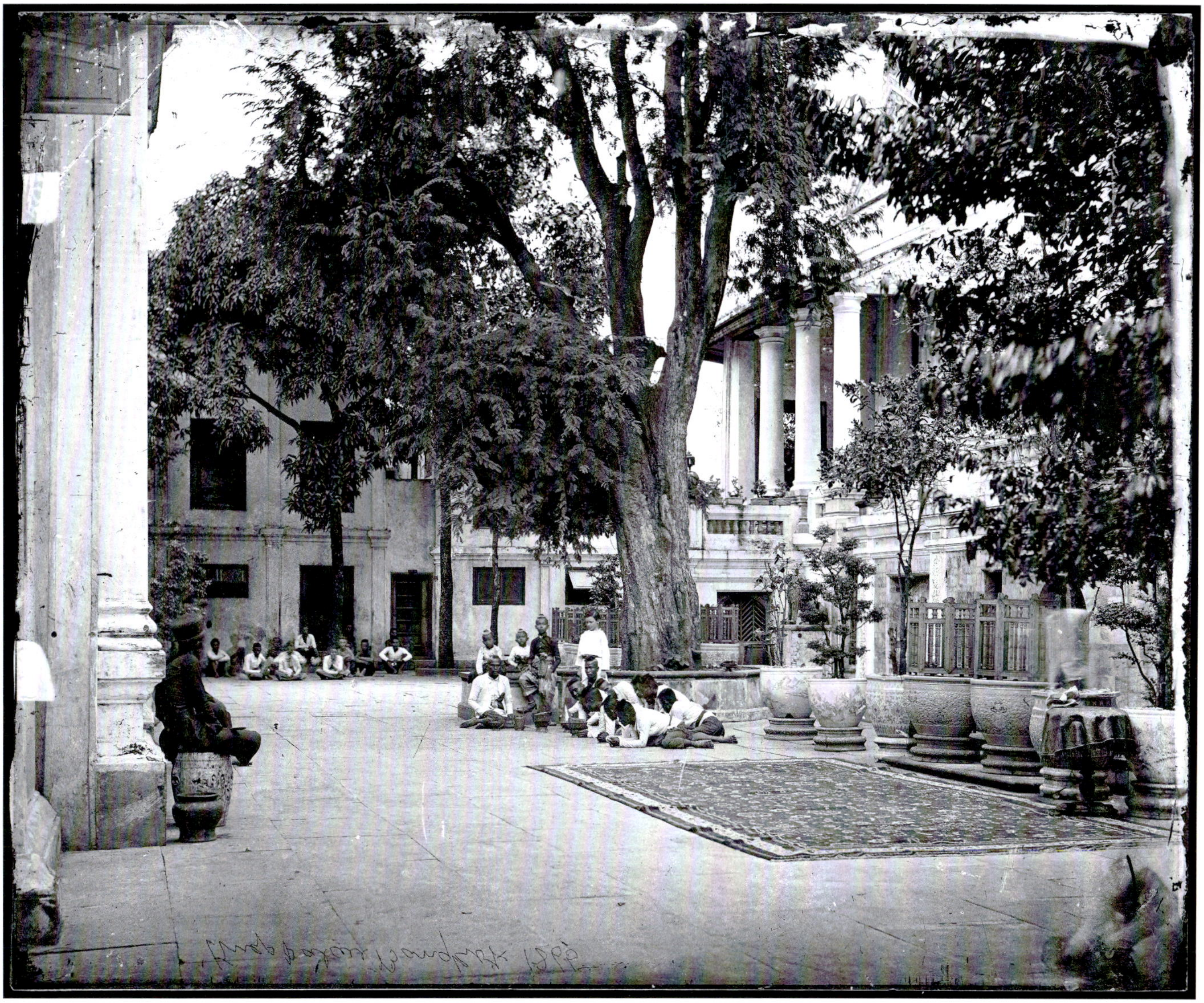

Prince Chulalongkorn, two of his brothers and attendants

Photo inscribed "King Palace Bangkok 1865"

The three princes sit at a low table under a large tamarind tree. The boy in the white sailor suit is Louis Thomas Leonowens (1856-1919), son of Anna, governess to the royal children, who in 1870 wrote a colourful account of her Bangkok life during 1862-67 entitled *The English Governess at the Court of Siam.*

The same location was used for all the royal portraits as, being outside, it provided plenty of light.

YOUNG BOY

Sometimes Thomson's simplest pictures are the most arresting. The young boy, identified as Sudjai Bunnag (later Phraya Rajanuprabhandhu), sits in front of a wooden partition. He wears a Chinese-style shirt with a slight pattern and plain silk *jonggraben*, knotted at the waist and secured by a belt with a metal buckle.

The photograph has only rarely been published in literature in Thai on John Thomson's work. Nevertheless, his intense gaze makes this one of Thomson's finest portraits.

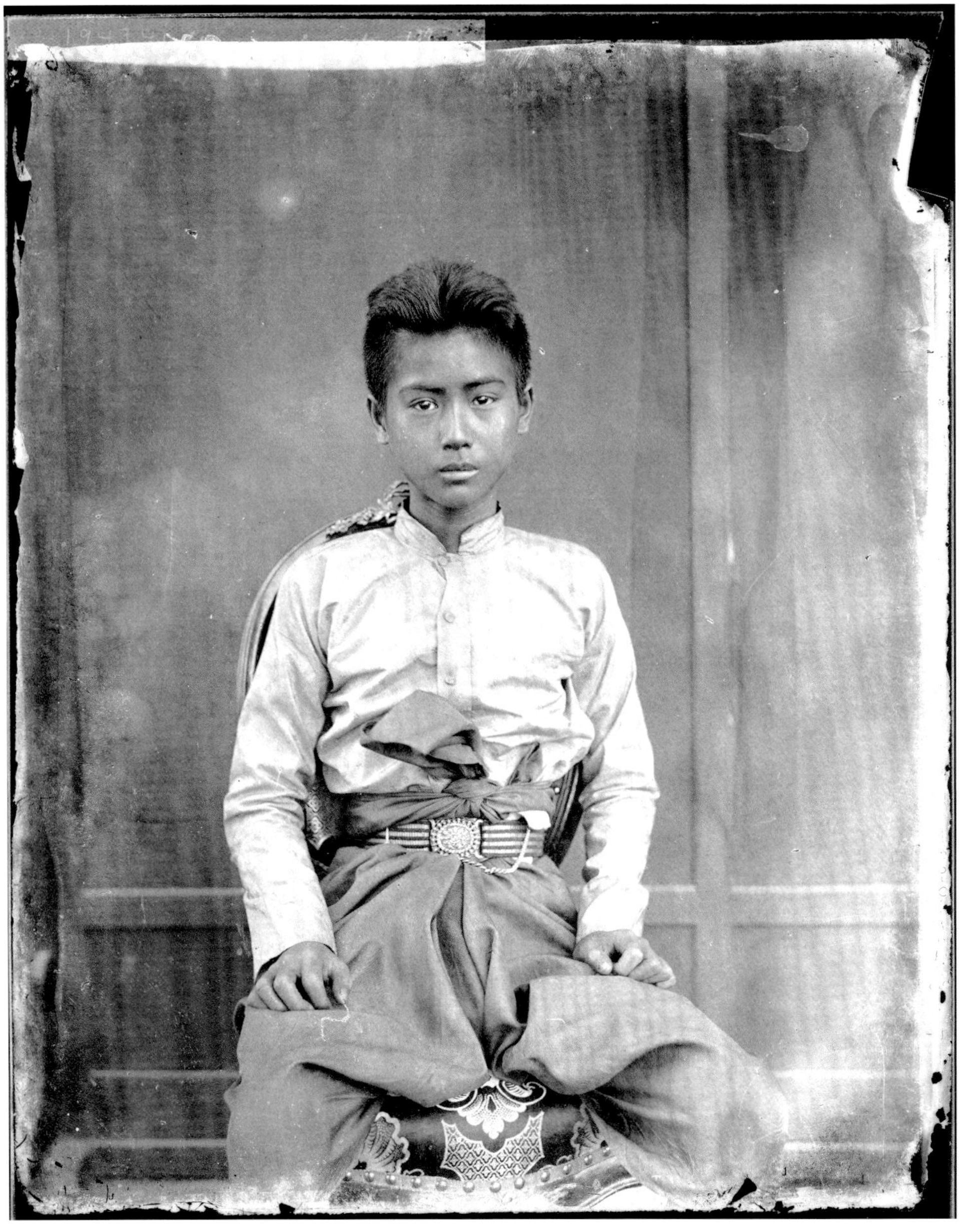

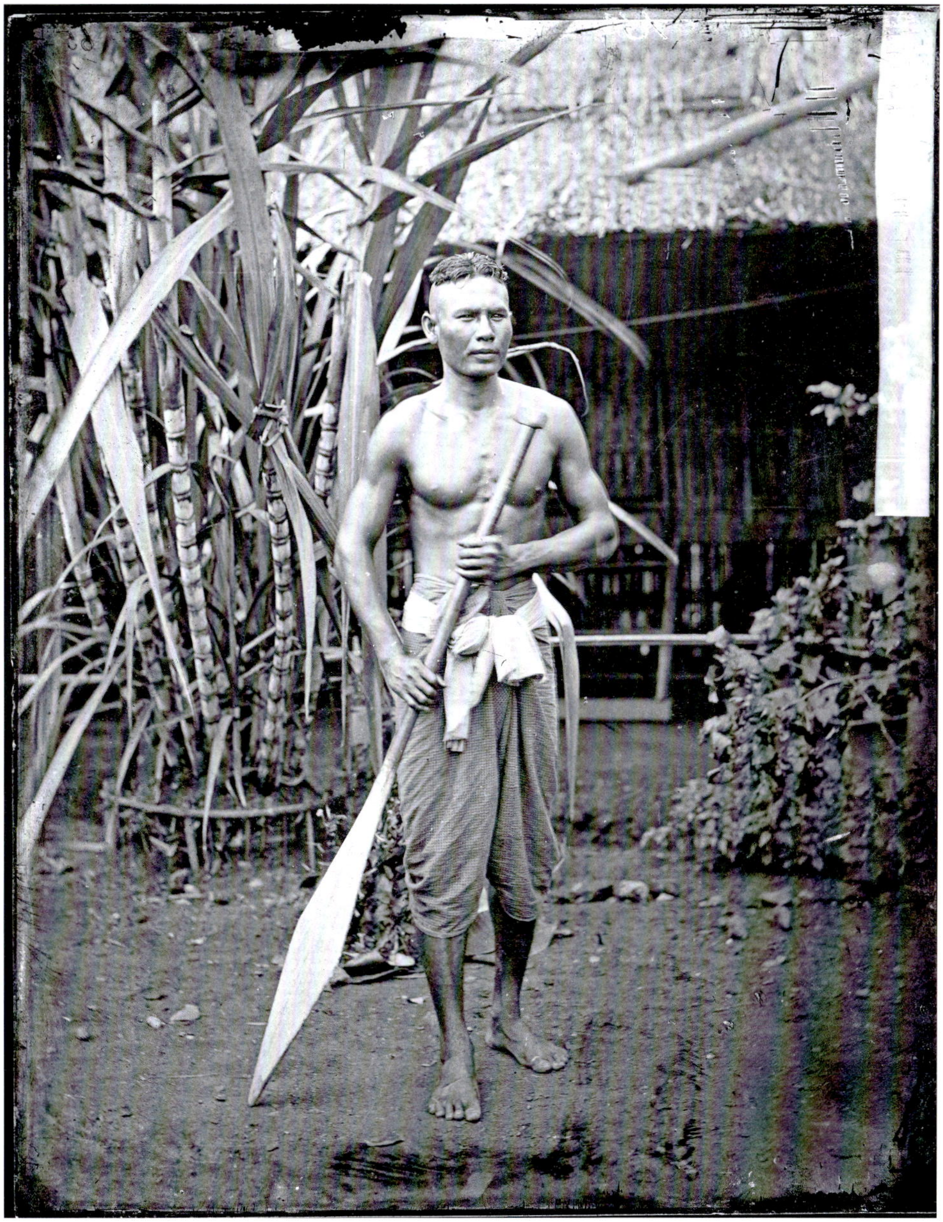

OARSMAN

The background of sugar cane and a thatched dwelling suggest the photograph was taken during Thomson's trip to Phetchaburi.

During the reign of King Mongkut many new canals for waterborne transport were dug. Settlements grew up along waterways with markets developing where canals entered the main river. The major canals dug by Chinese labourers in this reign were Padung Krung Kasem, Hualampong, Maha Sawat and Pasi Charoen. These were able to take steamboats carrying rice and served as a means of public transport.

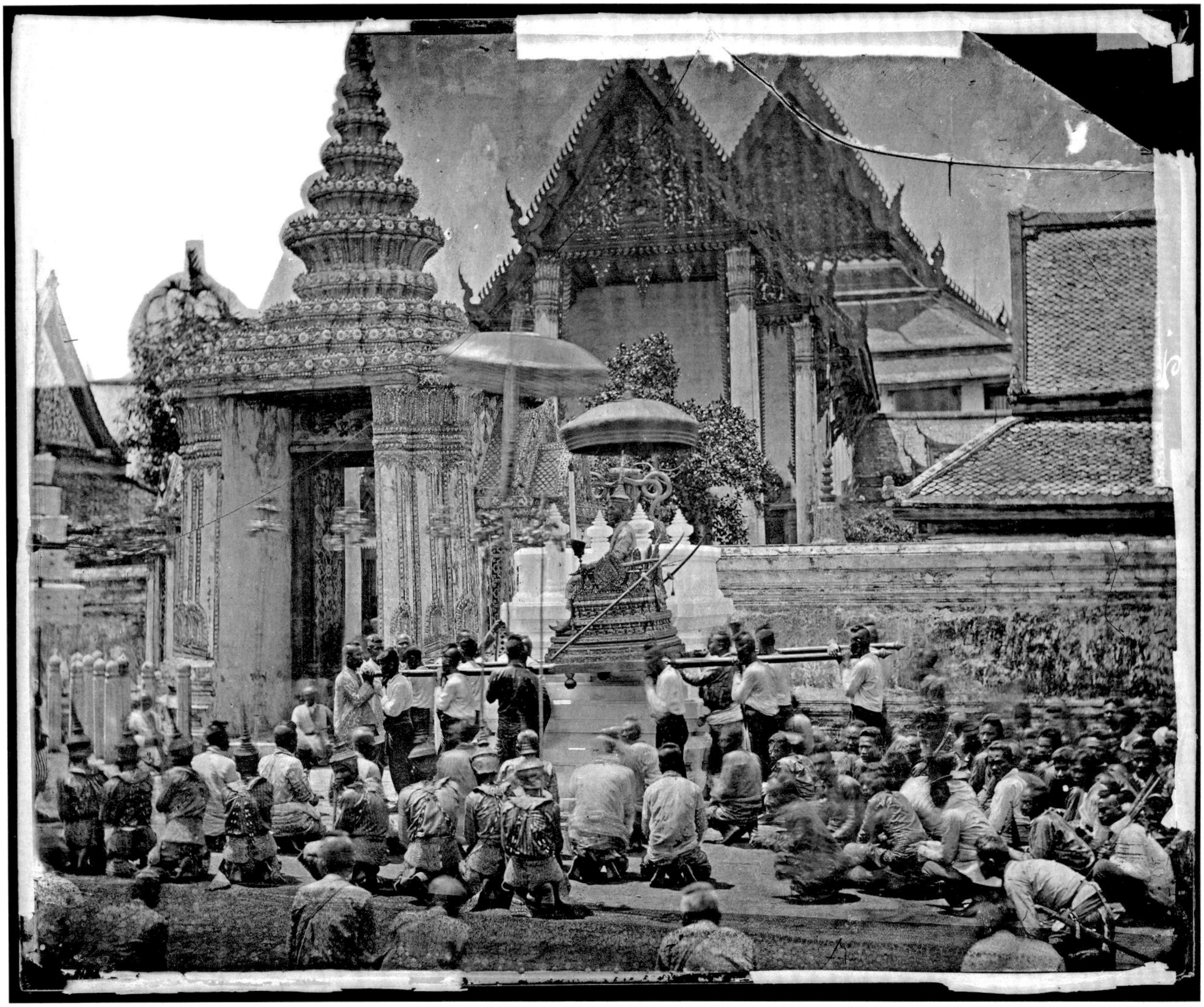

PRESENTING LENTEN ROBES AT WAT PHRA CHETUPON

October, 1865. Bangkok

King Mongkut is seen arriving at Wat Phra Chetupon (The Temple of the Reclining Buddha, Wat Pho) to present new robes to the monks after the annual rains. He is seated on the Phuttan Kanjanasinghad Throne, carried on two poles as a palanquin, and wears the Maha Kathin Crown and a gold-embroidered gown. Two war scythes used in elephant battles flank the throne. An attendant holds a parasol over his head and another, out of focus, waits inside.

When the procession arrived at the eastern gate, the king must have paused for Thomson to take the photograph. A few of the attendants turn to stare at the camera.

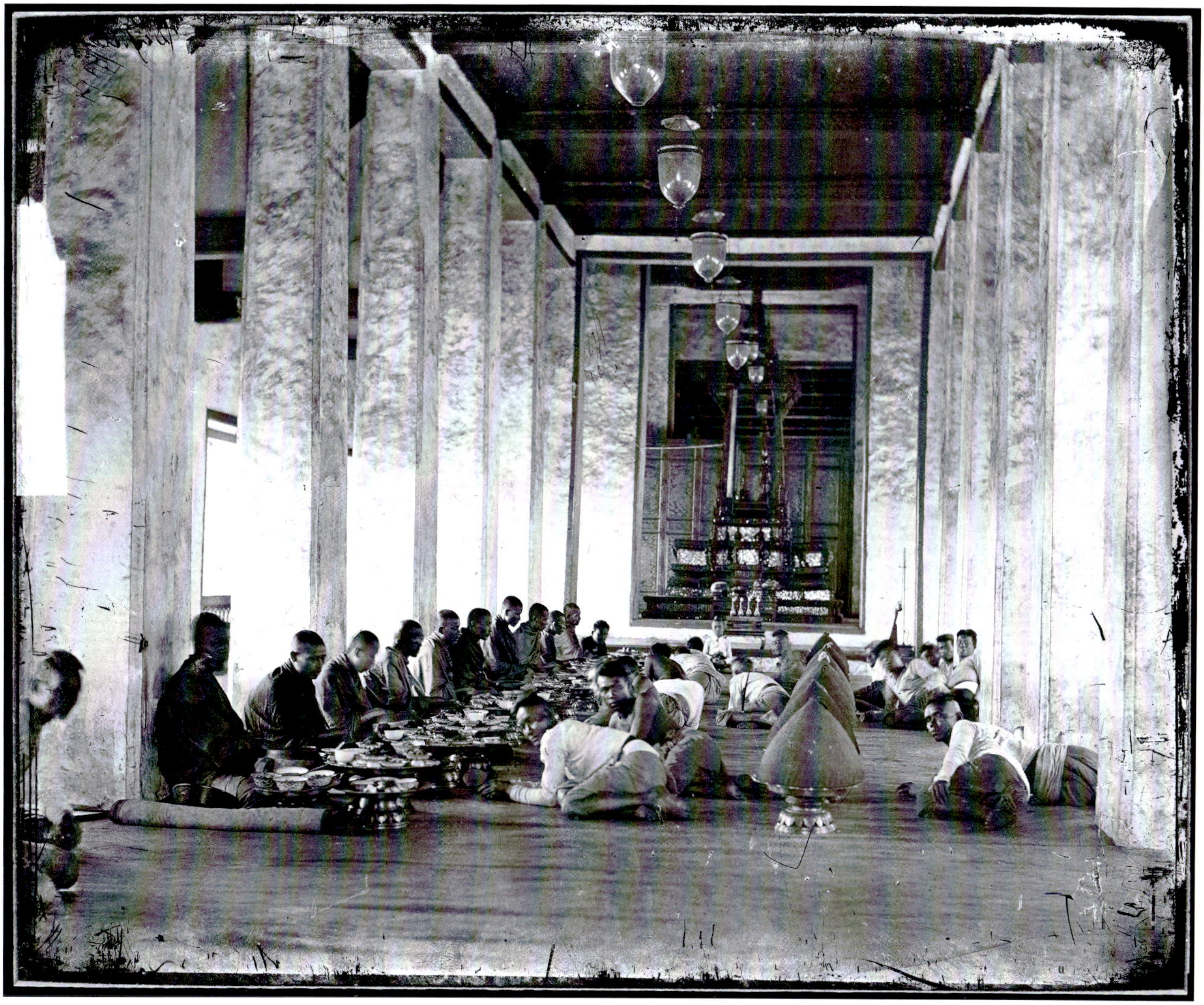

Offering lunch to Buddhist Monks, Sutthai Sawan Throne Hall

Inside the Throne Hall ten Buddhist monks eat from their individual alms' bowls. In front of them crouch palace attendants who have presented the food. The row of brass offering trays with conical cloth covers would have held the desserts.

In the Buddhist tradition, monks have one meal a day which must be finished before 12 noon. At the back of the hall in front of the throne, a small prince, HRH Prince Thongtaem (1857-1919), the son of King Mongkut and Chao Chom Manda Sangwan presides over the ceremony. The gilded throne inlaid with glass mosaic houses a standing and seated Buddha image. In front of the throne is a set of food offerings for the Buddha images as is traditional.

MONK HOLDING A FAN

Grand Palace, Bangkok

The fabric of the monk's robe has a diamond pattern, which is no longer used. Monks' robes consist of three pieces of cloth. The inner ones (not visible), are the *antarvāsa* (Thai: *ungsa*) and *uttarāsaṅga* (Thai: *sabong*), with the outer garment, *saāghṅti* (Thai: *jiworn*), wrapped around on top. Here, one shoulder is exposed, as is common when inside the temple, but during ceremonies both shoulders are usually covered.

Fans are part of a Buddhist monks' paraphernalia and are held in front of the face during chanting. This particular type was presented by the king to those who had passed levels 3-9 of Buddhist examinations equivalent to a university degree.

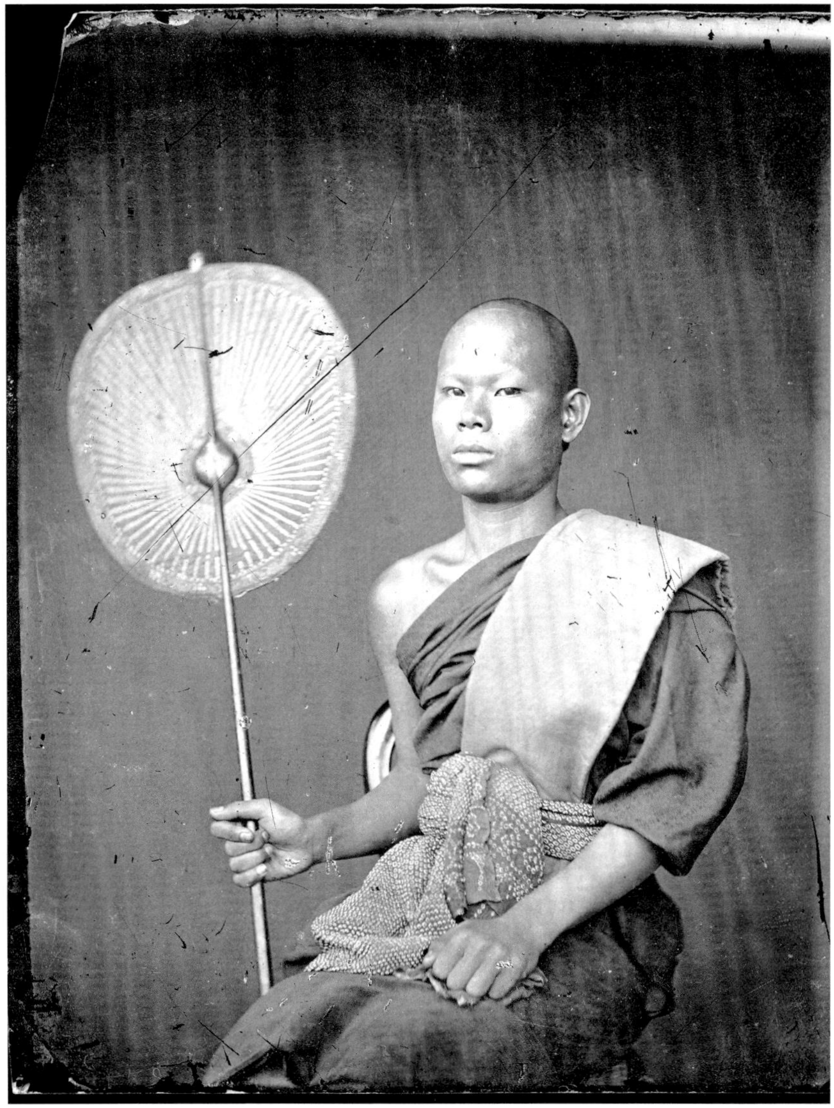

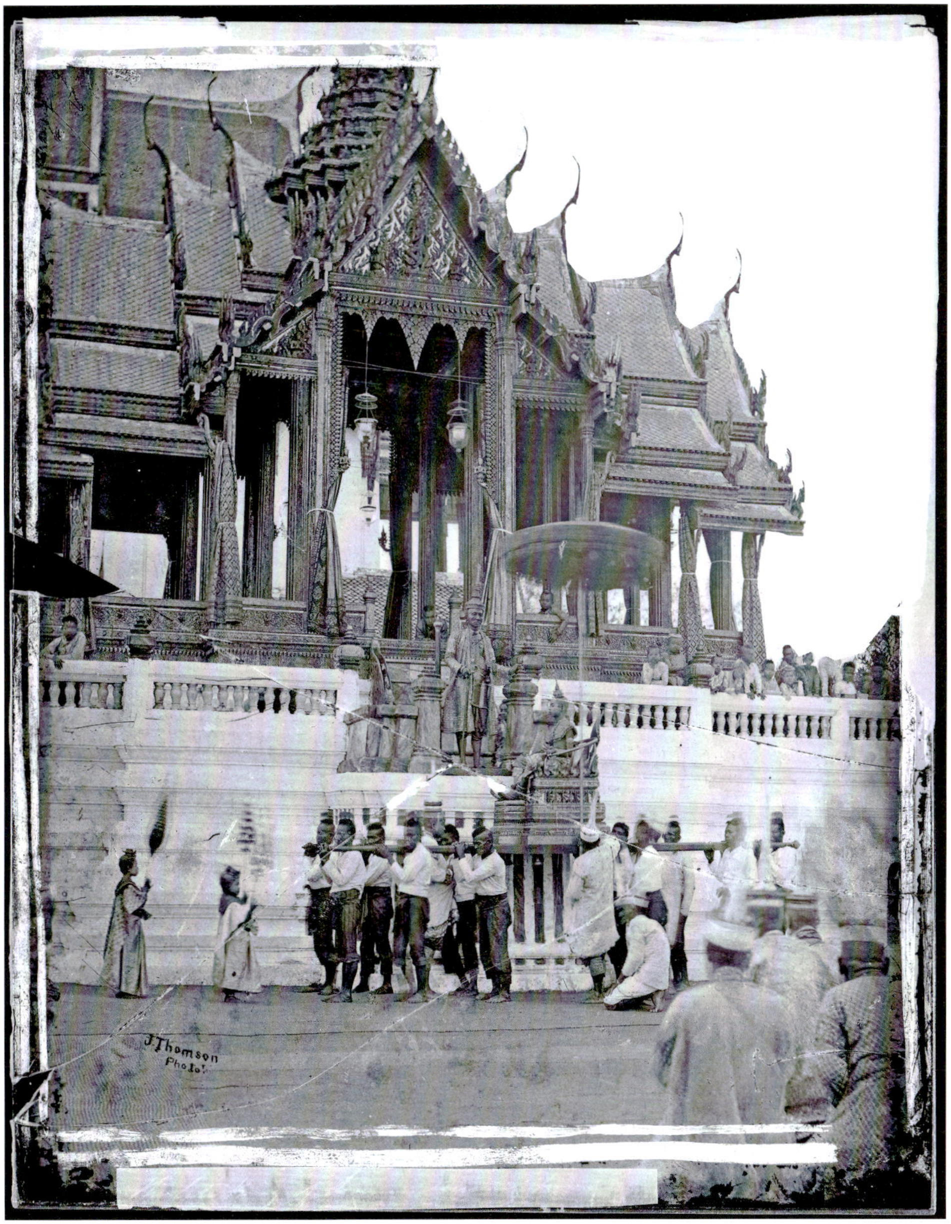

Tonsurate ceremony of Crown Prince Chulalongkorn, early morning, Thursday 4th January 1866 (Day 1)

Signed "J. Thomson photo"

The tonsurate ceremony was an elaborate rite of passage, taking place over three days. King Mongkut is wearing full regalia and crown, with a short sword is tucked into his belt and a walking stick in his right hand. He stands in front of the Aporn Phimok Prasat to send off Prince Chulalongkorn seated on the Kong royal palanquin, after a ceremony in the Dusit Maha Prasat Throne Hall. The prince still has the topknot, secured by a special gold and diamond studded covering and wears many bangles and bracelets. Some of his half brothers and sisters watch from the balcony.

Aporn Phimok Prasat, built early in the Fourth Reign, is in classical Thai style with porches on all four sides and a *prasat*-style spire in the middle.

Second Day of the Tonsurate Ceremony, 5th January, 1866

Signed "J. Thomson" along the base of the platform

For this photograph Thomson has moved in slightly closer to show the porch with King Mongkut from a different angle. Prince Chulalongkorn is seated on the Puttarn Thong palanquin as was customary after the tonsurate ceremony had been completed in the Dusit Maha Prasat Throne Hall. While the king is dressed in similar fashion to the previous day, Prince Chulalongkorn is dressed in the regalia of a royal prince with the bearers in red shirts instead of white.

The print shows that the negative has been retouched with white paint in order to emphasise the details, or perhaps because the exposure was slightly too long. This is very apparent on the crown worn by the prince and on the conical hat of his parasol bearer.

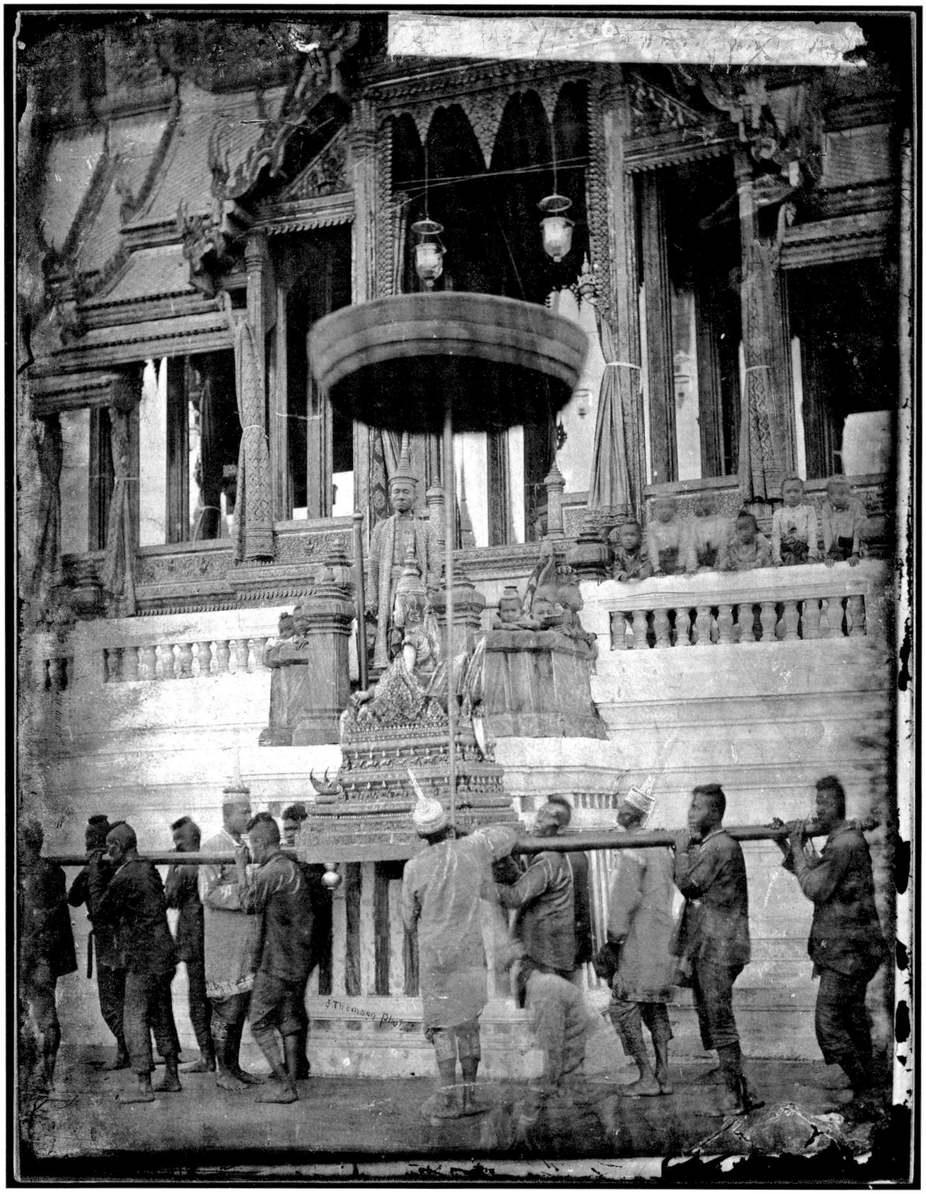

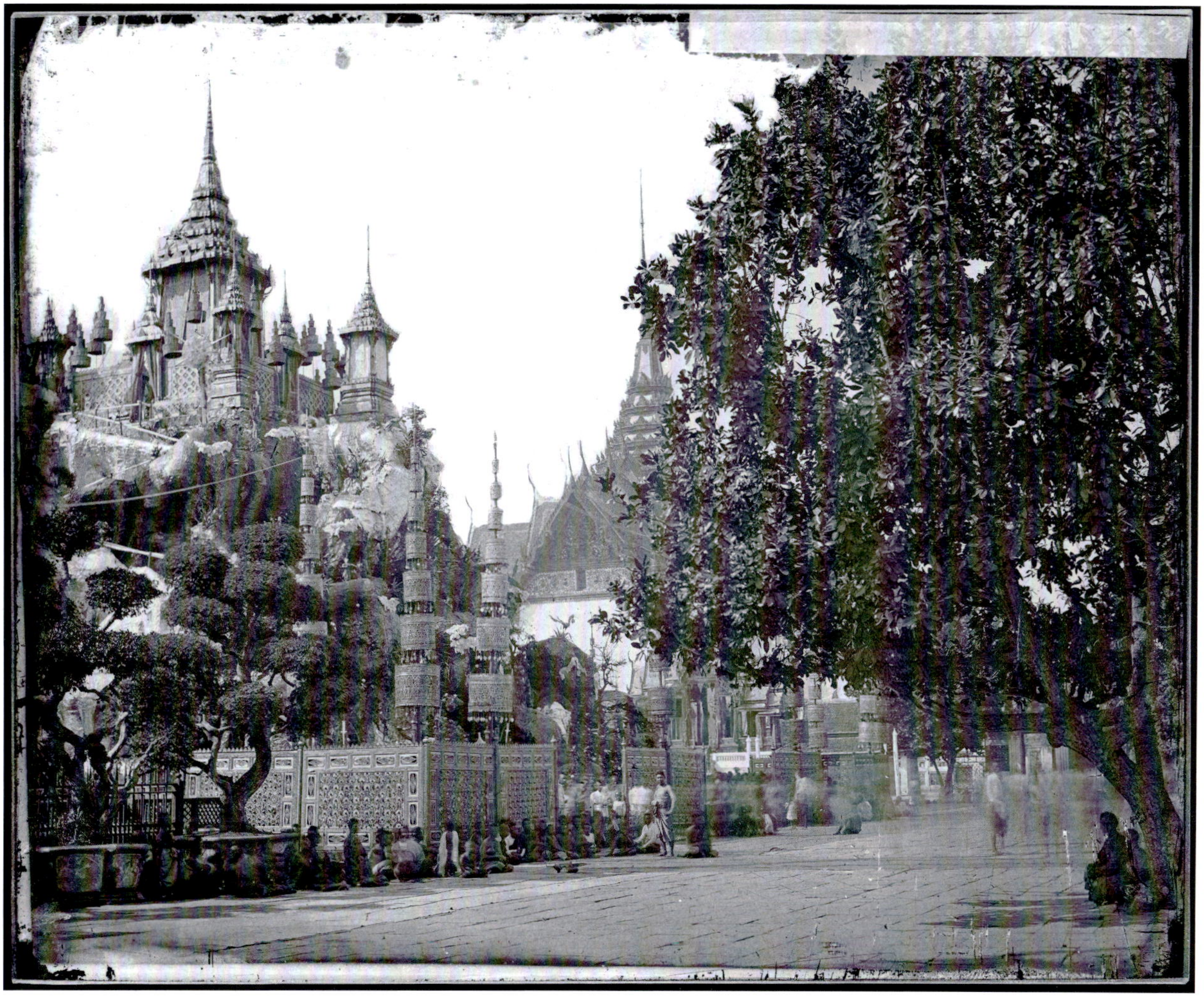

Mount Krailas Ceremony, 3rd Day of Tonsurate Ceremony

6th January, 1866.
Grand Palace, Bangkok

This photograph shows the three venues associated with the Tonsurate ceremony. In the background, is the Dusit Maha Prasat Throne Hall built in 1789 and used for the lying-in-state of kings, queens and high-ranking princes and princesses, tonsurate ceremonies and the coronation. In the middle ground, just discernible through the tree is the Aporn Phimok Prasat.

In the foreground and to the left, is Mount Krailas, an elaborate papier maché construction representing the abode of Shiva, the supreme god in the Brahmanic tradition. Once the prince had undergone a ritual bath, a senior Prince representing Shiva would descend from the *mandapa* to take him to the summit, where he bestowed a blessing before returning him to the earthly realm.

Although Prince Chulalongkorn is not present in the photograph, everything is ready with the officials waiting by the entrance to Mount Krailas.

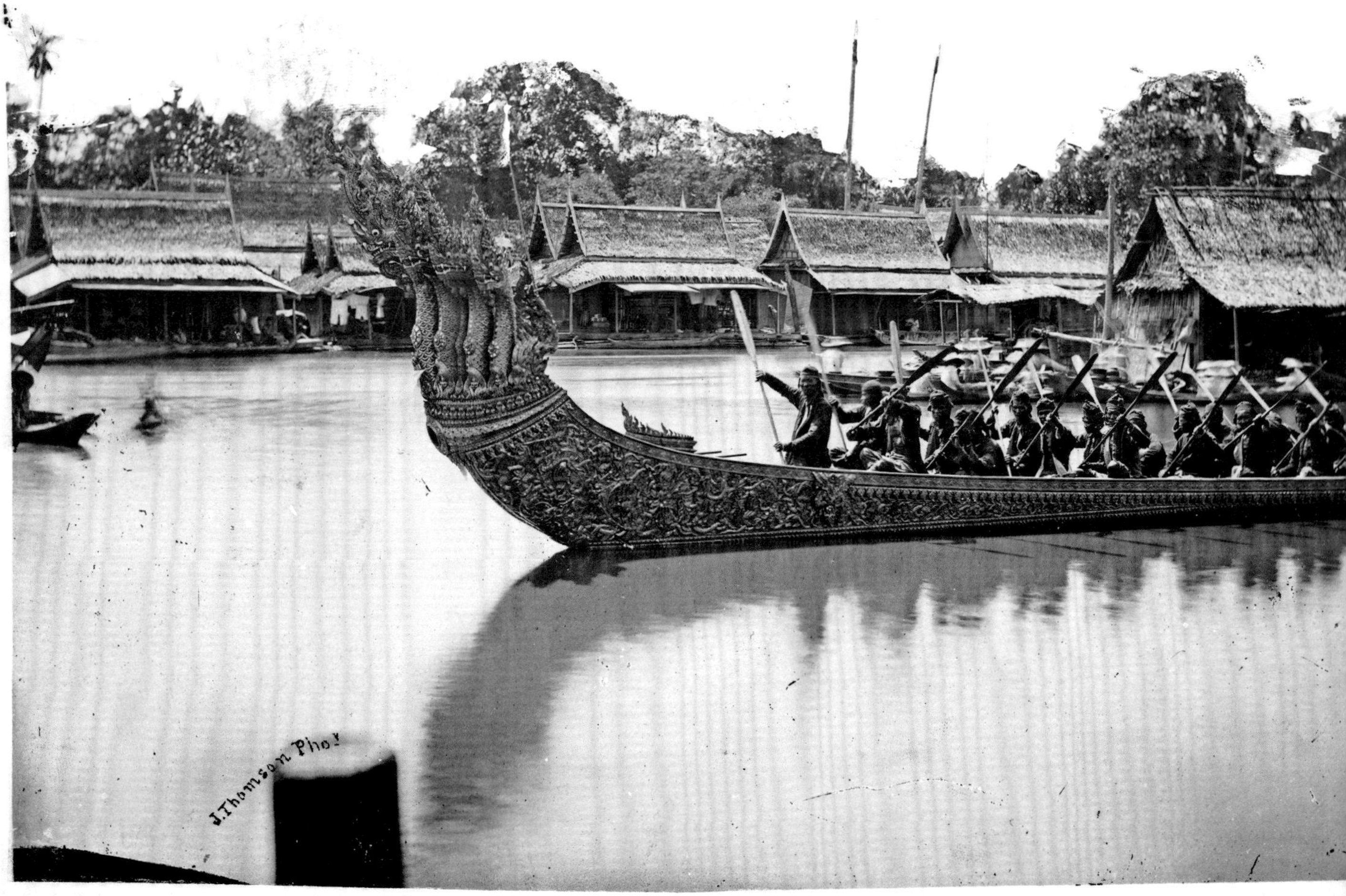

Royal Barge Procession for the Kathin Ceremony

14th October 1865. Signed "J. Thomson photo" on the left foreground post

For the water procession to distribute Lenten robes to royally-sponsored temples, King Mongkut used the *Ananta Nagara* barge shown here. The name refers to the king of the *nagas* (water serpents), who in Southeast Asian mythology controls the waters. Two glass plates were needed to photograph the whole boat, moored in a canal after the ceremony.

The oarsmen demonstrate the 'bird in flight' stroke and all look at the camera.

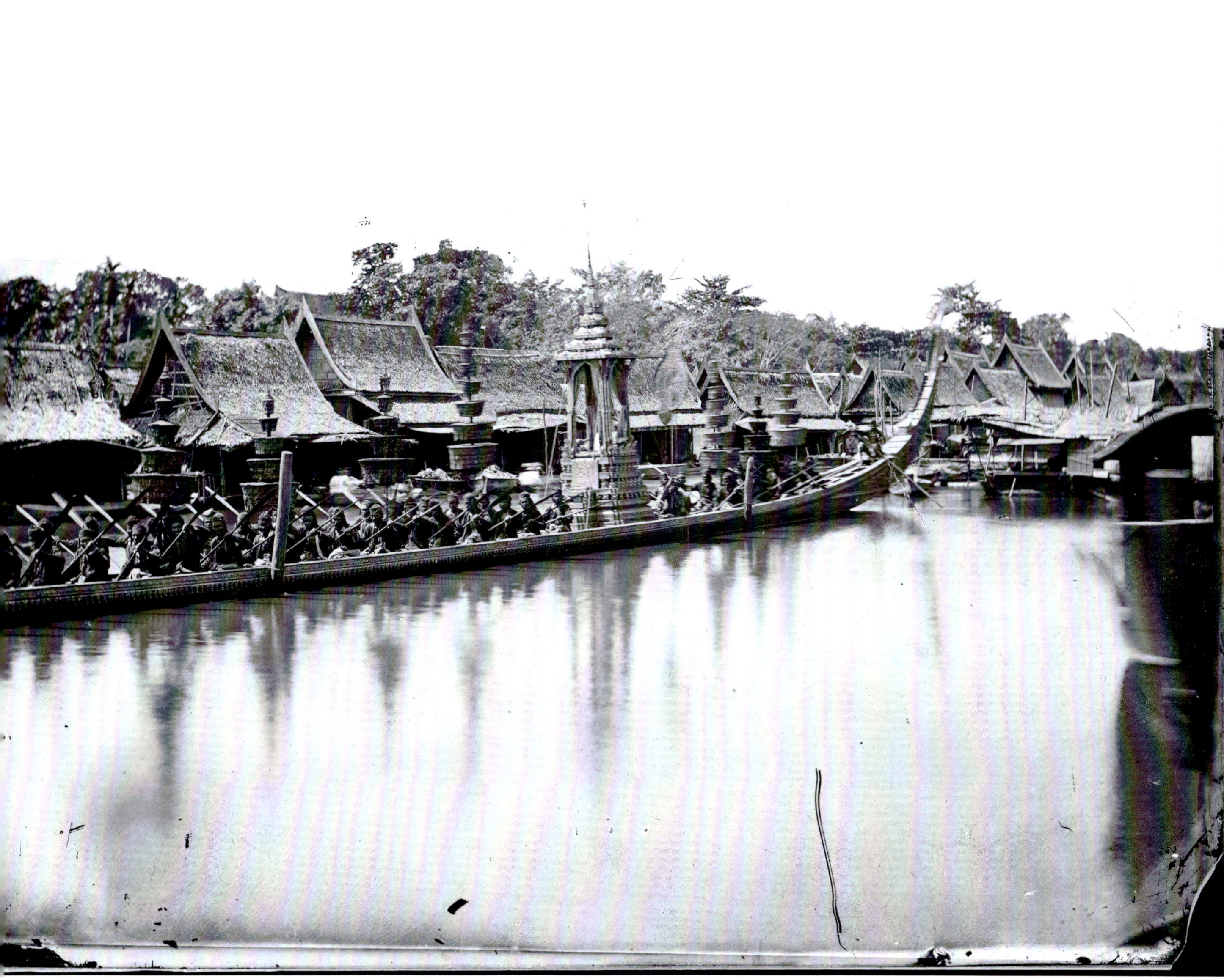

Behind the barge are floating houses of woven bamboo and pandanus thatch, typical of this period. The barge, constructed in the reign of King Mongkut, is today in the Royal Barges Museum, Bangkok. At 42.95 metres long x 2.95 metres wide, it requires 54 oarsmen, with two steersmen at the back and two at the front. The entire boat is carved with gilded nagas and adorned with glass mosaic.

FUNERAL *MERU* FOR KING PINKLAO, THE SECOND KING (1808-1865)

Thomson took two photographs of this elaborate wooden structure before leaving on 27th January 1866 for Cambodia. The *meru*, symbolising Mount Meru the centre of the universe and abode of the gods, was constructed on Sanam Luang (Royal Ground), the open area to the north of the Grand Palace. The king's urn is housed inside.

King Pinklao was the full younger brother of King Mongkut and was crowned as the Second King. He had died on 7th January 1865 but the construction of the *meru* took a full year. He was finally cremated on 17th February.

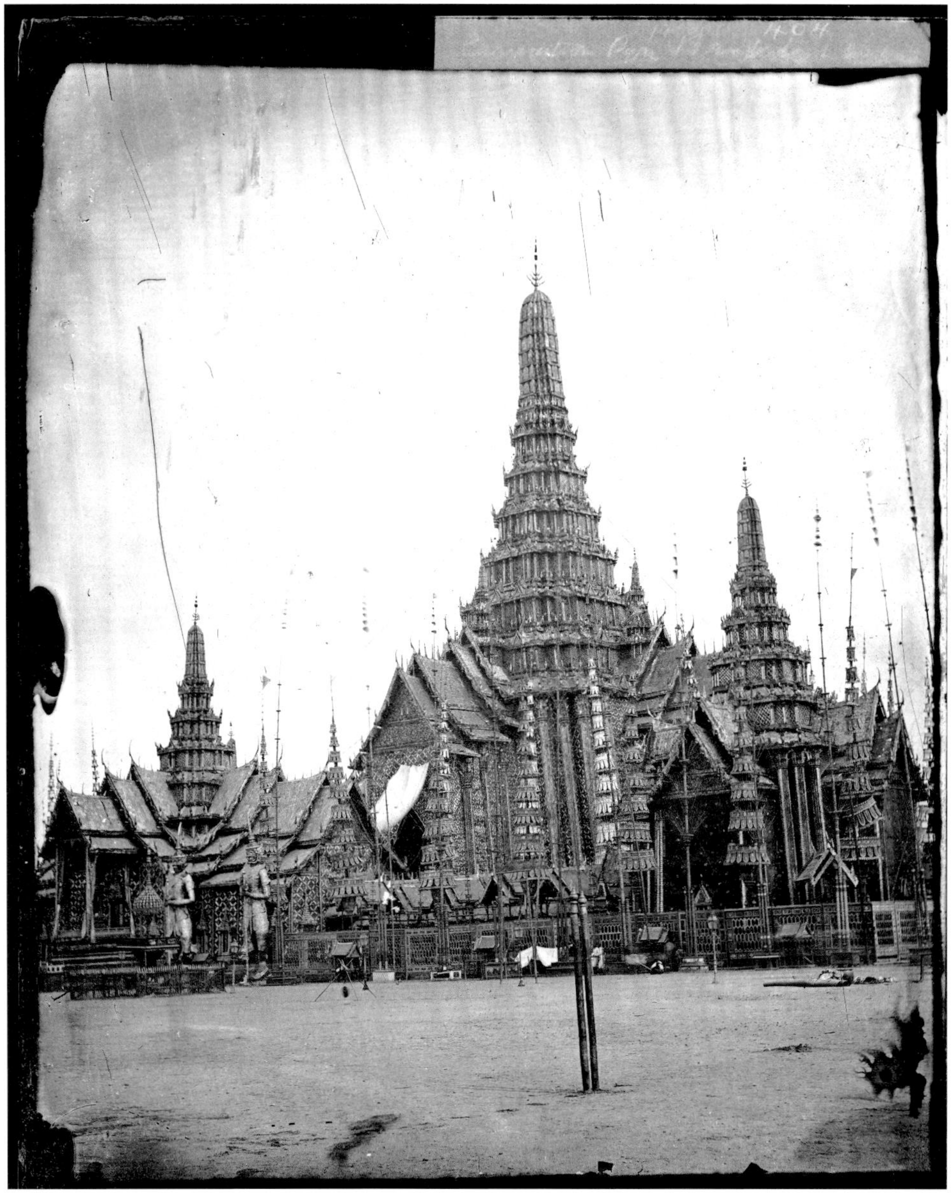

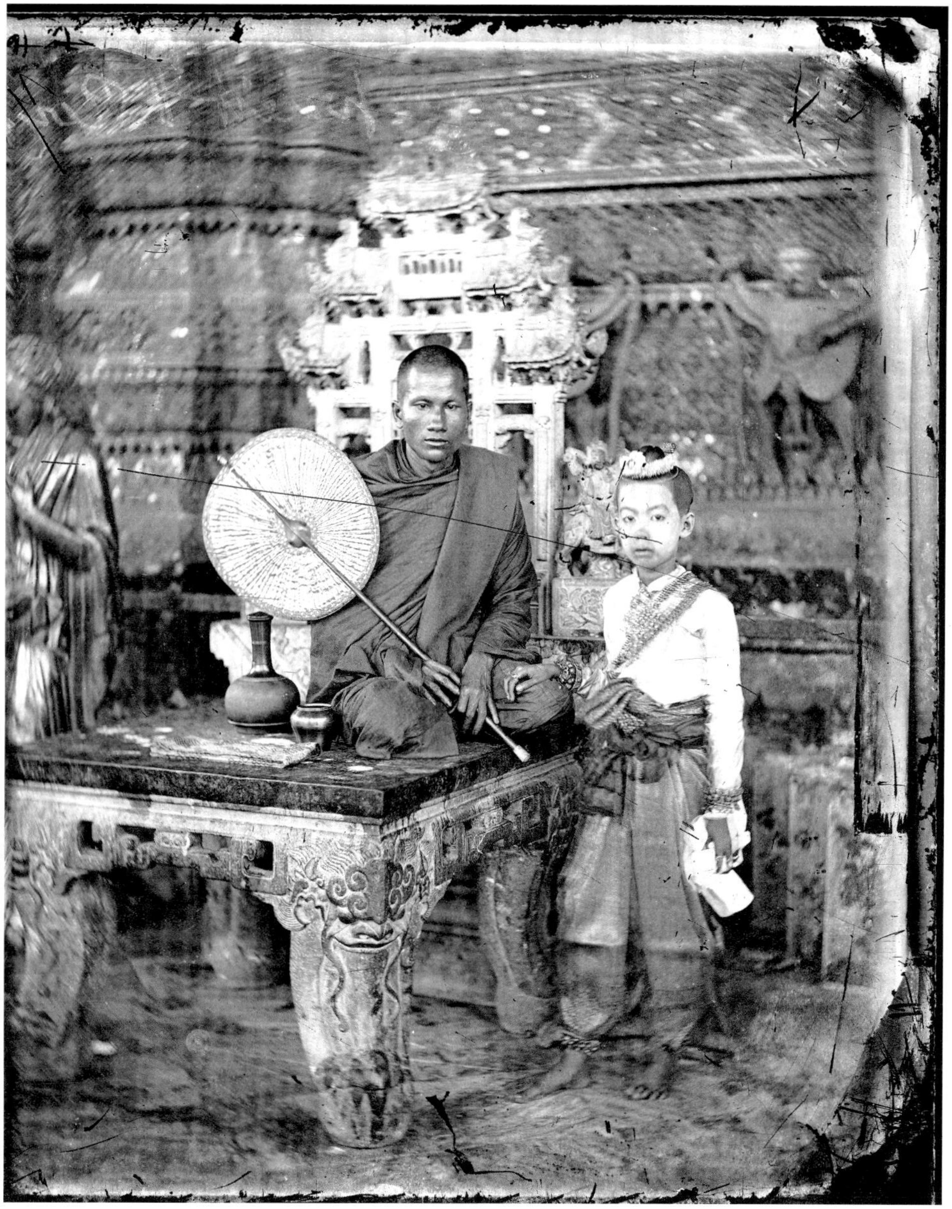

MONK AND YOUNG PRINCE

1865. Verandah of the Emerald Buddha Temple, Bangkok

A Buddhist monk sits on a marble and granite table, while next to him stands HRH Prince Krisdapinihan (later HRH Prince Nares Varariddhi, 1855-1923). The monk holds a circular fan (*talapat*) of the type used when chanting on royal holy days and at royal funeral ceremonies. Beside him are a spittoon and ewer. The young prince is in full regalia similar to that worn for the topknot-cutting ceremony. The stone carving in the background is a miniature triple-entrance Chinese doorway.

Verandah outside the Chapel of the Emerald Buddha

The chapel of the Emerald Buddha was built in the reign of King Rama I (1782-1810), the founder of Bangkok. Situated within the Grand Palace compound, it is a masterpiece of Siamese architecture and design. The central entrance on this north wall was reserved for the king and the royal family. The exterior wall is covered with low relief stucco, gilded and inlaid with glass mosaic. The sidewalls of the deep porch have gilded Chinese-style guardians standing on lions, while the door panels, inlaid with mother of pearl, portray mythological beasts from the Himavamsa forest.

Chinese porcelain with flowers and birds has been used for the risers on the steps, while granite stools were imported as ballast in junks during the reign of King Rama III (1824-1851) when maritime trade with China was at its height.

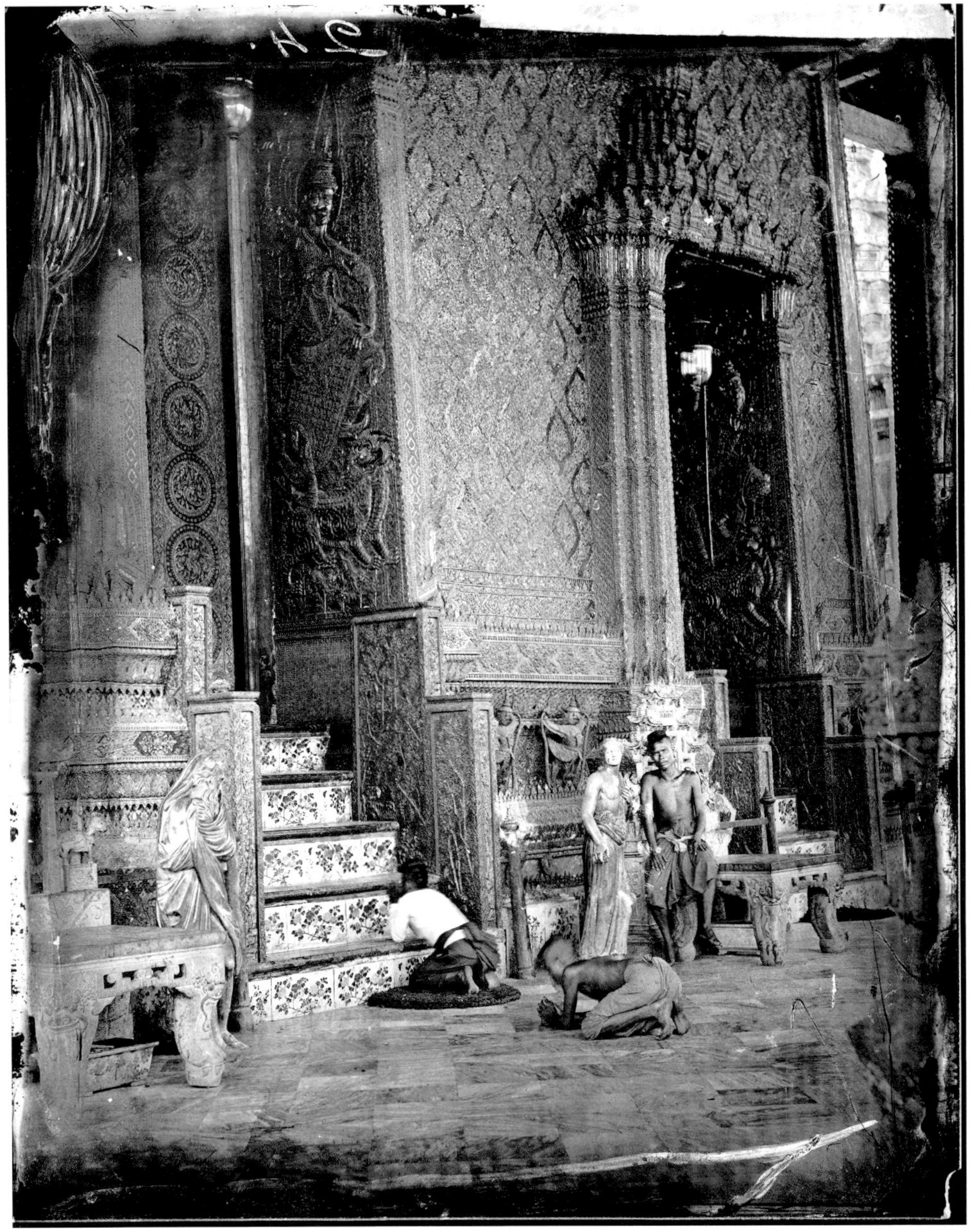

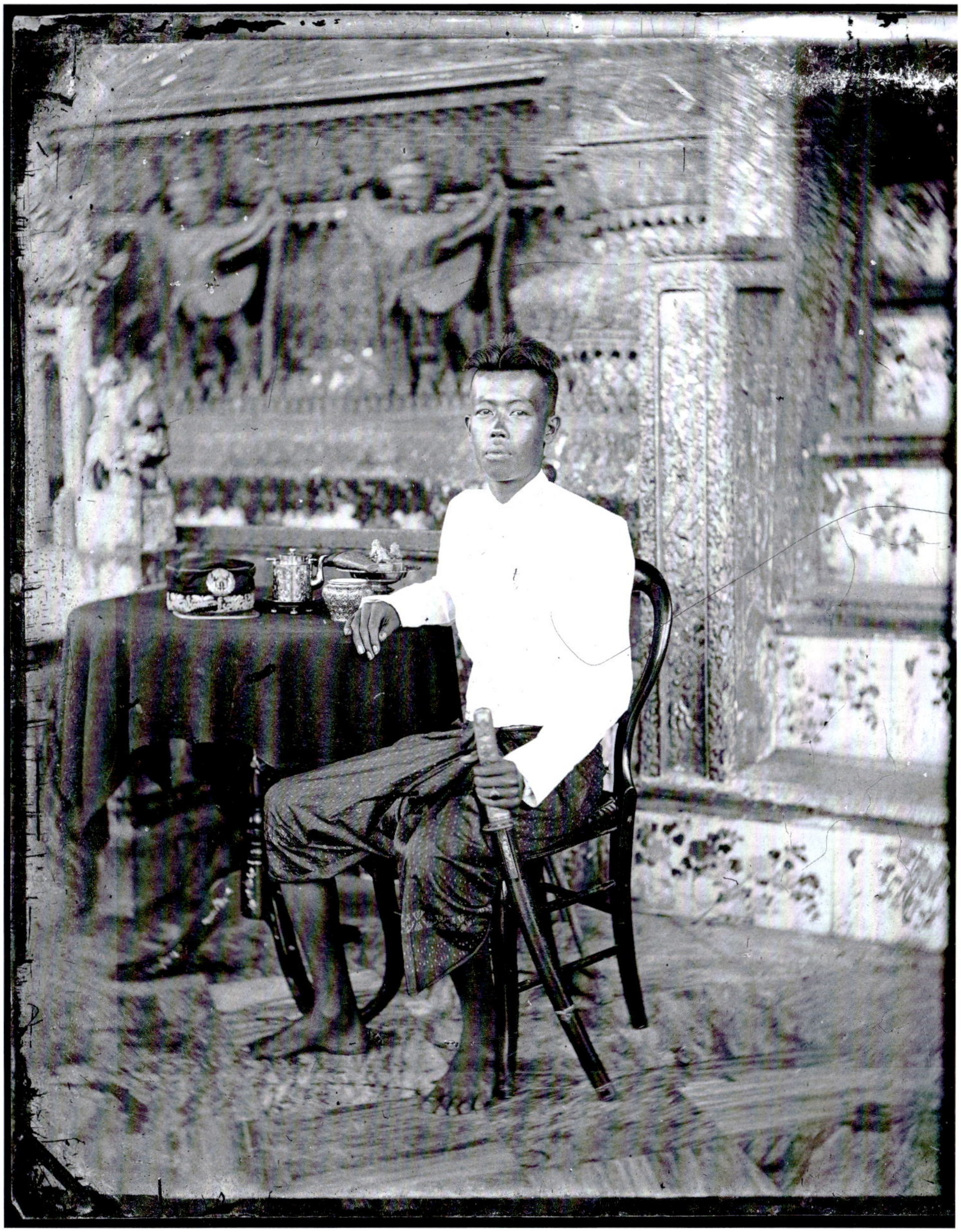

Young man with a Samurai sword

1865. Verandah of the Emerald Buddha Temple

The young man wears *jonggraben* of *mudmee* silk, probably woven in Cambodia, and a simple white shirt. His hair cut was very fashionable at that time and he holds a Samurai-style sword.

The rosewood side table is inlaid with mother-of-pearl (see on the legs) and covered with a baize cloth. The wool cap suggests the man is a palace official. Next to the cap is a small gold and enamelled Bencharong porcelain spittoon, a small cylindrical tea pot on a silver tray, and a silver pedestal tray with a betel leaf holder and three, square silver boxes with large lion handles, crafted by Shanghainese silversmiths. The pole used to steady his head during the long exposure is just visible at his neck.

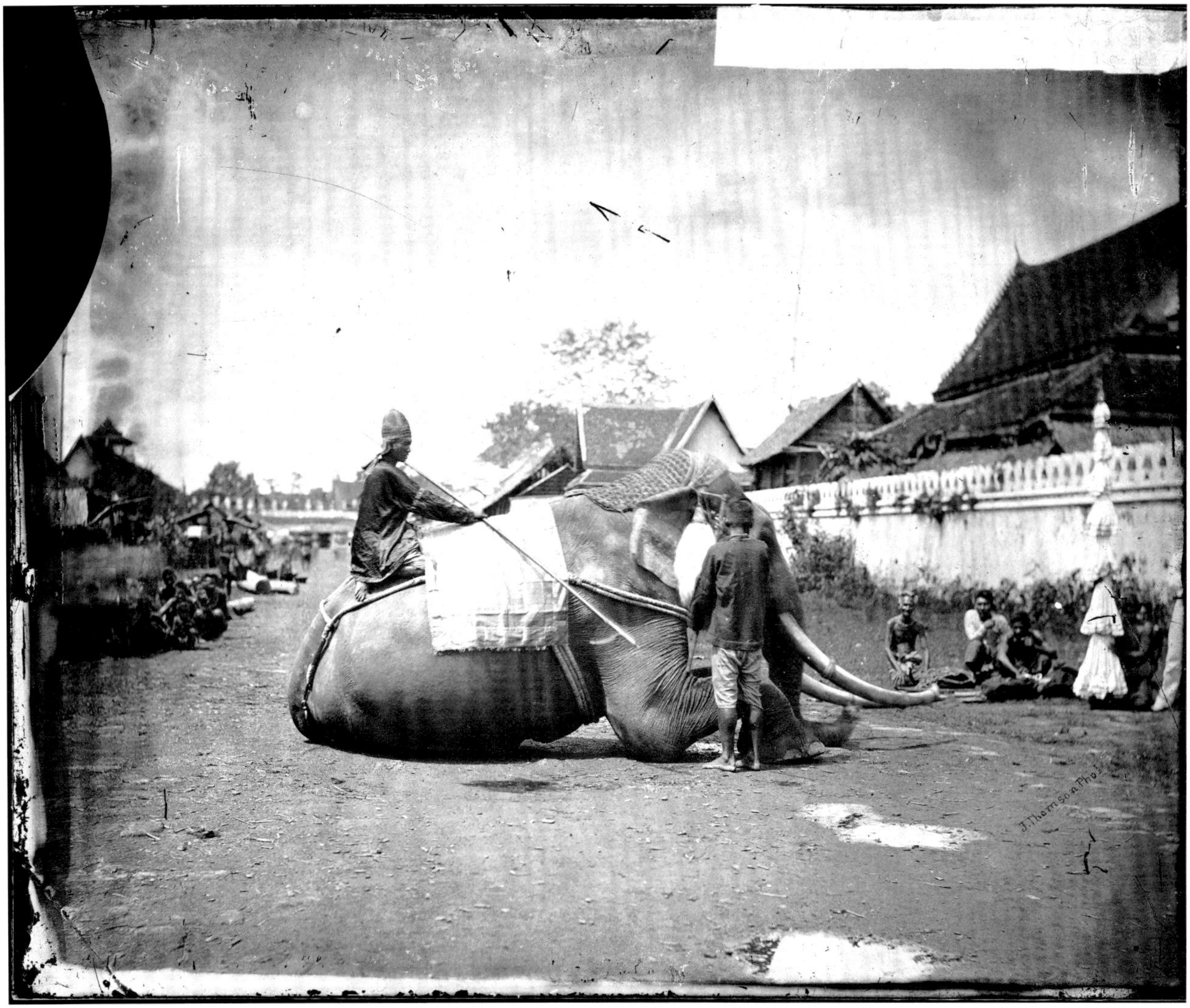

THE KING'S WHITE ELEPHANT

Signed "J. Thomson photo" on the bottom right of the photograph. Outside the Grand Palace, Bangkok

Based on its costume and mahouts, this elephant must be one of the 12 auspicious white elephants belonging to King Mongkut. Such animals received special regalia such as the brocade headband with a net of crystal beads covering his neck; a white yak tassle with a gold lotus-shaped finial; gold bangles inlaid with rubies on his tusks; a brocade cloth edged with gold thread on his back.

The mounted mahout wears a conical cap with flaps. The other is training the elephant to kneel using an elephant goad with a hook (an *ankusa*). By the palace wall, attendants sit casually. The rolled-up seven-tiered parasol was also part of white-elephant regalia.

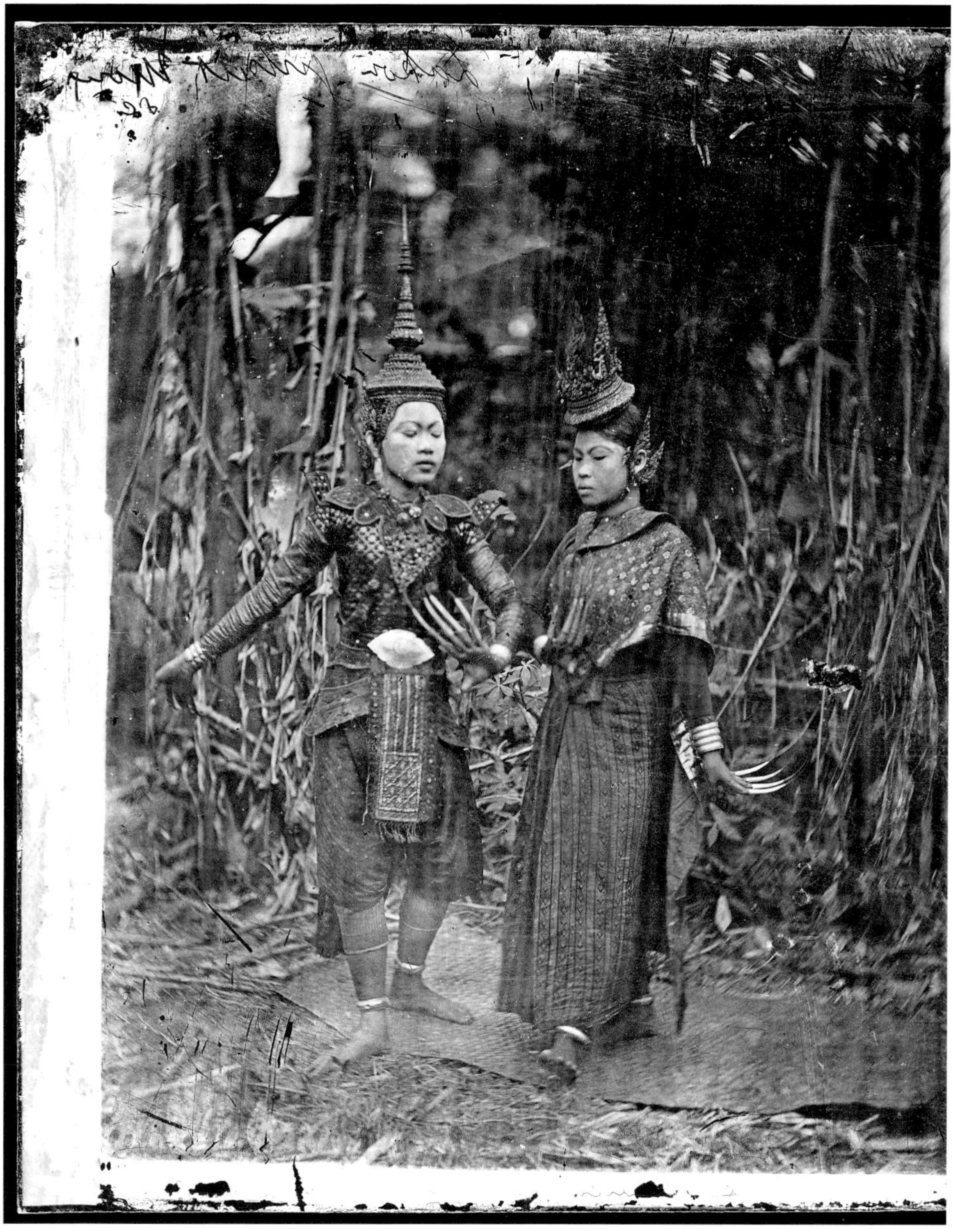

Two Siamese dancers

The dancers were most probably photographed on Thomson's trip to Phetchaburi.

Both wear extremely long and unusal metal nails. The male character (left) is played by a woman, wearing a fine headdress similar to those from court workshops. The wide collar is also unusual. The metal belt buckle is in Malay style. The frontal pleat is embroidered with metallic thread and sequins, and at the top are two side flaps similar to those on adorned Buddha images. The silk *jonggraben* with flower pattern is worn over a thin pair of trousers. Plain silver bracelets are worn around the ankles.

The female dancer has an elaborate flame-like headdress, worn slightly slanted and towards the front of her head, a fashion typical of the Ayutthaya and early Bangkok periods.

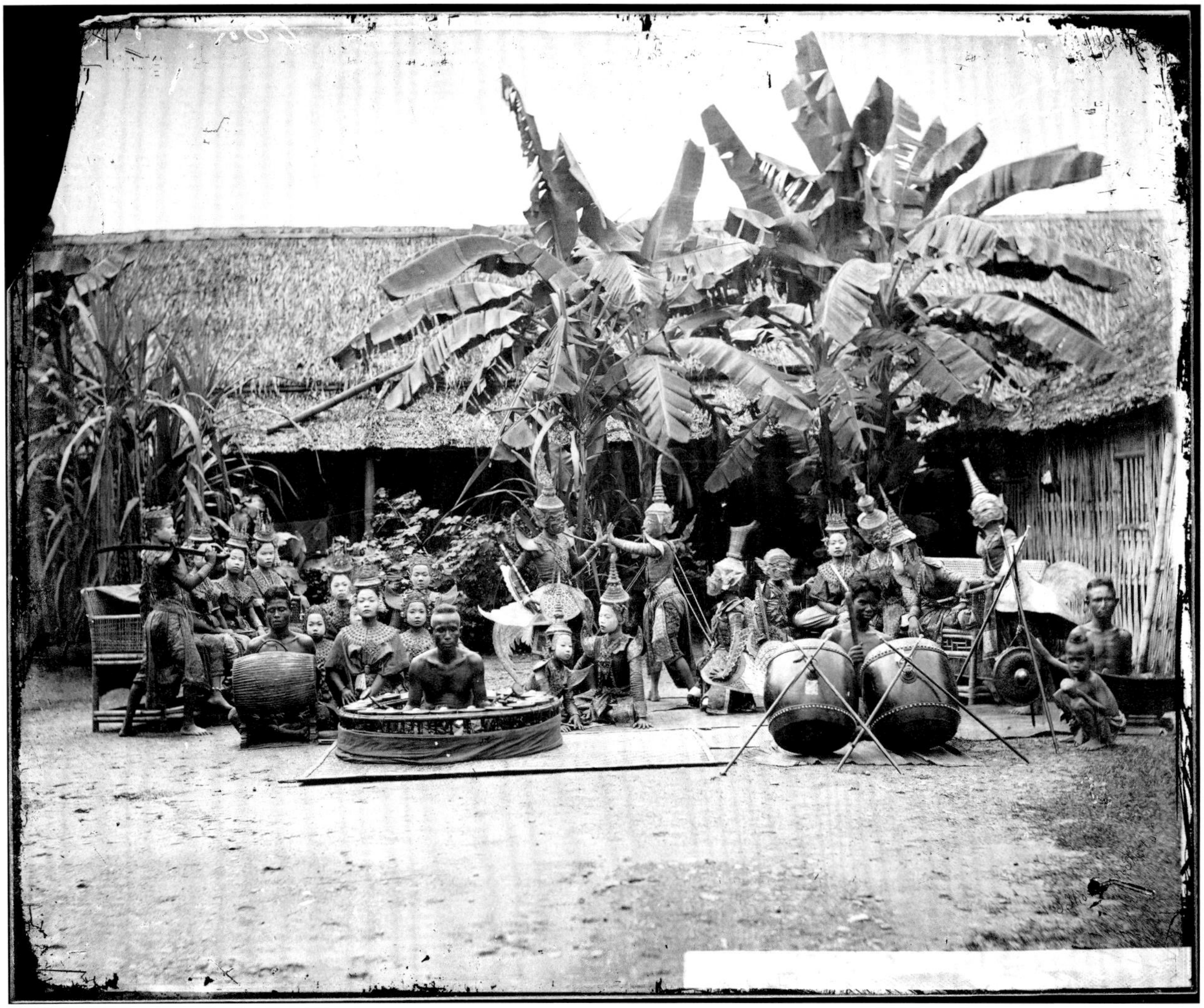

KHON AND LAKHON TROUPE

The *Ramakien*, derived from the Indian *Ramayana* epic, tells how Phra Ram and Phra Lak must rescue Sita, Phra Ram's wife, from Tosakanth, the evil giant king and his army, who live on the island of Lanka.

Performances of *khon* (masked dance drama) and *lakhon* (plays) were an integral part of Siamese court life, with performances accompanying many ceremonies and festivals.

This group, combining both, must have been staged for Thomson, as usually they do not appear together. There are a diverse range of costumes and masks and a traditional five-piece orchestra. Of the 26 people in the photograph, many are likely children as they are very small. Male characters were often played by women.

The six *khon* performers (wearing masks) seem to be dressed for the *Ramakien* dance drama, although the scene is not identifiable. In front, the four musicians play, from left to right, a two-sided drum, a large gong circle, a double timpani, a gong and a soprano bamboo xylophone.

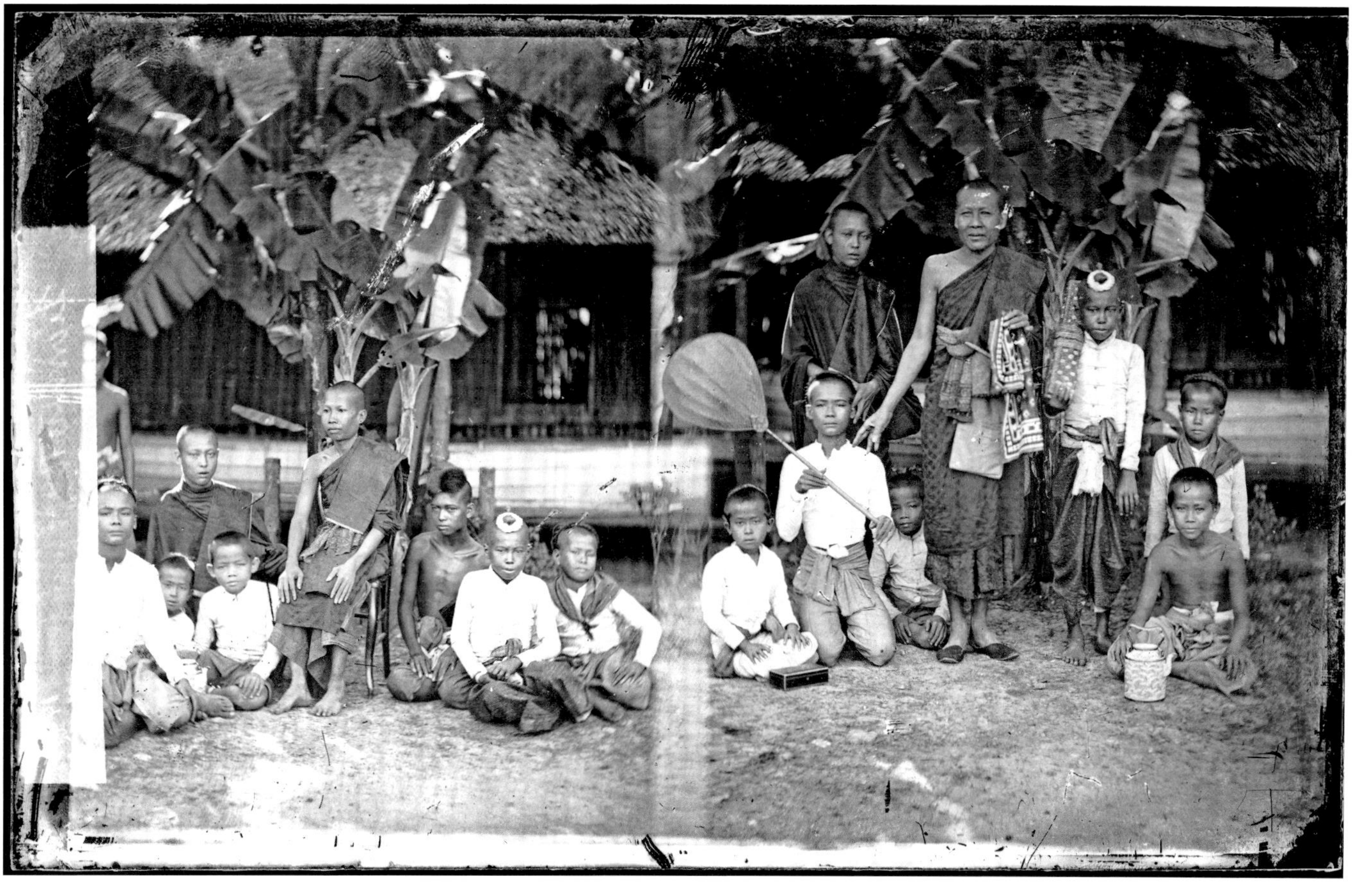

MONKS AND THEIR ASSISTANTS

This photograph is unusual in that two images have been combined into one, with several of the characters and the background appearing twice.

The senior monk is shown standing only on the right. A younger monk stands on his right and three young disciples flank the monks on either side. Among these are three young Chinese boys, their pigtails pinned on the top of their heads. Four of them look after the monk's paraphernalia such as a rush mat, a fan, a teapot and a box.

On the left, the younger monk from the right-hand side is kneeling, while a different monk sits in the chair. All six of the boys from the right-hand side are present (one partially covered by tape at the far left) plus a further one.

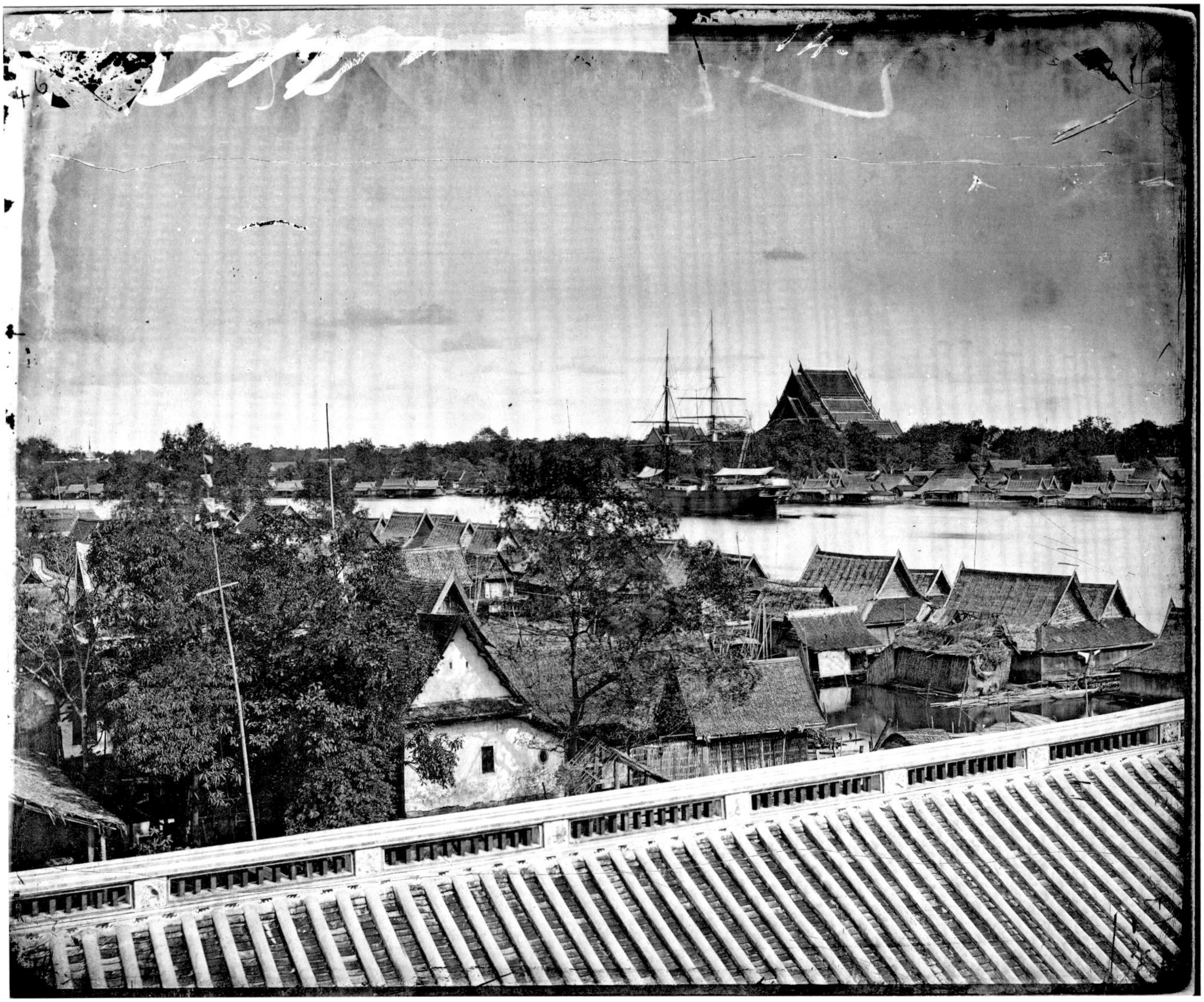

The main vihara of Wat Kalayanamitr

The vihara is the imposing building in the background, while in the foreground are the tightly packed, thatched roofed houses of the riverine community on the Bangkok side. The two-masted merchant ship pointing downstream would have had to pay taxes at the Customs House at Ta Tien, a short distance from where it is moored.

Chao Phraya Nikornbodin (Toh), founder of the Kalayanamitr family and Prime Minister during the reign of King Rama III, donated his home and land to the king in 1825 in order to build the temple, so King Rama III named it Kalayanamitr temple in his honour and built a royal vihara within the complex together with a large Buddha image.

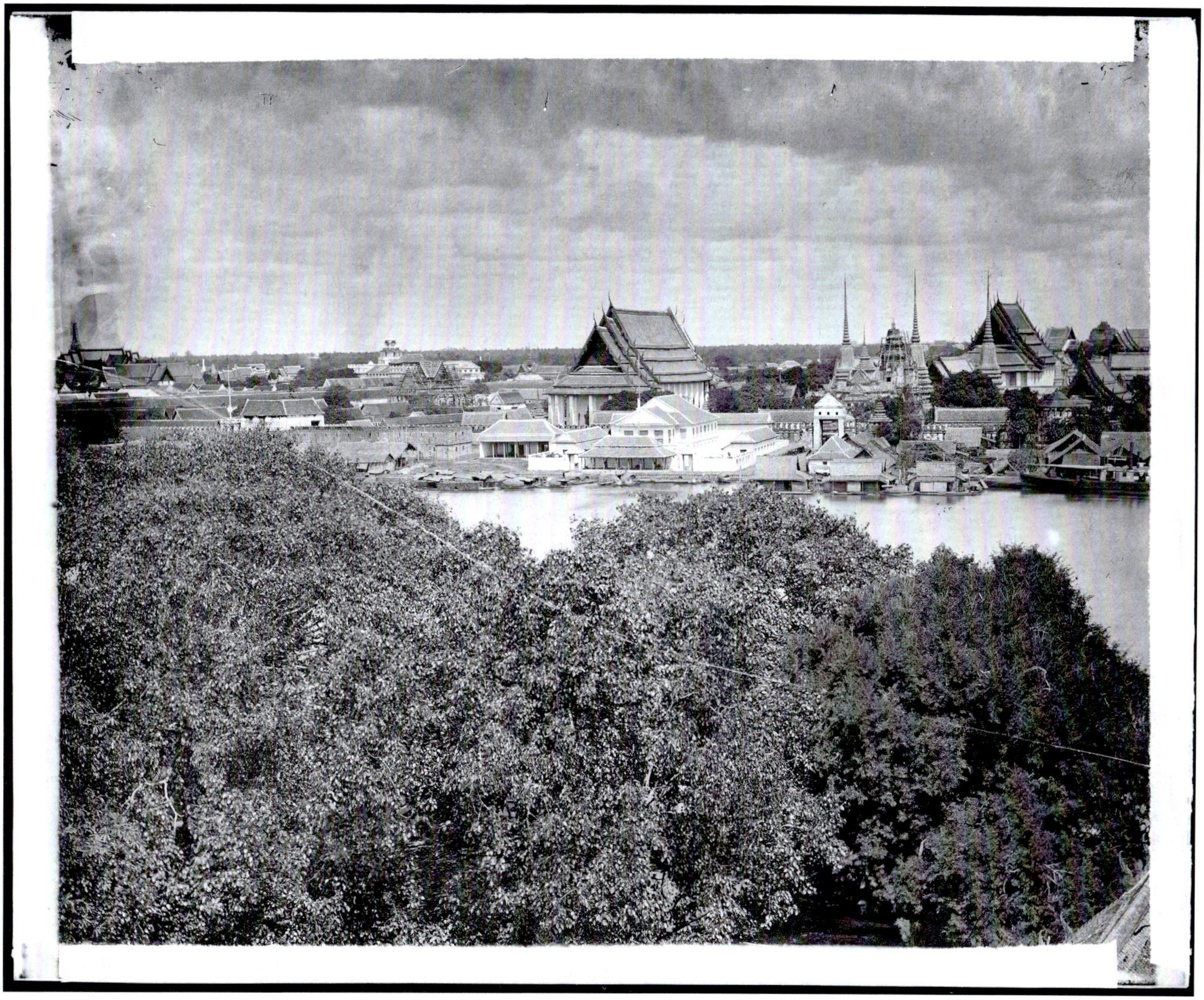

PANORAMA: THE CHAO PHRAYA RIVER AND RATTANAKOSIN ISLAND, FROM WAT ARUN

This photograph and those on pages 56-57 look across from the Thonburi side to show Rattanakosin Island and the Chao Phraya River as they were 150 years ago. In the middle and to the right is the large complex of Wat Pho.

Traditional wooden and floating houses line the river bank, beginning at the Grand Palace and running south as far as Pak Klong Talad. In front of what today is a land-based fruit and vegetable market are a multitude of small boats plying their trade.

This photograph gives an excellent view of the thickly clustered floating raft houses which lined the river bank. In the background is the bell tower. Note in the foreground, the Chinese style roofs of the pavilions in the compound of Wat Arun from where the photograph was taken.

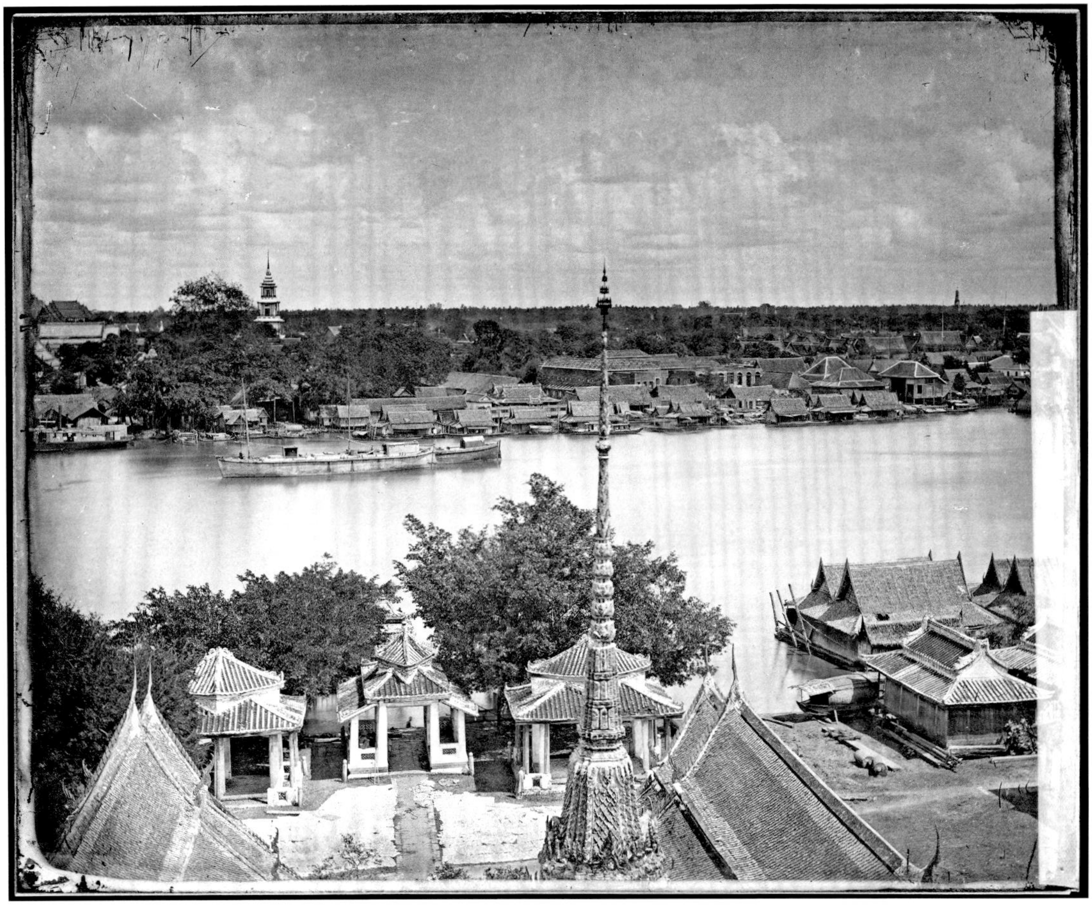

The same view taken from the identical spot today.

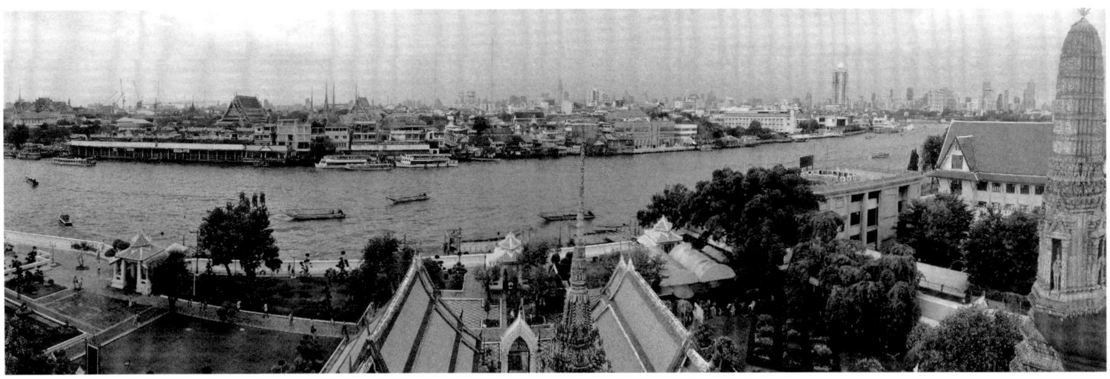

In the right foreground of the photograph is one of the four prangs surrounding the central one. In the niche is the Wind god on his horse. Thomson's signature is just discernabe on the roof.

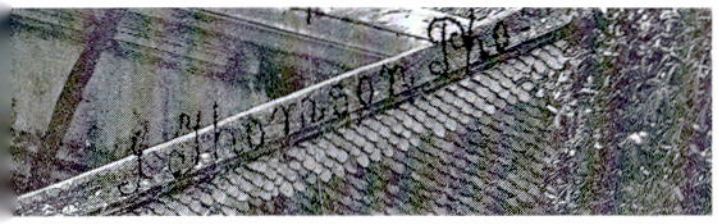

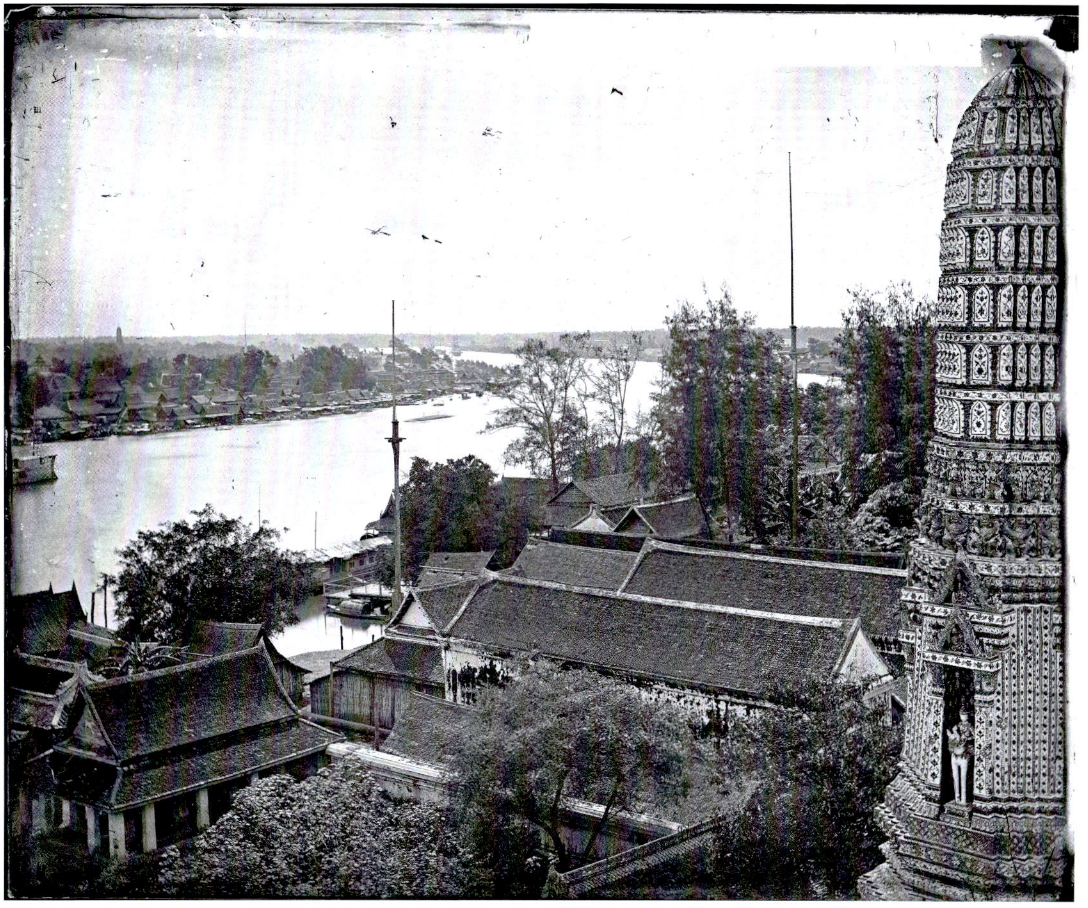

Below: A wide-angled view taken shortly after 1866 by Francis Chit from the same spot. The large group of white buildings the newly-built Theatre of Chao Phraya Mahindrasak Damrong (Peng Penkul). On the far right is the *vihara* of Wat Kalayanamitr.

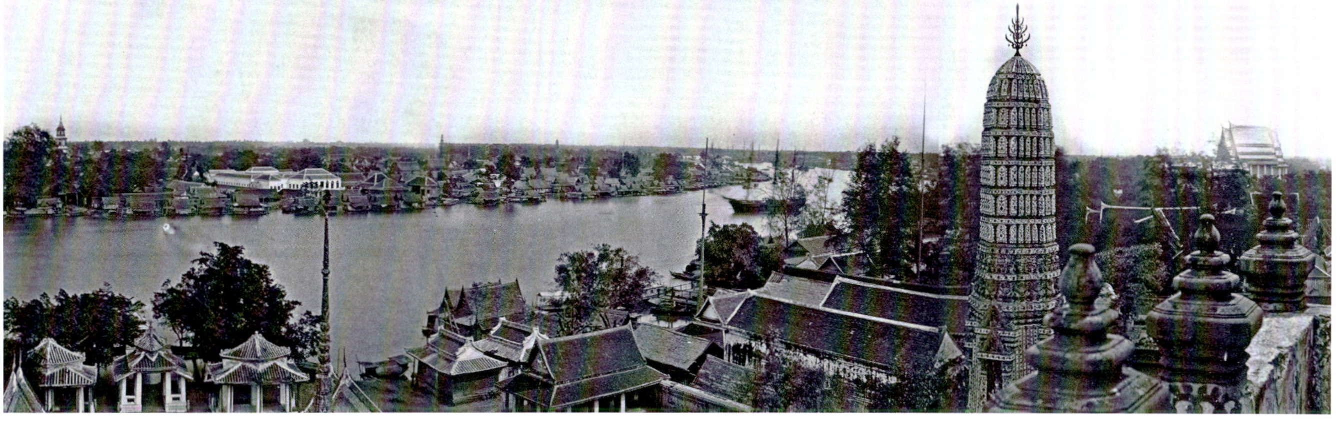

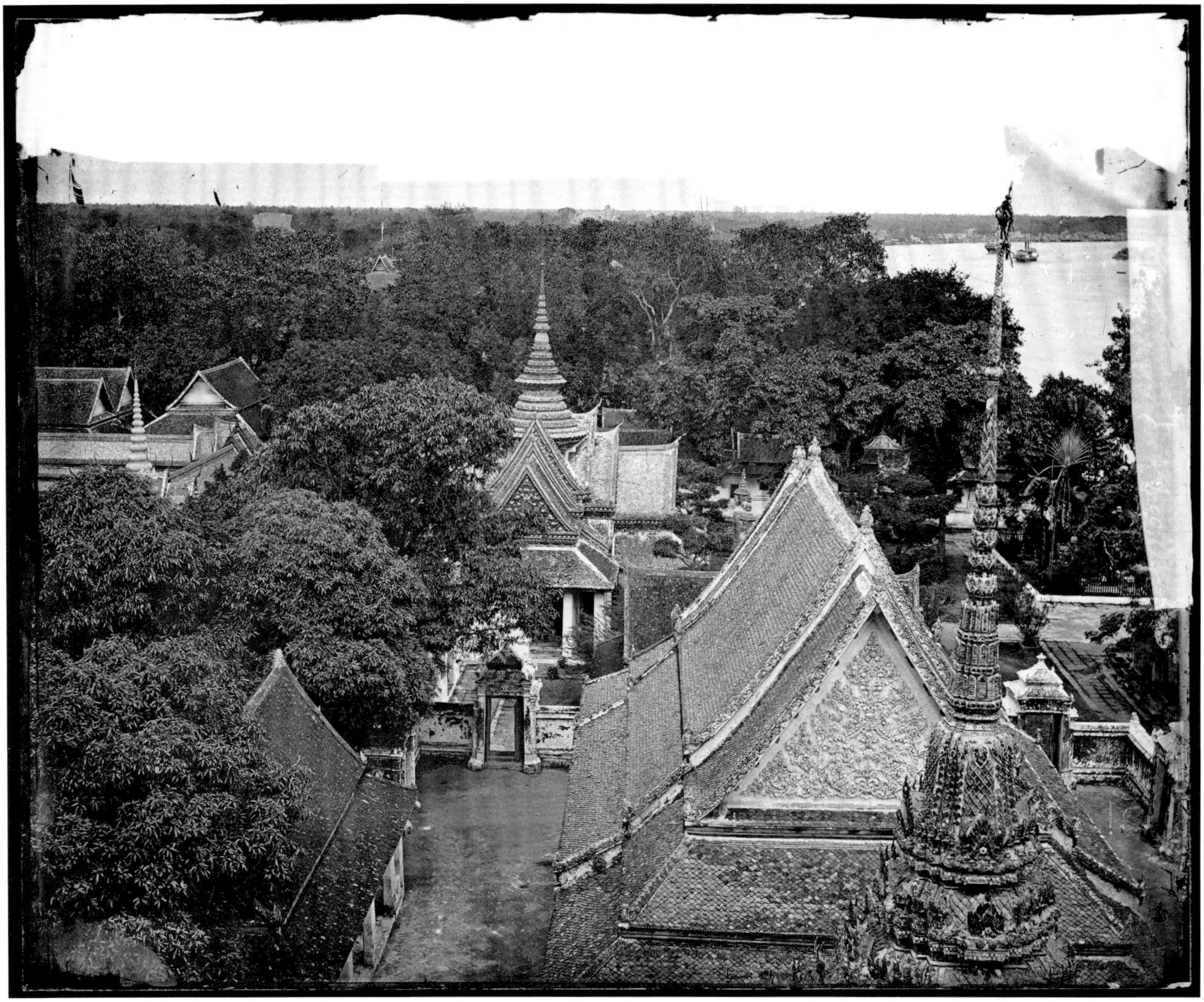

LOOKING NORTH OVER THONBURI FROM WAT ARUN

Wat Arun was built in the reign of King Rama II on the west bank of the river, the Thonburi side. This part of the compound was photographed from the central *prang* looking north.

In the right foreground is the finial of one of the directional mandapas and behind it the accompanying vihara, with, to the left, a pavilion for listening to sermons. In the middle ground and the centre of the photograph is the entrance porch added during the Third Reign and used by the King when he came to present Lenten robes.

At this time the area further up river behind the temple was filled with fruit orchards belonging to the Rear Palace (the relatives of the sister of King Rama I).

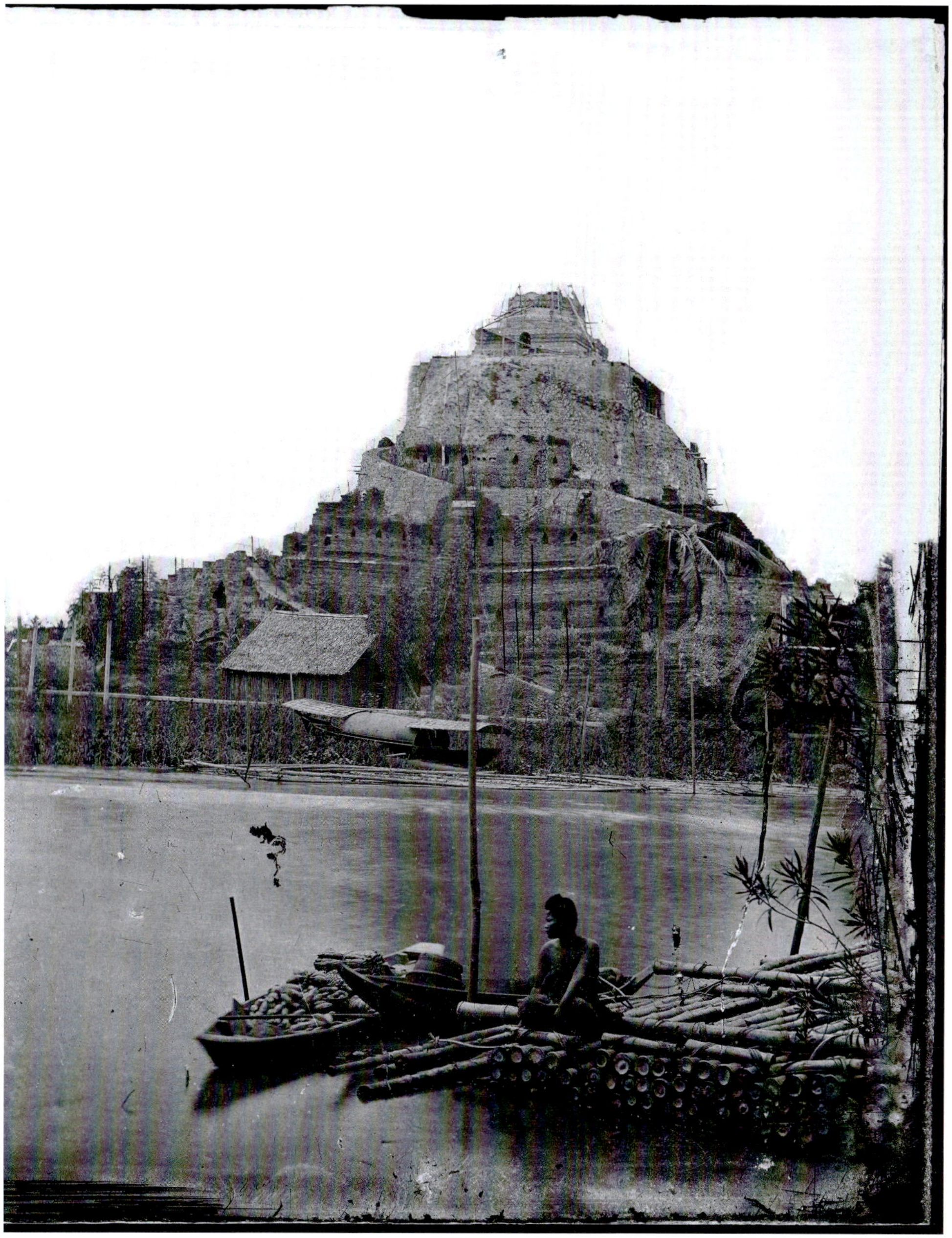

THE GOLDEN MOUNT

The construction of this temple was ordered by King Rama III, who wanted to copy the Golden Mount in Ayutthaya. Klong Mahanak was dug around the base so that Bangkokians could celebrate the Loy Kratong festival, when boats with lights were floated on the water. However, building was halted when the foundations proved inadequate.

In the reign of King Mongkut work was restarted but the design was changed. To reinforce the massive base (330 metres in diameter), two circular staircases were added, and a bell-shaped stupa was designed for the top. When Thomson took his photograph, the chedi was under construction with the former structure still in evidence and scaffolding at the top.

In the foreground is Klong Mahanak with Klong Saen Saeb on the left. These canals formed part of an important communication artery and, as a result, this spot became a busy trading hub, particularly for agricultural produce.

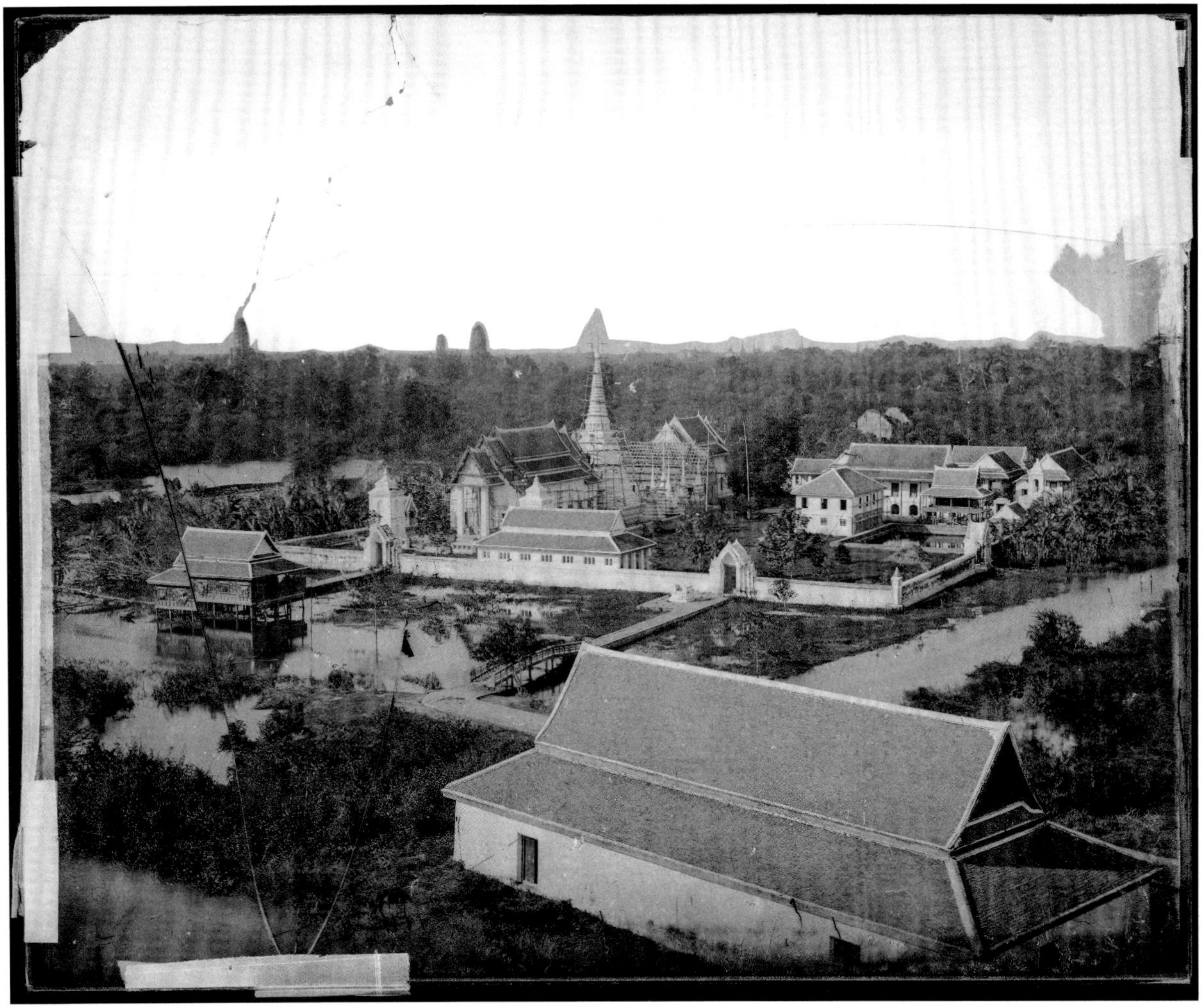

Wat Sena Sanaram, Ayutthaya

After the sack of the former capital by the Burmerse in 1767, Ayutthaya lay in ruins for many decades and quantities of bricks were removed to build the new capital, Bangkok. In 1863, King Mongkut order the restoration of some temples including this one previously know as Wat Seua. The photograph shows that work was still in progress as many structures still have scaffolding. The plan is typical of Fourth Reign temples.

Thomson's photography must have been taken from the Phisai Sanrak tower, a four-storey building reign of King Narai and rebuilt by King Mongkut on the same base. Looking west across the city islands, the ruined prangs of other temples are visible in the distance.

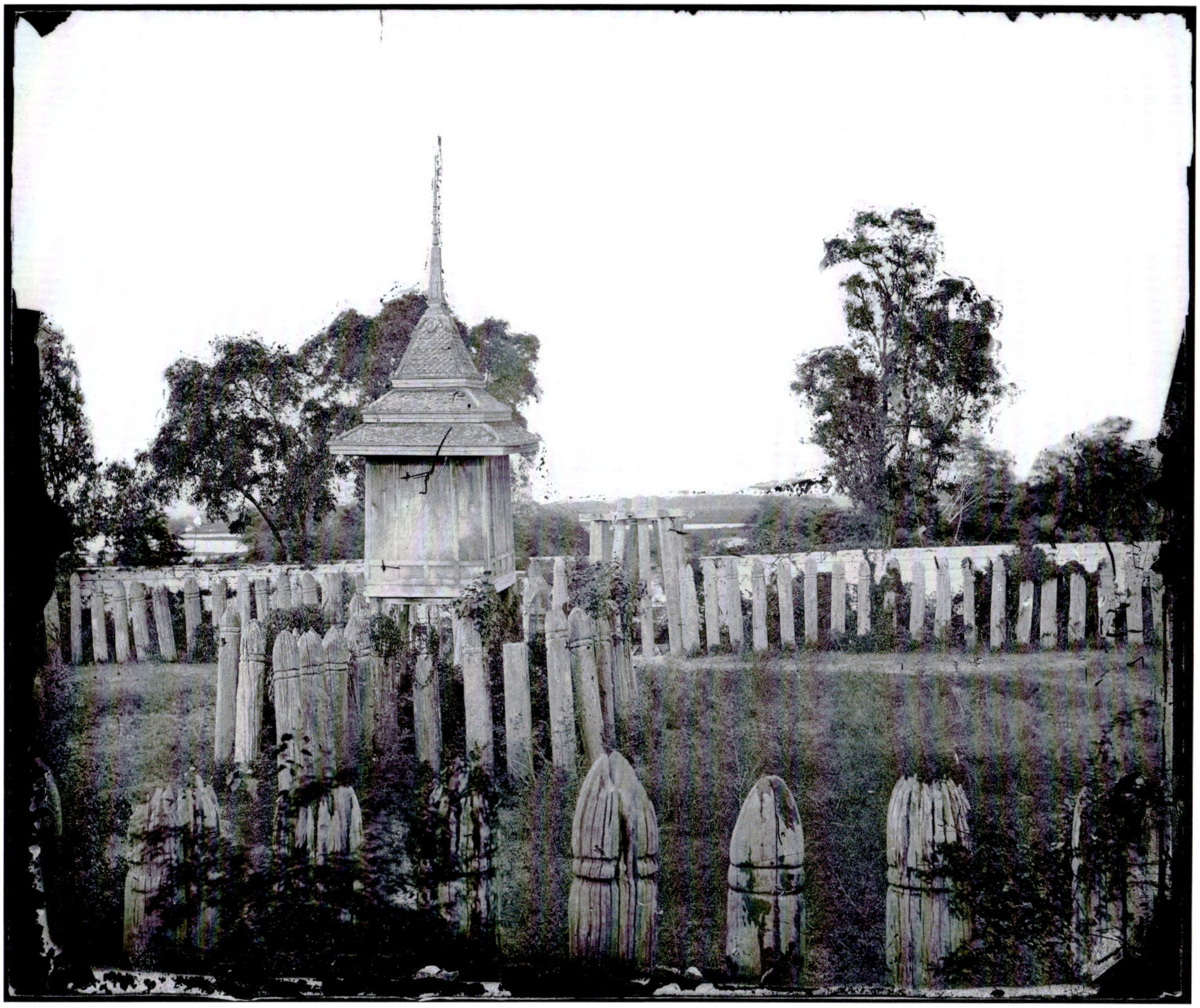

The Elephant Corral, Ayutthaya

This is where wild elephants were corralled in front of the king and other spectators. In a ruinous state after the sack of the former capital in 1767, it was renovated during the reigns of King Rama I, King Rama III and King Rama V.

The corralling of wild elephants was something that Westerners often commented on, as can be seen in the journal of Chevalier de Chaumont, French ambassador to the kingdom during the reign of King Narai the Great.

The outer layer was for all the elephants before selection. Those who had noble characteristics as listed in the *Gaja Shastra* (Elephant Treatise) were taken to the inner enclosure created by hundreds of teak pillars. In the centre was a shrine to the elephant god, Ganesha.

Thomson journeyed up river to Ayutthaya by steamboat together with three companions.

Wat Chumpon Nikayaram, Bang Pa-In district, Ayutthaya

After the sack of the former capital in 1767, Ayutthaya lay in ruins for many decades and bricks were used for the new capital, Bangkok. However, King Mongkut ordered the restoration of several temples, including this one in 1863 just two years before Thomson's visit.

This temple, built by King Prasat Thong (r. 1630-1656) in 1632, stands next to the royal palace of Bang Pa-In. It may also have been where troops were assembled in times of war with Burma, hence its name (*chumpon* = gathering of troops).

The style is typical of temples built or renovated in the reign of King Mongkut, with a low wall and two lower porches at the front and back. The window surrounds are in prasat style topped by a thin *prang* and with small pediments bearing the king's emblem of a crown. In the foreground is one of a pair of two stupa on a high, redented base.

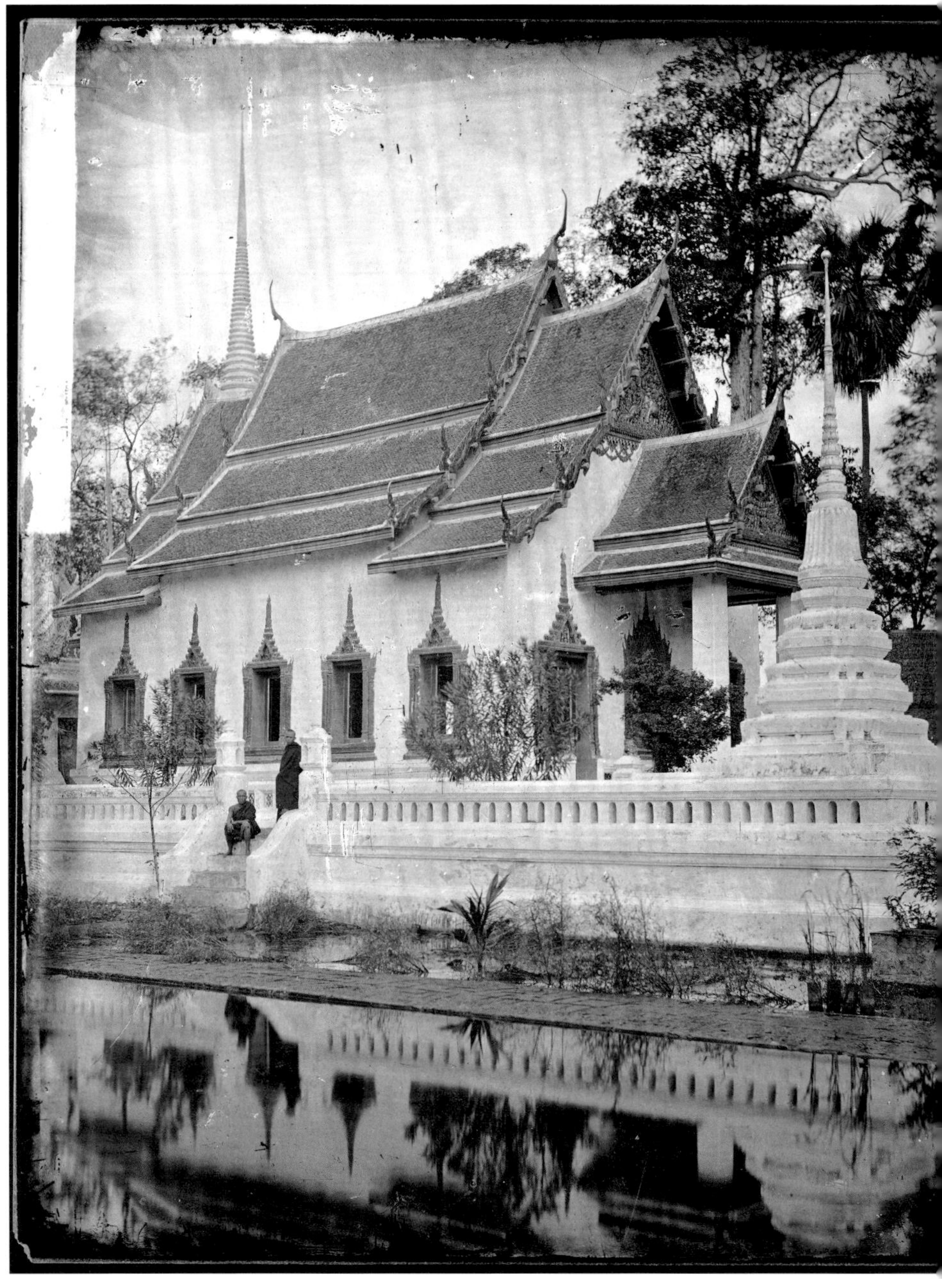

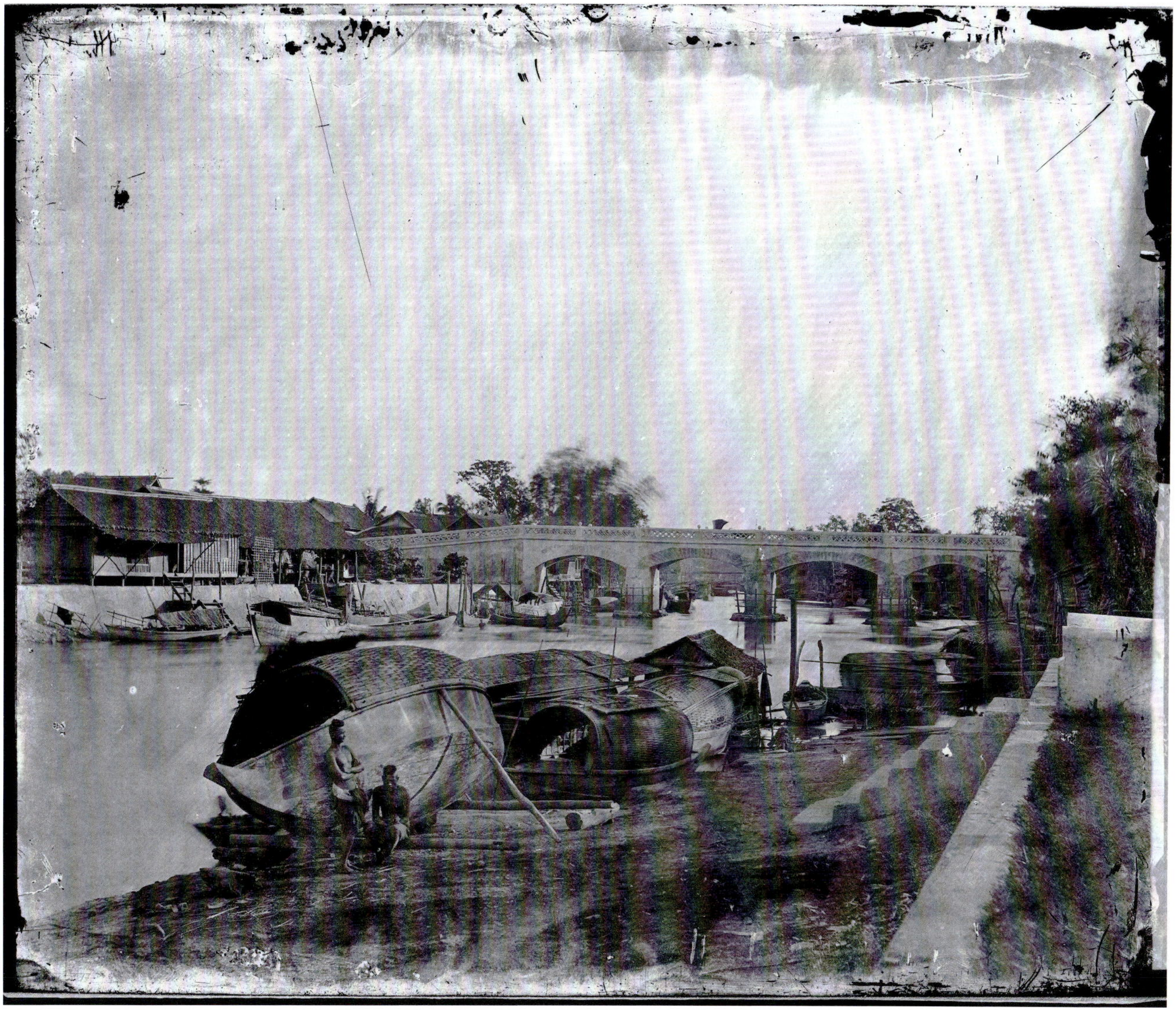

Phra Chom Klao Bridge, Phetchaburi

Thomson travelled to Phetchaburi by boat together with the Rev. Dan Beach Bradley, famous missionary and printer. Whilst in the town, they went on horseback to visit Phra Nakhon Khiri Palace, with six people carrying the photographic equipment.

The bridge over the Phetchaburi river was built at the beginning of King Mongkut's reign. At first it was called Hua Chang bridge (Elephant Head's bridge), but later the local populace changed the name to honour the king, who was particularly fond of Phetchaburi and liked to stay in a palace he built on a hill overlooking the town.

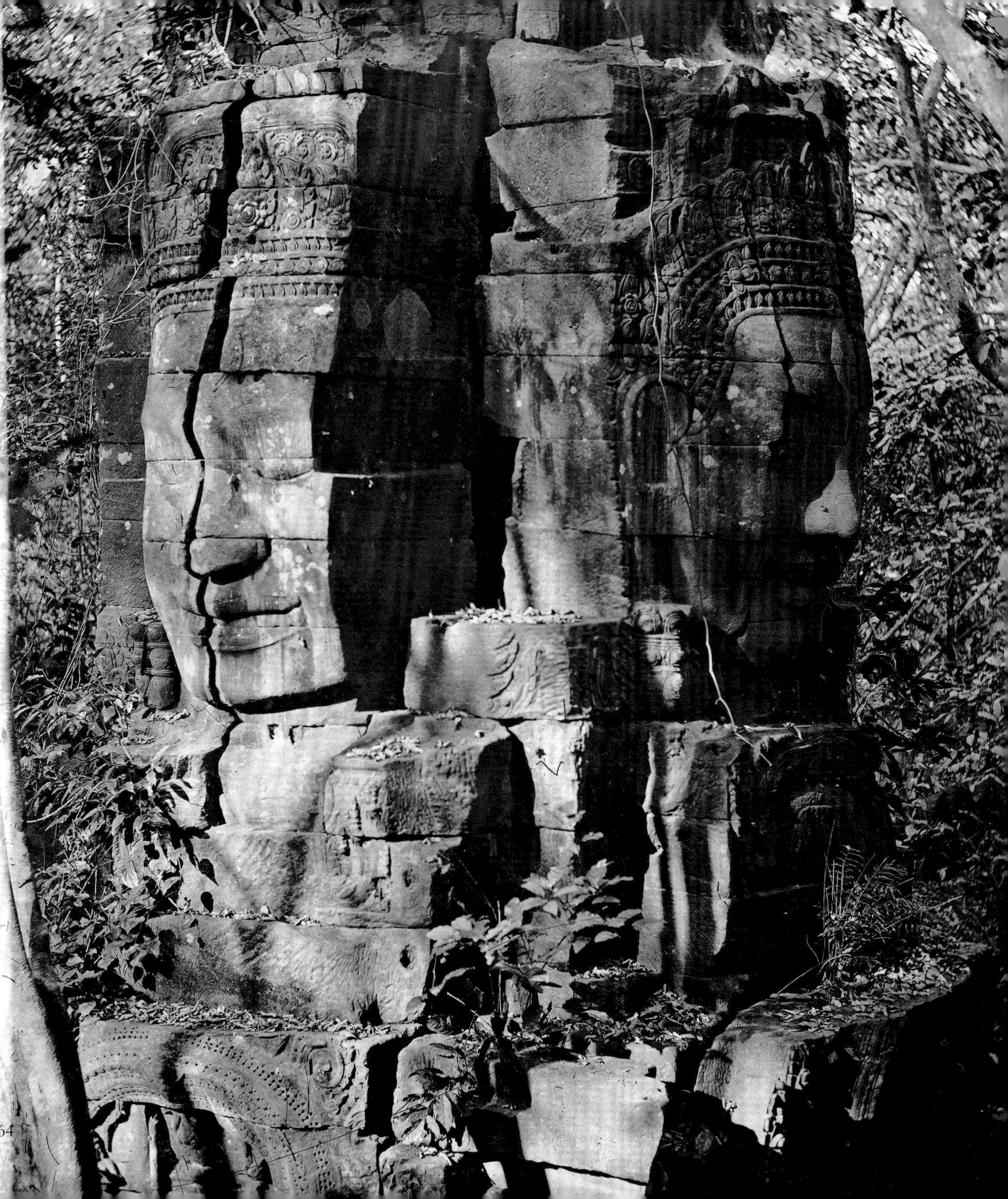

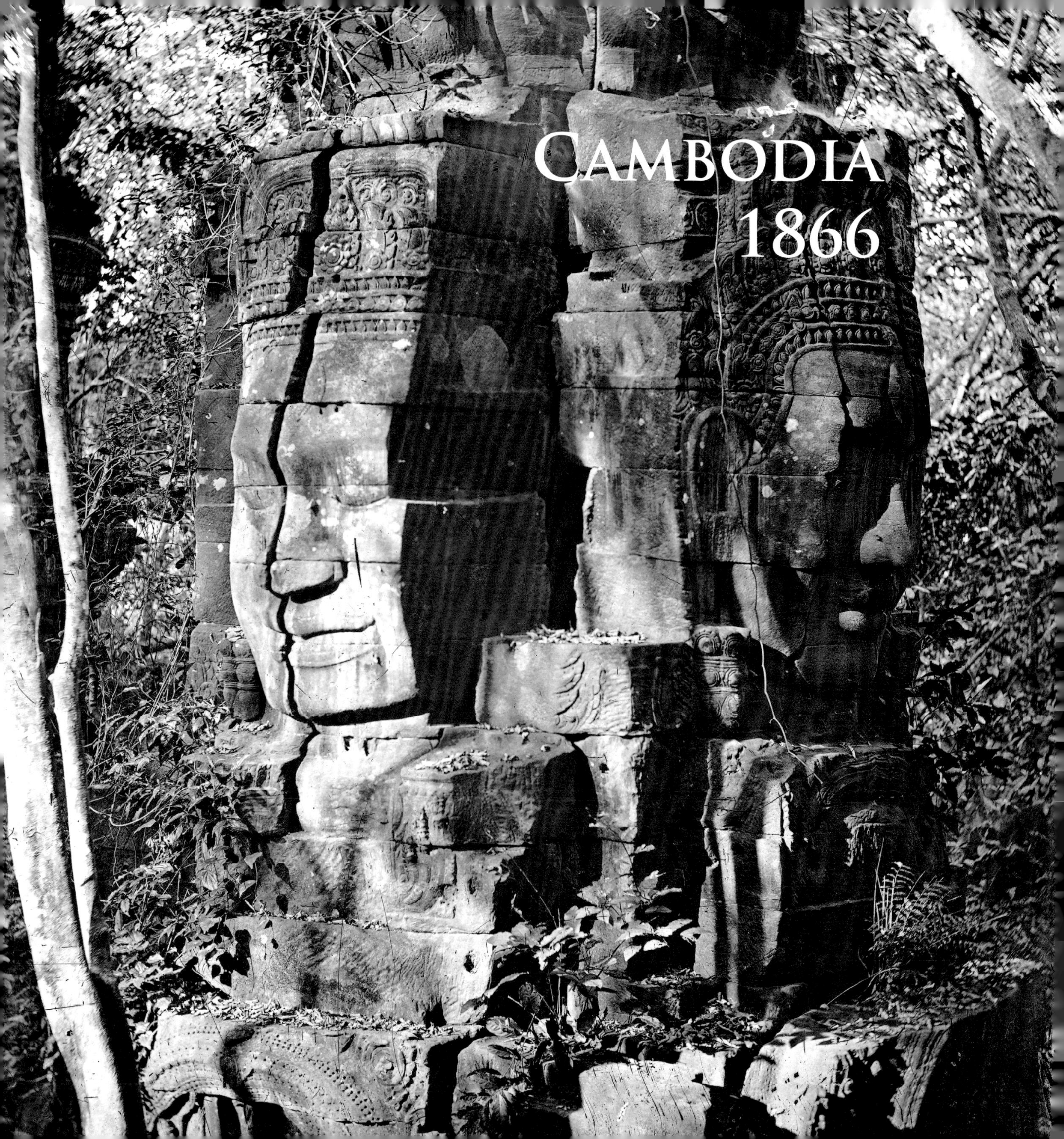
CAMBODIA
1866

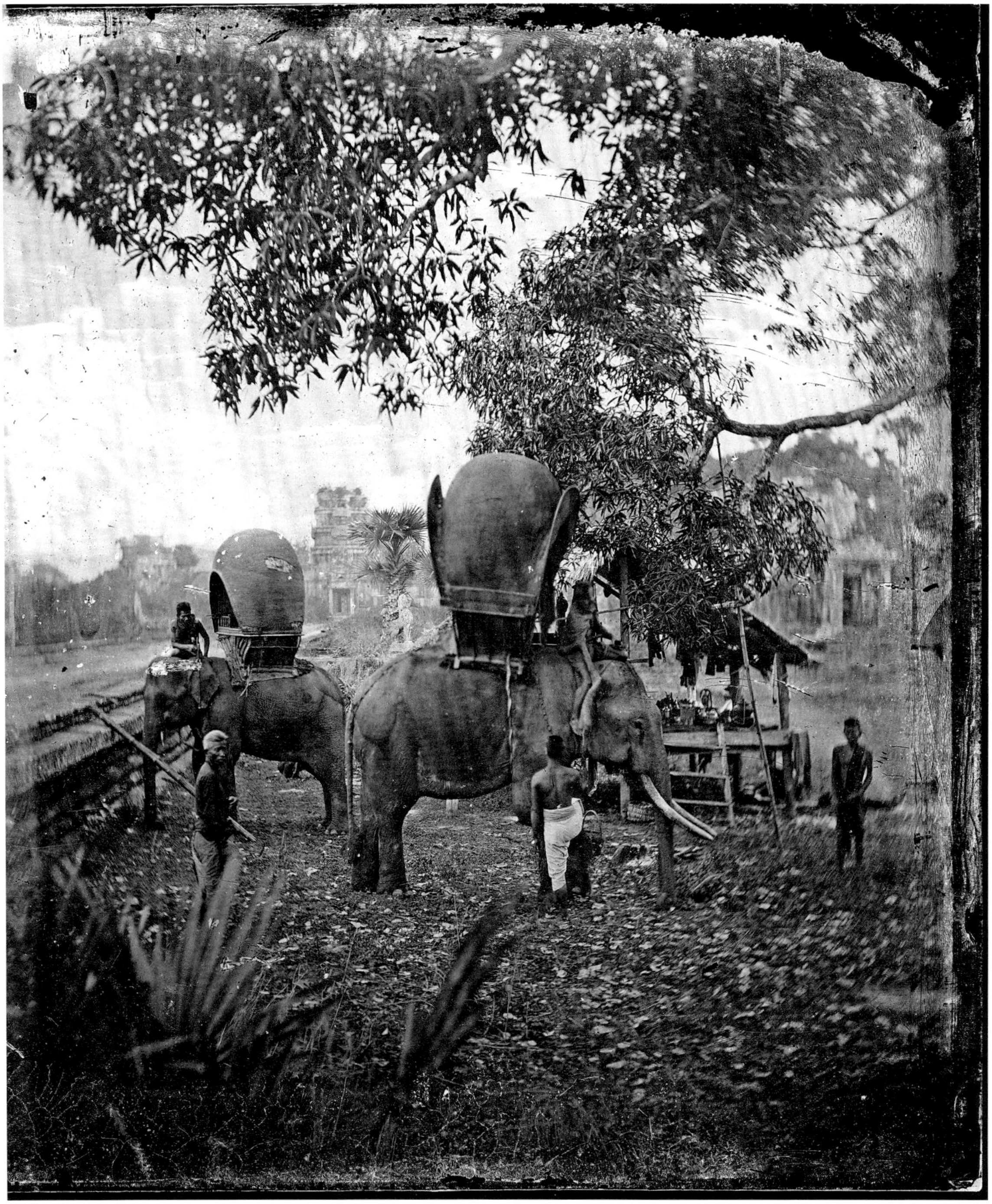

Elephants outside Angkor Wat

On 27th January 1866, inspired by explorer Henri Mouhot (1826-1861), Thomson left for Cambodia to photograph the temple of Angkor Wat. With a letter from King Mongkut as a passport, Thomson took a long boat from Bangkok together with Mr H. G. Kennedy from the British consulate, eight Thai rowers, and four assistants.

By 31st January they had reached Prachinburi by river, and when the elephants didn't turn up, made the overland trip on pony to the Tonlé Sap Lake. A hired boat took them across the lake, and only then did the elephants arrived to take them to Angkor thanks to the Siem Reap governor. Thomson was greatly impressed by his first encounter with an elephant and probably took the photograph in early February 1866.

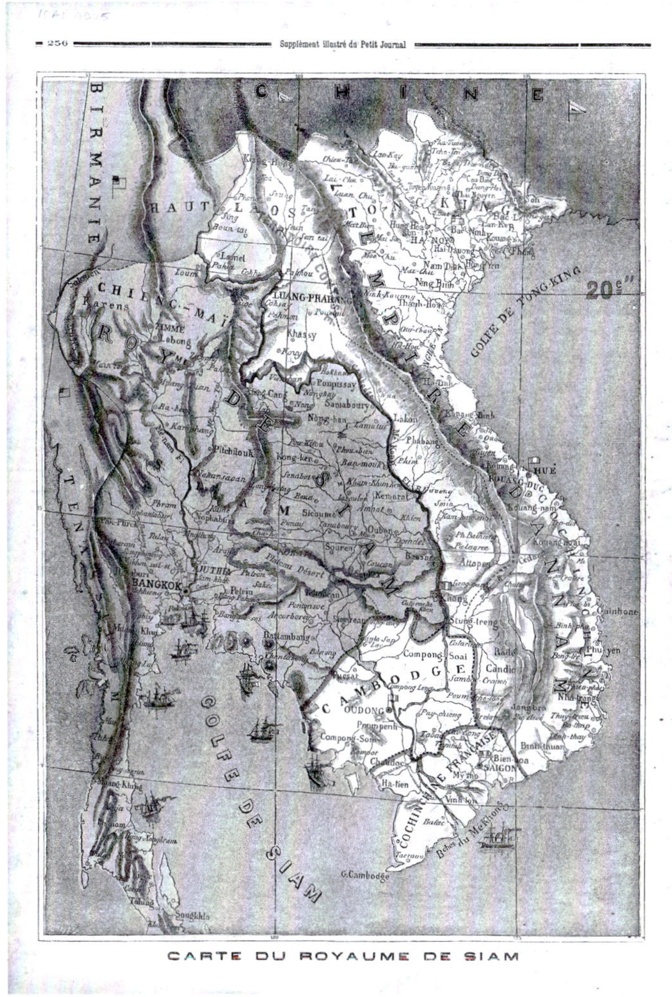

At that time, although Cambodia had recently become a French protectorate Siem Reap and the temples of Angkor were still administered by Siam.

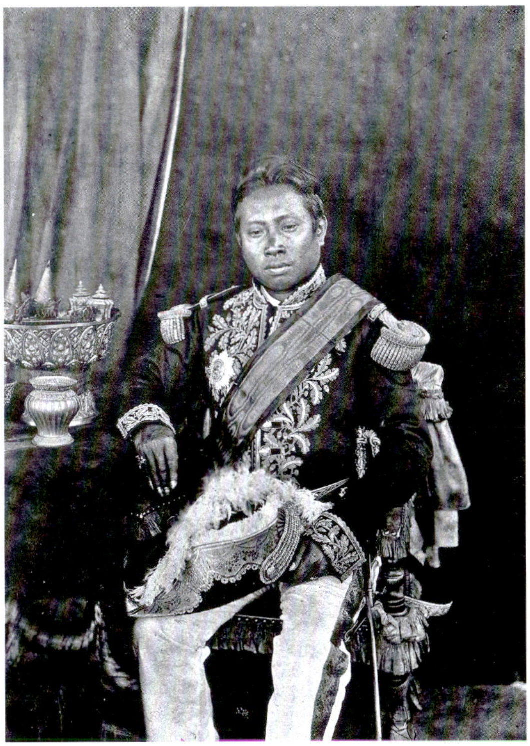

King Norodom of Cambodia in full dress naval uniform wearing medals created by Thai craftsmen.

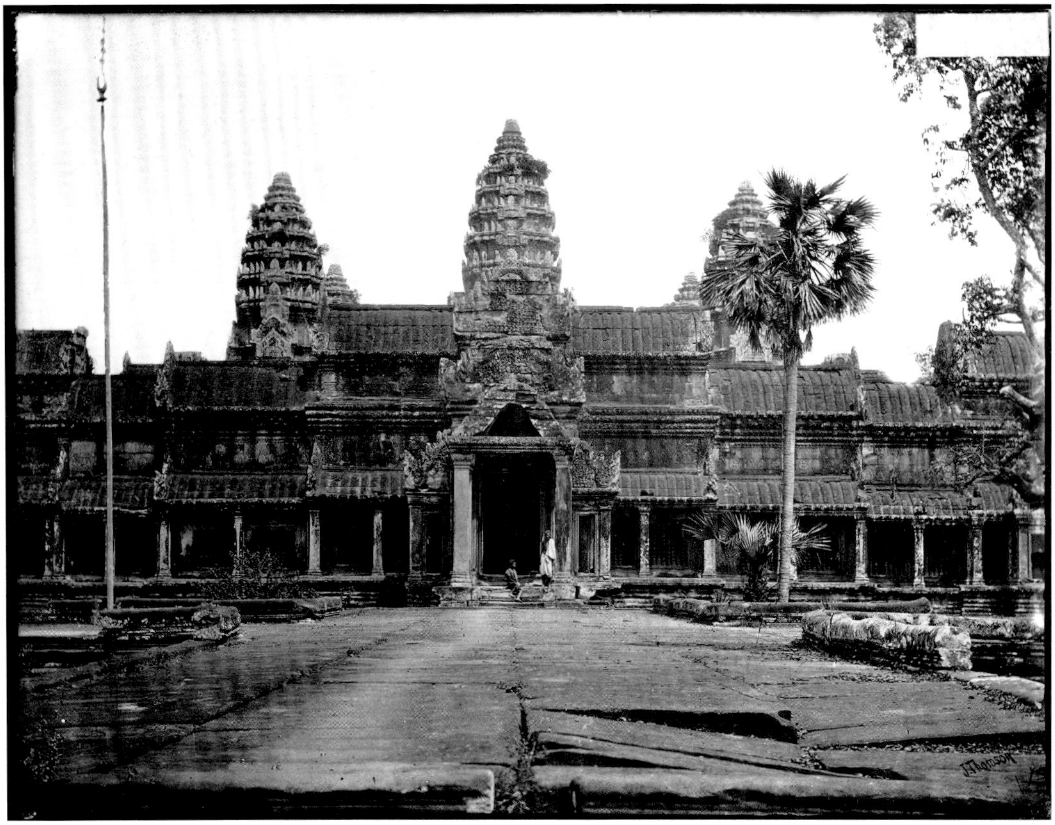

ANGKOR WAT

Angkor Wat, the largest religious monument in the world, was built in the first half of the 12th century (1116-1150) by King Suryavarman II (r. 1113-1145/1150) as his state temple and eventual mausoleum. Unusually, the temple faces west and was dedicated to Vishnu. It is built as a temple mountain, with a central tower and four corner towers, symbolising Mount Meru, the abode of the gods, surrounded by a gallery of carved reliefs, which stretch for some 600 metres. In addition, the entire temple is carved with pediments and lintels with scenes from the *Ramayana* or *Mahabharata*, while the walls are adorned with *Devata/Apsaras*, or celestial female guardians.

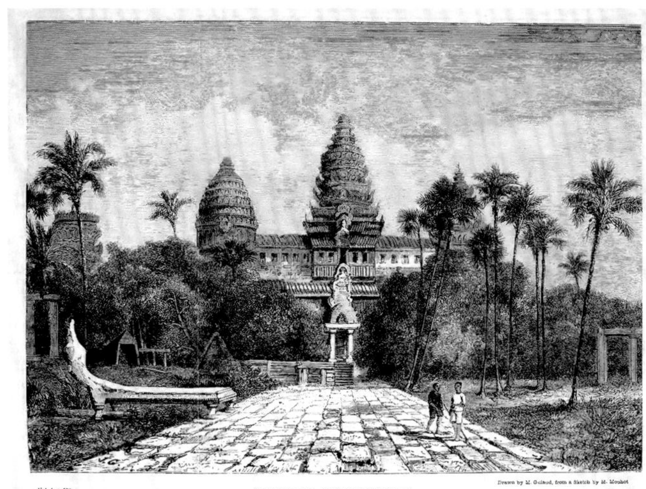

Vol. I. p. 279. FAÇADE OF THE TEMPLE OF ONGCOR-WAT. Drawn by M. Guiaud, from a Sketch by M. Mouhot

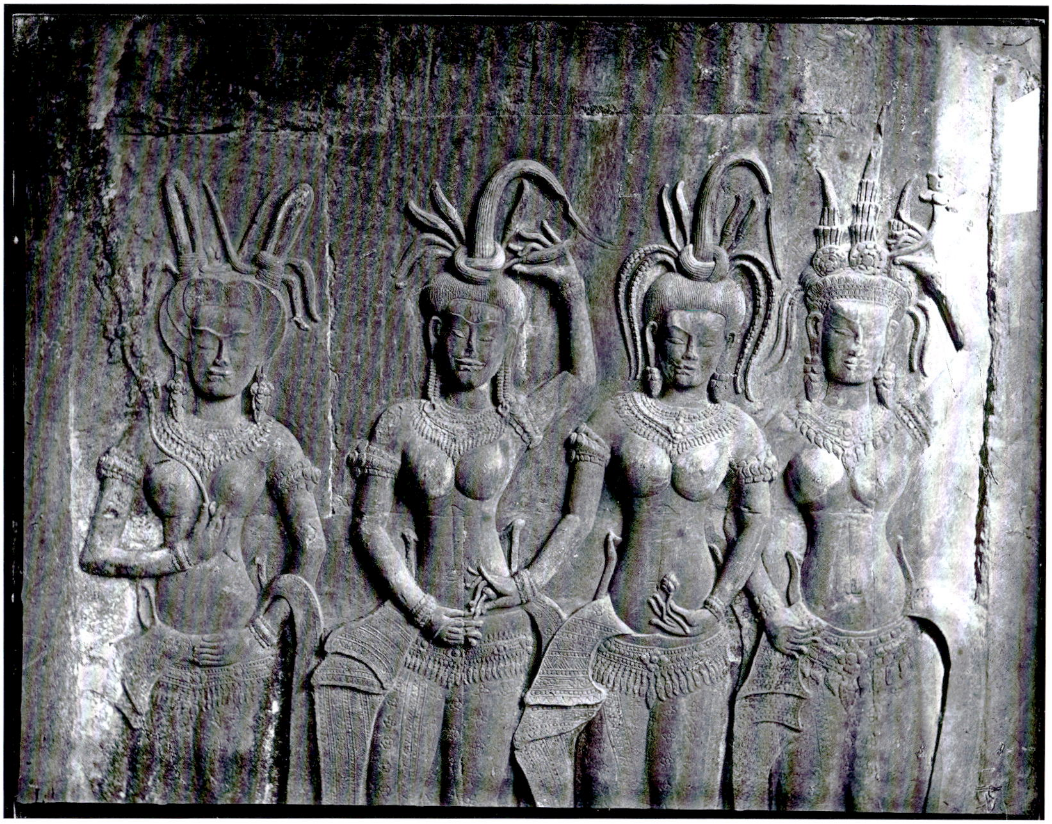

DEVATA/APSARAS, ANGKOR WAT

Carvings of celestial maidens are carved on many of the walls, some 1769 in all with diverse hairstyles, apparel and jewellery. Commonly referred to as *apsaras* they were believed to have been one of the miraculous things created during the Churning of the Ocean of Milk, when, under Vishnu's instruction, the gods and demons battled to obtain the sacred elixir or *amrita*. This scene is depicted in the Gallery of Reliefs on the lower level of the temple.

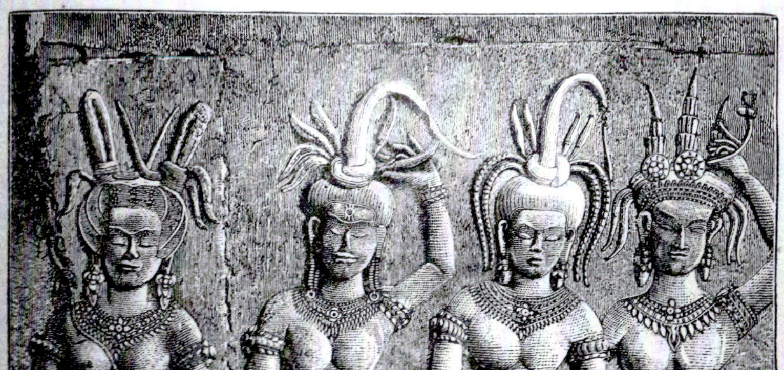

CAMBODIAN FEMALE HEAD-DRESS. ANCIENT SCULPTURE.

THE FACE-TOWERS OF THE BAYON

This dark sandstone temple (built between 1181-1219 CE) stands within the walled city of Angkor Thom and was the state temple of King Jayavarman VII (1181-1219), the Buddhist king who expanded the borders of the empire to its greatest extent. Jayavarman VII was a Mahayana Buddhist, but the temple also has many Hindu shrines.

There were 51 face-towers in all, an iconographic innovation of Jayavarman VII, although today only 37 remain. When Thomson visited 150 years ago, years of neglect and the incursions of the forest had created a "Romantic" and mysterious air no longer in evidence today.

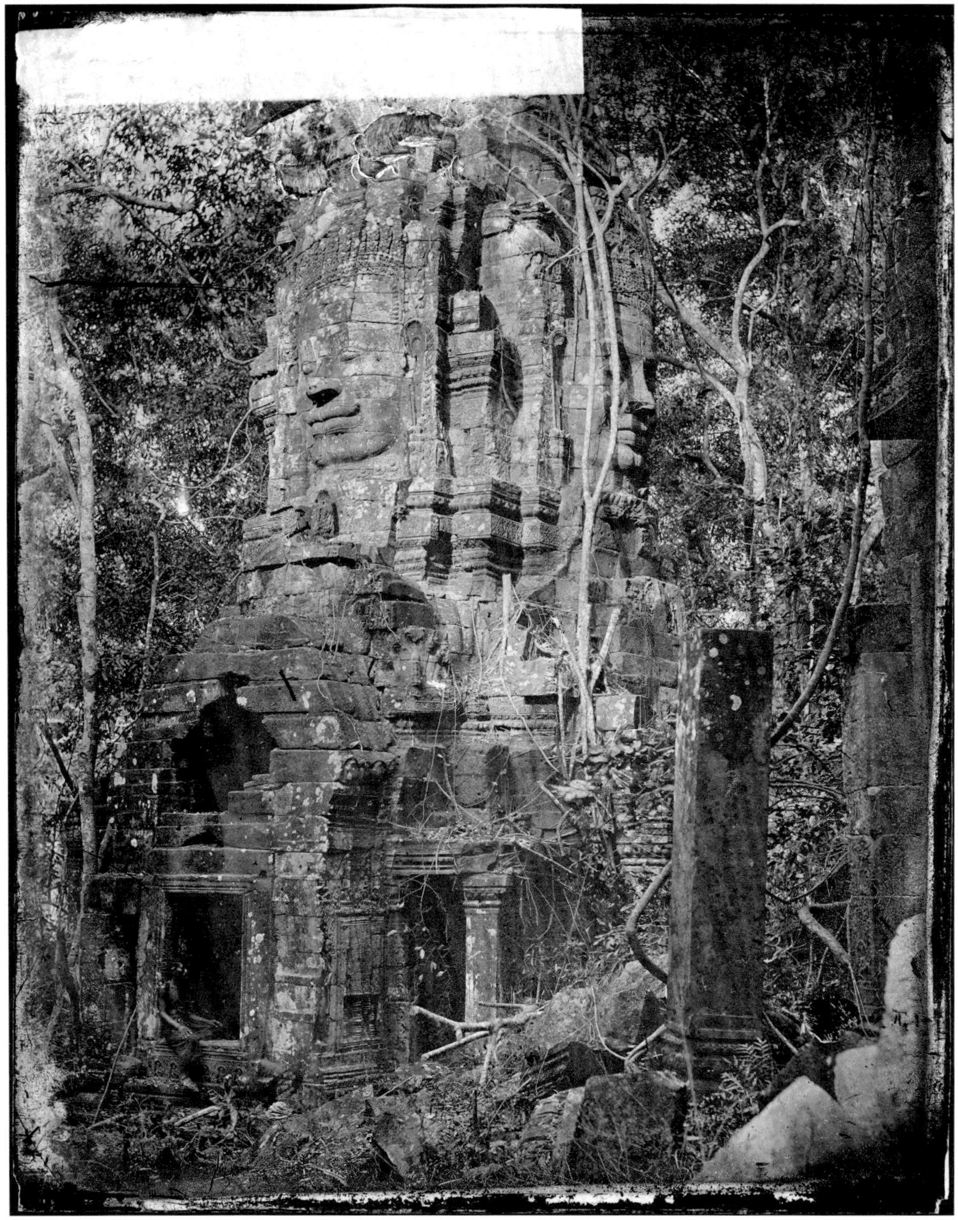

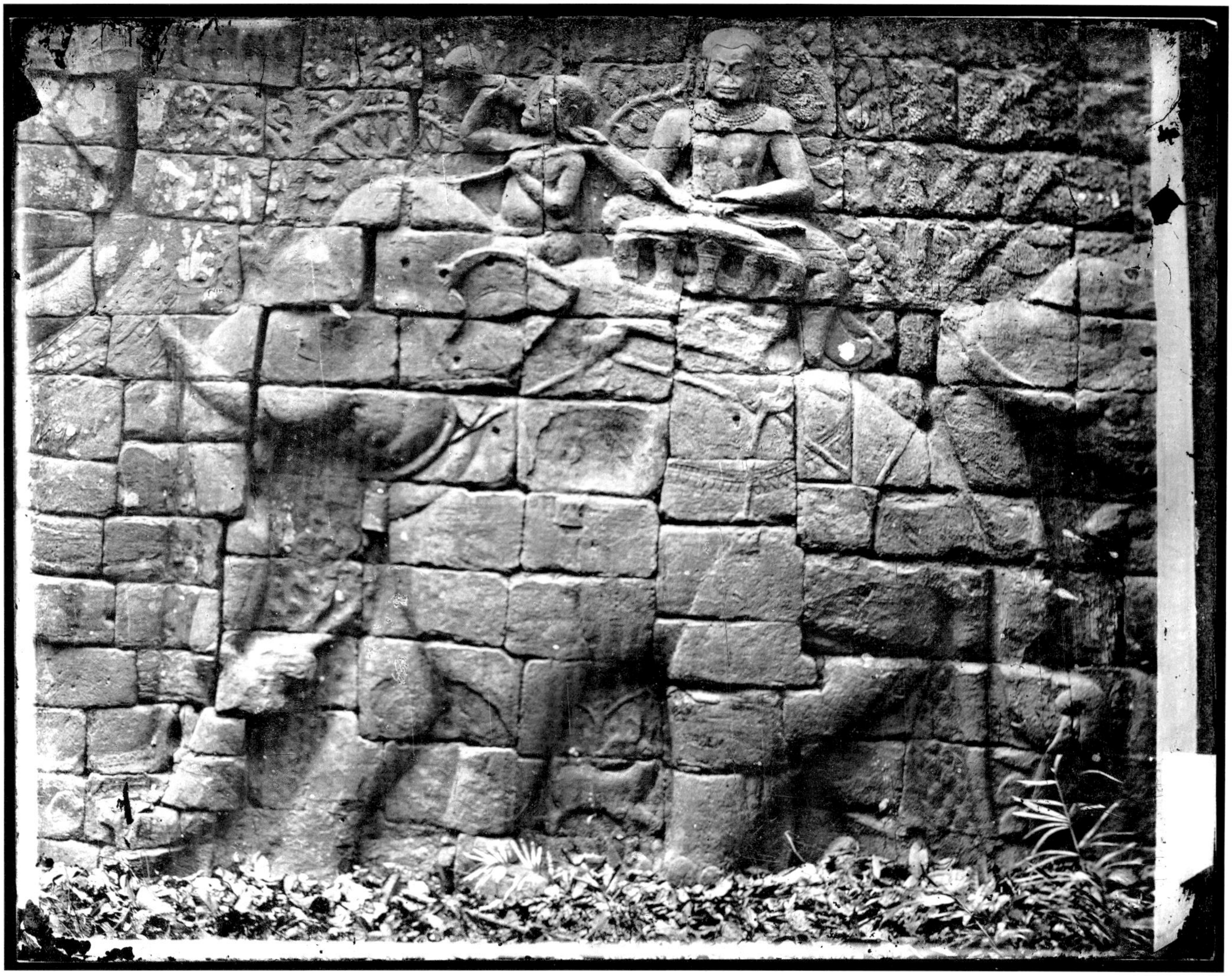

War Elephant, Terrace of the Elephants, Angkor Thom

This photograph of a war elephant with its commander and mahout was carved in high relief on large sandstone blocks. The animal is a part of the 350 metre-long Elephant Terrace situated almost in the centre of Angkor Thom. The terrace built in the late 12th century by King Jayavarman VII, faces east towards a large open area known as the Royal Ground. From here the king surveyed military processions and ceremonies.

On top of the terrace, there was most likely a wooden pavilion.

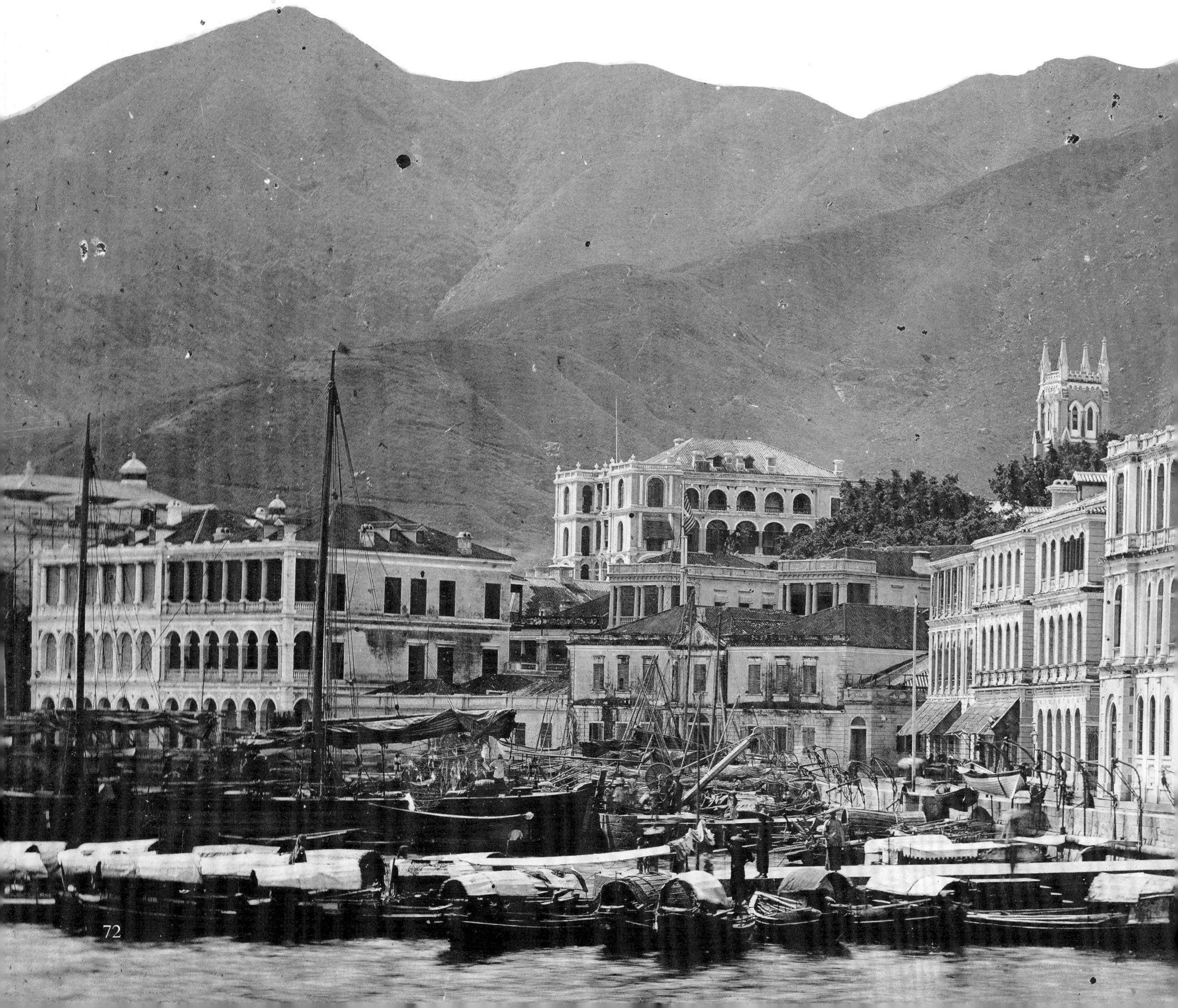

China
1868-1872

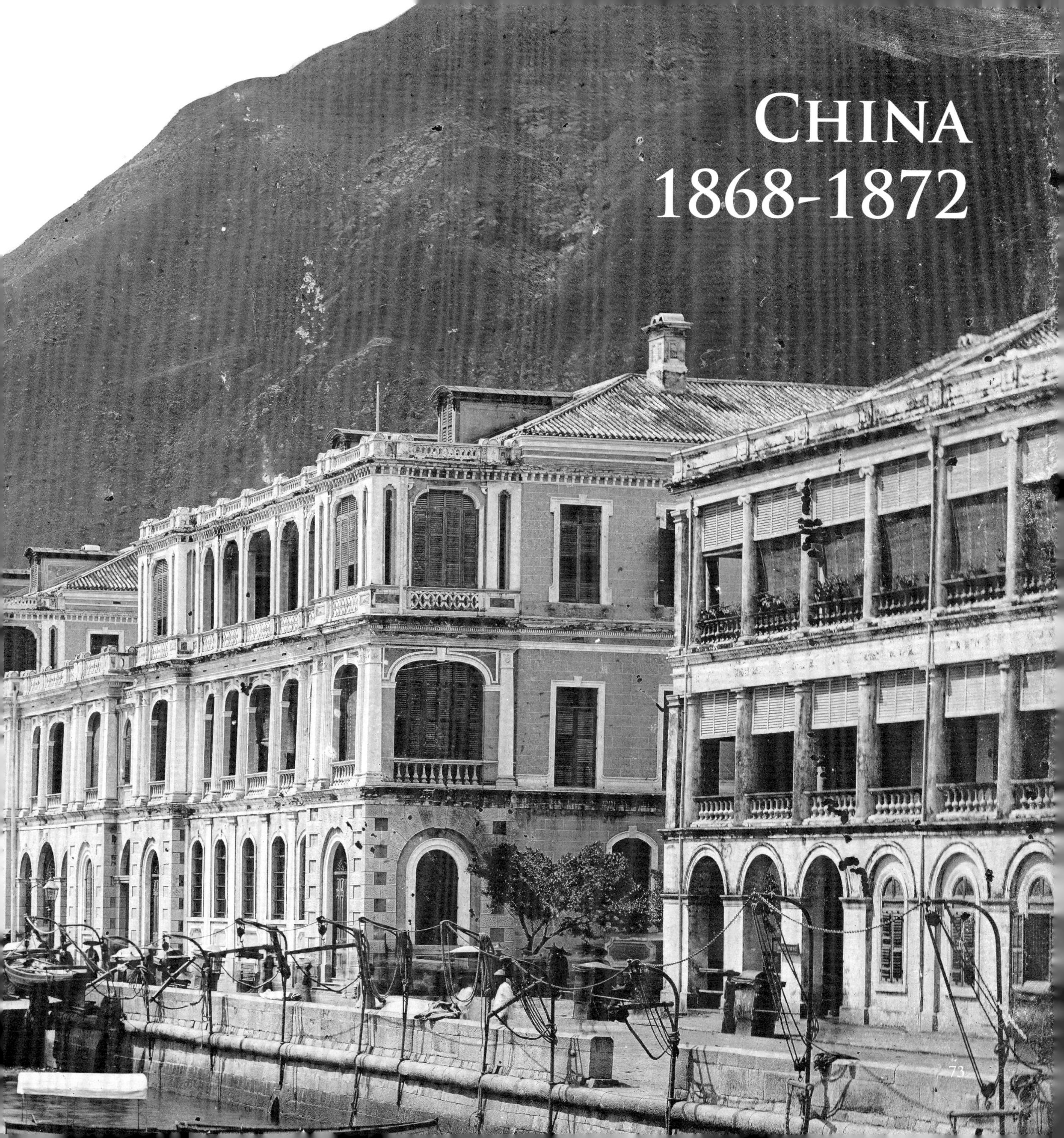

CHINA

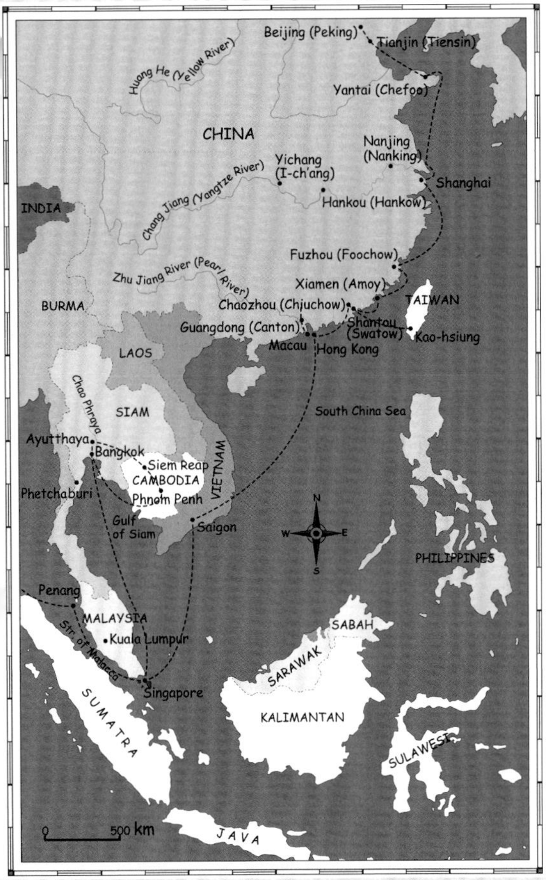

Map of John Thomson's Journeys to the Far East 1862-1872

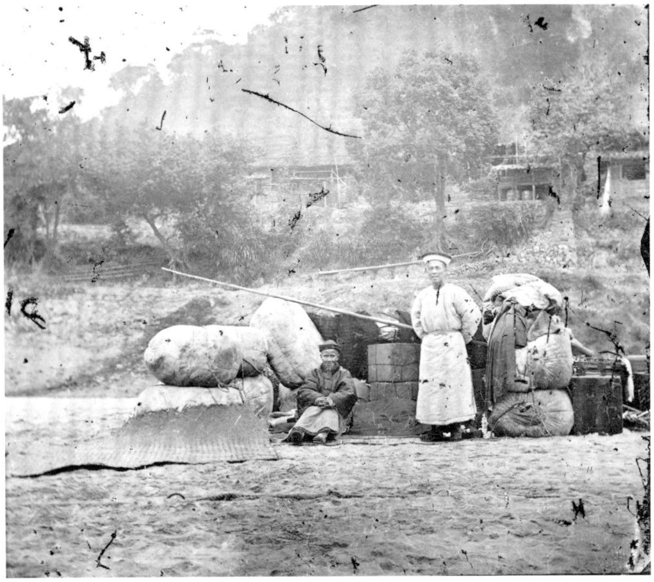

Two of John Thomson's porters and photographic equipment piled up on the bank of the River Min after running aground on rapids, 1870/1871. Print from photographic negative by John Thomson. Wellcome Collection no. 18816i.

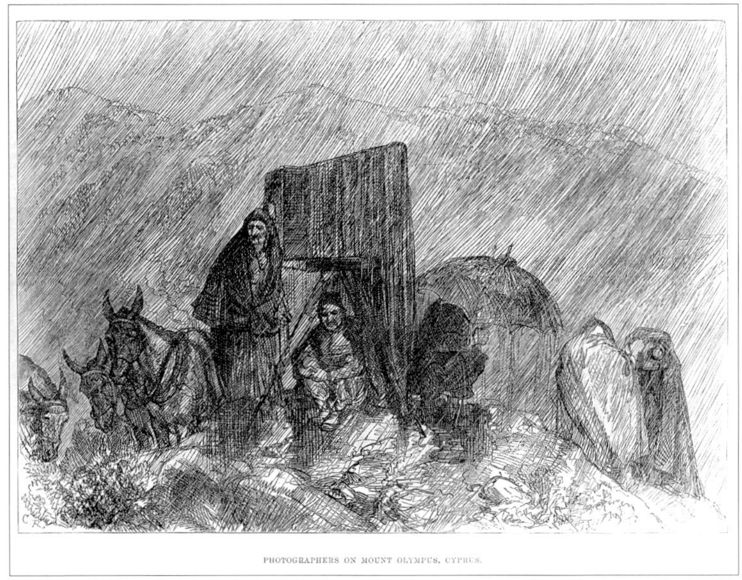

John Thomson's porters (one sheltering under the camera tripod) on Mount Olympus, Cyprus. Wood-engraving after a drawing by Thomson published in the Illustrated London News, 9 November 1878. Wellcome Collection.

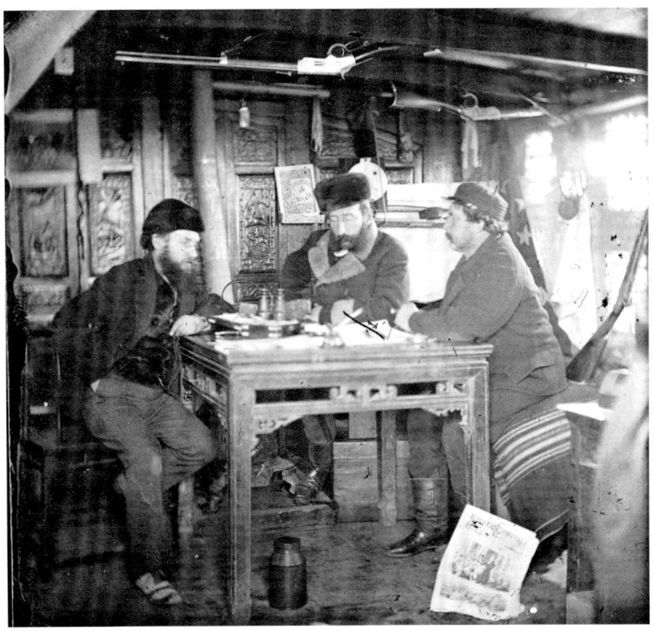

John Thomson (left) and two companions in their cabin on the Yangtze river, ca. 1871. Print from photographic negative by John Thomson. Wellcome Collection no. 19898i.

John Thomson: London to China, China to London

William Schupbach, Wellcome Collection, London

We are in the London of Sherlock Holmes. Through the fog walks an elderly man with a stick. He taps his way along the streets in the smart West End with its lavish new office buildings in the classical style. He is on a trip from his modest home in Streatham in south London to see a new collection that has gone on public display: the exhibition, in a showroom in Wigmore Street, of historic artefacts belonging to the wealthy American pharmaceutical manufacturer, Henry S. Wellcome.

The elderly man is the photographer John Thomson, and the date is 1920, when he is 83 years old. In his youth and middle age he had been a great traveller, photographer and writer. The reason for his visit to Wellcome's museum and library is to see whether Wellcome's institute would be a worthy recipient of Thomson's own professional archive of negatives. How Thomson came to be a man of such accomplishments and to build up that archive is itself a remarkable story, which is told in detail in the invaluable monograph by Richard Ovenden.[1]

Born in Edinburgh in 1837, Thomson received an education which, though he could not have known it at the time, was an ideal base for his future career as a photographer. At the age of fourteen, he was apprenticed to an optician. Opticians supplied lenses for telescopes, cameras and microscopes as well as for spectacles. Thomson supplemented his expertise in optical hardware by studying chemistry at the Watt Institution and School of Arts in Edinburgh, the forerunner of today's Heriot-Watt University. He thus acquired a training in the basic aspects of photography of his day: acquiring glass of suitable optical quality to serve as the negatives; making up the chemicals with which to coat the glass plate negatives; and exposing the glass plates to light through suitable lenses.

It was a family connection that led him to travel to the East in 1862: his brother William had already set up as a watchmaker in Singapore. After arriving there John Thomson practised as a portrait photographer and spent the best part of three years exploring and photographing not only Singapore but also Penang and the remaining country of present-day Malaysia. From there in 1865 he travelled to Bangkok: his arrival there must have been very similar to that later described in the opening paragraphs of Joseph Conrad's *The Secret Sharer* (written in 1909 and published in *Harper's Magazine* in 1910). After a successful spell as photographer at the welcoming court of King Mongkut, he travelled on to Cambodia and took the first photographs of the colossal ruins of Angkor Wat and Angkor Thom.[2]

He returned to Great Britain in 1866. There he publicised his photographs of Angkor, which astounded his British audiences. He also took advantage of his return home to find a wife: he married Isabel Petrie, of an Isle of Man family with Scottish connections. Many years later their son William would assist Thomson as partner in his photographic studio.

In 1867, having established a reputation in London, Thomson returned to the Far East, this time to Hong Kong. This was the beginning of

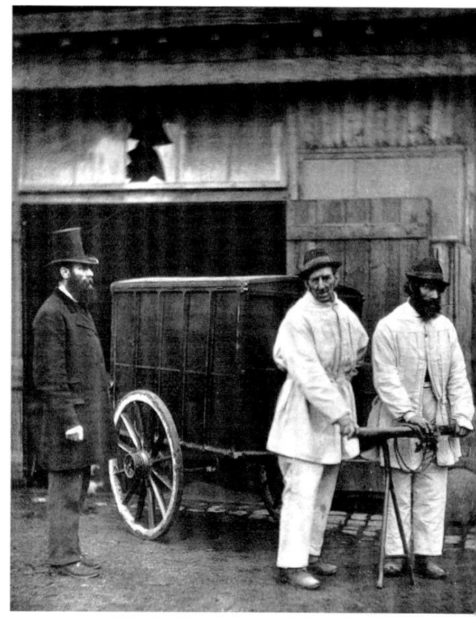

Men gathering infected clothing for fumigation, London. Woodburytype after John Thomson 1874.

1. Richard Ovenden, *John Thomson (1837-1921) photographer*, Edinburgh: National Library of Scotland, The Stationery Office, 1997
2. Joel Montague and Jim Mizerski, *John Thomson: the early years, in search of the Orient*, Bangkok: White Lotus, 2014

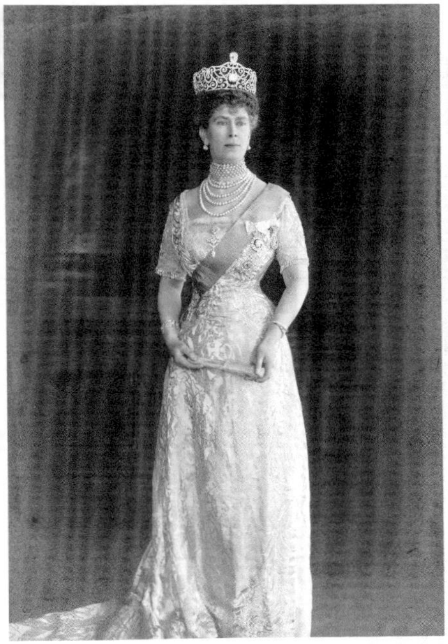

Queen Mary (May of Teck). Photograph by John Thomson, ca. 1910. Wellcome Collection no. 569580i.

his Chinese travels, which would become the central achievement of his life. This book shows the areas to which he travelled: from Hong Kong to Formosa (Taiwan), to the Treaty Ports (Shanghai, Guangzhou, Fouzhou, and Xiamen); westwards to Hubei in central China, and northwards to Beijing. These journeys and others within China lasted from 1868 to 1872.

Thomson's journeys were physically arduous. Wherever he went, his photographic equipment had to be transported; it consisted of heavy glass plates, and bottles of dangerous chemicals, cameras, tents and tripods. On his frequent trips by Chinese river boats, shipwreck was a constant danger: one photograph (Wellcome Collection no. 18816i) shows his equipment piled up on the river bank after running aground on the River Min rapids. In Thailand and Cambodia he struggled with malaria. In Shantou, as he tried to photograph an ancient bridge over the river, the people on the bridge pelted him so that he was forced to defend himself with the tripod of his camera.

His later travels outside China, to Persia and Cyprus, also took him to some rough terrain. A wood-engraving in the *Illustrated London News* (9 November 1878) shows Thomson after he and his bearers had made their way to the top of Mount Olympus in order to take photographs from the summit. As soon as they arrived at the summit, there was a mighty cloudburst, the party and all the equipment were drenched, and photography was impossible.

His hardships were softened by the company he kept. He was often accompanied by Scottish and American missionaries, diplomats, doctors and traders, especially if they could speak Chinese. A photograph set up by Thomson (Wellcome Collection no. 19898i) shows him (with a full beard, on the left) and two companions sitting snugly in their cabin on the Yangtze river. A copy of *Harper's Weekly* is prominent in the foreground, a copy of *Appleton's Journal* on the wall behind. Ominously, however, the three travellers each has a Winchester rifle within easy reach: piracy was a notorious hazard on the river.

Thomson returned to Great Britain in 1872, never to revisit the Far East. He settled in London and exploited his Far Eastern experiences in several ways. First, while his memories were still fresh, he wrote his magnum opus, the four magnificent volumes entitled *Illustrations of China and its people* (1873). This was followed by other books such as *The Straits of Malacca* (1874) which enlightened many British about a part of the world of great economic importance to them.

Second, the skill which he had acquired in photographing the street dwellers of Beijing and Guangzhou was turned to good use in a remarkable book about their London equivalents: *Street life in London* (1877), a classic visual record of Dickensian London.

Thirdly, there was demand from other explorers and geographers for training in documenting their travels. This training was provided by Thomson in his capacity as Instructor in Photography to the Royal Geographical Society, then based in Savile Row.

Fourthly, Thomson set up his own photographic studio in the West End of London. There he took photographs of the wealthy aristocrats and financiers of Victorian England. In the 1880s he obtained a Royal Warrant, signifying approval of his work by the Royal Household. In that capacity he photographed Queen Victoria and, much later, Princess of May of Teck, subsequently Queen Mary (1867-1953). Thomson's unobtrusive blind-stamped signature on the mount of this and other photographs is often overlooked by collectors.

It was with this lifetime of experience behind him that Thomson set off to check out the Wellcome historical exhibition in 1920. There, Thomson would have seen a corridor lined with photographs already in Wellcome's possession: it was a small display and had much about Africa but nothing about China. So, on 12 May 1920, Thomson wrote to the curator of the gallery as follows.

Dear Sir, I don't know if Mr Wellcome intends to have a room in the museum set apart for the exhibition of photographs. If he does, selections from the photographs taken by me during my eastern travels would prove useful, seeing that each photograph was taken to represent something peculiar to the lands and to the people I visited. Each series includes antiquities, arts, architecture, industries, and evidence of evolution. The regions include Siam, Cochin China, Cambodia, China and the islands of Formosa and Cyprus. I would supply the negatives and quotable notes to each subject. I am sure that such a series would add usefulness and interest to the wonderful collection of this museum. Kindly let me know your views on the subject. Yours sincerely, J. Thomson.

That letter was the beginning of the process which has led to the worldwide touring exhibition. If Thomson had not written it, it is unlikely that the photographs in this exhibition would exist today: there were few institutions at the time which could have taken on the responsibility of preserving such a huge weight of old glass, making positive prints from the negatives, making a catalogue of them, and making them available worldwide for exhibition and research.

Thomson's hope that Henry S. Wellcome would provide a home for his photographs was a reasonable one: Wellcome was himself an enthusiastic amateur photographer, he manufactured photographic chemicals, published a photographer's annual diary, and was building up a collection of historic photographs which would include works by many master photographers: views of Mexico by Désiré Charnay, records of mediaeval France by Édouard-Denis Baldus, portraits of native Americans by Edward S. Curtis and Frank A. Rinehart, portraits of English men and women by Julia Margaret Cameron, and prize-winning studies of Kashmir by Samuel Bourne. Within this treasure-house of fine photographs, Thomson, along with Felice Beato and William Pryor Floyd, would represent those who had photographed China in the nineteenth century.

Thomson died before the negotiations to add his photographs to the collection were concluded, and Wellcome subsequently bought them from Thomson's heirs. As a result, three wooden steel-lined crates containing nearly 700 precious negatives were delivered to the Wellcome offices, and subsequently became part of the Wellcome Collection, where the crates and their original contents are preserved today. Since 1981 they have been catalogued and studied with the aid of many scholars from China, Thailand, Scotland, England, France, and America. In the course of these studies, the collection was found to contain many photographs which Thomson had not been able to include in any of his publications: these negatives are the sole surviving witnesses of the scenes which they show. Others were published but in a cropped form, so that readers of Thomson's publications only saw the people in the centre of a composition, unaware that the uncropped original negative showed the people sitting in a palace garden or out on the Bund.

Given the size and range of Thomson's work, there is still much scope for further study and enjoyment of his art. The Wellcome Collection is therefore delighted that the exhibitions and this publication will continue to bring Thomson's most humane and evocative photographs to new audiences.

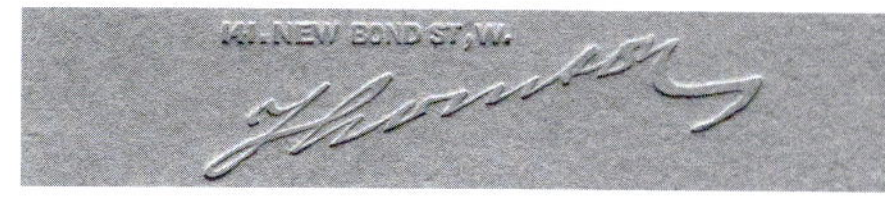

Thomson's unobtrusive blind-stamped signature on the mount of this and other photographs is often overlooked by collectors.

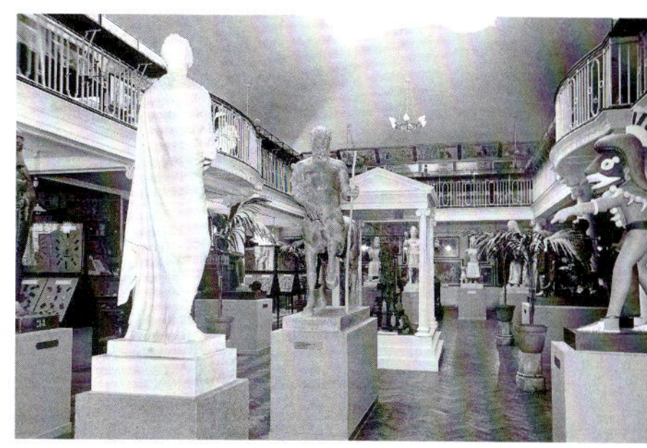

Statues of deities in the Wellcome Historical Medical Museum, London, ca. 1920. (Photo: Wellcome Collection, London)

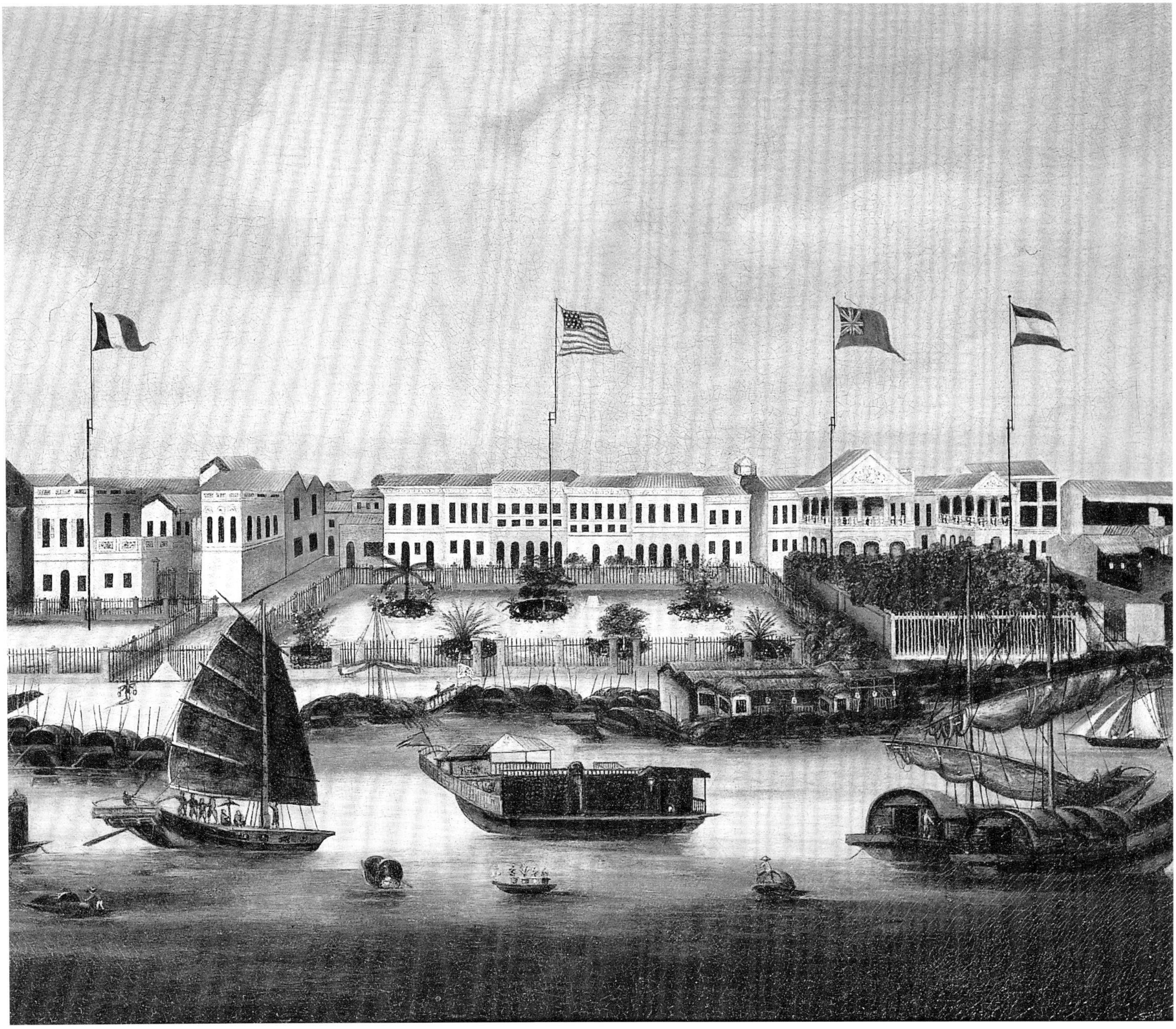

Canton: the 'Factories' or 'Hongs', Chinese artists, c.1842. (Courtesy Martyn Gregory Gallery, London)
This painting of some of the "Thirteen Factories", was made towards the end of the First Opium War in 1842. It shows the area of the Pearl River where Western merchants could operate.

The Turbulent Years

Betty Yao MBE

In July 1867 John Thomson set sail for his second journey to Asia. He landed in Singapore, went on to Vietnam, and there spent three months in Saigon. He then travelled on to Hong Kong where he settled for the next five years, establishing a photography studio there in 1868. In 1869 his bride-to-be, Isabel Petrie, joined him and they were married in November of that year.

The achievements from Thomson's first journey to Asia were outstanding. He had produced an impressive collection of photographs of Siam, which included royal portraits of King Mongkut (Rama IV) and of his heir Prince Chulalongkorn. He had documented major festivals and ceremonies rarely seen by outsiders. He was also the first person to have photographed the temple ruins of Angkor Wat in Cambodia. His printed album *The Antiquities of Cambodia* had been published in early 1867. In the previous year, 1866, he had not only become a member of the Royal Ethnological Society of London (now the Royal Anthropological Institute), but also been elected a Fellow of the Royal Geographical Society.

Why would a young man from Edinburgh, of modest means and with few contacts, have chosen to venture to Singapore in 1862 and then to Hong Kong in 1868? To understand this requires some knowledge of the political context of the time. The 19th century was traumatic for the Chinese, and in their eyes a century of humiliation. This feeling is still embedded in the Chinese psyche today. The birth of photography in 1839 coincided with a period during which China was forced to open up to western traders, missionaries, and travellers. For 2,000 years Europeans had only intermittent access to China. But, from the mid 18th century the Qing dynasty government came under increasing pressure to open the Chinese market to the West.

First, in 1756, with the aim of confining trade with the West to one city only, the southern trading port of Canton (Guangzhou) was established. Foreign merchants operated from the Thirteen Factories, a designated area located along the banks of the Pearl River southwest of Canton. They were overseen by the Canton Customs Supervisor under the authority of the Governor of Guangdong and Guangxi. Foreign traders were strictly confined to their compounds.

The Opium Wars (the First, from 1839 to 1842, and the Second, from 1856 to 1860) dramatically altered this. These wars had their roots in the tea trade. Since the 18th century as tea had become more and more popular in Britain, the cost of purchasing and importing it had become an increasing burden to the British government's coffers. Traders, searching for something to sell to the Chinese to redress the gaping trade deficit, settled on opium. Although opium was banned by the Qing government, smugglers and corrupt local officials allowed it to spread. This had a devastating effect on the Chinese population. In the late 1830s the Qing court instructed the governor of Canton, Lin Zexu (1785-1850), to put an end to this contraband trade. In June 1839 Governor Lin blockaded the British and American trading bases in Canton and destroyed 20,000 chests of the illicit drug. Furious and indignant, the British declared war on China in late 1839. Numerous blockades and several battles ensued, resulting in a British victory in 1842. The Treaty of Nanjing was signed on 29th August 1842 by Prince Gong (1833-1898), the younger brother of the Emperor. Later, in 1870, he was photographed by John Thomson. Hong Kong was ceded to Britain as a colony and five Chinese ports were forcibly opened to western traders. In addition to Canton (Guangzhou), these were Amoy (Xiamen), Foo-chow (Fuzhou), Ningpo (Ningbo) and Shanghai. British consular officials were allowed to reside in these treaty ports and all British nationals were granted 'extraterritoriality' enabling them to live and work outside Chinese law. The Chinese government had to pay a crippling reparation of over 21 million silver dollars, with 6 million of this as compensation for the opium that had been confiscated, 3 million for the debts the Chinese merchants owed the British, and 12 million for the cost of the war.

After the First Opium War more and more publications and exhibitions on China appeared in the West. Public interest, especially in Britain and the United States, grew and this led to more travellers setting off for the Far East. By 1850 this new influx of travellers felt frustrated by their confinement to the five treaty ports. The British were clamouring for more rights and privileges and called for the complete opening up of China to their merchants and missionaries. They also called for the legalisation of the opium trade and the right to place a British ambassador in Beijing. Tensions grew, but during this period the Qing government was otherwise occupied by the Taiping Rebellion (1851-1864), a revolt which led to civil war and caused millions of deaths. With this terrible internal war raging and the Chinese military enfeebled, one single act in October 1856 lit the fuse that led to the Second Opium War.

In Canton, some local government officials impounded the *Arrow,* a ship that flew the British flag, because it was suspected of illegally carrying opium. This act led to the bombardment of Canton and British troops stormed the city. By March 1857 the British Parliament was calling for war and appointed Lord Elgin as an envoy to China with the remit to open the whole of China to western trade. James Bruce, 8th Earl of Elgin (1811-1863) became the High Commissioner and Plenipotentiary to China. British military units were dispatched from India and Singapore and joined forces with the French troops. They seized Canton in December 1857 and forced the Chinese to sign the Treaty of Tianjin, extending gains from the earlier Treaty of Nanjing. When the Qing government refused to ratify these harsh terms, tensions escalated. In August 1860 Elgin gathered an expeditionary force. When the Chinese captured the British consul Harry Parkes in September 1860 the British and French troops attacked Peking. In October 1860, the Second Opium War culminated in the infamous sacking of Yuanmingyuan, the original summer palace of the Qing emperors.

Set in a large 3.4 square kilometre park, Yuanmingyuan palace consisted of hundreds of imperial buildings and gardens. The palace was originally developed by Emperor Kangxi (1654-1772) and further extended by Emperor Qianlong (1711-1799). There were lakes, waterways and artificial hills, hundreds of pavilions, temples, and it included a maze designed by the Italian Jesuits for the Qing court. Yuanmingyuan palace was filled with imperial treasures, porcelain, paintings, jades, bronzes, and textiles. On the night of 6th October 1860, the French and British soldiers arrived and were amazed by such magnificent treasures the like of which they had never seen. The soldiers ransacked and looted with abandon. What the soldiers could not take they smashed to smithereens. It was indiscriminate plunder and wanton destruction. Twelve days after that night, Elgin ordered the complete destruction of the Yuanmingyuan palace. Thousands of troops were marshalled to torch the complex. The blaze took two days to burn out. It is estimated that over 1.5 million objects were looted or destroyed. Many of the looted pieces are now scattered across the world in museums and private collections.

In an act of final humiliation, at the Convention of Peking on 24th October 1860, the Chinese were forced to ratify and extend the Treaty of Tianjin. 6 million taels of silver had to be paid to Britain and France as war reparations. Kowloon, the peninsula across from Hong Kong island, was ceded to Britain forming the colony of Hong Kong. Foreign delegations were allowed to reside in Peking. Further cities and ports such as Nanjing, Shantou, Yantai and Haikou were opened to traders. Foreigners were allowed to travel to the interior of China and missionaries were given freedom of movement. Opium was legalised.

John Thomson's photographs of China should be seen in this historic context. In 1867 this adventurous young man armed with a camera and his recently acquired skill of photography, set sail to the new colony of Hong Kong and established a photography studio. In 1869 Thomson received his first major commission, to photograph the official commemorative book recording the visit of Prince Alfred, Duke of Edinburgh, younger son of Queen Victoria. This was the first royal visit to a new colony. Thomson's portrait studio thrived because many merchants and government officials wanted to have a set of photographs recording their time in the East to take home to show their families.

We can trace the footsteps of Thomson's journeys from Canton, Amoy, Foo-chow, Shantou, Shanghai, Peking, and Tianjin, following the route of treaty ports, opened as a result of the two Opium Wars. He befriended the English and Scottish civil servants, American missionaries and British traders who lived and worked in these treaty ports. Some, having learned the Chinese language, offered help crucial to Thomson's work. Thanks to these introductions, he was able to photograph Prince Gong and some of the ministers in the 'Zongli Yamen', the Office for Foreign Affairs. He was introduced to the Chinese merchant Yang Fang, who gave Thomson access to the women of his family, enabling Thomson to photograph them in the inner courtyards, where men were normally not allowed. He received help to plan and navigate his various photography journeys. Thomson went to Foo-chow and up the Min River with American missionary, the Reverend Justus Doolittle (1824-1880). He travelled with Scottish missionary Dr James Laidlaw Maxwell (1836-1921) to photograph the island of Taiwan. He photographed the new Summer Palace, Garden of Clear Ripples, adjacent to the ruins of Yuanmingyuan accompanied by Dr John Dudgeon (1837-1901), a Scottish physician, translator, and medical missionary who had worked in Beijing since 1864. Thomson could never have taken his photographs had he not received help in this way.

The two Opium Wars created a dramatic shift in the British and European public perception of China. It was no longer a mysterious place. But the forced way in which China was pried open shaped the way the 19th century Western world viewed the country. It easily led to prejudiced interpretations. John Thomson, however, documented the people and the landscape of China more even-handedly. He photographed the rich and the poor with equal respect and empathy. After his return to London in 1872 Thomson published several books – *Foochow and the Min River, Illustrations of China and its People,* and *Through China with a Camera.* He continued to give lectures and provided a picture of China that the Victorian public could relate to. Showing stunningly beautiful landscapes, ancient architecture, and lively street scenes with traders going about their day-to-day business, he became known as 'China Thomson'.

Photography is a social medium. Thomson's images of women, children, street traders, all give life to the Chinese people and continue to resonate with us today.

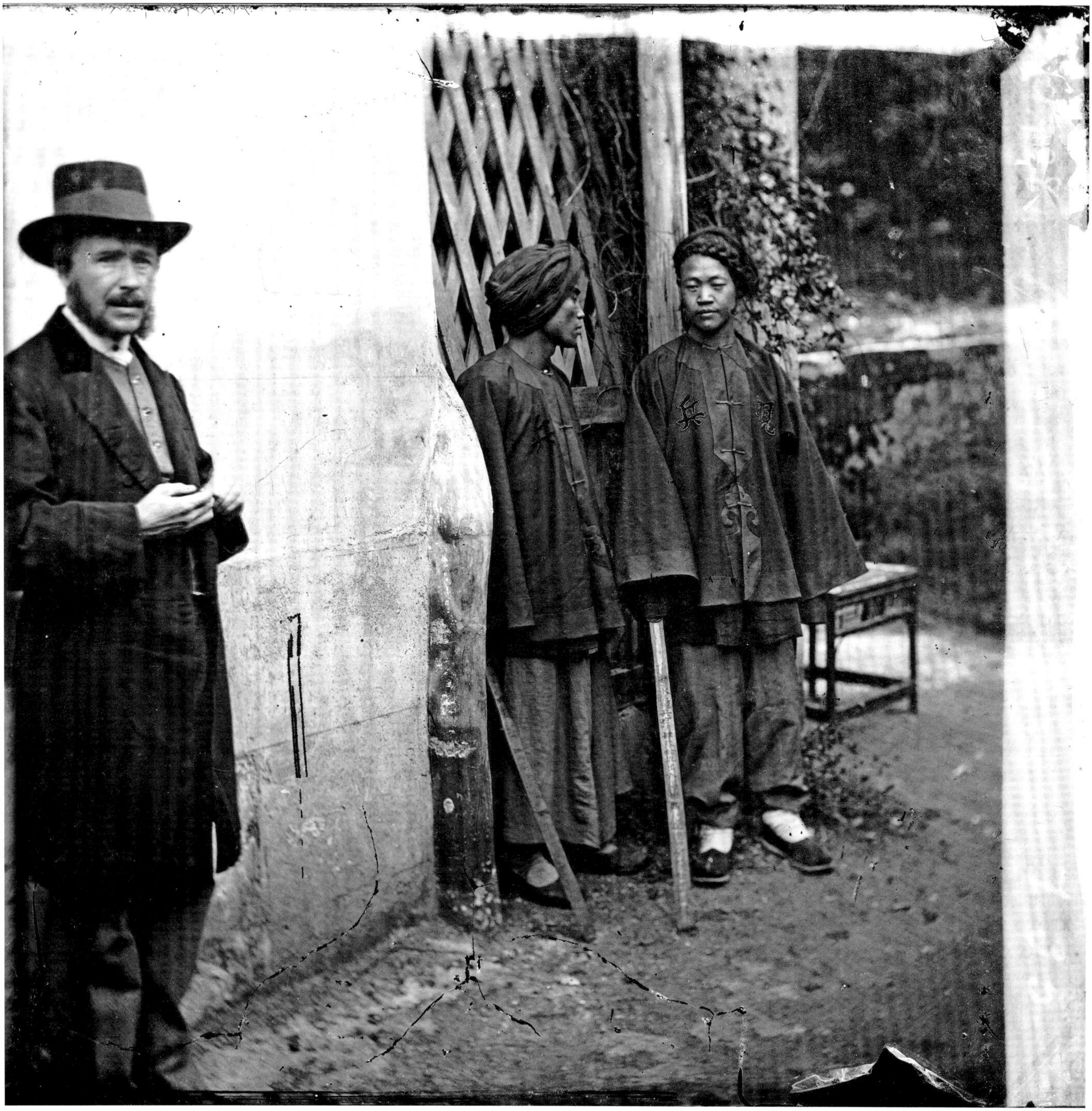

John Thomson's China: 1868-1872

Professor Nick Pearce, Richmond Chair of Fine Arts,
University of Glasgow

We cannot be certain why John Thomson (1837-1921) decided to make his future in the Far East or why he embarked upon a career in photography. Circumstances, opportunities, education and training can all be seen to have played a part. Born and brought up in Edinburgh of the 1840s and 50s, in relatively modest circumstances, Thomson was apprenticed to an optician and attended evening classes in Natural Philosophy, mathematics and chemistry at Edinburgh School of Arts, now Heriot Watt University.[1] His training in the manufacture and operation of optical instruments and the scientific environment of Edinburgh at the time, not least the pioneering work of David Octavius Hill (1802-70) and Robert Adamson (1821-48), in photography, would all have had an influence on the young Thomson. Indeed it is likely that he was apprenticed to optician and optical instrument maker James Mackay Bryson (1824-94), whose father, Robert Bryson, had been associated with Hill and Adamson and who was himself a keen photographer and traded in photographic supplies.[2] Thomson was therefore immersed in the scientific and photographic crucible that surrounded him.

Thomson's move to the Far East followed in the wake of his elder brother, William, who left for Singapore in August 1859 to set up a watch-making business. Just over two years later, John joined William, arriving in Singapore in the spring of 1862.[3] As a major trading colony, the opportunities that Singapore could offer men of ambition were considerable and it may have been John's original intention to join his brother once William had established himself in business. Surviving evidence suggests that while both brothers operated the watch-making business, as early as 1863, John had also opened a photographic studio.[4] It was while in Singapore that Thomson began his travels as a photojournalist and in 1865 embarked upon a major expedition to Siam, Laos and Cambodia, photographing people, events, sites (notably Angkor) and taking portraits of both the King of Siam and of Cambodia. The result was *The Antiquities of Cambodia,* published immediately upon his return to Edinburgh in 1867.[5] This publication, his stock of photographs and the lectures which Thomson gave during his sojourn back in Britain, established both his reputation as a traveller and photographer and the pattern of his work during the rest of his professional life, that of publishing his photographs together with a narrative, particularly in book form. Thomson's next venture, in China, would see this pattern develop in a systematic way, for although he would spend only five years in China, this period resulted in the bulk of his photographic work which would sustain him and his reputation for the rest of his life.

China

Early in 1868, Thomson re-established his photographic studio, this time in Hong Kong, teaming up with printer and stationer J.J. da Silva.[6] Hong Kong was an ideal base for a photographer, it being a port of growing commercial significance, within easy reach of Canton and Shanghai and, as a British colony, having a regular turnover of customers requiring photographic

Opposite: Thomson with two Manchu soldiers, Xiamen, Fujian 1871. It is rare for Thomson to appear in a photo, here with two Manchu soldiers. Amoy, or Xiamen, was the southern frontier of the Qing empire. Although the Manchu finally managed to conquer the region, it continued to cause great difficulties to the imperial rulers.

1. For a detailed biography of John Thomson, see: Richard Ovenden, *John Thomson (1837-1921): Photographer,* Edinburgh, National Library of Scotland and The Stationary Office, 1997.
2. Ovenden, *John Thomson,* p. 2.
3. Ovenden, *John Thomson,* p. 6.
4. Ovenden, *John Thomson,* p. 6.
5. John Thomson, *The Antiquities of Cambodia*: A Series of Photographs Taken on the Spot, Edinburgh: Edmonston and Douglas, 1867.
6. Commercial Bank Building, Queen's Road, Central, The Chronicle and Directory for China, Japan and the Philippines, Hong Kong, 1869, p. 165. Thomson also issued an announcement in the China Mail of 11 March, 1868. See Ovenden, p. 14.

souvenirs of the region. Hong Kong, however, was already a well established and thriving centre for professional photographers, European and Chinese, so it was inevitable that Thomson would expand his enterprise in other directions, providing photographs for a variety of publications, including one of his own: *Views of the North River* and making a number of extended trips into mainland China to expand his repertoire.[7] Between 1870 and 1872, he made a series of journeys, each time extending further afield: Guangzhou, Shantou, Shanghai, Fuzhou, Taiwan, Fujian, Tianjin, Beijing and up the Yangzi River. These journeys resulted in a large corpus of Thomson's best known and often stunning photographs.

What marks out Thomson's time in China in addition to the extensive number and range of photographs he produced, was his network of contacts which allowed him to access particular sites, make the most of his time in the different parts of China he visited and also to reveal the life of a people and their activities experienced by very few westerners at that time. These contacts included missionaries, diplomatic personnel, and fellow photographers, albeit mostly amateur, all of whom assisted him in various ways, not least in his introduction to Chinese officials and members of the Chinese elite.

Thomson's iconic photograph of Yixin, Prince Gong (1832-98) and the series of images of members of the Grand Council (advisors to the throne) and the Chinese Foreign Office, were arranged through the offices of William Alexander Parsons Martin (1827-1916), an American missionary who was President of the Tongwenguan, a college established by the Chinese government to teach western languages, science and international law. Martin had come to China with the Presbyterian American Mission in 1850 and before taking up his post with the Tongwenguan in 1869, had been an interpreter at the American Legation in Beijing.[8] As a prolific writer and translator of scientific texts into Chinese, Martin was greatly respected by members of the Chinese government and it was through these connections that Thomson was able to photograph Prince Gong and other senior officials. Prince Gong is represented in Thomson's photograph as a formidable character, relaxed yet immensely strong, fixing the viewer with his direct stare. The image is in stark contrast to that taken of the Prince by photographer Felice Beato (1832-1909) in 1860, under very different circumstances immediately following the Second Opium War (1856-60). On that occasion Prince Gong was negotiating a peace treaty on behalf of his brother, the Xianfeng Emperor (r. 1850-61) and appears tense and pensive in Beato's photograph.[9] Thomson's photograph was taken at Prince Gong's residence, which might have contributed to the relaxed atmosphere and the photographer records that he was somewhat disarmed by the Prince's interest in photography.[10] The other officials were photographed in the grounds of the Foreign Office and like Prince Gong, strike very casual poses. Thomson was able to take several individual and group photographs during the session. One of the most senior ministers present, Bao Yun (1806-91), was moved to record the occasion in a poem in which he described the reaction of each of the sitters and remarked that the session lasted all day.[11] As to the physical appearance of the photographer: 'Thomson the visitor from overseas', wrote Bao Yun, had 'piercing eyes and dragon-like whiskers and a great forehead.'[12]

Thomson created a number of close personal contacts with Protestant missionaries across China, but those in the capital, Beijing, served him well during his lengthy stay in the autumn of 1871. In addition to Martin, his colleague, Dr John Dudgeon (1837-1901), who was Professor of Anatomy and Physiology at the Tongwenguan and Head of the London Missionary Society's Hospital, was also well connected and helpful to Thomson. A fellow Scot and a graduate in

7. John Thomson, *Views of the North River*, Hong Kong: Noronha & Sons, 1870.
8. For details of Martin's life and work, see: Jonathan D. Spence, *To Change China: Western Advisers in China*, Harmondsworth: Penguin Books, 1980, Chapter 5, pp. 129-160.
9. See: David Harris, *Of Battle and Beauty: Felice Beato's Photographs of China*, Santa Barbara: University of California Press, 2000.
10. John Thomson, *The Straits of Malacca, Indo-China and China, or Ten Years' Travels, Adventures and Residence Abroad*, London: Marston Low, Marston, Low & Searle, 1875, p. 512 and *Through China With A Camera*, London: Constable & Co. 1898, p. 235.
11. Baoyun, *Wenjinggong yiji* (文靖公遺集), juan 1, cited by Fung Min-chu, 'Decoding John Thomson's Figural Photographs from His China Travels', *National Palace Museum Bulletin*, vol.44, October, 2011, pp. 103-124, p. 107.
12. Fung Min-chu, 'Decoding', p. 107.

medicine of Glasgow University, Dudgeon had been appointed to the medical mission in Beijing in 1864. As well as being a talented doctor, he was also a keen amateur photographer of considerable ability.[13] Shortly after Thomson's visit to Beijing, Dudgeon published the first manual on photography in Chinese, Tuoying qiguan (脫影奇觀, How to Take Wonderful Photographs), in 1873 and we know from Thomson's own writings that Dudgeon accompanied him to various sites in the City and to the Summer Palace complex to the north.[14] These would have been familiar sites for Dudgeon and no doubt already captured by the amateur photographer. There is often a close correlation in terms of subject and camera position between extant photographs attributed to Dudgeon and those by Thomson; evidence, it may be suggested, of a close working relationship between the two men while Thomson was in Beijing. One example is of the marble archway to the Biyun Si (Temple of Azure Clouds), one of a group of monasteries in the Western Hills on the approach to the Summer Palace. Dudgeon photographed the archway from a very similar angle and one is tempted to see his guiding hand in Thomson's approach (Fig 1: John Dudgeon, 'The White Marble Archway and Vajra Thorne Pagoda, Temple of Azure Clouds').[15]

It is clear that Dudgeon was responsible for introducing Thomson to another amateur photographer, Yang Fang. Yang was a pawnbroker by profession who, through his wealth, had purchased his official rank. The two photographs of a Manchu official, can be identified as Yang, appearing rather stern in his spectacles and belying the friendly character which Thomson and other westerners attributed to him. Yang had been educated in Shanghai where he had come into regular contact with western life and technology, including photography and he seems to have continued his love of things western, meeting with visitors to the City whenever the opportunity arose. From his writings, Thomson obviously admired Yang and visited him and his family on several occasions: 'I had occasion to repeat my visits in fulfilment of a promise I gave Mr Yang, to show him how to make for himself certain photographic chemicals with materials which he could procure in Peking.'[16] We also have details from Thomson's and other accounts of Yang's love of mechanical contrivances, including a sawmill and a steam-driven water pump, which had been installed, along with gas lighting, by another photographer resident in Beijing, Thomas Child (1841-98).[17] Child was employed as a gas engineer by the Chinese Maritime Customs and as a friend of Dudgeon's would have met Thomson during his stay in the Capital. Thomson owed his opportunity to make a series of photographs of Manchu and Chinese women to Mr Yang, who opened his home for this purpose. In a society where women remained secluded this was an exceptional occurrence and points to a trust and friendship that must have developed between the two men.

Perhaps less comfortable to our sensibilities today are some of the other photos of human subjects, which are described by Thomson as racial 'types' in his *Illustrations of China and Its People* of 1874. The beautiful portrait of the Old Cantonese Woman, joins a group of three other 'Heads', under the title: 'Types of the Labouring Classes', and there are other occurrences in the pages of the book where character through physiognomic traits are considered to be representative of a particular race or type. Thomson was a member of the Ethnological Society of London, having petitioned to join soon after his return to Britain from Singapore (and his expedition to Siam and Cambodia), in 1866.[18] Thereafter many of his portrait subjects provided a physiognomic record (supported by a descriptive text), of his sitters, particularly those of the working classes. Additionally, Thomson, like other 19th century western commentators, was preoccupied with foot-binding, which

13. For examples of work attributed to Dudgeon, see Nick Pearce, *Photographs of Peking, China: 1861-1908*, New York: Mellen Press, 2005 and the same author's 'A Life in Peking: the Peabody Albums', *Journal of the History of Photography*, Vol. 31, No. 3, Autumn, 2007, pp. 276-293.
14. For details of *Tuoying qiguan, see: Pearce, Photographs*, pp. 28-29 and 'A Life', pp. 288-289.
15. Dudgeon's photograph appears in Pearce, 'A Life', p.292, fig. 13.
16. John Thomson, *Illustrations of China and Its People*, London: Sampson Low, Marston, Low and Searle, 1873-74, Vol. IV, text to Plate VII.
17. Colin Osman, 'Thomas Child (1841-1898), Photographer of Peking', *The Photo Historian Supplement*, No. 86A, Autumn 1989, p. 3.
18. Ovenden, *John Thomson*, p. 11.

though not by any means a universal practise in China, was the subject of much interest. In *Illustrations of China and Its People*, Thomson included a technical commentary on foot-binding provided by his friend Dr John Dudgeon to accompany his photograph (which was one of a series he took) of the woman from Xiamen displaying her unbound foot. Dudgeon was an opponent of foot-binding, as he was of opium smoking, although this did not prevent him from explaining its origins and social context.[19] Thomson himself wrote rather wryly of the practice, comparing it to the then equally damaging fashion for corseted waists in the West. As James Ryan has written, 'The ability of photography to apprehend visually the human body made it one of the most powerful mediums in the Victorian era for bringing the British viewing public imaginatively face to face with people different from themselves, both abroad and at home.'[20] Indeed later in his career Thomson joined with journalist and social commentator, Adolphe Smith, to publish *Street Life in London*, which followed a trend in the 19th century to study, analyze and classify the poor and working class of any nation.[21] Although from one perspective these 'photographs of the natives' may make us feel uncomfortable, Thomson's artistic ability with the camera has produced some images which are striking and iconic, in the sense that they are hugely memorable and continue to be used in publications today.

Thomson's inclusion of trades and occupations as a subject followed a tradition that began in China a century earlier with painting. During the 18th century it was fashionable for East India traders and ships officers to return with sets of paintings produced by Chinese artist that depicted the port cities that they had visited, principally Canton (Guangzhou).[22] Topographical views were popular, but so were scenes depicting the trades of the Chinese. Thomson took advantage of his journeys to capture scenes of industry in a much wider context but often using an iconography developed in the 18th century. Good examples are those taken in Beijing and include the knife-grinder), travelling fruit-seller and chinaware mender, all of which have corresponding images in the export watercolour tradition developed in Canton in the 18th century.[23]

The closest link with the watercolour tradition, however, is the stereoscopic photograph of the Portrait Artist, taken by Thomson in Hong Kong and recognisably a survivor of an occupation which would eventually be replaced by photography (Fig 2: Anon, 'Chinese Artist Copying a European Print').

While he was in Beijing, Thomson made a comprehensive record of both the Chinese and Tartar Cities – walls, gates and temples. The Imperial City itself was of course closed to him, but one of the more unusual buildings Thomson photographed was the Korean Legation. Situated in the south-east corner, immediately below the inner wall which separated the Tartar City from the Chinese City, the Legation also housed the embassies of other 'tributary' nations, Annam, Burma and Mongolia, collectively known as the *siyiguan* (四異館), the Four Barbarian's Residence.[24] Thomson was impressed with the Koreans, remarking upon their spotlessly white garments, although access to the premises proved difficult. His photograph was taken from atop the city walls and was obviously a challenge: 'It was with great difficulty, however, that I secured an illustration, but it was on that account all the more prized.'[25] In addition to exploring the capital, he made various excursions to sites situated in the Western Hills, north-west of the City. Mention has already been made of his visit to the Imperial Summer Palace in the company of John Dudgeon. Another excursion took him to the Ming Tombs and the Great Wall, on which occasion he was accompanied by Alexander Wylie (1815-87). Wylie was an extraordinary

19. Thomson's quote in *Illustrations* comes from: J. Dudgeon, 'The Small Feet of Chinese Women,' *Chinese Recorder and Missionary Journal* 2, Fuzhou and Shanghai: n.p., 1869), pp. 93–96.
20. James R. Ryan, Picturing Empire: *Photography and the Visualization of the British Empire*, London: Reaktion Books, 1997, p. 140.
21. John Thomson and Adolphe Smith. *Street life in London: With Permanent photographic Illustrations*. London: Sampson Low, Marston, Searle and Rivington, 1877-78.
22. For further details, see: Craig Clunas, *Chinese Export Watercolours*, London: Victoria & Albert Museum, 1984.
23. Thomson was probably familiar with such books as *The Costume of China* and *The Punishments of China*, both published by George Henry Mason in 1800 and 1801 respectively and which used Chinese watercolours as the basis of the illustrations.
24. Pearce, *Photographs of Peking*, pp. 148-149.
25. Thomson, *Through China*, p. 230.

figure with a life-story not dissimilar to that of Thomson. Apprenticed to a cabinet-maker, he became fascinated by the Chinese language which he picked-up via a Latin-Chinese grammar. He was helped by James Legge (1815-97), missionary and latterly Professor of Chinese at Oxford University, who recruited him to run the London Missionary Society's press at Shanghai. By the time of Thomson's meeting with Wylie in Beijing, the latter was agent for the British and Foreign Bible Society in China, with an established reputation in Chinese language and literature and had translated many key western scientific texts into Chinese.[26]

Wylie was the ideal companion for Thomson. Not only was he conversant in Chinese, but he had the necessary connections which allowed access to sites which were sometimes off-limits or were restricted. Wylie was also best qualified to accompany Thomson on his Great Wall journey as he was author of the first study and translation of the Buddhist texts and carved images found on the inner walls of the stone gateway through a stretch of the Great Wall known as Juyong Guan (Dwelling in Harmony Pass).[27] The gate was built between 1342 and 1345 by the Mongol Emperor Shundi (1333-68) and consists of relief carvings of Buddhist images on the face and on the inside of the archway and only on the inside of the archway, inscriptions in six languages: Sanskrit, Tibetan, Mongolian, Uighur, Tangut and Chinese. Framing the archway is a Garuda bird, carved in relief on the keystone, with two Naga kings on either side whose coiling bodies create a complex pattern. On the inside are the Four Heavenly Kings (Tian Wang), guardians of the Four Quarters, two on either side of the inner archway. Thomson's photograph is of Chiguo Tian Wang, the Guardian of the East, who is shown with his attribute, a lute. Thomson also photographed the Great Wall itself at the stretch at Badaling, a section still popular with visitors today, and Nankou Pass, the gorge south of Badaling, which although looking unpromising as a road, had, according to Thomson: 'some few parts of the ancient road which are still in comparatively good order.' Of the photograph he continues: 'At this point the pass narrows down considerably, and makes a sharp bend. On a rocky peak to the left rises a picturesque little edifice, dedicated to Kwei-Sing [Kuixing], the god of literature; on the opposite side of the ravine is a small two-storied temple, approached by a steep staircase cut into the face of the rock. The lower story is dedicated to Kwan-te [Guandi], the god of war, and the upper one is called the cave of Kwanyin [Guanyin], the goddess of mercy.'[28]

On the same journey, Thomson visited the Ming Tombs, the resting place of thirteen of the Ming emperors, beginning with the second, Yongle (1403-24), who established Beijing as the Ming capital. The Tombs pepper the hillside which is in the form of a semi-circle, open to the south. It was the approach to the tomb site – the line of giant limestone figures of animals and human figures that are positioned either side of the Spirit Road (Shendao) – that provided Thomson with one of his most iconic photographs. 'All the figures', wrote Thomson, 'wear an expression of tranquil repose, thoroughly in keeping with their duty as the guardians of the dead'.[29] The man standing next to the camel in the photograph is quite possibly one of Thomson's two loyal Chinese servants, Ahong or Akum, both of whom he had recruited many years earlier in Singapore and who remained with him during his time in China.

It is obvious from Thomson's writings that his contacts throughout China were hugely important in engineering the many carefully staged photographs of groups and individuals he obtained. We know from *Illustrations of China and Its People*, for example, that the group of women from Xiamen he photographed, had foreign employers who no doubt arranged for the sitting. The Manchu soldiers which he photographed in Canton, belonged to the contingent assigned to

26. For more information on Wylie, see: Henri Cordier, *The Life and Labours of Alexander Wylie*, London: Trubner & Co., 1887.
27. Alexander Wylie, 'On An Ancient Buddhist Inscription at Keu-yun-kwan, in North China', *Journal of the Royal Asiatic Society*, Vol. V, n.s. (1871), pp. 14-44.
28. Thomson, *Illustrations*, Vol. IV, text to Plate XXIII.
29. Thomson, *Illustrations*, Vol. IV, text to Plate XX.

the British Consul there, Sir Daniel Brooke Robertson (1810-80), and so their compliance would have been ensured. Thomson's way of creating an elegant and carefully balanced composition is clearly demonstrated in his images of the soldiers. Compliance of the subjects would also have been a relatively easy task at the Nanjing Arsenal, directed as it was then by fellow Scot, Halliday Macartney (1833-1906), who later went on to become British Secretary and Counsellor to the Chinese Legation in London. Thomson even engineers a self-portrait at the Arsenal, with him caught in the act of firing a Gatling Gun.

An important contact when Thomson visited the island of Taiwan (Formosa), in the spring of 1871, was Scottish missionary doctor James Laidlaw Maxwell (1836-1921), probably already known to Thomson from his Edinburgh days. Maxwell was resident in Tainan, the then capital city of Taiwan, as representative of the Foreign Missionary Board and the Presbyterian Church in England and where he operated a medical mission. He accompanied Thomson to sites in and around Tainan and into the interior of the island. Thomson first visited the port of Takao (165), then open to foreign trade, where he met another Presbyterian missionary, the Rev. Hugh Ritchie (1840-79), who with his wife was in the process of establishing a number of churches and missionary schools.[30] From there Thomson, accompanied by Maxwell, explored Tainan and its environs and then made an expedition inland to see the 'aborigines', as Thomson termed them. These were the Popohoan (平埔番), native to Taiwan and seen by both Chinese officialdom and westerners at the time as savages, although during his visit Thomson encountered nothing but friendliness and hospitality. The Popohoan provide Thomson with an opportunity to explore once again his interest in racial 'types', but also the physical surroundings, natural and domestic. The Popohoan house he photographed was comprehensively discussed in *Illustrations of China and Its People*, where he noted that 'The houses of the Popohoan are tolerably clean, well-arranged, and comfortable, and present a striking uniformity of design in the different settlements throughout the island. The entire dwelling makes up three sides of a square, of which the portion in the rear is occupied by the family, while the two wings are invariably used for sheltering cattle, pigs and poultry'.[31]

American missionary, Justus Doolittle (1824-80), was also instrumental in helping Thomson during the photographer's visit to Fuzhou and his trip up the River Min. Employed by the American Missionary Board and based at Fuzhou, where he remained for most of his career, Doolittle was also a social commentator, having published his *Social Life of the Chinese* in 1866.[32] Fuzhou and the surrounding area provided Thomson with a rich source of subjects ranging from portraits to the topographical. A memorable photograph taken during the visit is that of Jinshan Temple on the River Min, depicted as if floating on the water, the stillness of the river creating a perfect mirror-like reflection. His time in the Fuzhou area allowed him to visit a number of monasteries where he could be sure of a welcome and where he could be guaranteed of both beautiful and striking subjects. Yuanfu (Yuen-fu) Monastery in particular (86-88), situated in a cave on the summit of a mountain and surrounded by dense vegetation, provided Thomson with a 'romantic situation' and also a reminder of home: 'the scenery of the Trossachs' in Scotland.[33]

Thomson's relationship with his companion, Justus Doolittle, must have been cordial, for just a few year's later in 1873, he contributed a section on 'Photographic Chemicals and Apparatus' to Doolittle's *A Vocabulary and Handbook of the Chinese Language, Romanized in the Mandarin Dialect* (*Yinghua cuilin yunfu*, 英華萃林韻府).[34] Doolittle's dictionary was divided into three-parts, the third of which consisted of technical terms and specialized vocabularies relating to

30. John Thomson, *The Straits of Malacca*, p. 301.
31. Thomson, *Illustrations*, Vol. II, Plate III.
32. Justus Doolittle, *Social Life of the Chinese*, 2 volumes, London: Sampson Low, Son & Marston, 1866.
33. Thomson, *Illustrations*, Vol. II, text to Plate XVII. *Language, Romanized in the Mandarin Dialect* (Yinghua cuilin
34. Justus Doolittle, *A Vocabulary and Handbook of the Chinese yunfu*, 英華萃林韻府), 2 volumes, Shanghai 1873, Section XXVII.
35. Doolittle, A *Vocabulary*, Section LXII.

science and technology subjects such as mathematics, medicine, law, religion and commerce. Thomson provided eighty-five terms on chemicals and apparatus with Doolittle and his Chinese assistants providing the Chinese translation. Interestingly, John Dudgeon also collaborated on the book and provided 540 'Photographic Terms'.[35]

Although Thomson spent just five years in China, his huge output during that time secured his reputation as a travel photographer and forever associated his name with that country. He was helped in no small measure by the numerous contacts he made throughout China, many of them missionaries, who provided the necessary introductions, practical assistance and, on occasion, companionship. Thomson must have possessed charm, affability and determination in equal measure to have worked successfully with so many and often under difficult situations and we can only wonder at the achievement.

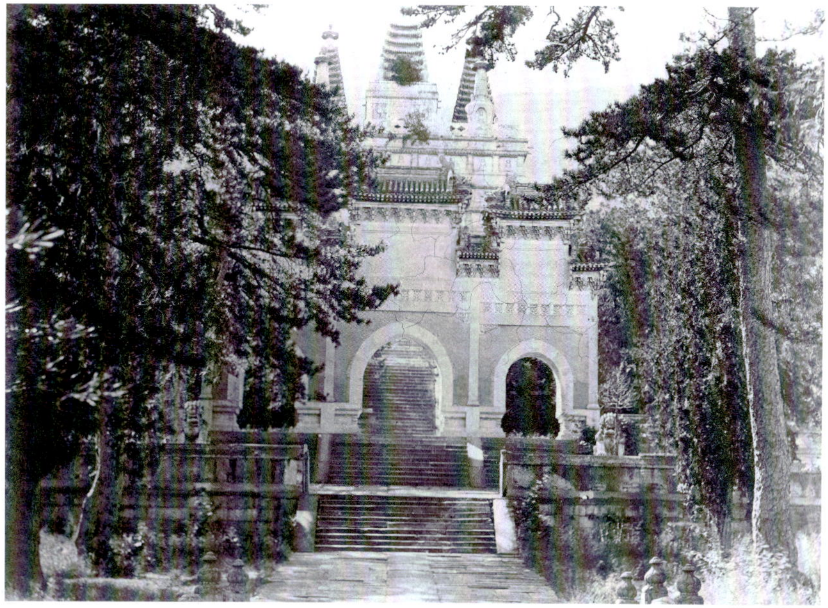

Fig. 1: John Dudgeon, 'The White Marble Archway and Vajra Thorne Pagoda, Temple of Azure Clouds', Albumen print, c. 1870. Reproduced courtesy of the Oriental Museum, University of Durham.

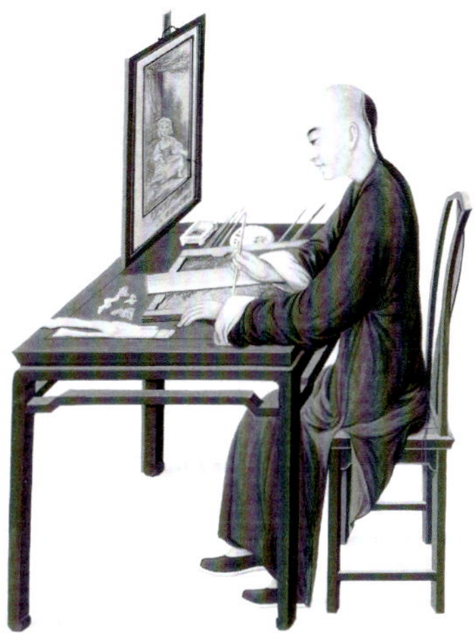

Fig. 2: Anon, 'Chinese Artist Copying a European Print', watercolour on paper, c. 1790. Reproduced Courtesy of the Trustees of the Victoria & Albert Museum. Permissions have been granted for reproduction.

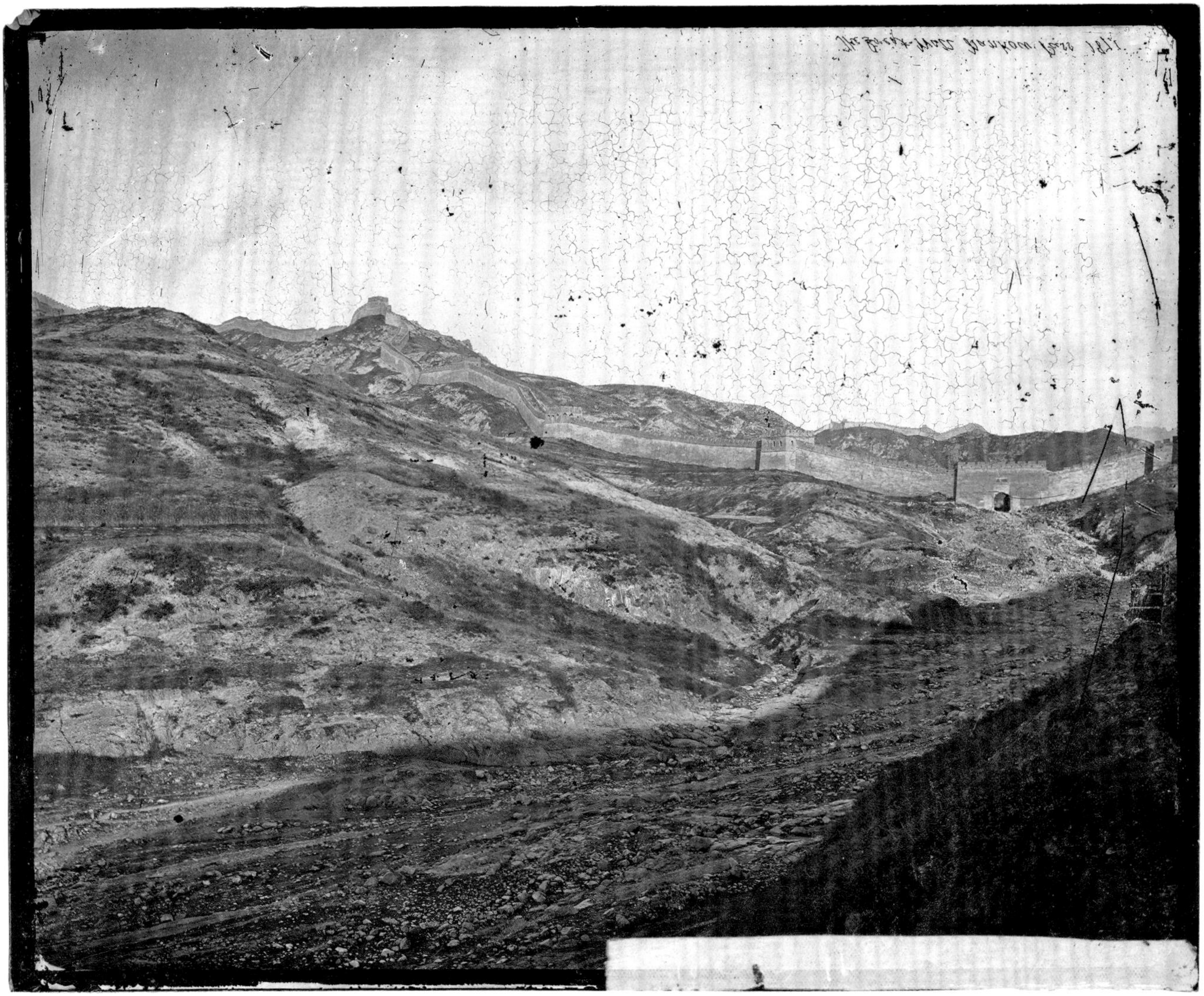

View of the Great Wall at Badaling

Beijing

Thomson regarded the Great Wall as an important symbol of China and thought it was an expression of the '*national characteristic of the Chinese race with China at the centre of the world*'. He further added that '*no illustrated work on China would be worthy of its name if it did not contain a picture of some portion of the Great Wall*'. This photograph was taken at Badaling near the Nankou Pass.

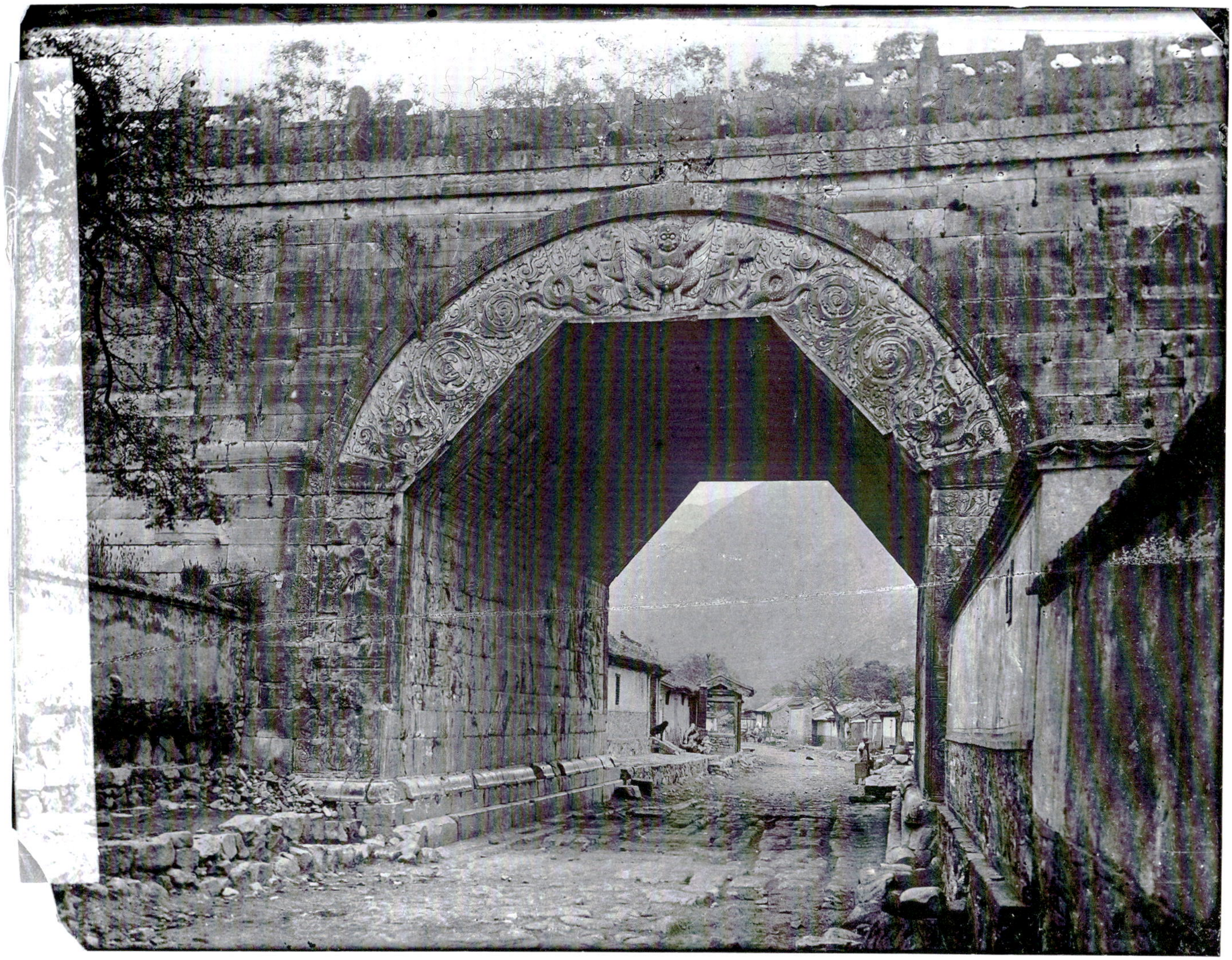

ANCIENT BUDDHIST ARCH AT JUYONG GUAN, NANKOU PASS

Beijing

The ancient Buddhist Arch at Juyong Guan is situated at the most important section of Nankou Pass. It was here that the Mongols first entered north China in the 13th century. This marble arch was built between 1342 and 1345 by the Mongol Emperor Shundi (1333-68) during the Yuan dynasty. It is decorated with relief carvings of Buddhist images on the face and on the inside. Framing the arch is a Garuda bird with two Naga kings on either side whose coiling bodies create a complex pattern. The interior is elaborately sculpted with inscriptions in six languages: Sanskrit, Tibetan, Mongolian, Uighur, Tangut and Chinese.

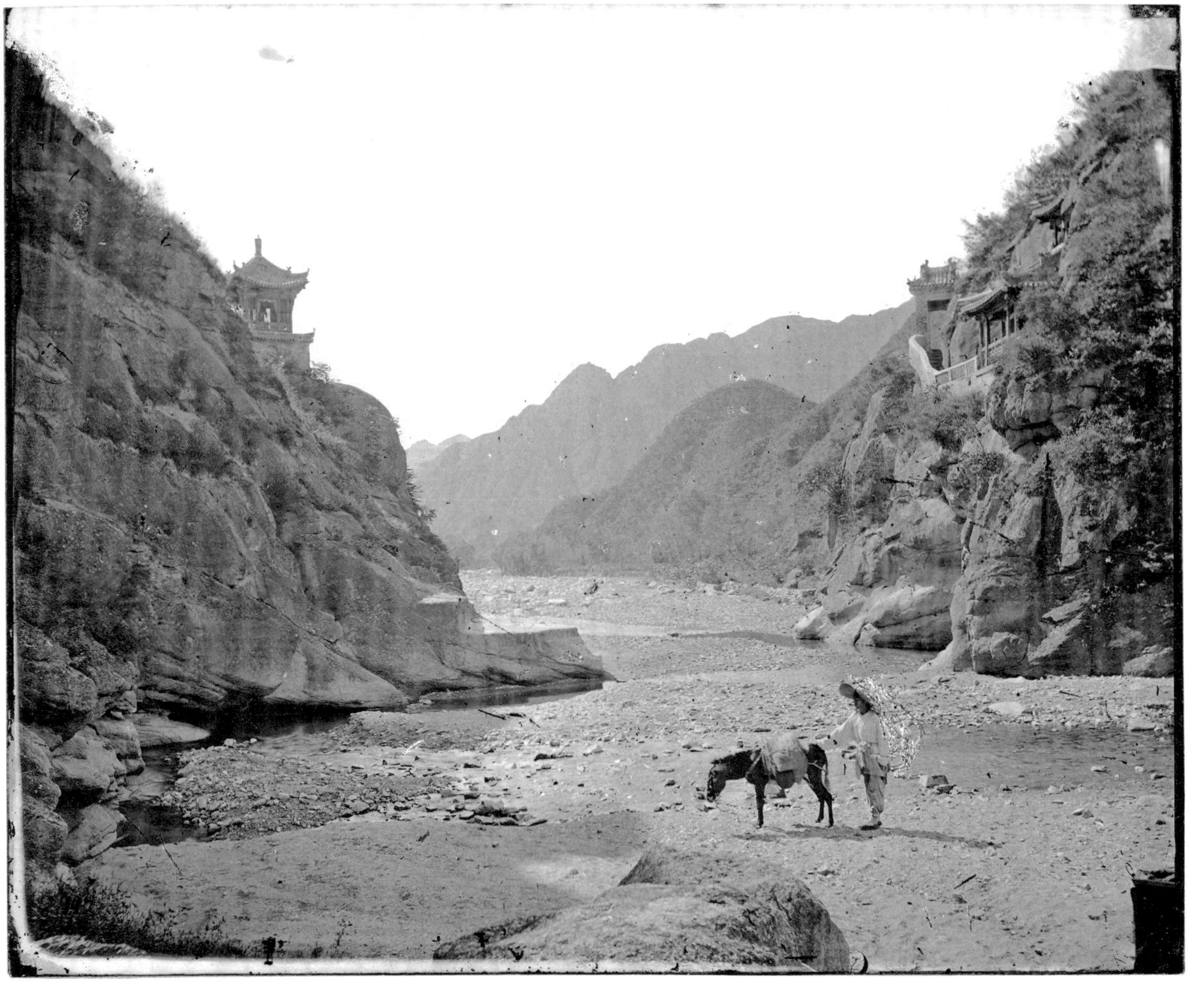

Nankou Pass

Beijing

Nankou Pass or the 'southern entry' is situated in Changping County in the suburbs of Beijing. Positioned between two high mountains, it has been of strategic importance throughout history. From here one can see the first spur of the Great Wall. Since the terrain of the Pass was difficult and very rocky, mules proved to be the ideal animals that were used by traders for the transportation of goods through and beyond the Pass.

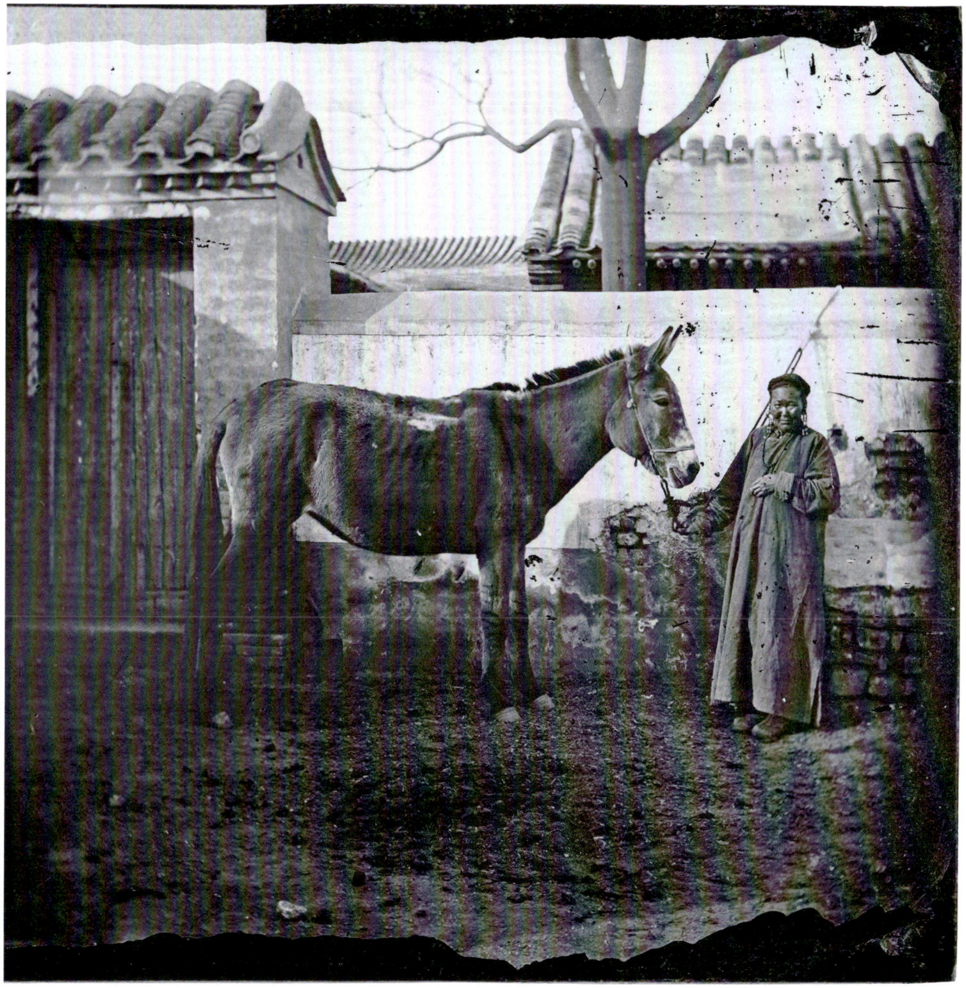

Mongol Woman with her Mule

Beijing

Mongols are nomads at heart. Thomson met this Mongol woman in Beijing, where her family had rented a home. To his surprise he found that the family stabled their horses and donkeys in the dwelling-house proper, while they themselves had set up their tents and lived in the courtyard. Such living arrangements were common practice among Mongols visiting Beijing at the time.

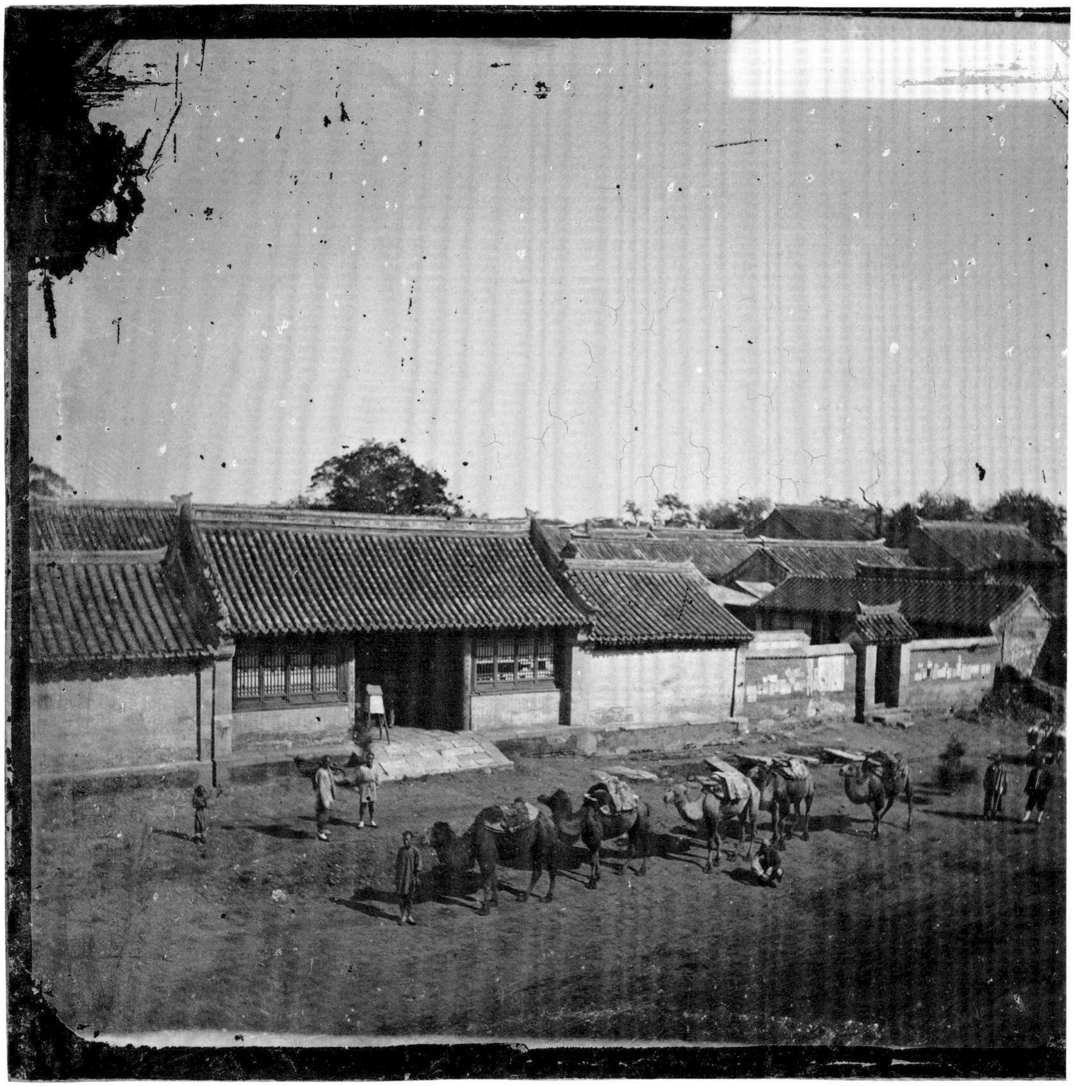

Camels with Brick Tea Leaving for Russia

Beijing

Thomson watched the departure of over 2,000 of these camels laden with black tea that was to be sold in Russian markets. During certain seasons of the year, tea-laden camels travelled in their tens of thousands across the Gobi Desert to Russia. In the absence of a common currency, black tea was a means of barter and exchange in Mongolia, Tibet, and Siberia. In addition to the transportation of tea, camels were also employed to transport coal and other commodities.

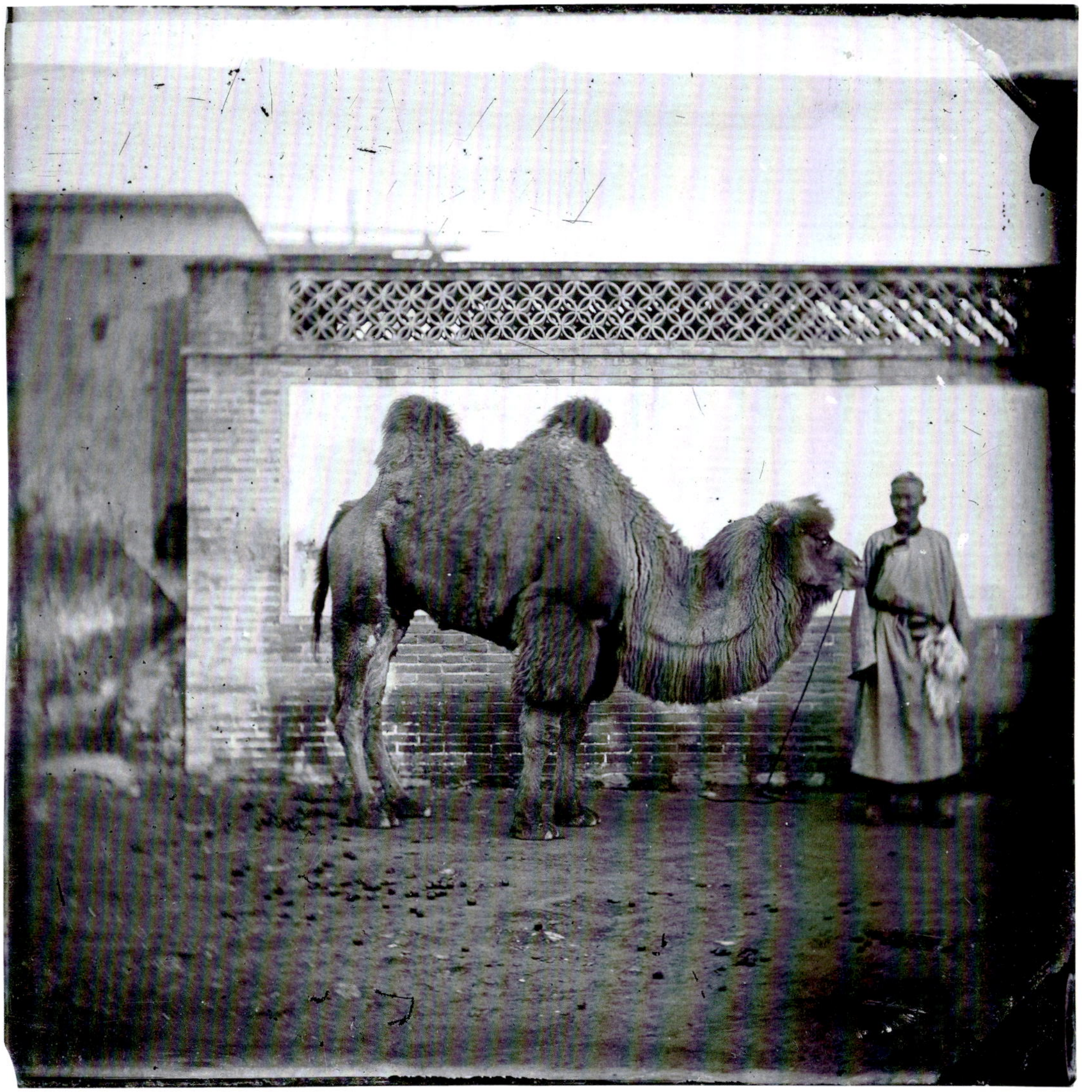

A Camel with its Owner

Beijing

Until the advent of railways, camels were the main form of transportation of goods throughout north China and into Central Asia. The Mongolian camel, with its tolerance for cold, drought, and high altitudes was physically well suited to cope with the challenges of crossing the sandy plains of the Gobi Desert. The camel's stomach contains bladders which enable it to carry a store of fresh water, while the humps store food in the form of fatty matter which can be absorbed in times of need. As such, camels were highly prized among the Mongols.

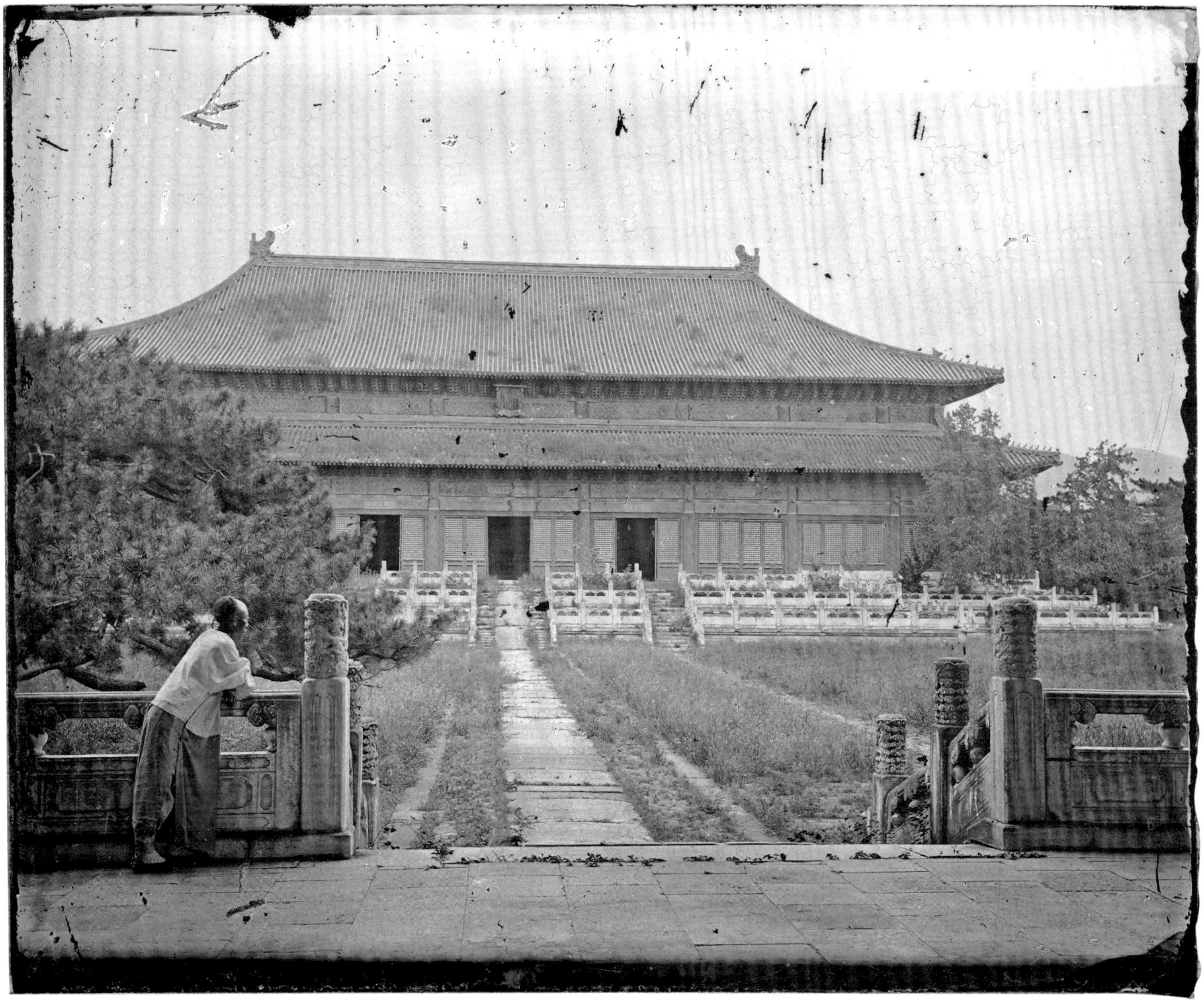

The Great Sacrifice Hall, Changling, the Ming Tombs

Beijing

Changling, tomb of the Yongle Emperor, is the most magnificent Ming tomb in Beijing. Completed around 1413, it was one of Yongle's many majestic projects. The Great Sacrifice Hall is situated in the second or sacrificial quadrangle, where imperial offerings were made to emperors of former dynasties. The hall has 32 pillars built entirely with teak from Yunnan province making it unique and the most impressive building within the complex. The ceiling is painted with many colours and the outer roof of the Hall is covered in yellow glazed tiles.

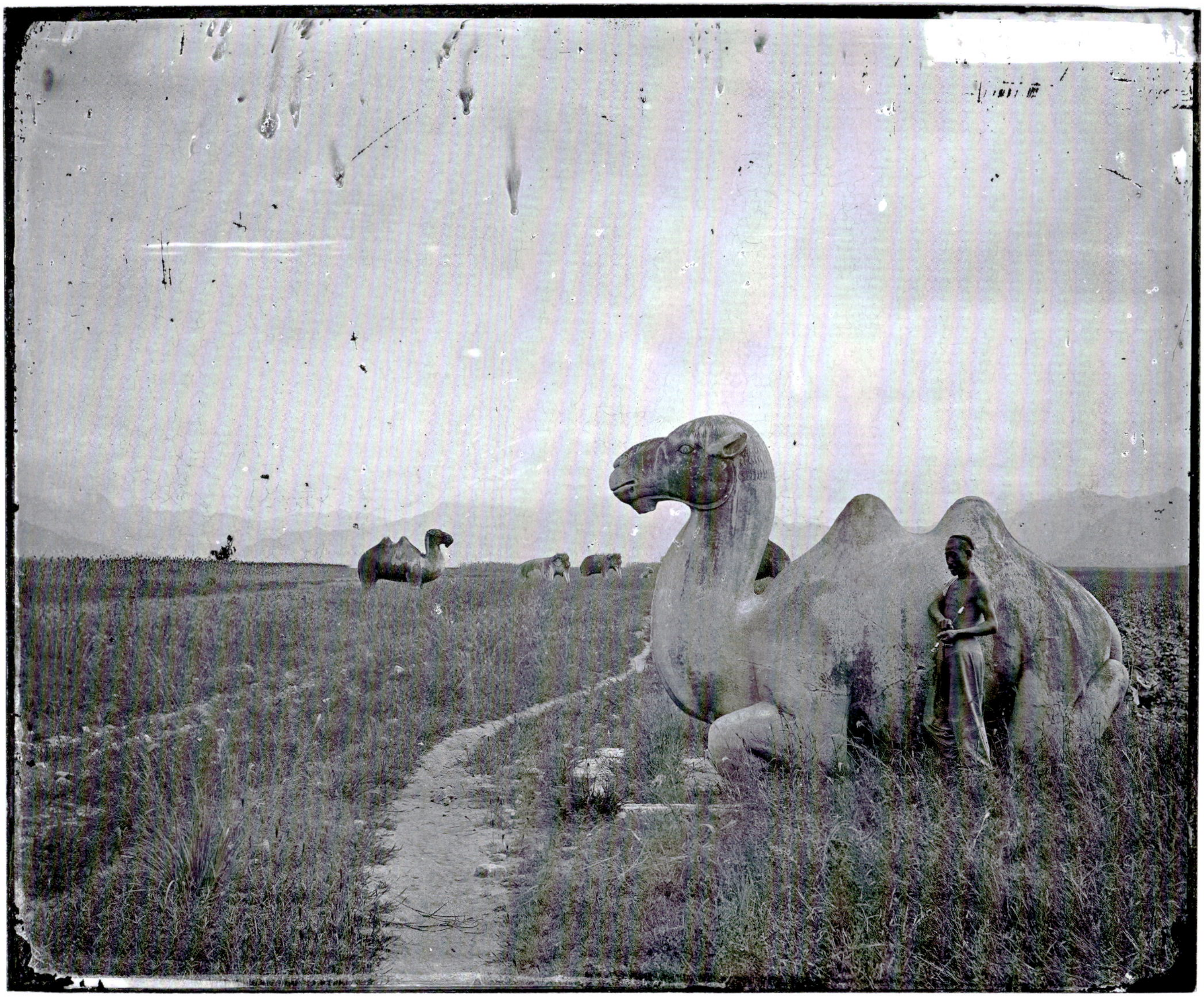

Stone Animals on the Approaches to the Ming Tombs

Beijing

The Ming tomb is approached through an avenue which was guarded by animals carved from limestone. 24 species of animals are represented, ranging from lions and elephants to camels, and mythical beasts such as the unicorn and 'qilin' (one of four divine animals). There are two pairs of each species, one pair kneeling in repose and the other standing on guard. The animals were carved with expressions of tranquil repose, which as Thomson noted was '*thoroughly in keeping with their duty as the guardians of the dead.*'

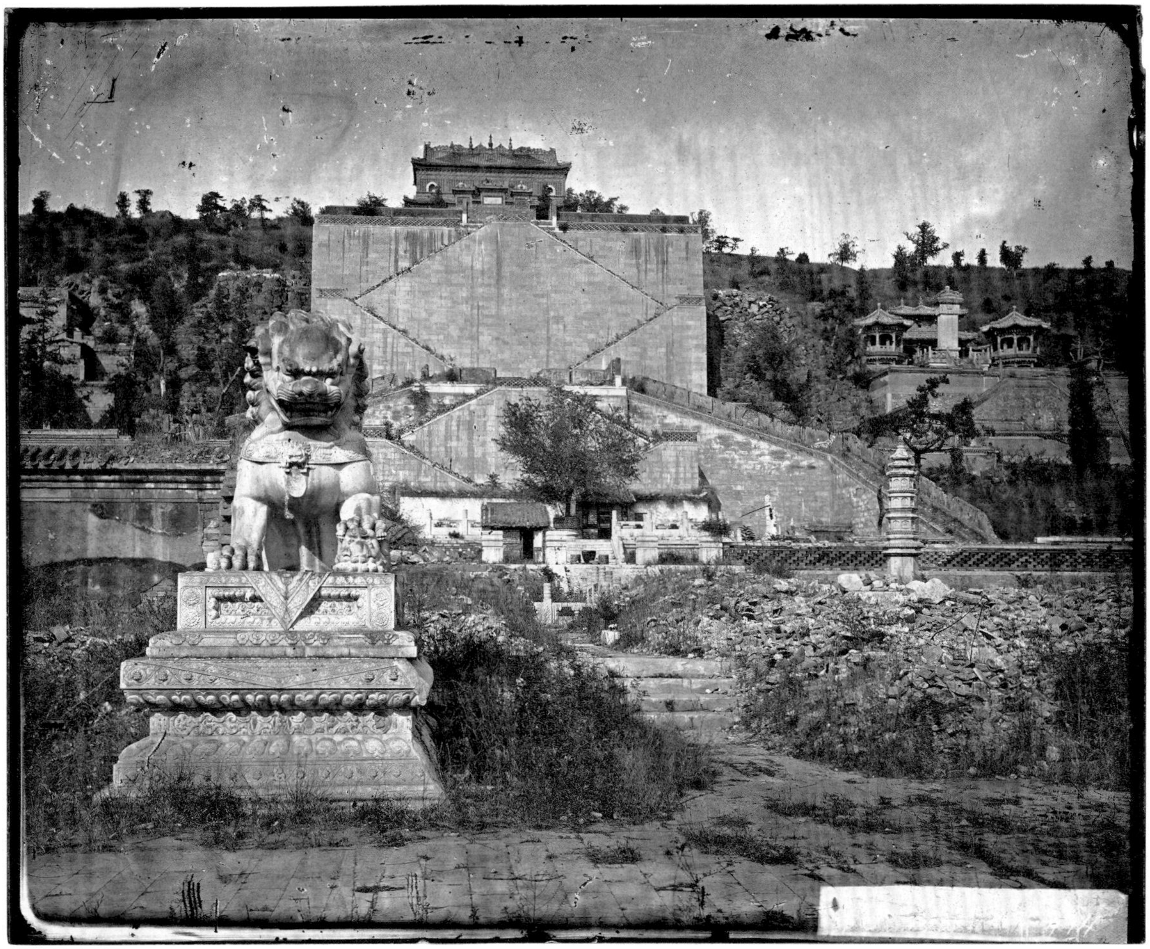

Ruins of the Sculptured Terrace, Longevity Hill, the Garden of Clear Ripple

Beijing

Building of the Garden of Clear Ripple began in 1750 under Emperor Qianlong and was completed in 1764. The Garden encompassed several architectural styles drawn from various palaces throughout China. Its artificial lake was modelled on the West Lake in Hangzhou and was named Kunming Lake so that it would be associated with the artificial lake built by Emperor Wu of the Han Dynasty. Longevity Hill, standing 60 metres high in the centre of the Garden, was built using earth excavated from the Lake. The name 'Longevity Hill' was given by the Emperor in celebration of his mother's birthday. In 1860 the Garden was looted and torched by British and French troops during the Second Opium War, also known as the Arrow War. Empress Cixi ordered its restoration in 1868, renaming it the Garden of Nurtured Harmony. As her new summer resort, it became widely known as the Summer Palace.

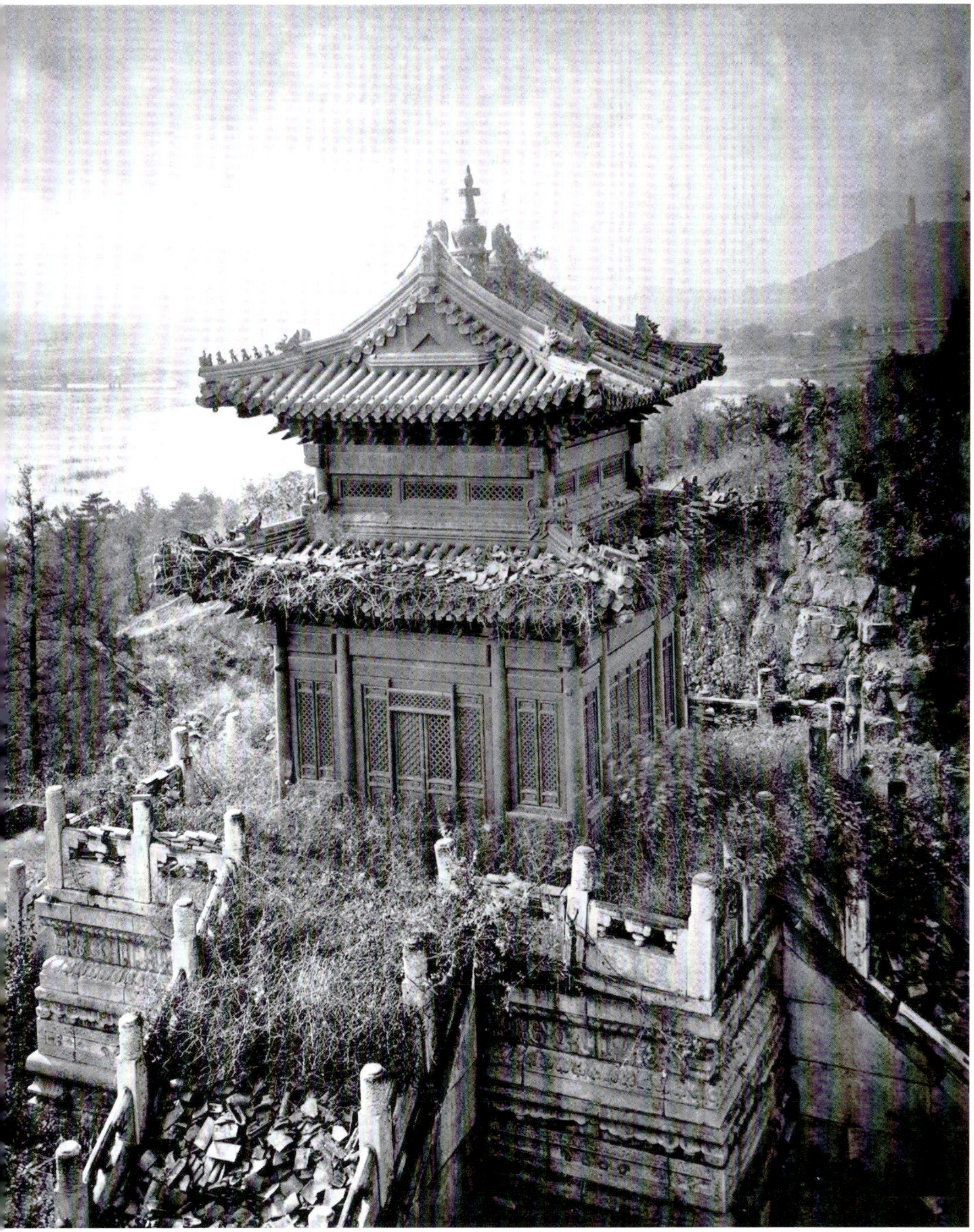

Ruins of Bronze Temple, Garden of Clear Ripple

Beijing

The Bronze Temple was one of the most impressive buildings on Longevity Hill within the Summer Palace. Formally called Cloud Dispelling Hall, the Temple was first built in 1755 at the foot of Longevity Hill. It was, according to Thomson, '*a very perfect example of Chinese temple architecture, showing, as it does, the most minute details of construction, and the skill with which the Chinese can work in metals, and adapt them to almost every use*'. In subsequent years the Temple was used for prayer whenever the Tibetan Lama visited the imperial capital. It contained numerous Buddhist objects made of bronze, including a statue of Siddhartha Gautama. Although many of these items were looted by the French and British troops in 1860, the building itself survived.

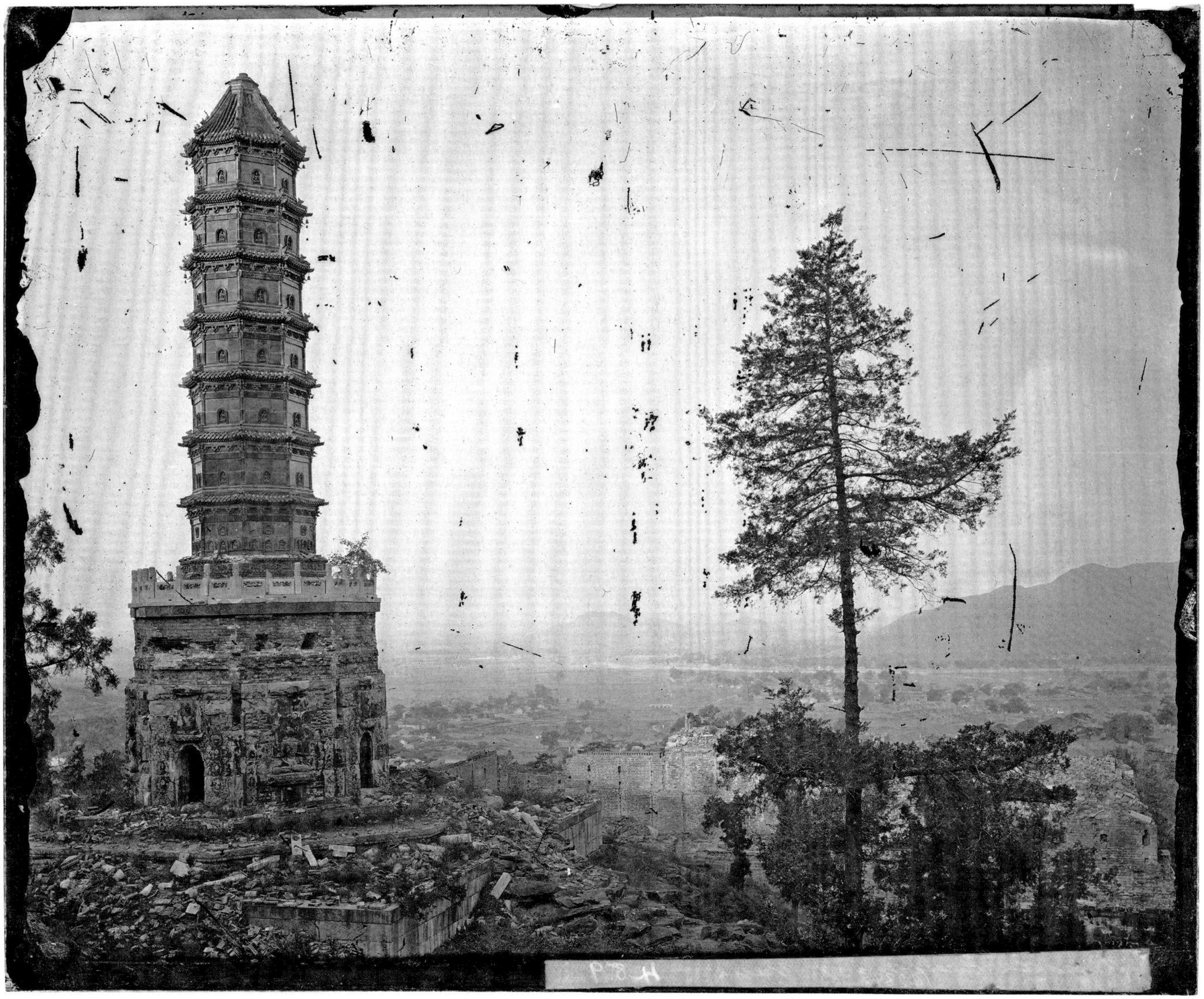

GLAZED TILE PAGODA AT THE GRAND ZONGJING MONASTERY, FRAGRANT HILL

Beijing

This octagonal pagoda is 40 metres tall and stands seven storeys high on an octagonal stone base. It was first completed in the mid-18th century as a part of the Fragrant Hill project, another one of Emperor Qianlong's great constructions. Alongside the pagoda stood the Grand Zongjing Monastery, which was built to accommodate the sixth Panchen Lama during his stay in Beijing in 1780. Although the monastery was burned down by French and British troops in 1860 the pagoda miraculously survived.

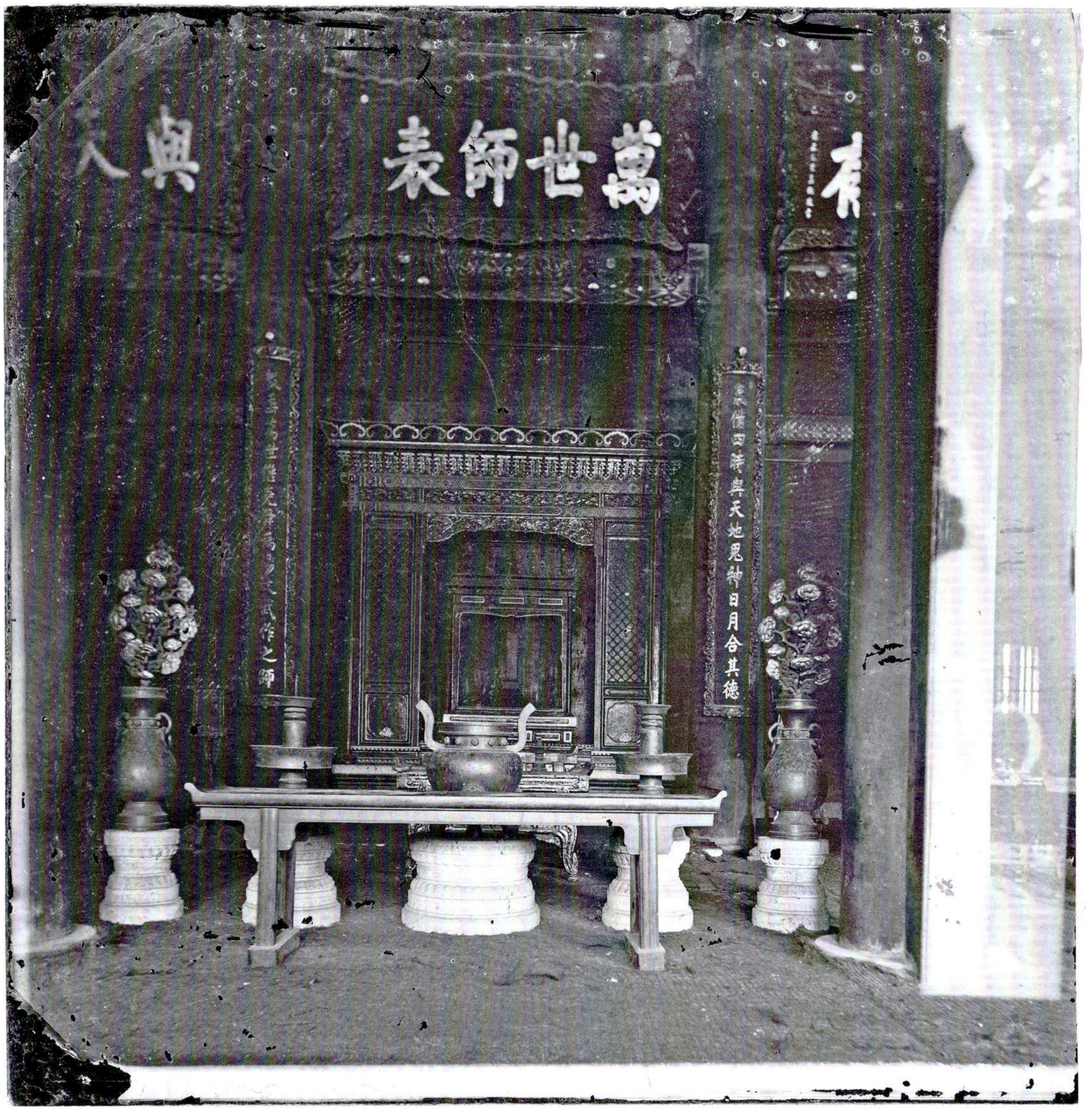

THE GREAT PERFECTION HALL AT THE TEMPLE OF CONFUCIUS

Beijing

Situated next to the ancient National University, or Guozijian, the Temple of Confucius was a shrine where people paid homage to the great Sage throughout the Yuan, Ming and Qing Dynasties. The Great Perfection Hall, situated in the centre of the Temple, is one of the most imposing examples of imperial architecture in Beijing. Both inside and outside the Hall, there are inscriptions by nine Qing emperors added since the time of Emperor Kangxi. The large, gold-lettered inscription above the Hall, by Emperor Kangxi himself reads 'The teacher and example of ten thousand generations.'

Prince Gong (1833-1898)

Beijing

Prince Gong was the youngest brother of Emperor Xianfeng. He was little known to the west before the Second Opium War. In 1860 the Emperor fled the capital to escape advancing British and French armies. On behalf of the Emperor and the Qing government, Prince Gong met General Gordon and the allied powers and negotiated the peace treaty. Following this, the prince held several high military and civil appointments including membership of the Supreme Council. He was also in charge of the Office for Foreign Affairs (Zhongli Yamen). In this portrait Thomson intended to show a senior Chinese government member who was a moderniser and a pro-Western figure. Thomson remarked that Prince Gong was a man '*quick of apprehension, open to advice, and comparatively liberal in his views*'.

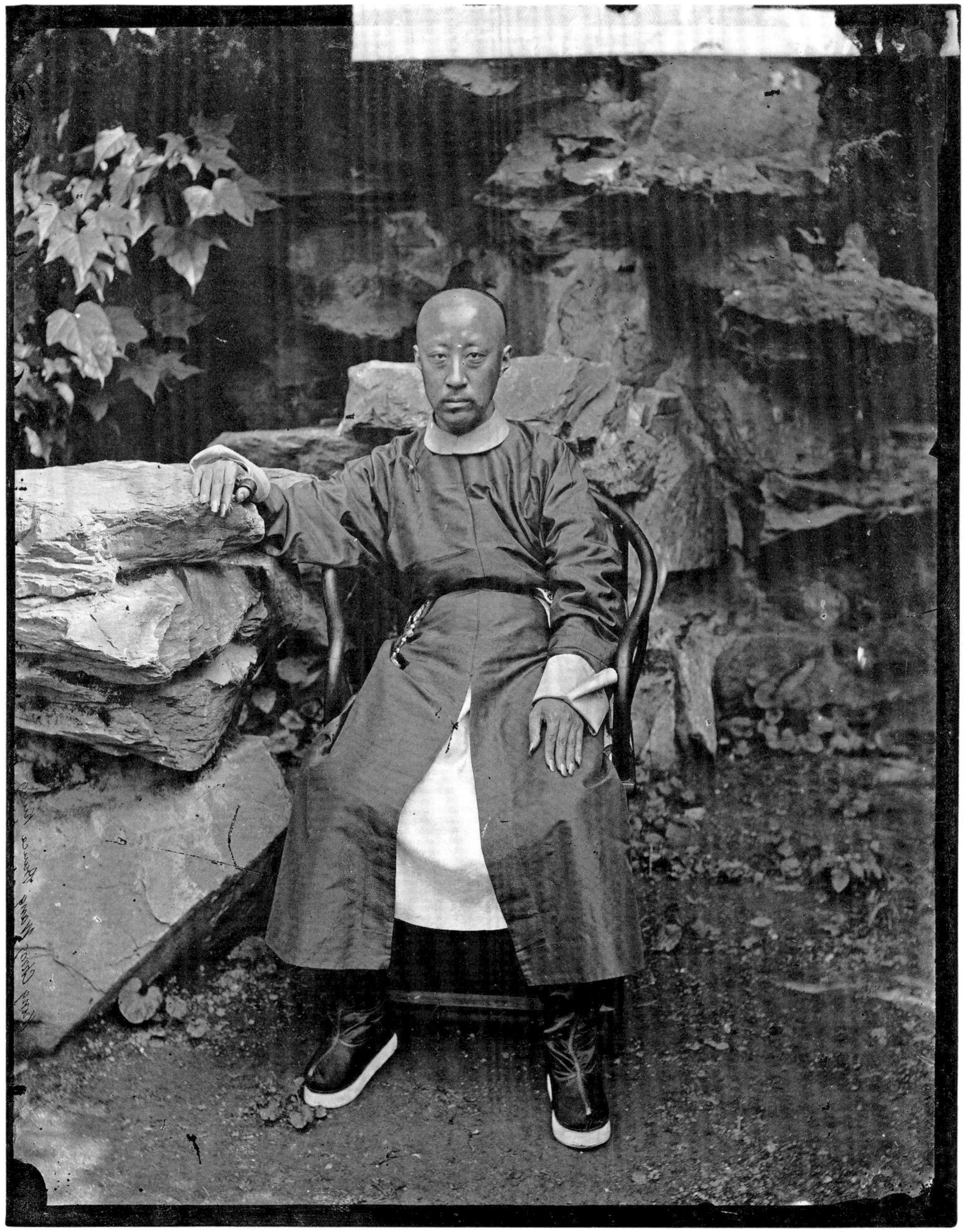

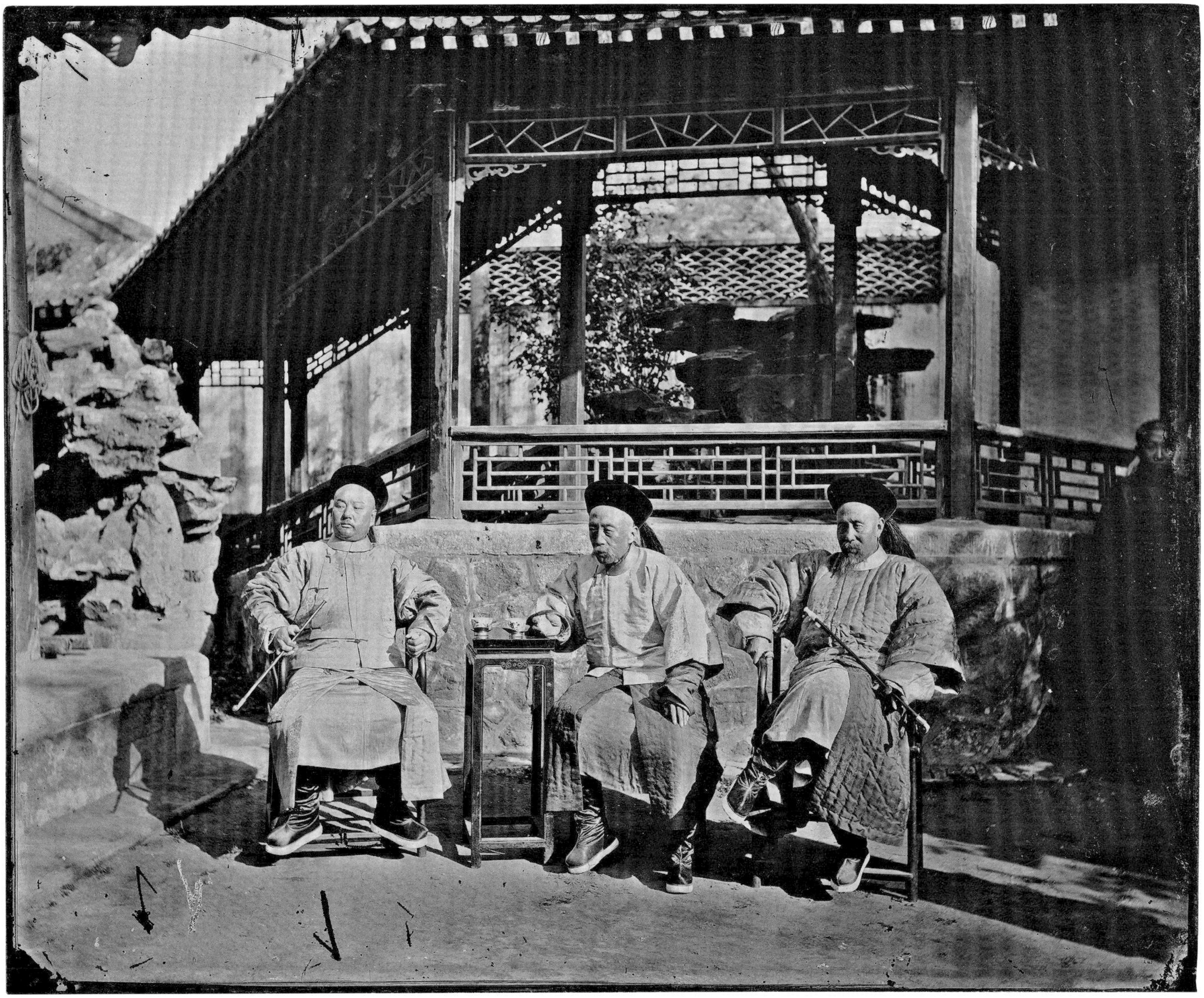

Three Manchu Ministers at the Office for Foreign Affairs

Beijing

The three Manchu ministers at the Office for Foreign Affairs were, from left to right, Cheng Lin, Bao Jun and Wen Xiang. Of the three, Cheng Lin was the youngest at forty-five. Bao Jun, aged sixty-five, was also a member of the Grand Council and one of the Presidents of the Board of Finance. Wen Xiang, born in Mukden in 1817, ranked next to Prince Gong in the Office for Foreign Affairs, holding that position since 1861. He was also a member of the Grand Council, President of the Board of Civil Service and Member of the Imperial Cabinet. A man of rare intellect and with his long experience in high office, he was seen as the most influential late Qing statesman.

Three Chinese Ministers at the Office for Foreign Affairs

Beijing

From left to right are Shen Guifeng, Dong Xun and Mao Changxi. A native of Jiangsu, Shen Guifeng was best known for his anti-opium policy and for his contributions to the state-run modernising movement – the 'yangwu movement' or Self-Strengthening Movement. In this portrait, Thomson wanted to show that Chi nese officials did not spend their time in idleness and luxury, rather they led hardworking lives and dressed in simple robes. Thomson remarked that these three individuals '*were as fine-looking men as ever our own Cabinet can boast. All of them had an air of quiet, dignified repose*'.

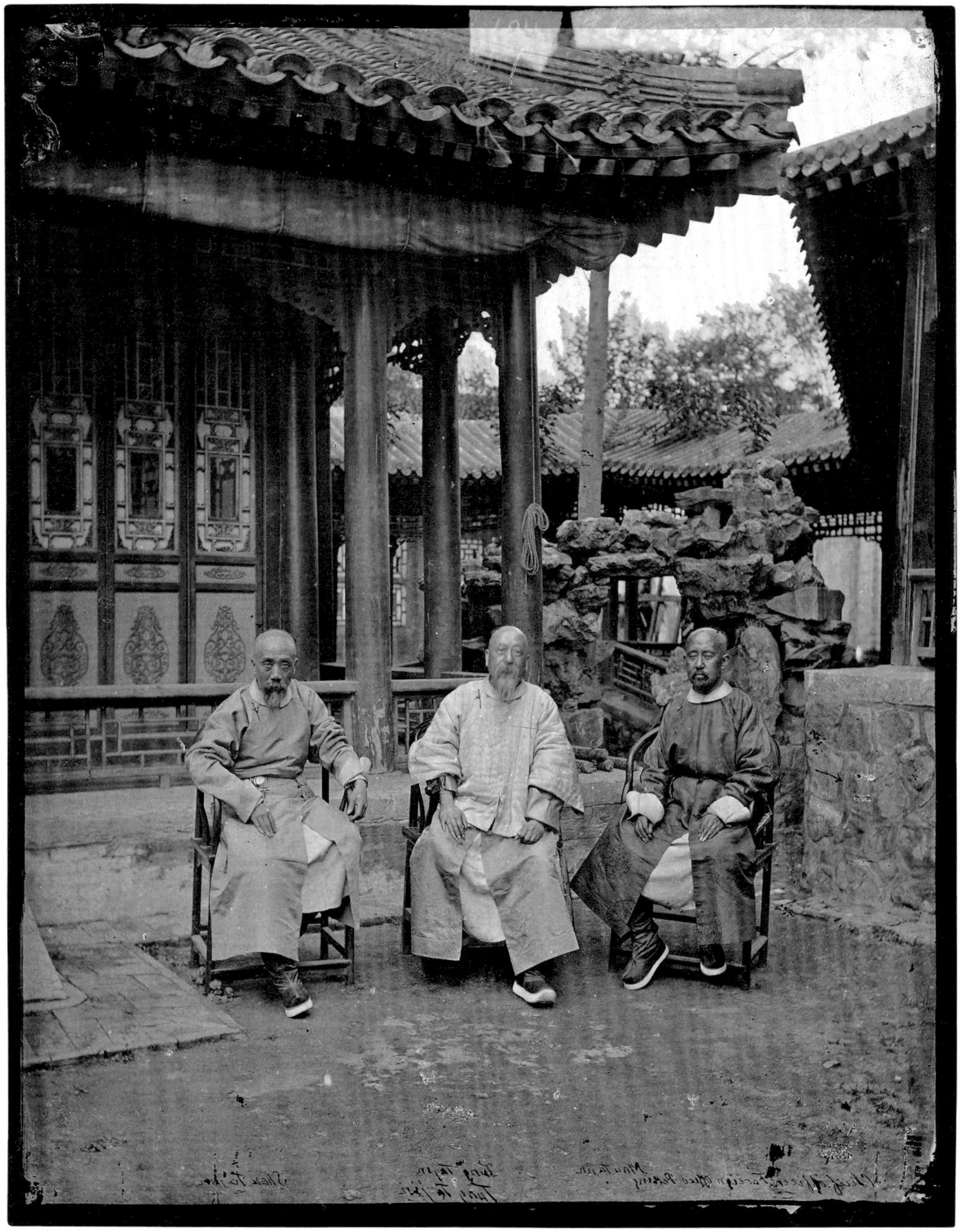

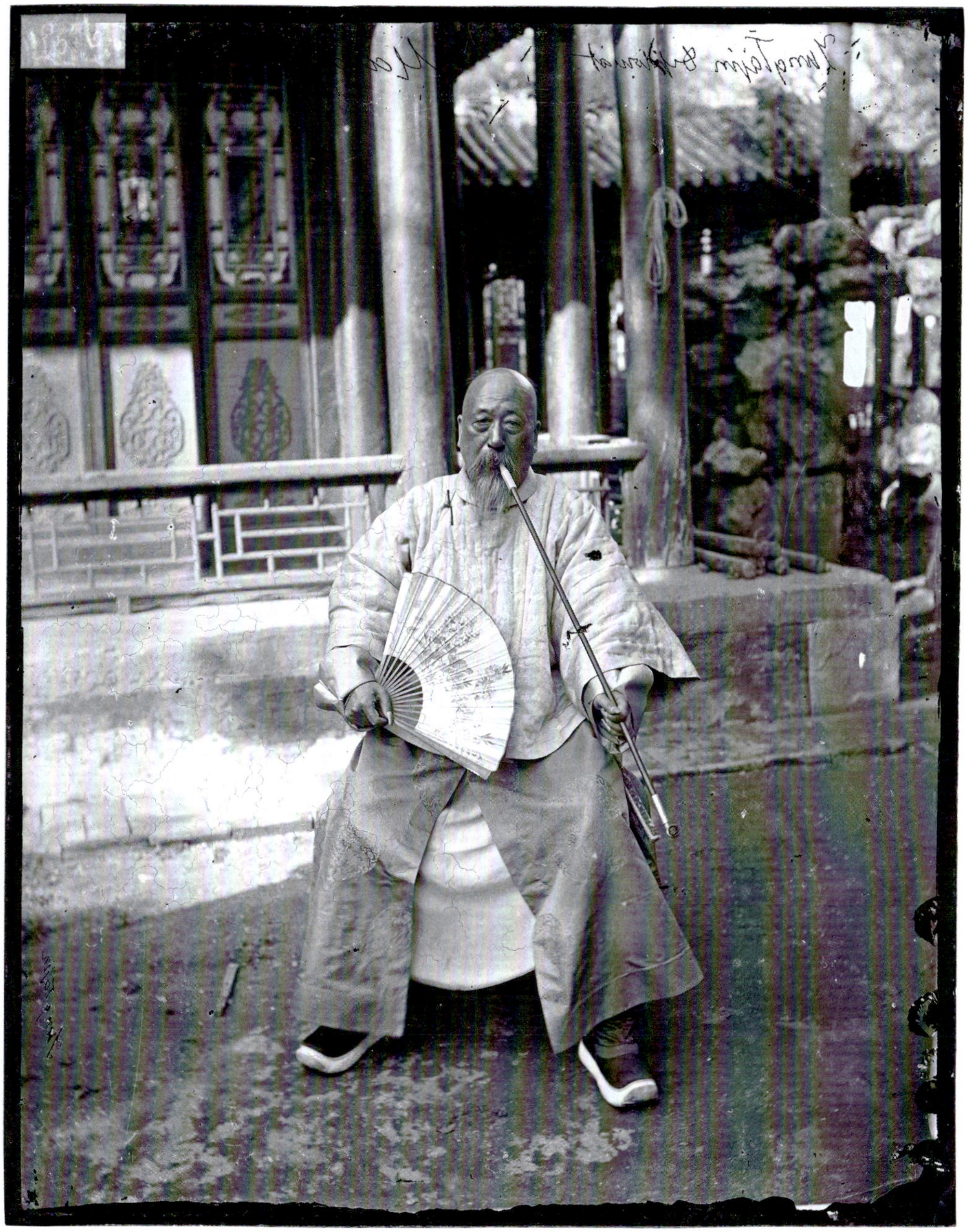

DONG XUN (1810-1892), MINISTER OF FOREIGN AFFAIRS

Beijing

Dong Xun was one of three Chinese ministers in the Office for Foreign Affairs. During his time in office, he negotiated on behalf of the Qing government, including the signing of several international trade treaties with Belgium, Britain, the United States, Russia, and others. Dong Xun was an extremely learned man and a prolific author. Dong was also a well-known authority on hydrography, and he impressed Thomson with his plans to improve irrigation and drainage throughout China.

MAO CHANGXI (1817–1882), MINISTER OF FOREIGN AFFAIRS

Beijing

The Office for Foreign Affairs (Zhongli Yamen) was set up in 1861 to deal with international relations and state-run modernisation projects. Mao Changxi was one of the three Chinese ministers appointed to this Office, the other three being of Manchu descent. A native of Henan, Mao entered government service through imperial exams and rose to government office of the highest rank after his success in suppressing the Taiping northern army. Unlike many of Thomson's portraits of Chinese officials, Mao is photographed looking away from the camera.

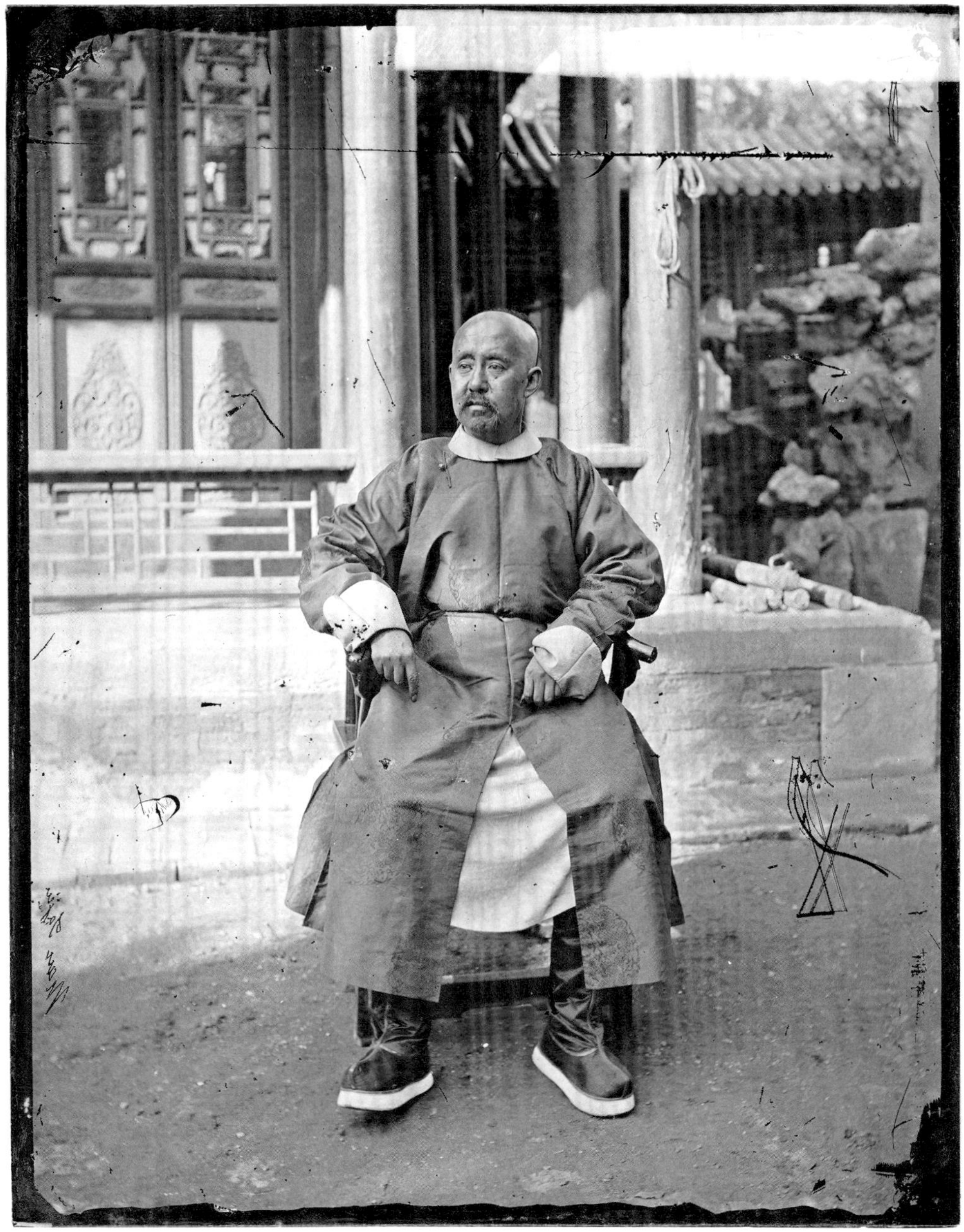

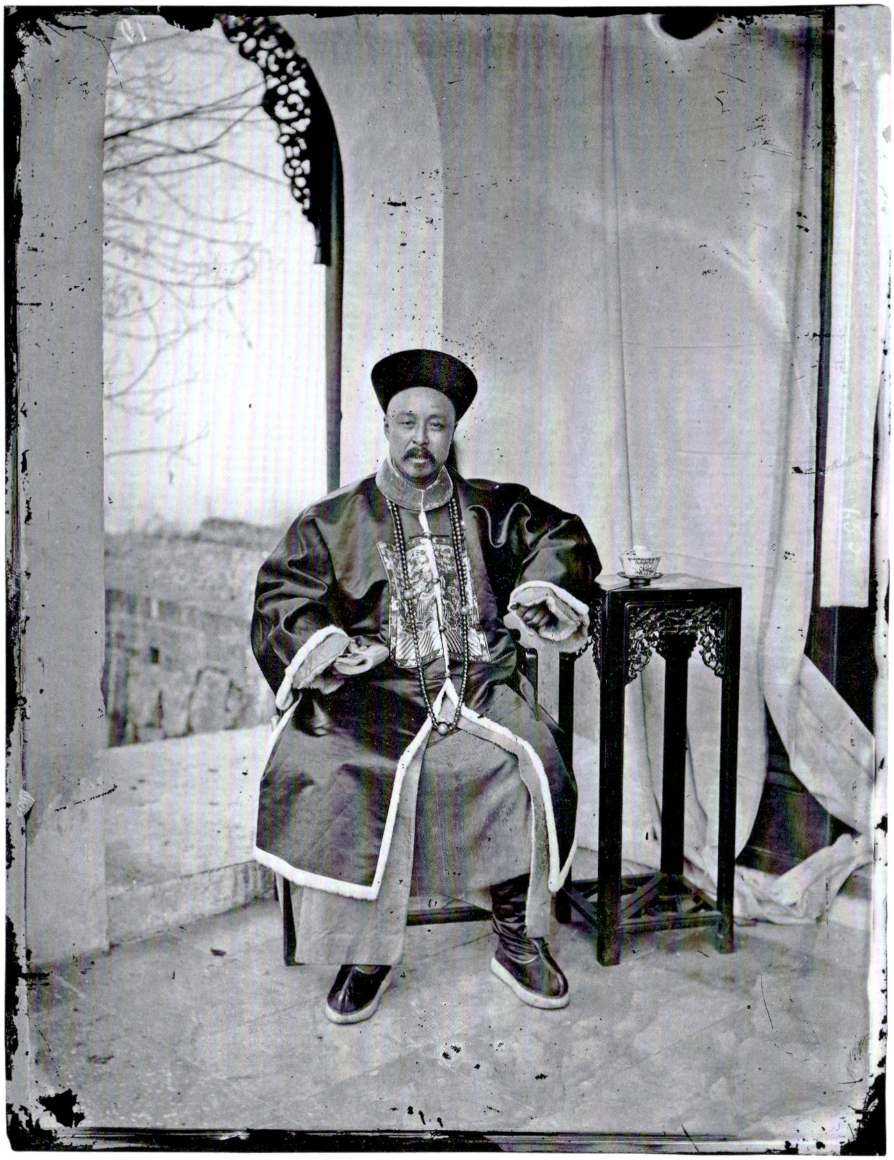

A Mandarin Official

Beijing

In imperial China, a bureaucrat was called a Mandarin, who entered office through imperial examinations. There were two types of Mandarin: those who held civil office and those awarded a military one. They were then graded into nine ranks and were distinguished by the robe, rank badge and hat they wore. Rank badges or Mandarin Squares, as seen in this portrait, were sewn onto, or woven into the wearer's robe. Civil official ranks were represented by different birds corresponding to their rank, while animals denoted military officers.

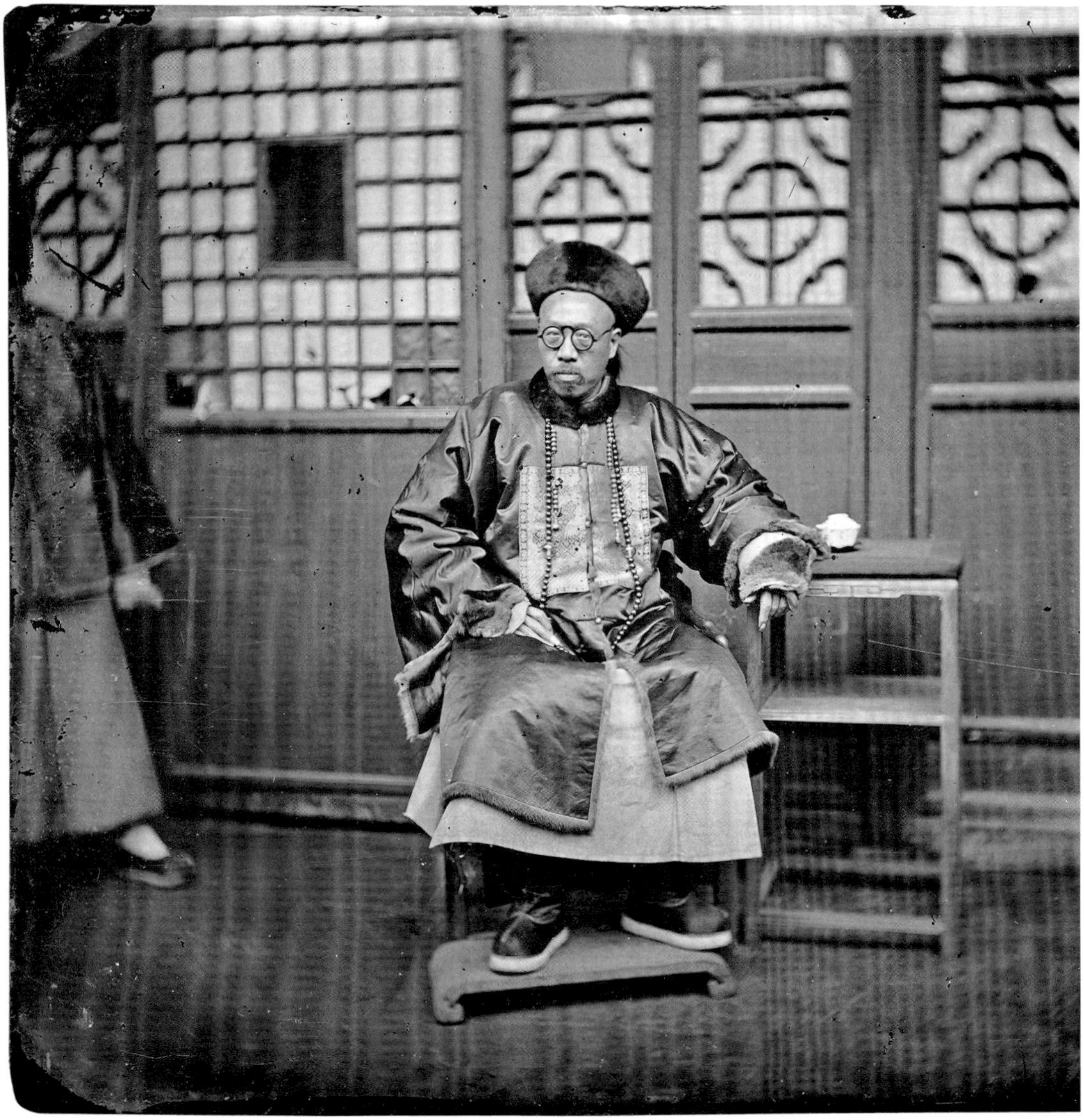

A Manchu Official

Beijing

This seated portrait of a Manchu official is purported to be Mr Yang Fang, a wealthy businessman who invited Thomson to his home, giving him rare access to photograph women of the household. This was unheard of in a society where women were prevented from meeting men who were not immediate family members.

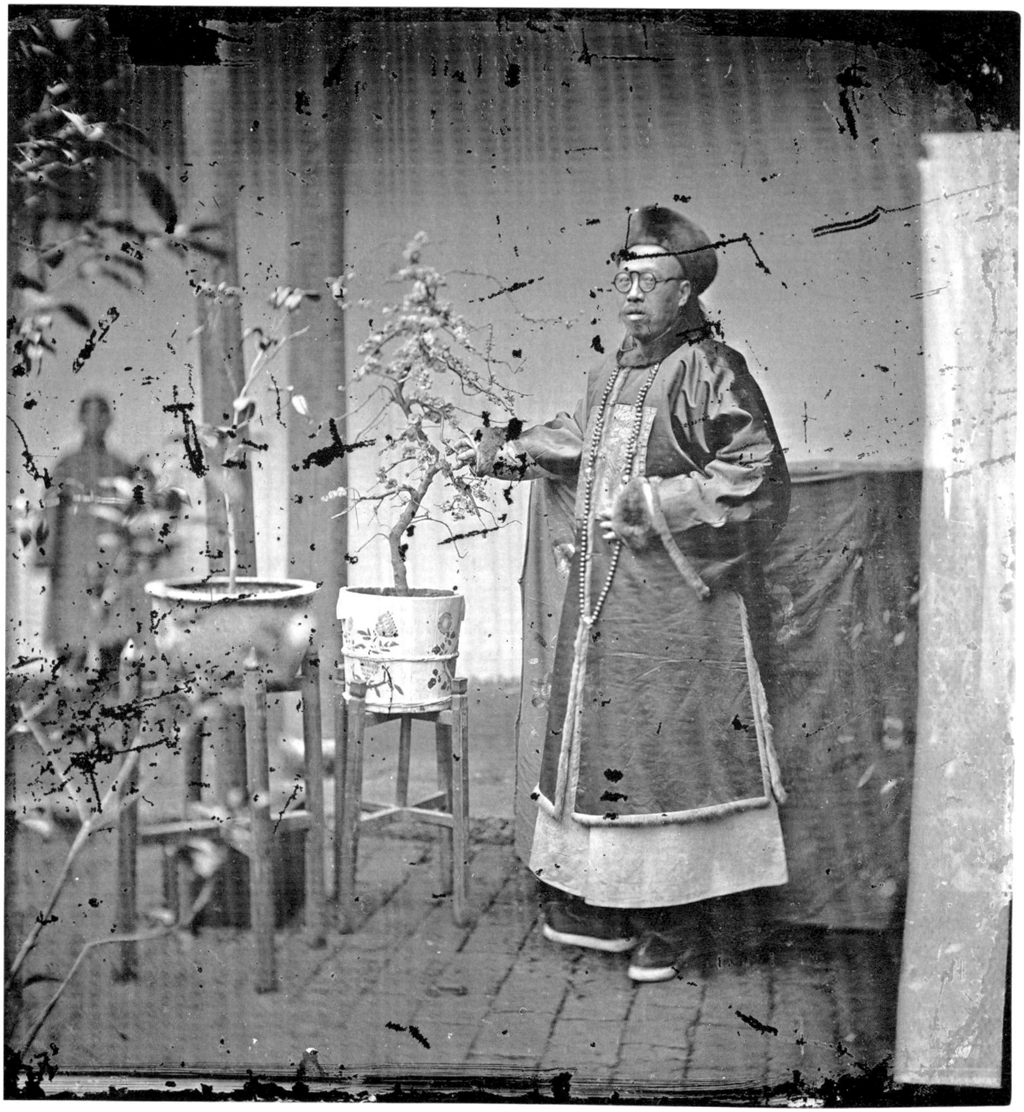

A MANCHU OFFICIAL

Beijing

This portrait of a standing Mr Yang shows him wearing a Manchu-style silk robe, hat and spectacles, an outfit that suggests he is wealthy and the holder of an official rank. The foreign spectacles further convey his interest in western accoutrements. Mr Yang's interest in photography and eagerness to learn from Thomson allowed the Scotsman a unique opportunity to photograph women in his household.

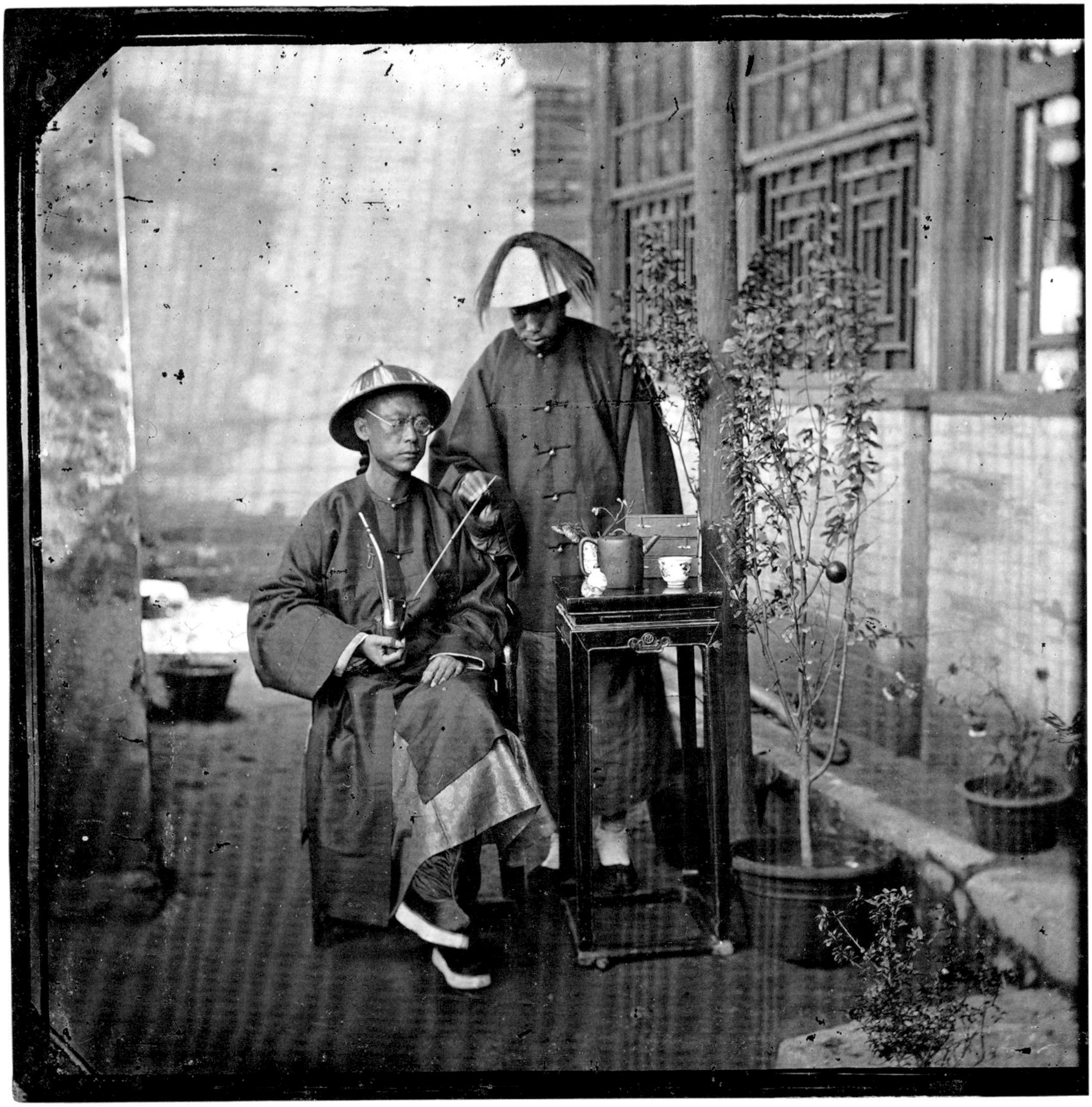

A Manchu with Servant

Beijing

The seated man holding a pipe is dressed in a Manchu robe whilst his servant stands to his side. Both men wear plumed hats. On the side table are a Yixing ware teapot, a porcelain tea bowl, flowerpot, and a snuff bottle. These kinds of objects usually accompany a formal style of portraiture, more often seen in Thomson's studio portraits.

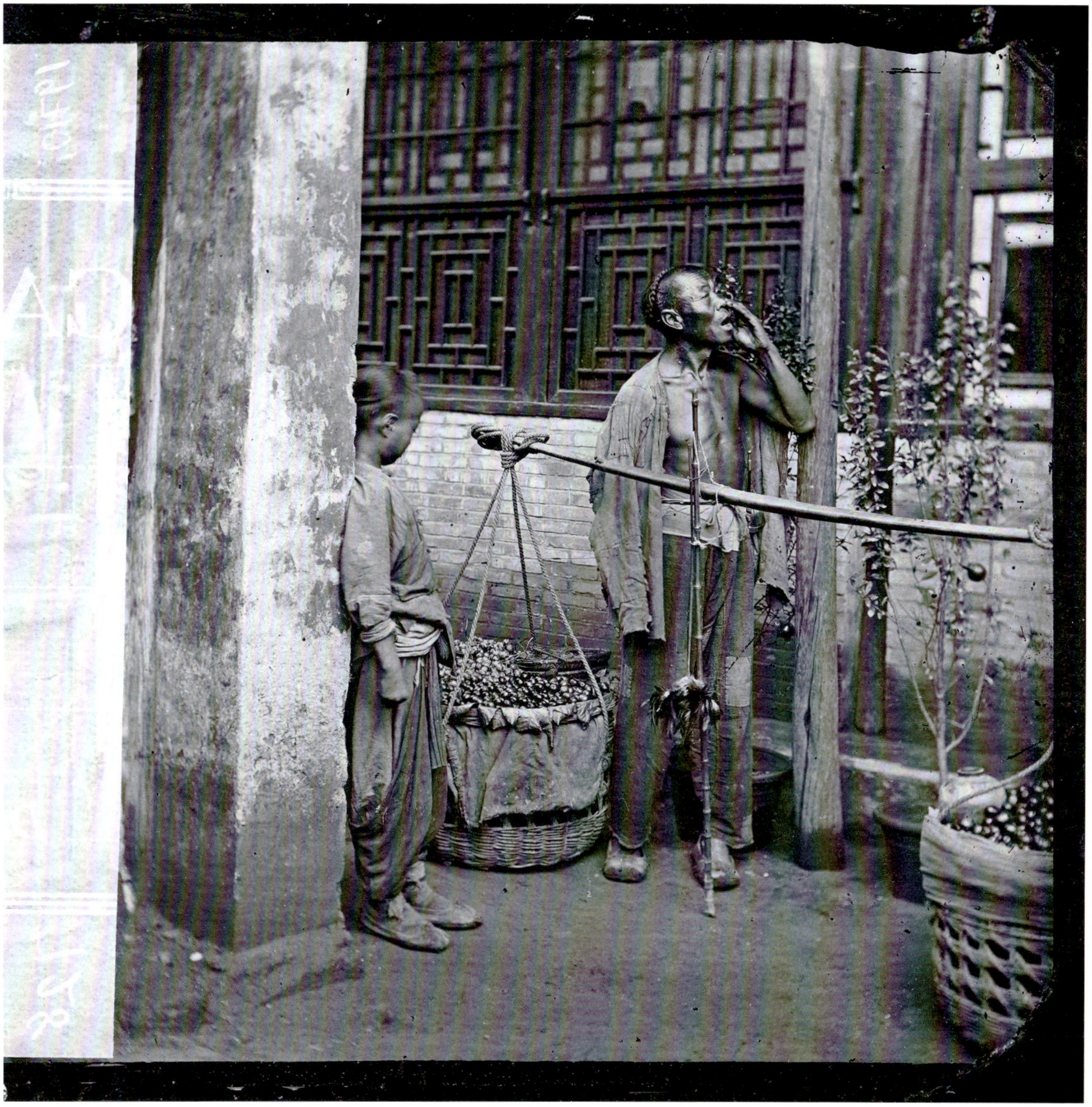

A TRAVELLING FRUIT-SELLER

Beijing

In imperial Beijing, shop-owners and street vendors were mainly Han Chinese or Muslims. Street vendors would carry their wares in baskets balanced on a pole over their shoulders, walking around narrow lanes of the 'hutongs' whilst calling out to advertise their wares. As they each used a distinctive 'call' or music instrument, residents would immediately know what goods or services were available at their doorstep. These calls by street vendors formed an essential part of the typical sounds of the city, especially in quiet residential neighborhoods.

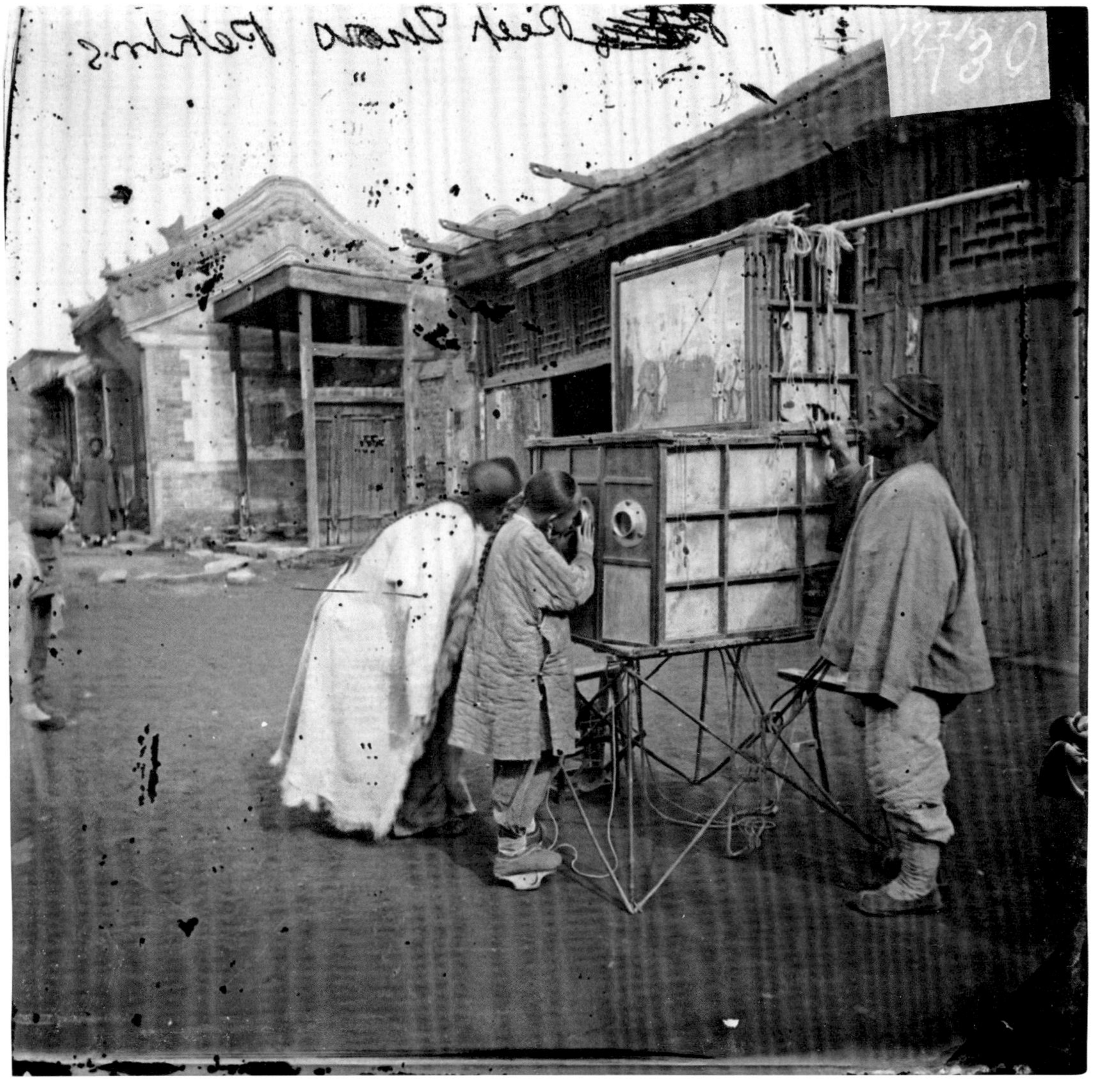

'Magic lantern' Peep Show

Beijing

Slide or 'magic lantern' shows were a novelty in China in the late 1860s. Thomson described how the lantern was considered '*truly ingenious beyond belief*' and soon attracted a mass audience. People in China who had never travelled could learn about foreign places through the slide show, discovering a world beyond the confines of their home village or province. Usually, a showman would deliver a running commentary on the scenes as he introduced them to his viewers, sometimes with musical accompaniment. To attract more customers, presenters sometimes included a few images of naked women in the middle or at the end of a show.

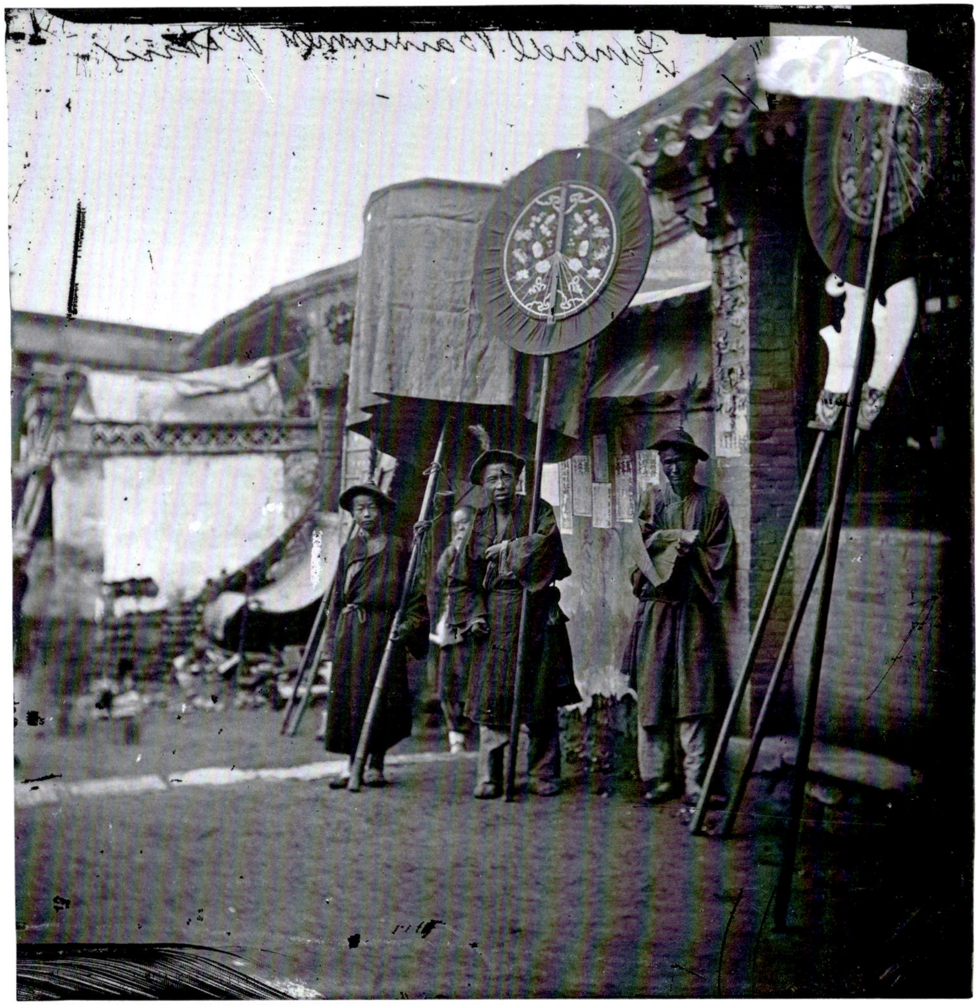

Hired Bannermen in a Manchu Funeral Procession

Beijing

A Manchu funeral procession in imperial China was an elaborate and expensive affair. Sometimes the coffin would be carried by as many as 64 men. The canopy covering was often decorated with embroidered white satin. Wailing female members from the household would follow the procession in carts.

Created in the 17th century under the Qing dynasty, the eight banners were administrative/military divisions into which all Manchu households were placed. In war, the Eight Banners functioned as elite armies, but later the banner system became the basic organisational framework of Manchu society. Membership in the Banners became hereditary, and Bannermen were granted land and income. Over time, the Eight Banners became synonymous with Manchu identity even as their military strength waned. Banners and paraphernalia, integral to any Manchu funeral, differed a great deal from the ornaments used in Han Chinese funerals. The Qing government gave an allowance towards the costs of Manchu funerals so sometimes beggars would be hired to act as the Bannermen for the procession.

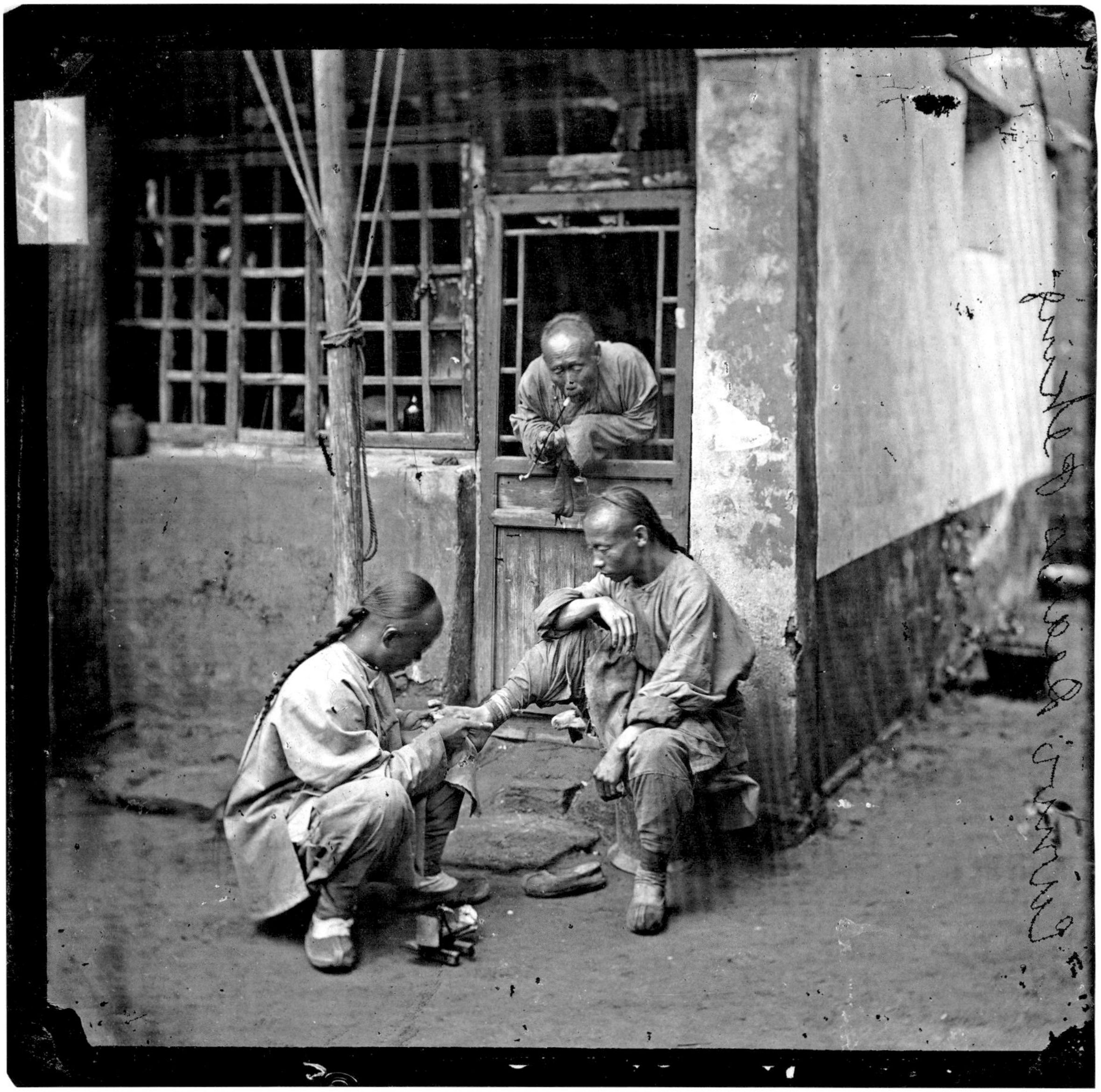

A Travelling Chiropodist

Beijing

Until the advent of modern medicine, many people in China sought help from untrained doctors and used herbal remedies to treat their ailments. In the late Qing period, the streets of major cities were full of such men, many of whom also practised as barbers and ear-cleaners. In this photograph, an itinerant chiropodist is operating on a painful corn and dressing the toenails of his patient.

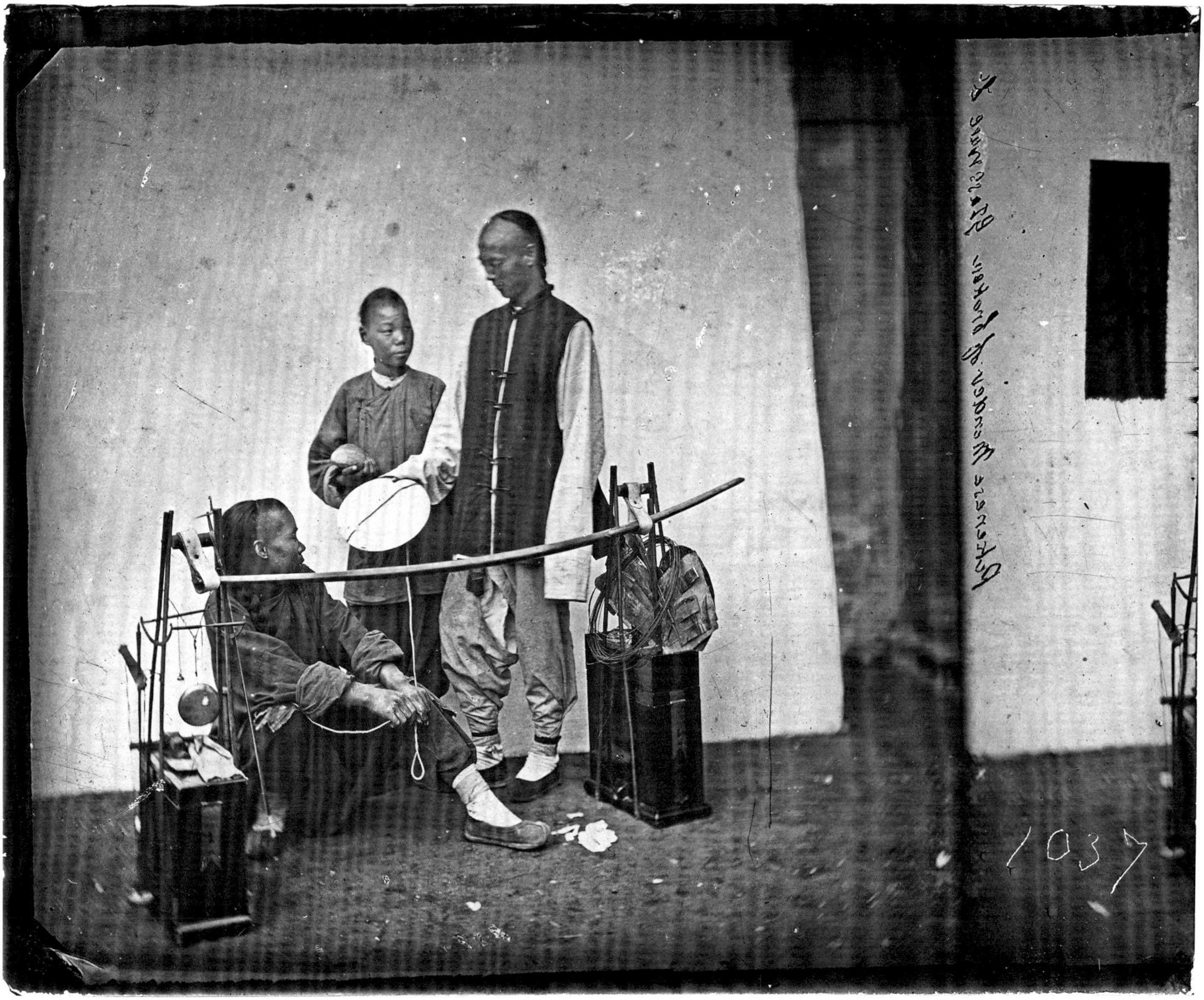

A MENDER OF BROKEN CHINAWARE

Beijing

During his visit to Beijing, Thomson noted that artisans plied their trades on every vacant space in the streets and hutongs (narrow lanes) of the city. Here, a man and a boy are standing holding a plate, the other, the mender, is sitting with a yoke and panniers containing the tools of his trade.

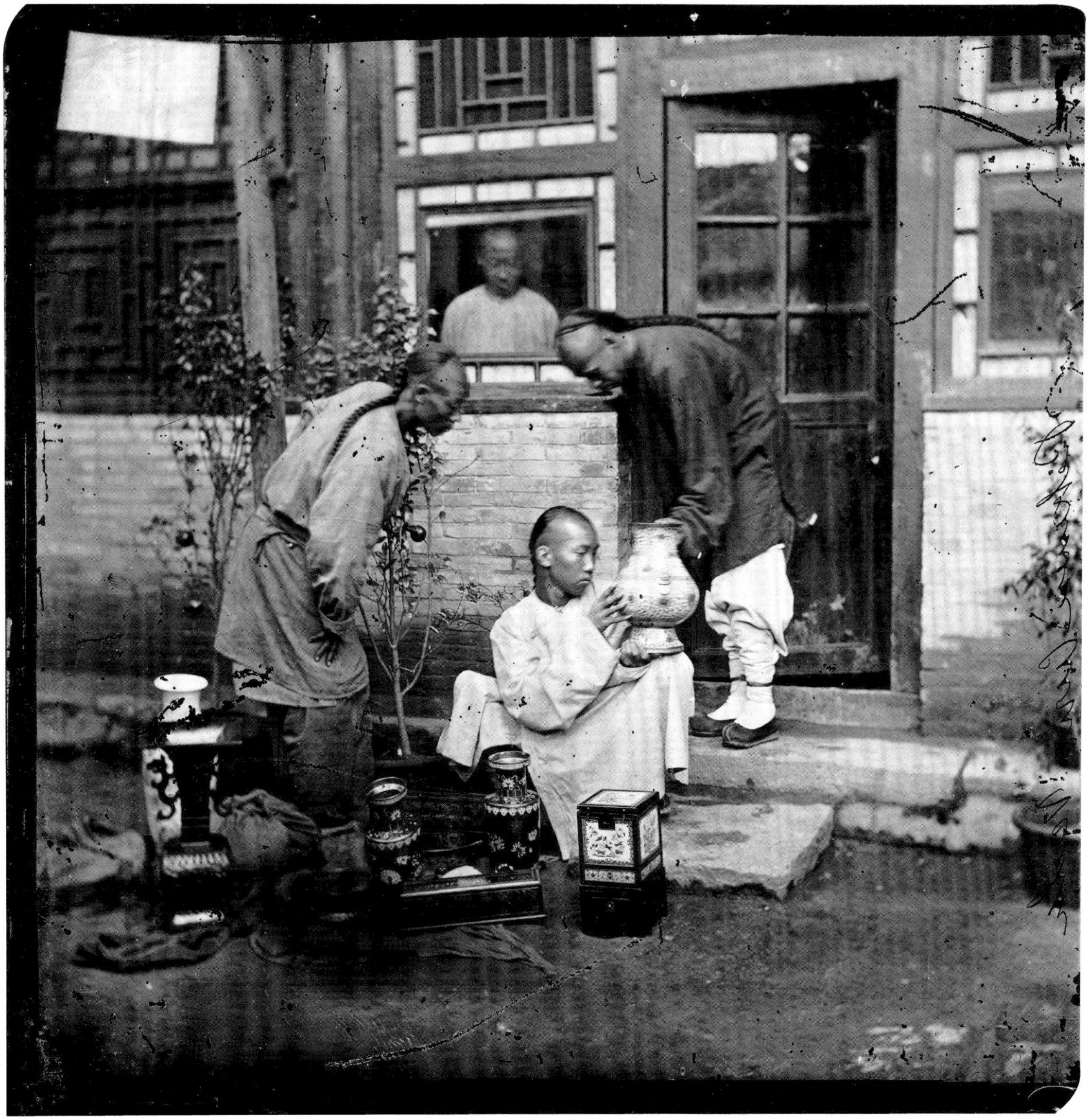

A Dealer of Curiosities

Beijing

In the second half of the 19th century foreign visitors to China were often a target for antiques dealers who charged them high prices. One evening Thomson found himself waited on by a dozen such dealers who sought to sell him old porcelain bowls, dishes, and various other items at exorbitant prices. These dealers were introduced to him by a former servant. It was common practice for household servants to introduce dealers to foreigners, with the servants receiving a good portion of the profits.

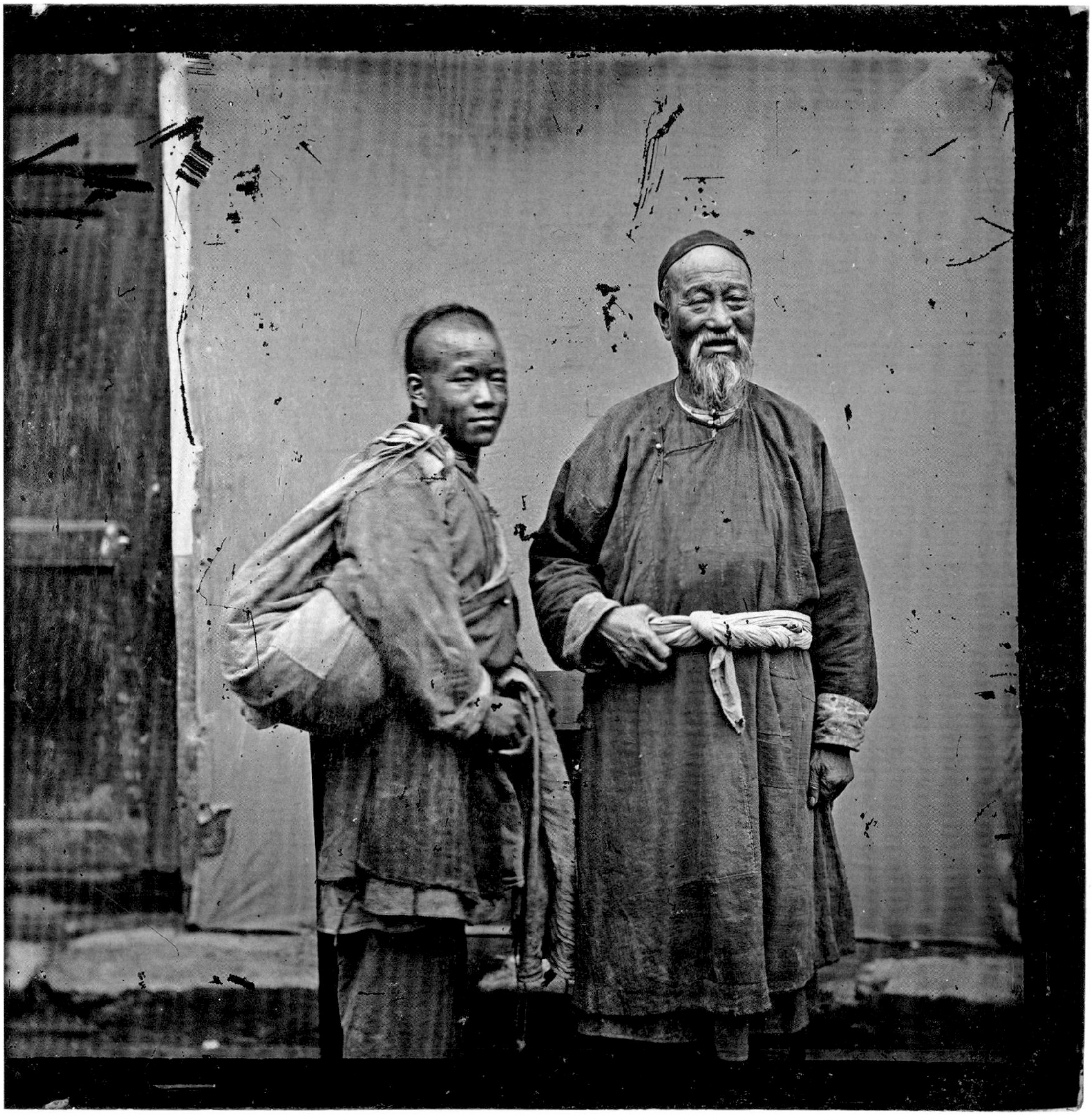

An Old Muslim Cook with His Assistant

Beijing

Many Muslims in Beijing worked as butchers or ran cheap eating houses and bakeries in the city. Muslim butchers were known for their good-quality meat and carving skills. The older man in this photograph had a small cook's shed in the Qianmen area. In front of his shop was a series of brick ovens and open fire pits from where, as Thomson noted, a constant aroma of roasting wafted out. The shop specialized in various baked and stuffed breads with both savoury meat and sweet fillings. While the older man presided over the cooking and stuffing of the bread, his assistant rolled the dough.

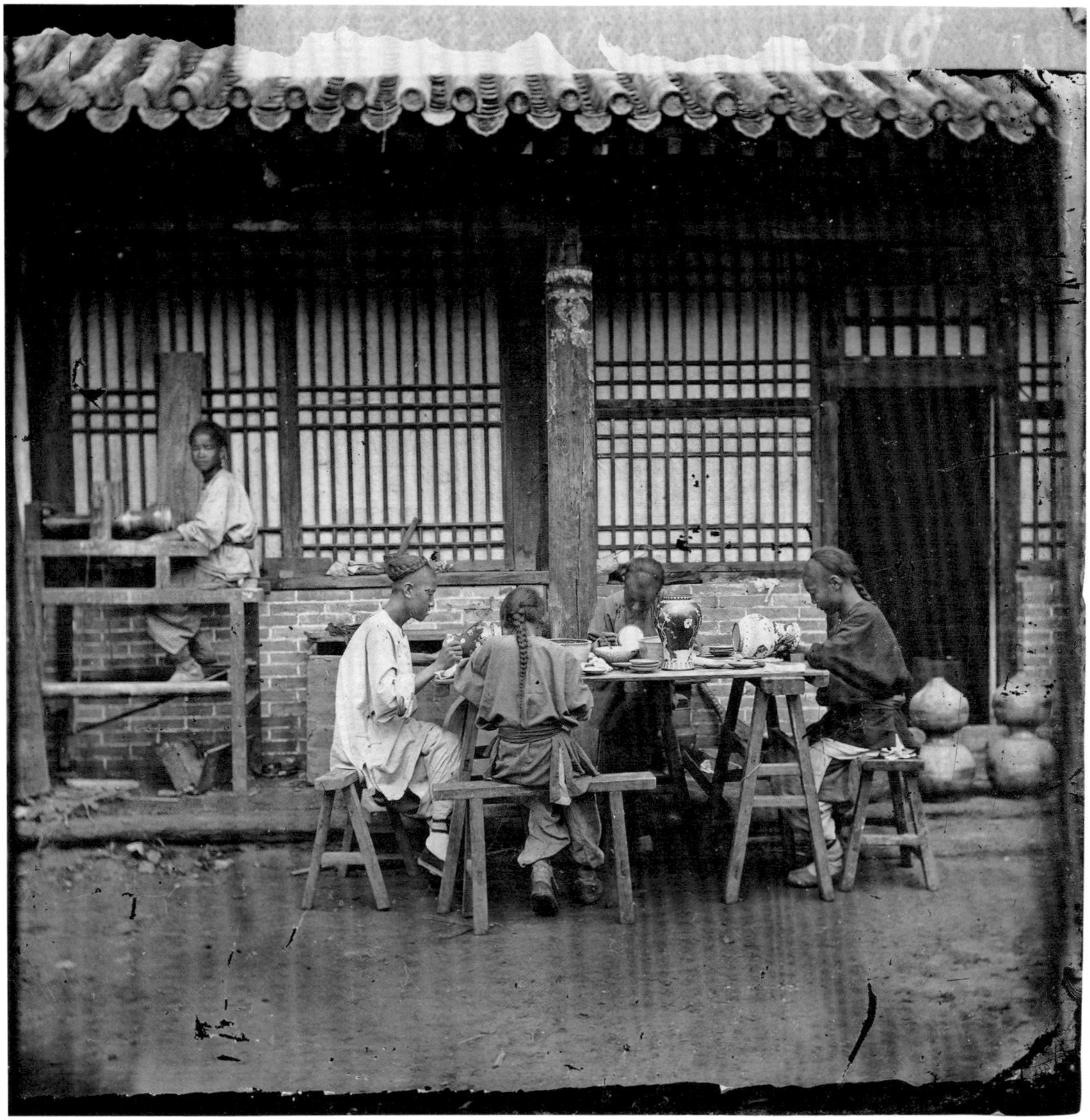

Enamellers

Beijing

In the late Qing period enamelware became hugely desirable and fetched extremely high prices in the marketplace. However, the art of making enamelware was becoming a rare skill, with only one or two shops in Beijing managing to carry on the tradition. The shop shown here was owned by a Manchu and was situated not far from the French Legation quarter in Dongjiao Minxiang. Despite their youthfulness Thomson was very impressed by their expert skill in colour-blending.

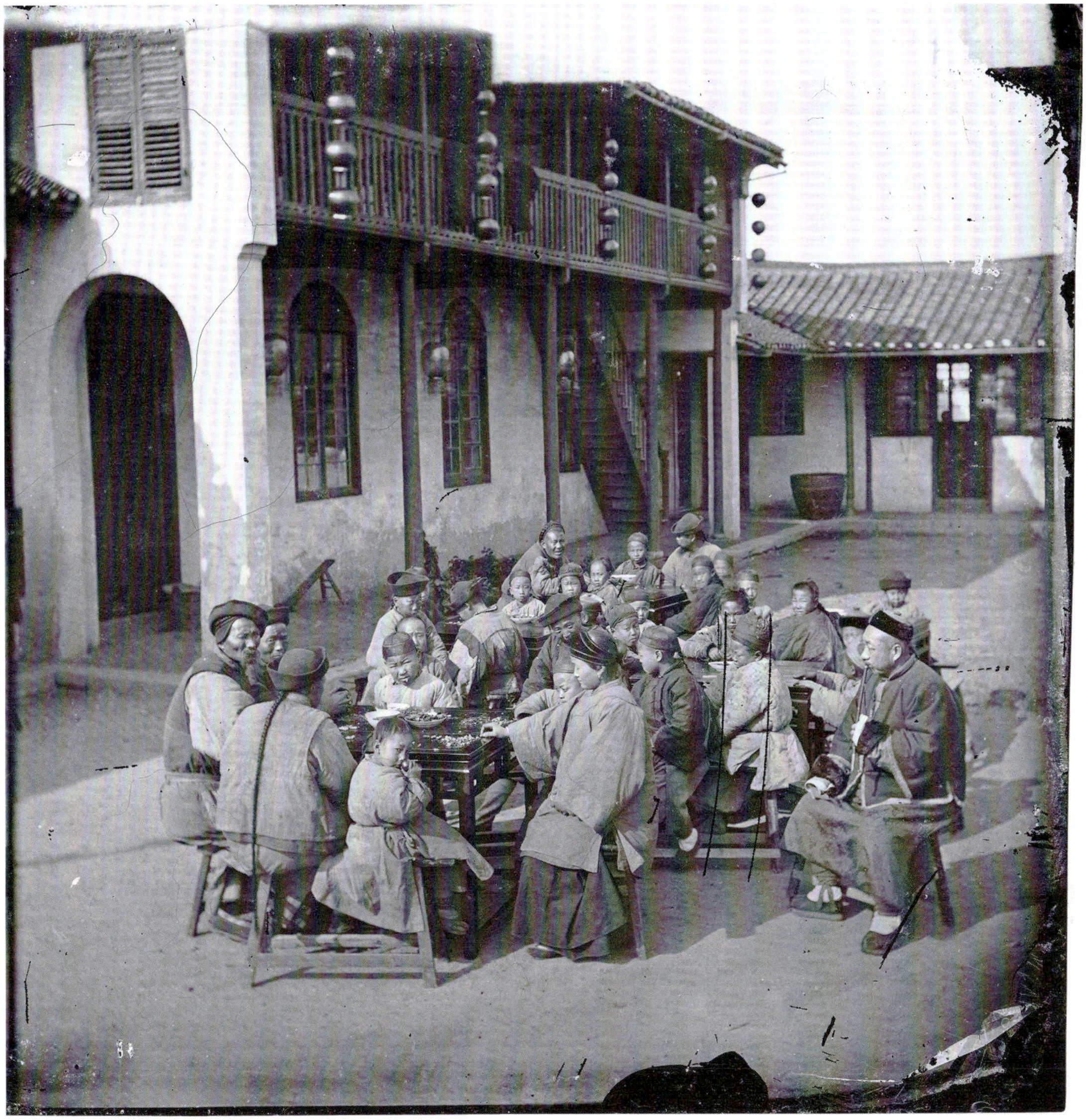

Mission School

Beijing

'Modern' western-style education did not begin in China until 1905. In Beijing, as well as in some coastal areas, a few privately run missionary schools had been established around 1860s. With a few exceptions, such as those run by Jesuits, most of these were at elementary level and devoted entirely to instruction in religion and Chinese classics. This only began to change after 1877. During the Protestant general conference that year, it was agreed that China's mission schools were to provide a secular education, although textbooks with secular content did not appear until 1890. This change made it possible for a small number of Chinese students to receive a Western secular education.

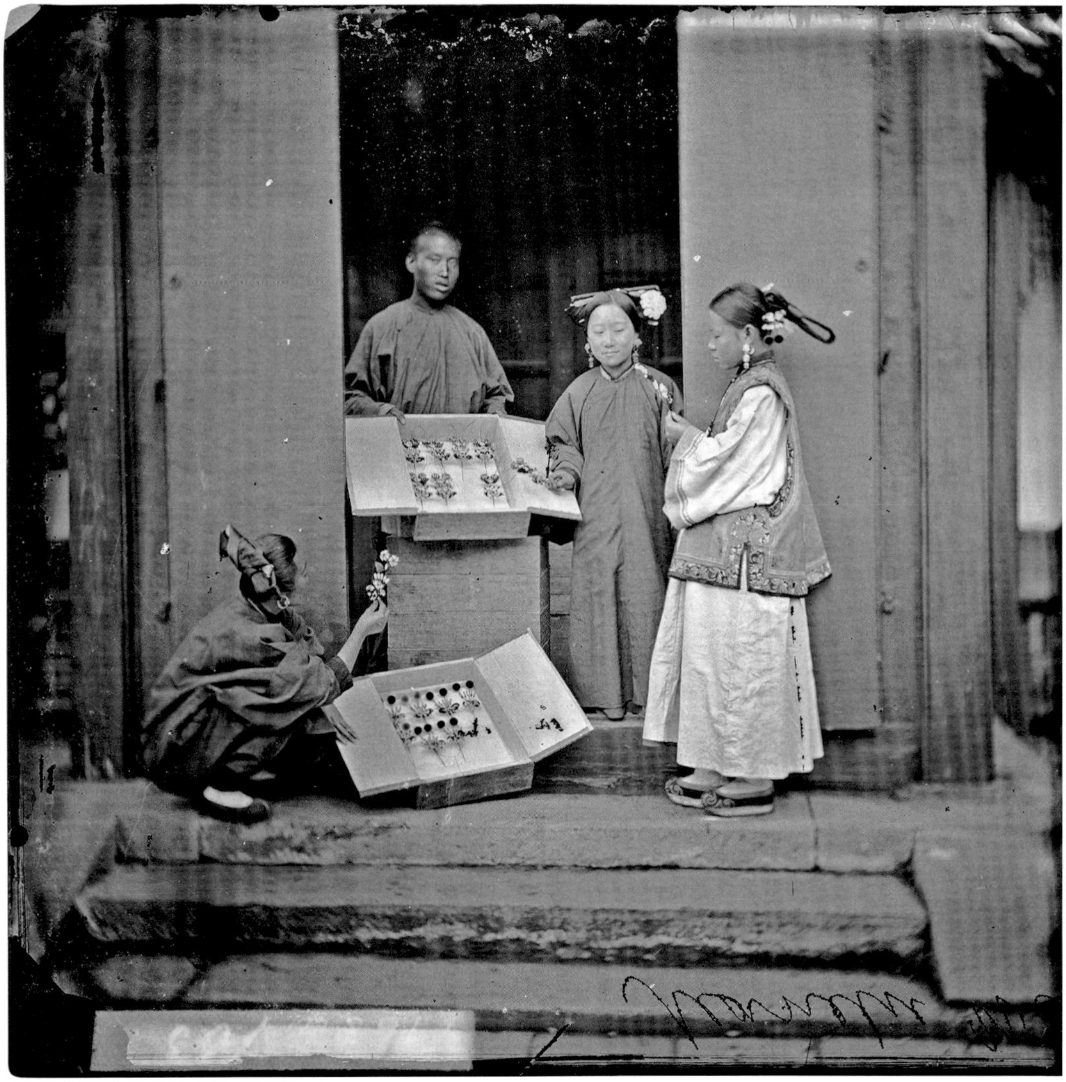

Manchu Women Buying Flowers for Their Headdress

Beijing

As a marker of ethnic identity, the headdress played an important part in the life of a Manchu Bannerwoman. The headdress would have been elaborately decorated with tassels, jeweled ornaments, and fresh or artificial flowers.

Young girls would wear a single pigtail hanging behind with the front hair cut into a fringe. After marriage, women had to arrange their hair on the top of their head using a fan-shaped hair coronet. This hairstyle was called 'Qitou' (which means hair style for the Manchu nobility) or 'Jingtou' (which means hair style of the capital city).

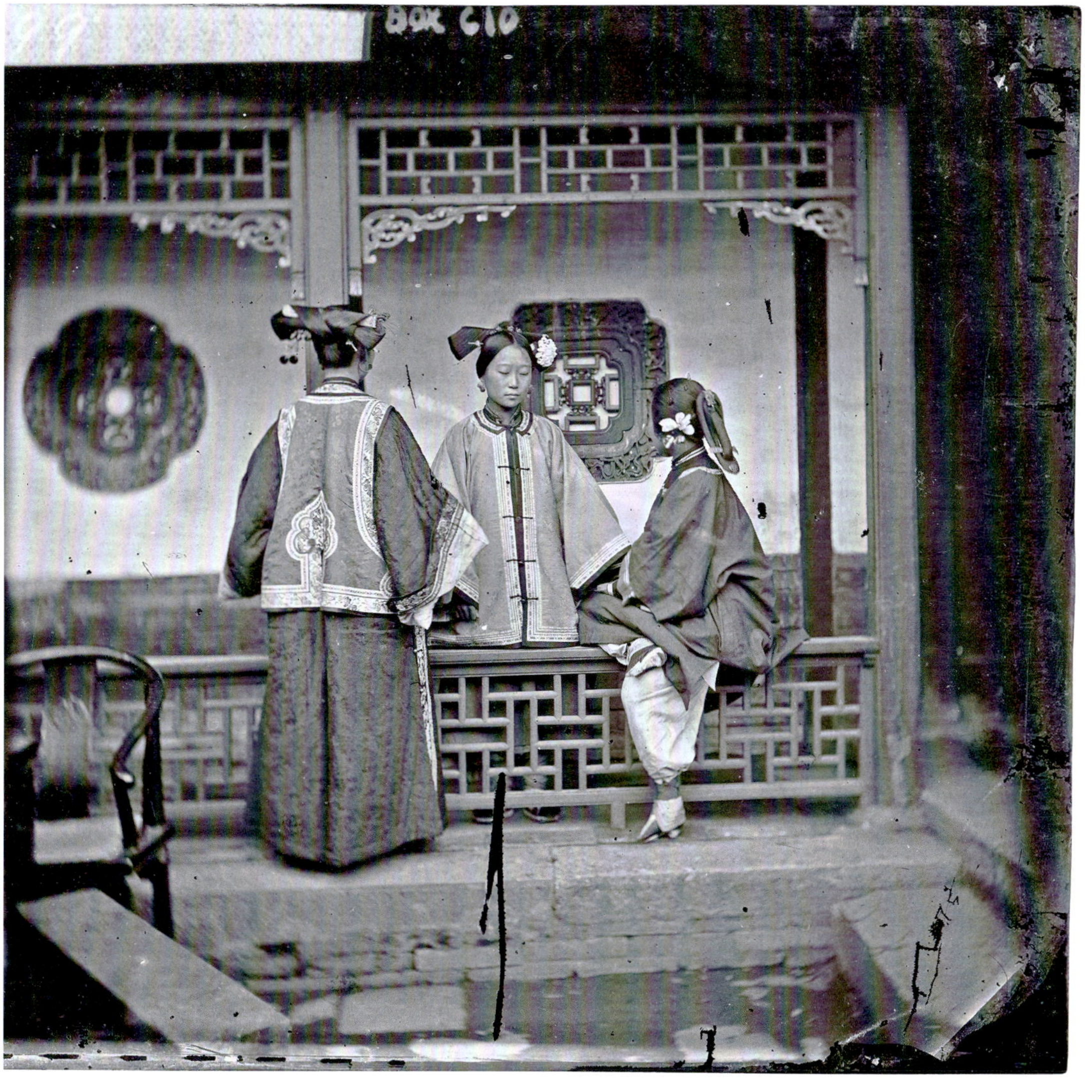

MANCHU AND CHINESE LADIES INSIDE A COURTYARD

Beijing

This scene shows how Manchu women, unlike Han Chinese women, did not follow the custom of having their feet bound. One Manchu woman faces the camera, another stands with her back towards it, while the Chinese woman on the right is seated sideways to show her bound foot. Foot-binding originated in the 10th century, originally practised among the elite women. By severely altering the shape of the foot it produced a particular sort of gait that was considered erotic. By the Qing dynasty this practice had spread to the lower social classes in order to improve marriage prospects. Manchu emperors attempted to ban foot binding in the 17th century but failed.

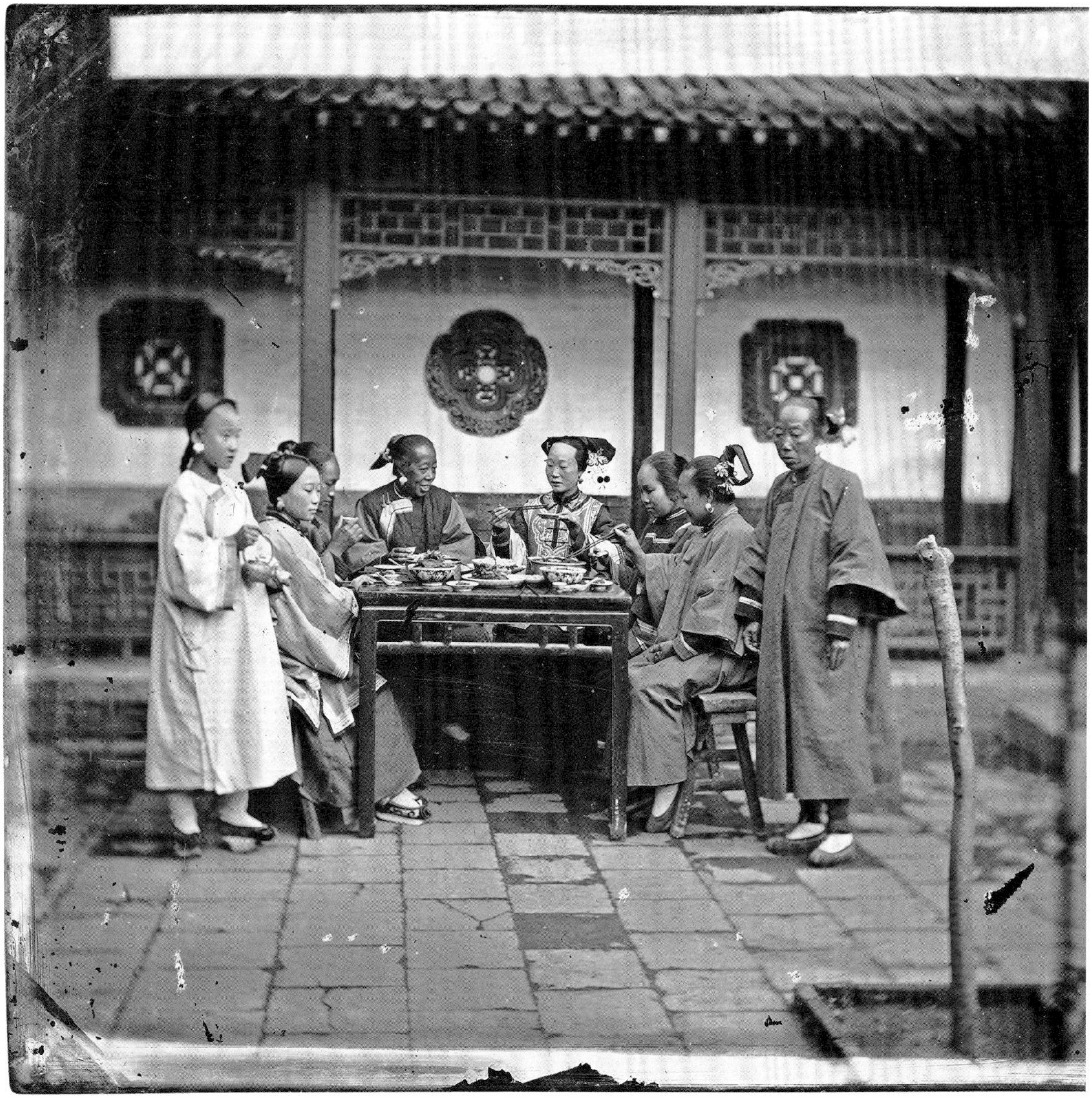

Manchu Ladies at Table

Beijing

Thomson regarded himself extremely lucky to have been admitted into '*the sacred precincts of the mysterious Chinese dwelling*', where he had the opportunity to gain insights into the daily life of women in Beijing at the home of Mr. Yang Fang. Thomson befriended Yang by teaching him techniques of photography. Thomson was impressed by the women's grace and beauty, and by their elegant and richly coloured robes. Here a group of Manchu ladies are enjoying a meal in a courtyard, eating from a porcelain set that appears to be decorated in over-glaze enamels and made at Jingdezhen.

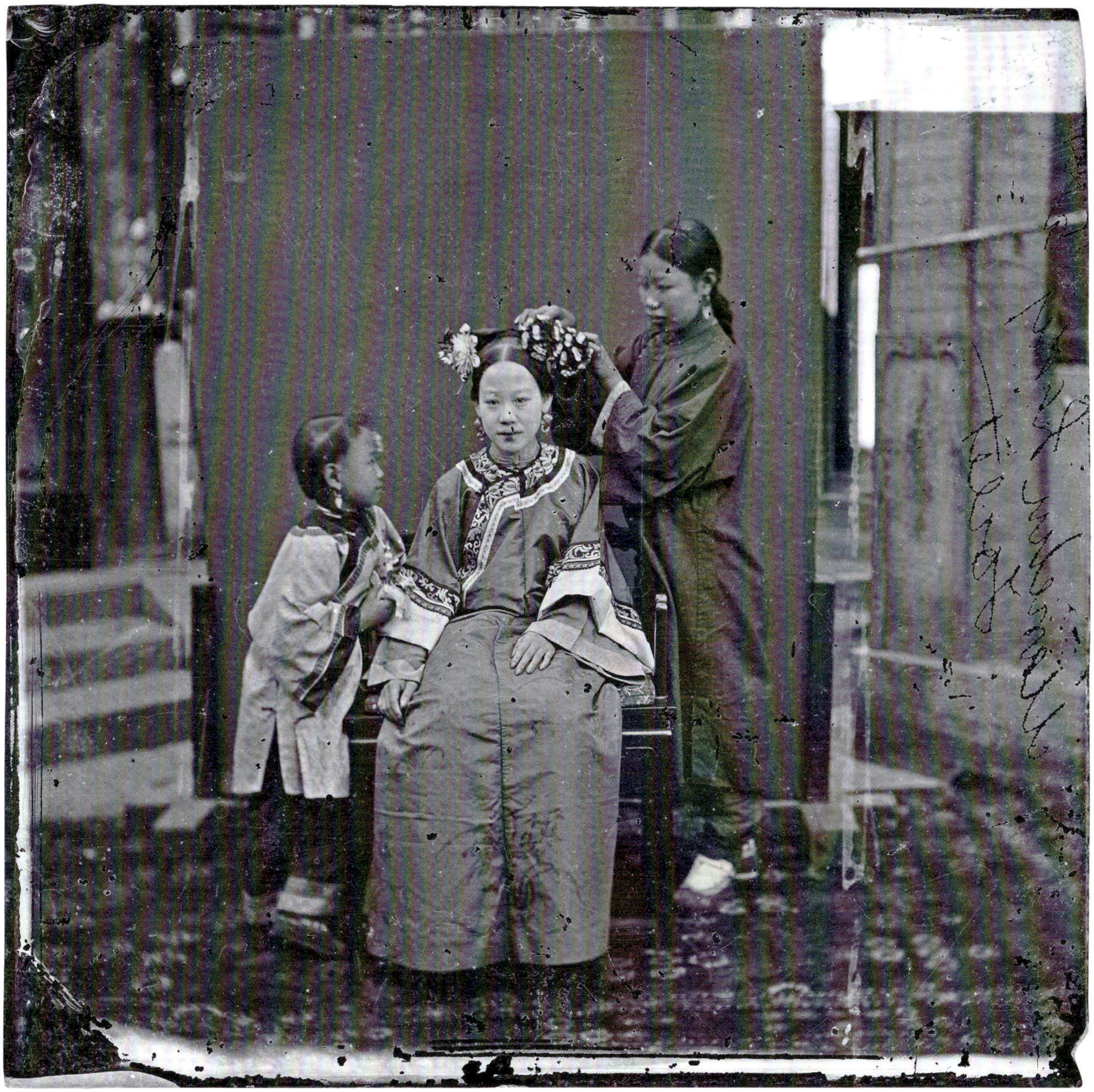

A Manchu Lady having her Hair dressed

Beijing

Thomson had the opportunity to observe the detailed, often tedious routines of a Manchu lady being dressed by her servant girl with hairdressing being perhaps the most important ritual. In general, it took one to two hours for the servant to dress her lady's hair. The 'Liangbatou' was created by twisting the wearer's hair up and around a flat strip, known as the 'bianfang'. It features two handfuls of hair, parted to each side of the head. When completed, the coiffure extended out at the back as well as to both sides. Flowers or tassels were often attached to the hairstyles to make it more impressive.

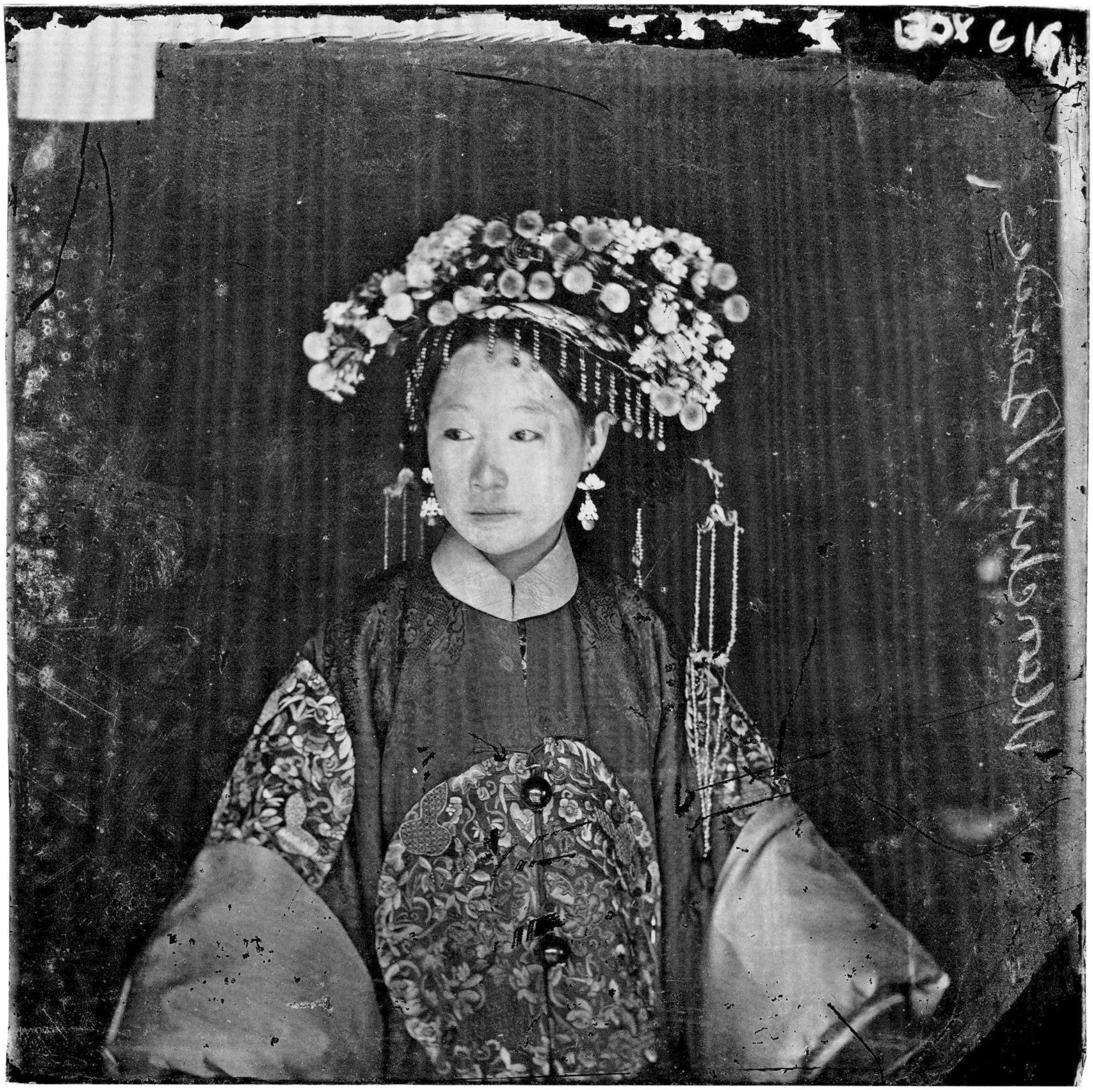

A Manchu Bride

Beijing

Manchu custom dictated that girls could not be betrothed until they were fourteen years old. Thomson was sympathetic to the lives of these young brides, which he reckoned to be one of slavery, in which the wife '*is even liable to be beaten by her mother-in-law, and husband too, if she neglects to discharge her duties as general domestic drudge*'. This photograph shows Thomson's great sensitivity towards his subject capturing a feeling of apprehension through her eyes.

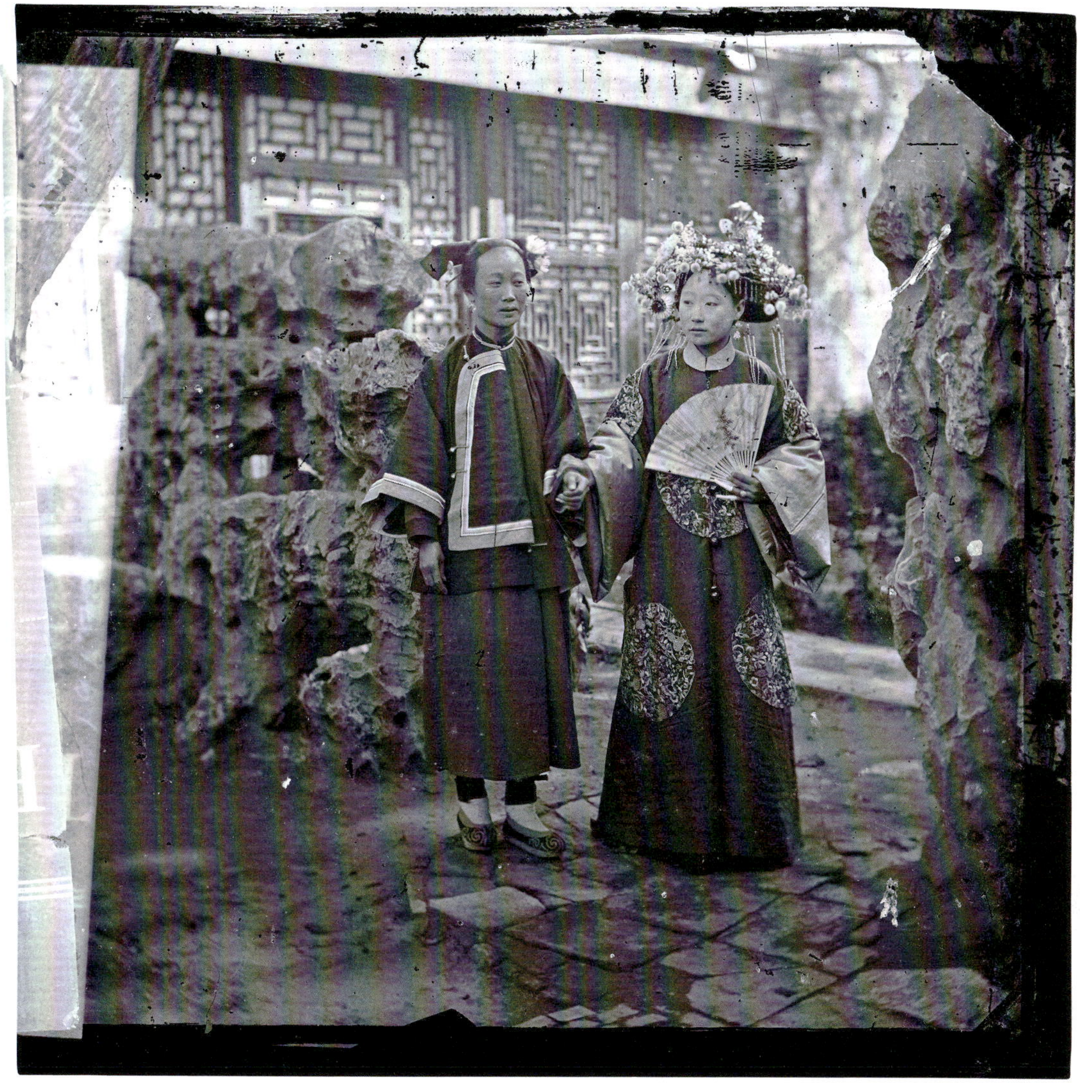

A Manchu Bride with Her Maid

Beijing

The costume for a Manchu bride was normally red, the colour of celebration and the decoration of the customary eight roundels was dictated by her father's position in the social hierarchy. Here the roundels are embroidered with narcissus flowers and prunus blossom with double gourds, all signifying good fortune and prosperity. The elaborate headdress was also particular to weddings, with hanging strings of freshwater pearls (or glass for poorer families) and red pompoms amongst enamel, or kingfisher feather decorated, flowers. On her wedding day, the bride was carried to her husband's home in a sedan chair decorated with crimson cloth. Her head was covered with a veil that was also crimson and richly embroidered.

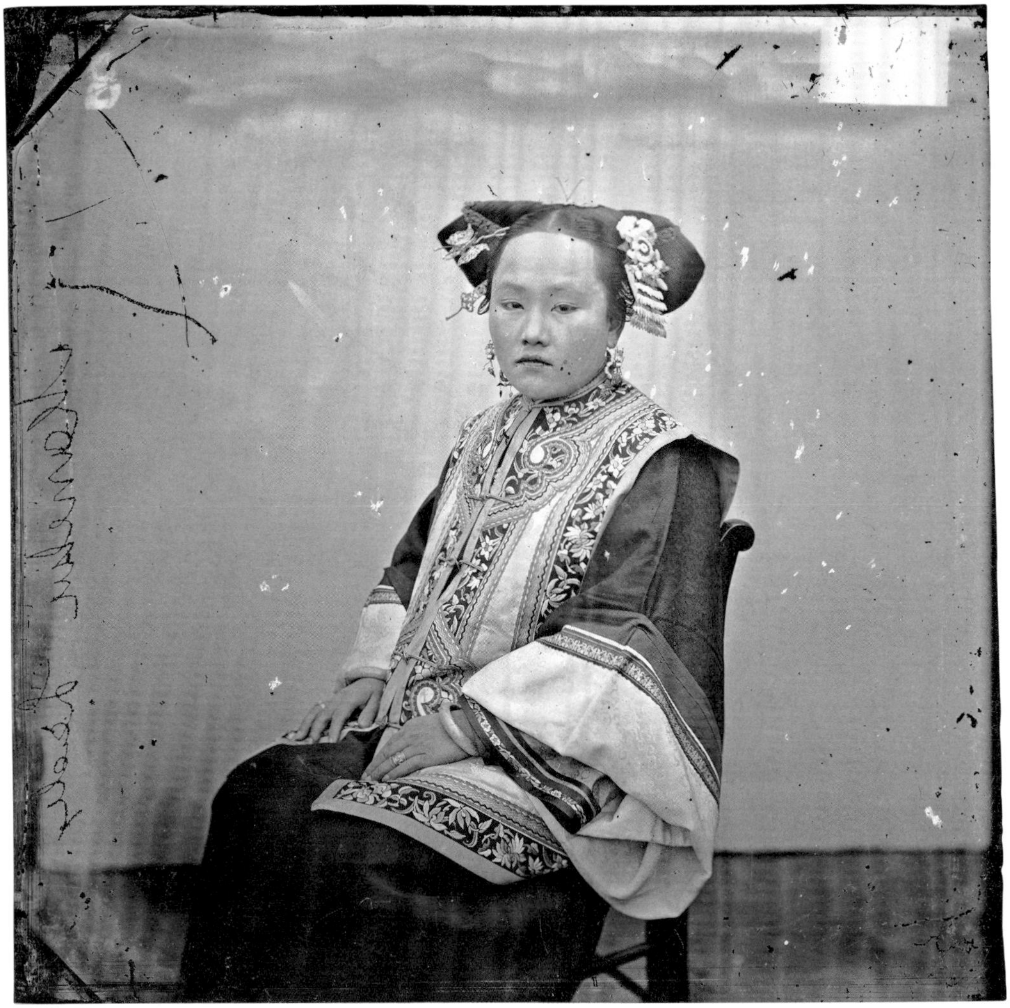

A Seated Manchu Lady Wearing a Coiffure

Beijing

The photograph is in the mode of classical portraits, whether painted or photographed, and evokes the Western tradition of portrait painting where the subject wears their finest apparel to proclaim their status. The lady's serious face contrasts with her festive Manchu dress and its many layers. Her elaborately styled hair is embellished with colourful hairpins and combs, with a large butterfly prominently displayed on one side. Her richly embroidered sleeveless waistcoat has a curiously shaped front opening created with two *ruyi*-heads, echoing the shape of the Daoist fungus of long life and representing a 'wish-granting gem'. The wide, turned back cuffs of her robe in a pale material contrast effectively with the dark silk of the long robe, itself woven with a damask pattern which is barely visible in the photograph. Peeping out under the cuff is a third costume, its be-ribboned edge hinting at yet more finery.

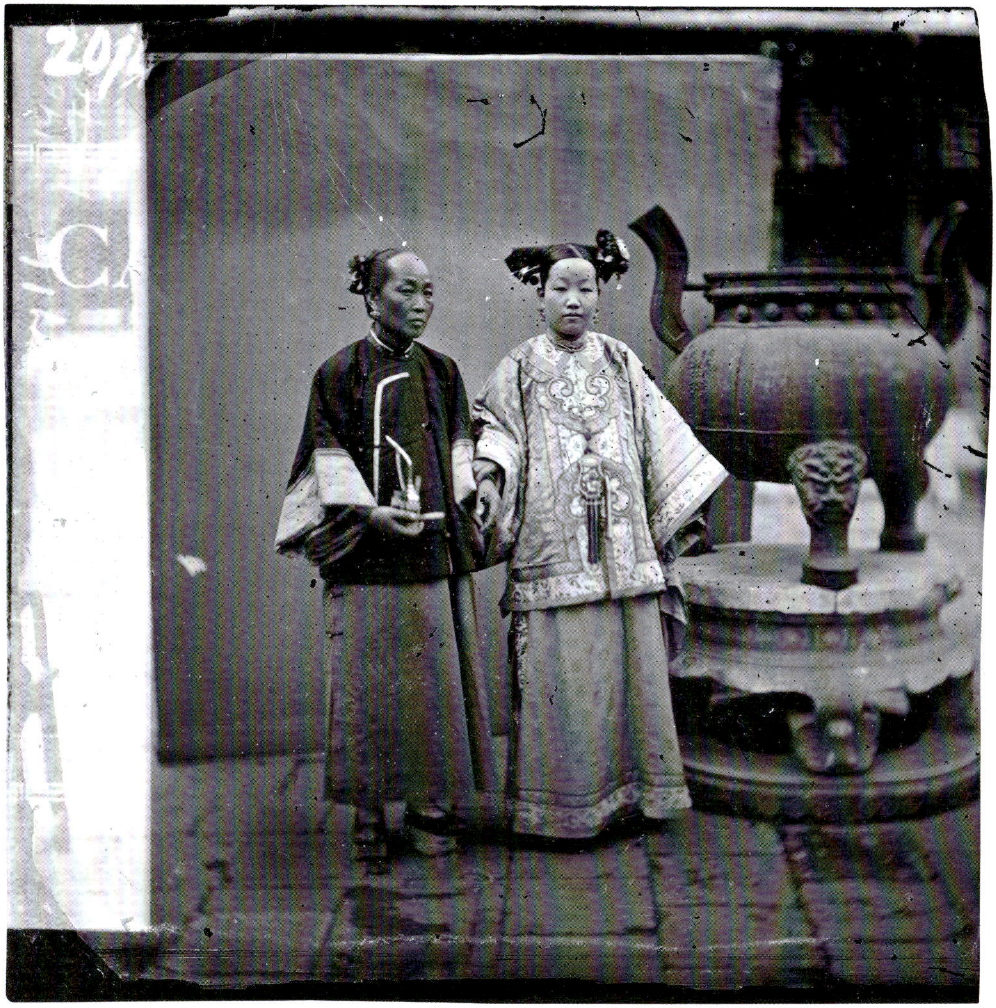

A Manchu Lady and her Maid beside a Bronze Brazier

Beijing

An outdoor portrait, contrasting a wealthy Manchu lady with her maid. The former wears a Han-style jacket and skirt, adopted by the Manchu upper classes, with wide-sleeved silk jacket edged with white silk embroidered borders and inner bands of woven ribbon. The front opening has two large heart-shaped designs of Chinese *ruyi*-shape as in the photograph opposite. A tasselled ornament hangs from one of the front buttons. Her sophisticated hairstyle contrasts with her companion's simpler style and altogether plain form of dress. The maid holds a smoking set, a popular pastime of the period, and stands on typical Manchu platform-style shoes.

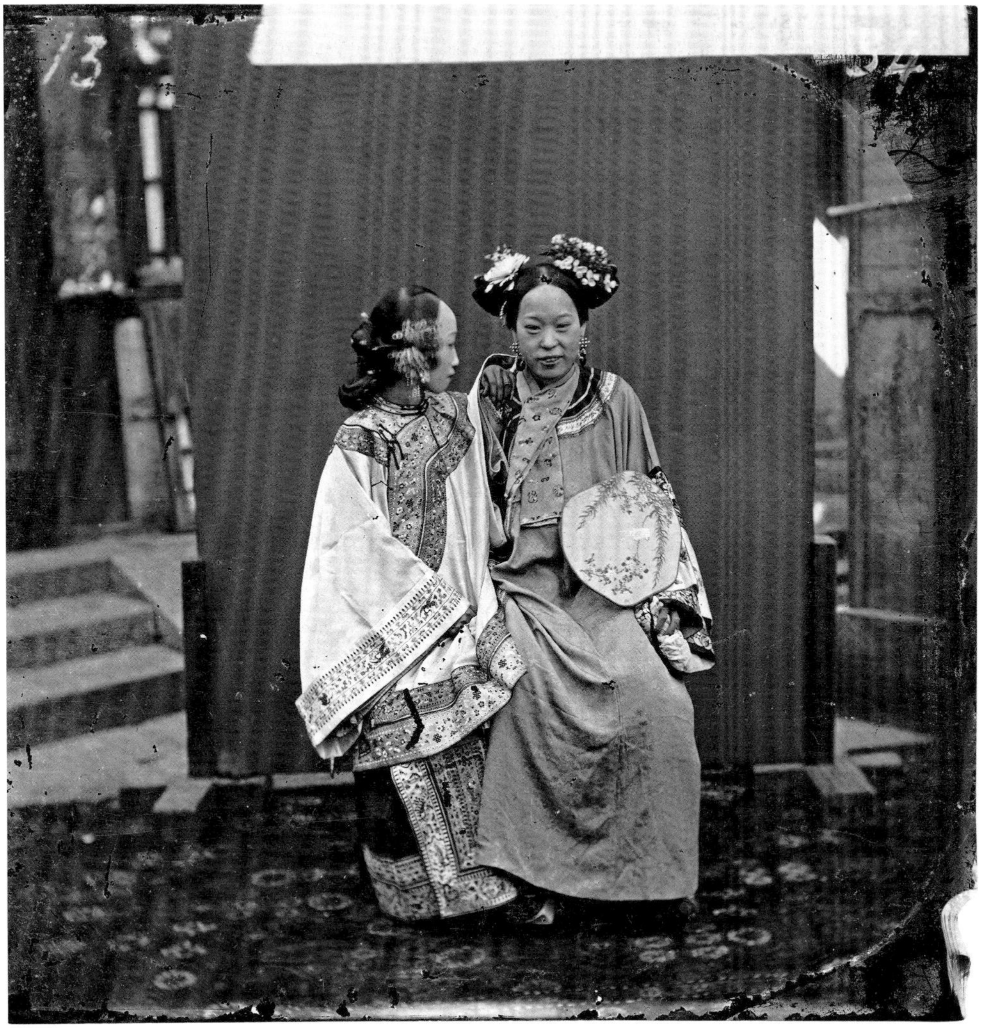

A Manchu Lady after having her Face Painted

Beijing

After a woman's hair had been dressed, her face was then painted. In Qing China, Manchu and Han women, in particular those from wealthy families, covered their faces and necks with a thick white paste. When the paste was dry, it was smoothed and polished. Afterwards, a blush of rose-powder was applied to the cheeks and eyelids, and the surplus rouge left on the lady's palms, as the colour rose-pink on the hand was thought to be particularly attractive. The ladies are wearing Han Chinese jackets and skirts with the Manchu style long costume for semi-formal occasions, along with the elaborate hair styles worn by wealthy women. By the time of Thomson's visit the style of dress for the Manchu and the Han had become interchangeable. For the wealthy, costumes were of silk in a variety of colours, with elaborate borders in contrasting colours, finely embroidered with figures in gardens, landscapes, or flowers and birds, all enhanced by elaborate jewellery.

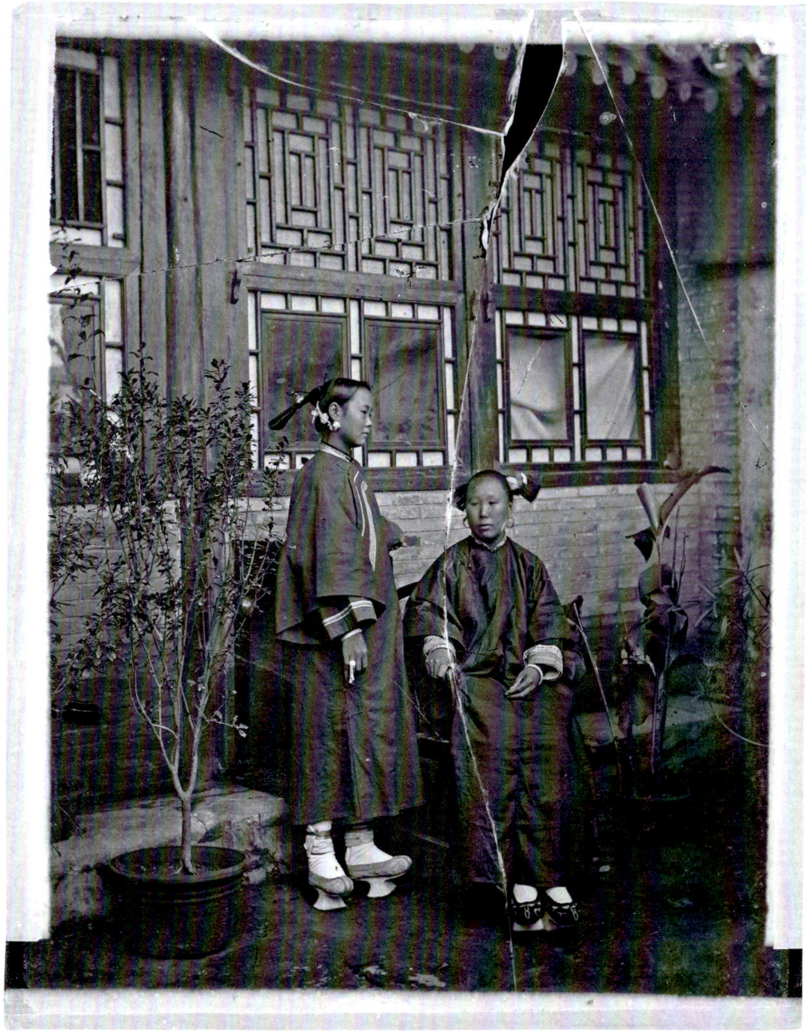

A Manchu Lady with her Daughter

Beijing

In this photograph, Thomson shows clearly the unbound feet of Manchu women. They did not adopt the Han Chinese custom of foot binding but wore platform shoes that imitated the gait of the Han Chinese women with bound feet. The lower portion of the shoe was a high platform heel made of wood. The upper portion was made of fabric and often with embroidery.

This photograph also shows the difference between the hairstyle of the mother who wears a 'liangbatou' (two-handled style) of a married woman and the younger unmarried daughter with a 'magpie' hairstyle.

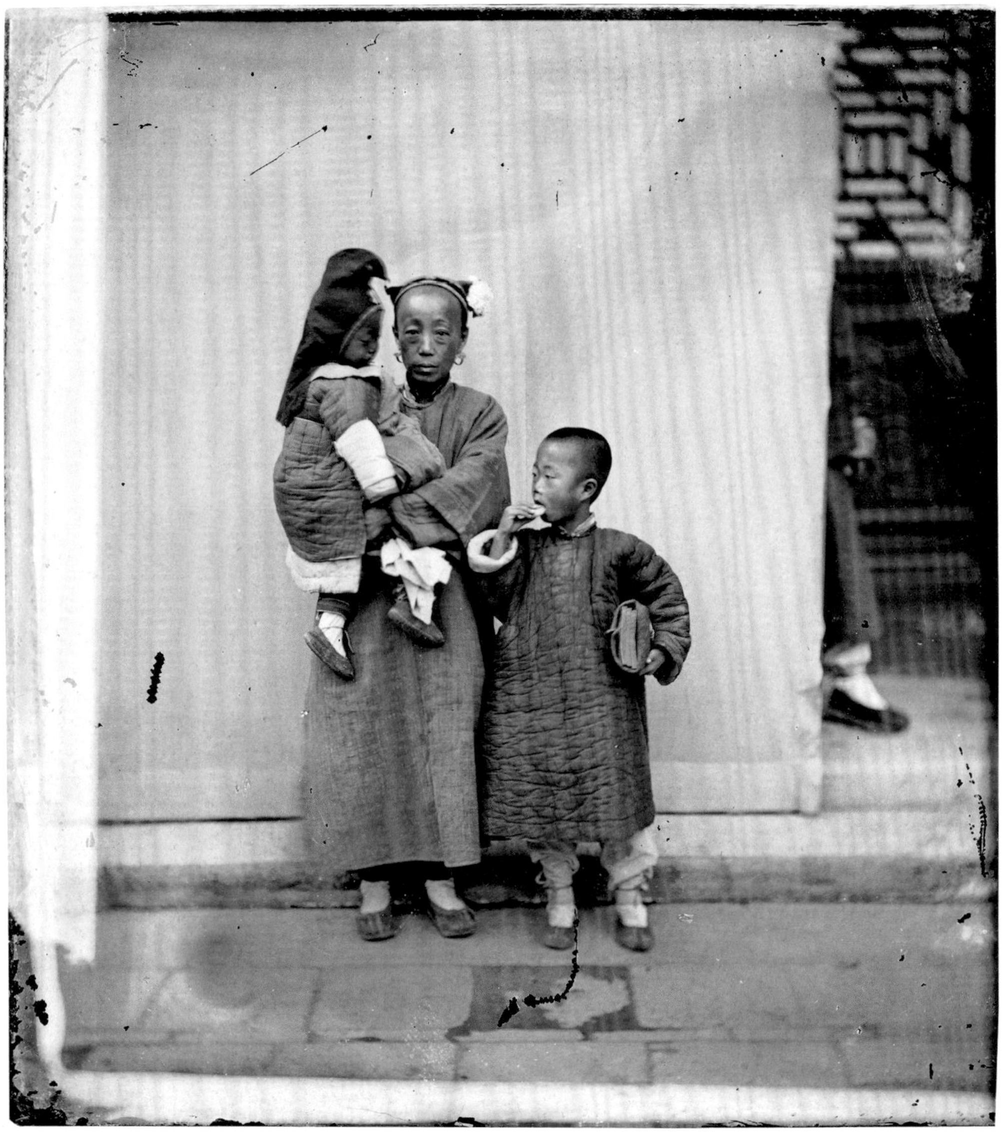

Mother with Two Children

Beijing

Thomson described the streets of Beijing as '*highly picturesque and interesting*', and the people formed an essential part of its charm. In many works he betrayed a great deal of sympathy towards the poor. Here a woman is holding a child in her arms; next to her, looking away from the camera, stands a boy eating a piece of pastry. Thomson met them in front of a butcher's shop while touring the Qianmen area of the city. They are dressed in plain but warm and clean clothing, outfits that indicate they are not from a wealthy family.

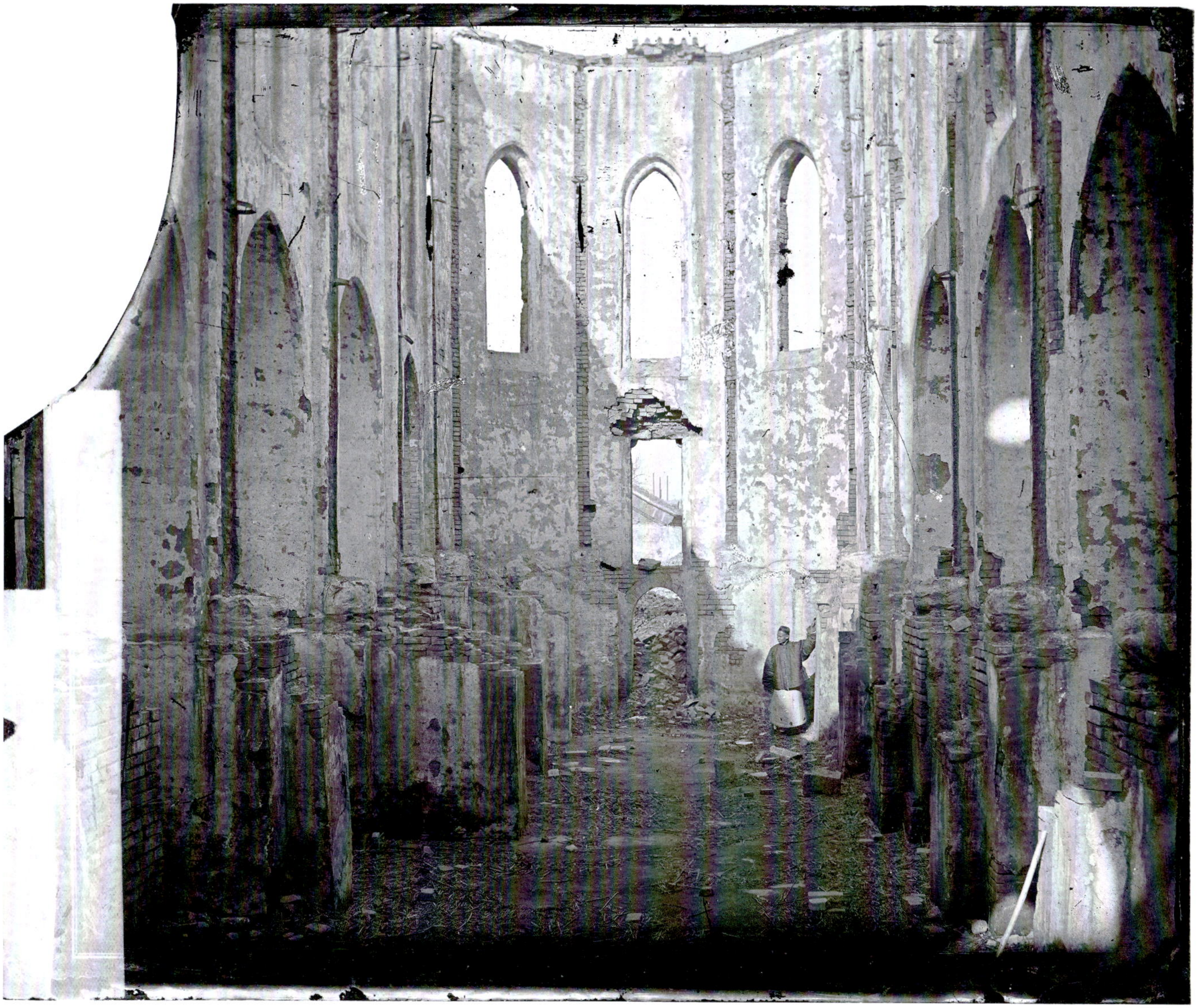

Interior Ruins of the Chapel of the Sisters of Charity

Tianjin

The Sisters first arrived in Tianjin in 1862 to perform charitable works. In 1870 in response to a cholera epidemic nearby, they received many sick children in the convent. A large number of these children died there, and due to a shortage of coffins, two or three were frequently buried together, causing a public outcry. On 21 June, angry Chinese burned down many foreign mission stations, and massacred 21 foreigners in Tianjin, including ten nuns of the Sisters of Charity. The incident became known as the Tianjin Massacre. This photograph was taken not long after the event.

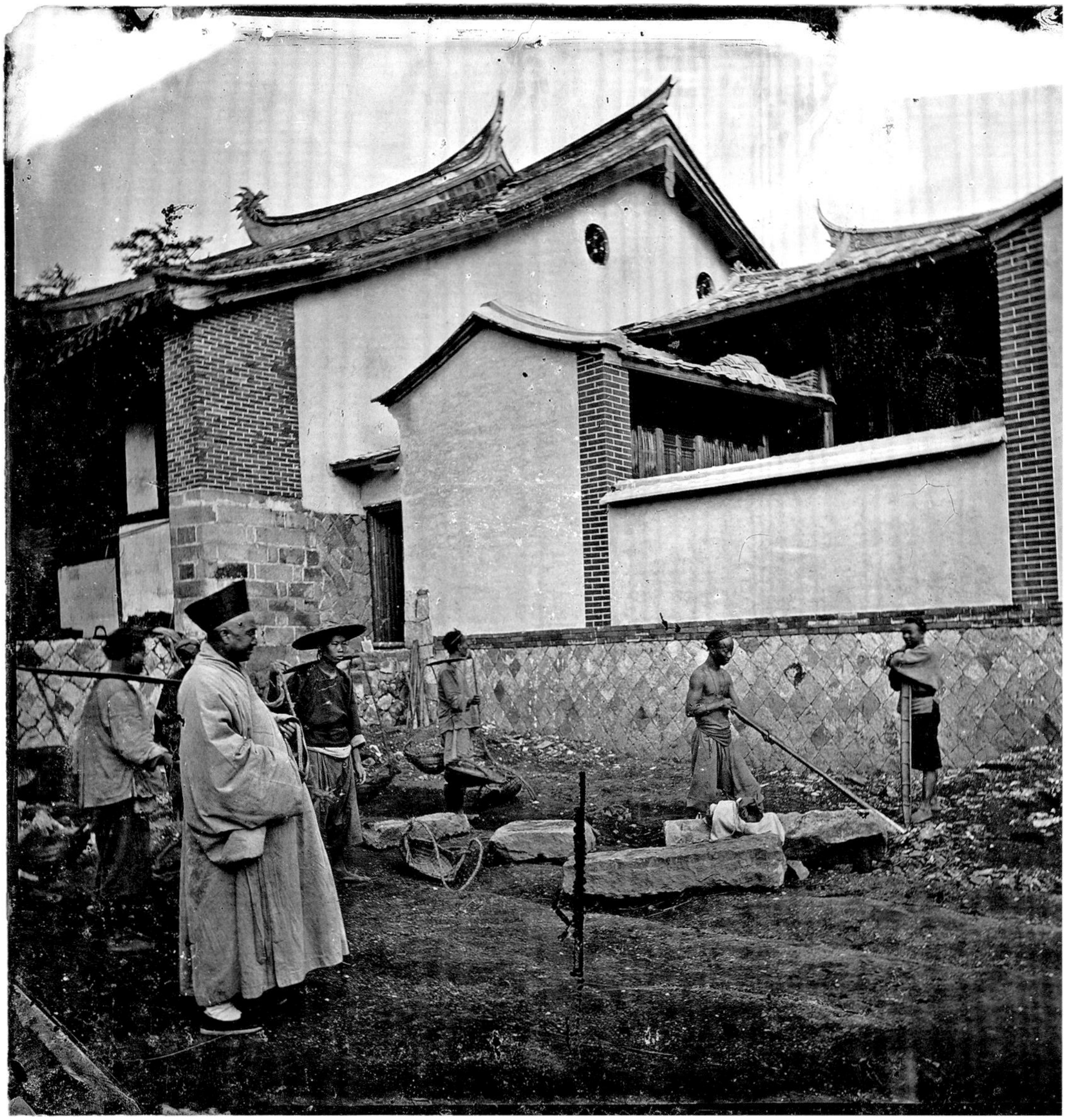

Reconstructing the City of Nanjing

Nanjing

In 1853 Taiping rebels captured the ancient 'southern capital' Nanjing and made it its 'Heavenly Capital'. Some ten years after, in 1864, Qing and foreign troops crushed the Taiping's Heavenly Kingdom and sacked Nanjing. When Thomson visited Nanjing a few years later, the city had literally become '*many dreary acres of demolished streets with not a single occupant*'. He noted that an active restoration programme had just begun. This photo shows a group of labourers at work near a temple, while a Buddhist priest supervises them.

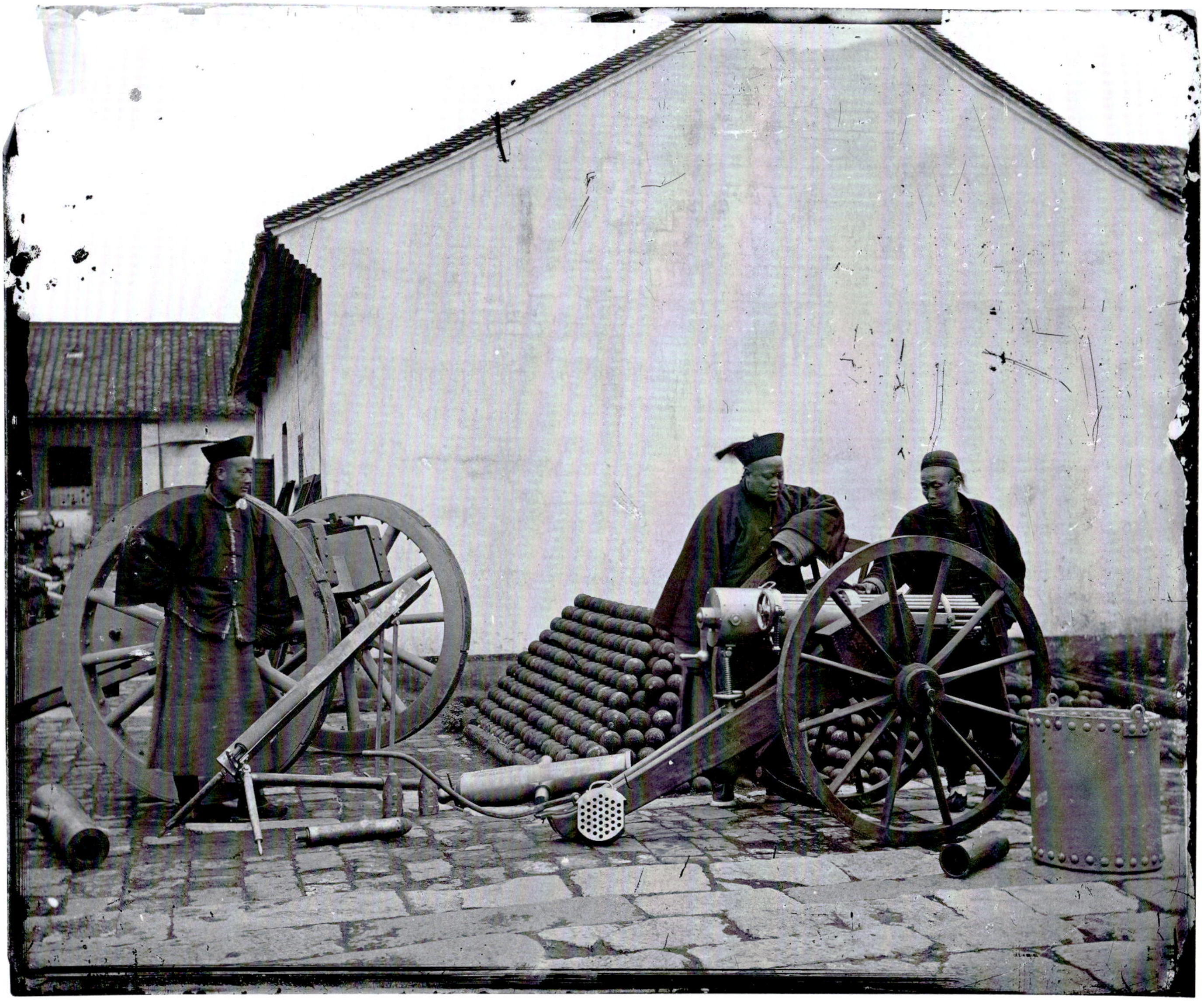

NANJING ARSENAL

Nanjing

The Nanjing Arsenal was built in 1865 under the auspices of Li Hongzhang, the renowned Qing general and statesman, who negotiated with western powers on behalf of the government and who also advocated modernising the Chinese army. The Arsenal was first of its kind in China, and under the supervision of Sir Halliday McCartney, was run on the most up-to-date scientific and military principles. Hundreds of tons of guns and ammunition were manufactured there annually. The photograph shows the new Gatling gun.

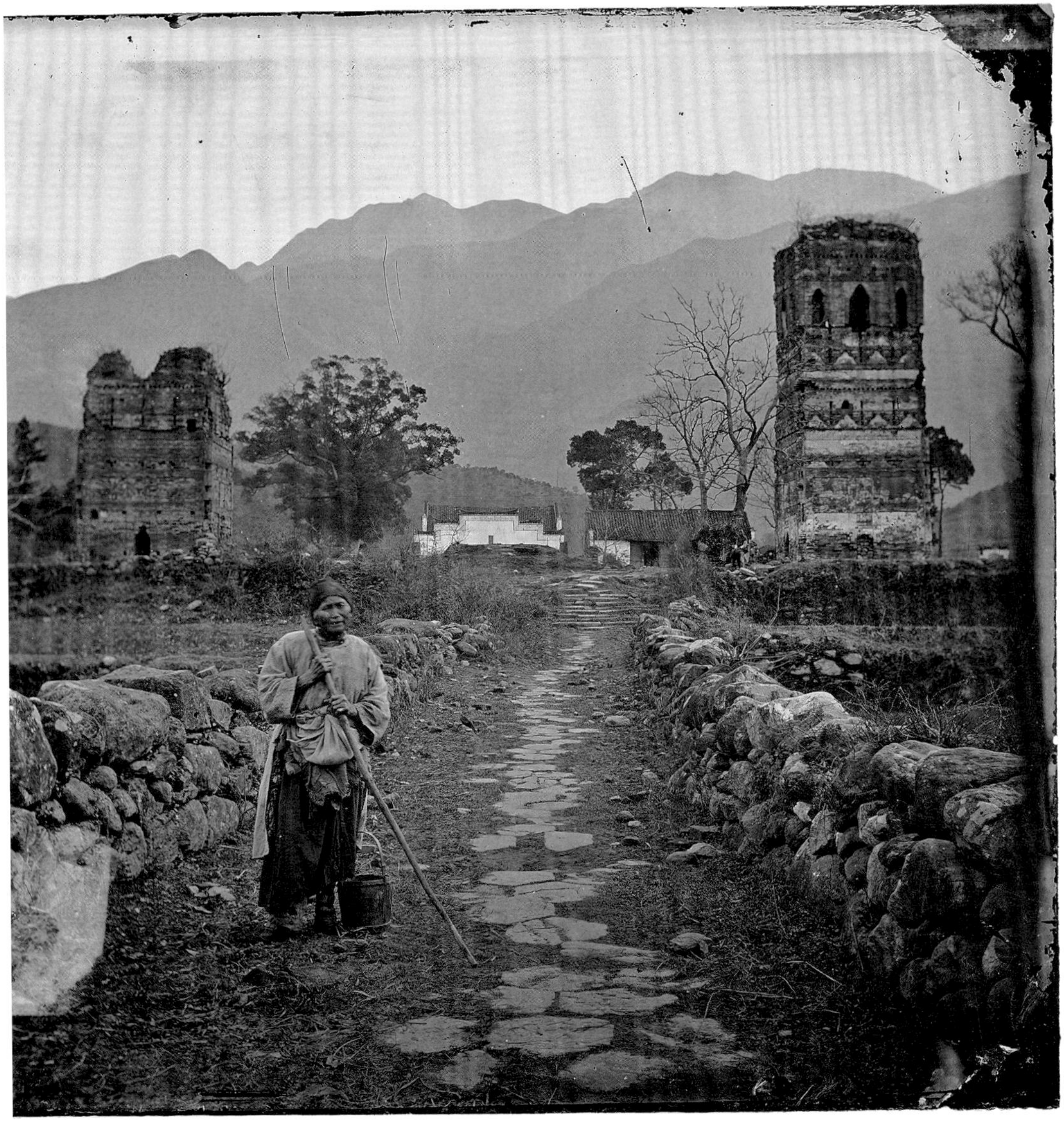

A Religious Ruin

Jiujiang, Jiangxi

According to Thomson this photograph was taken in a small town called Taipingkang about ten miles from Jiujiang. The area was close to Bailu Cave in Mount Lu where the celebrated neo-Confucian scholar Zhu Xi once stayed. Although Thomson was told this was once a famous Buddhist monastery, he thought the ruin resembled the pointed Gothic apertures of a medieval European building and surmised at one point that it might have been a Jesuit mission. However, Matteo Ricci only stayed in the Nanchang area and there is no evidence of him building a mission near Mount Lu.

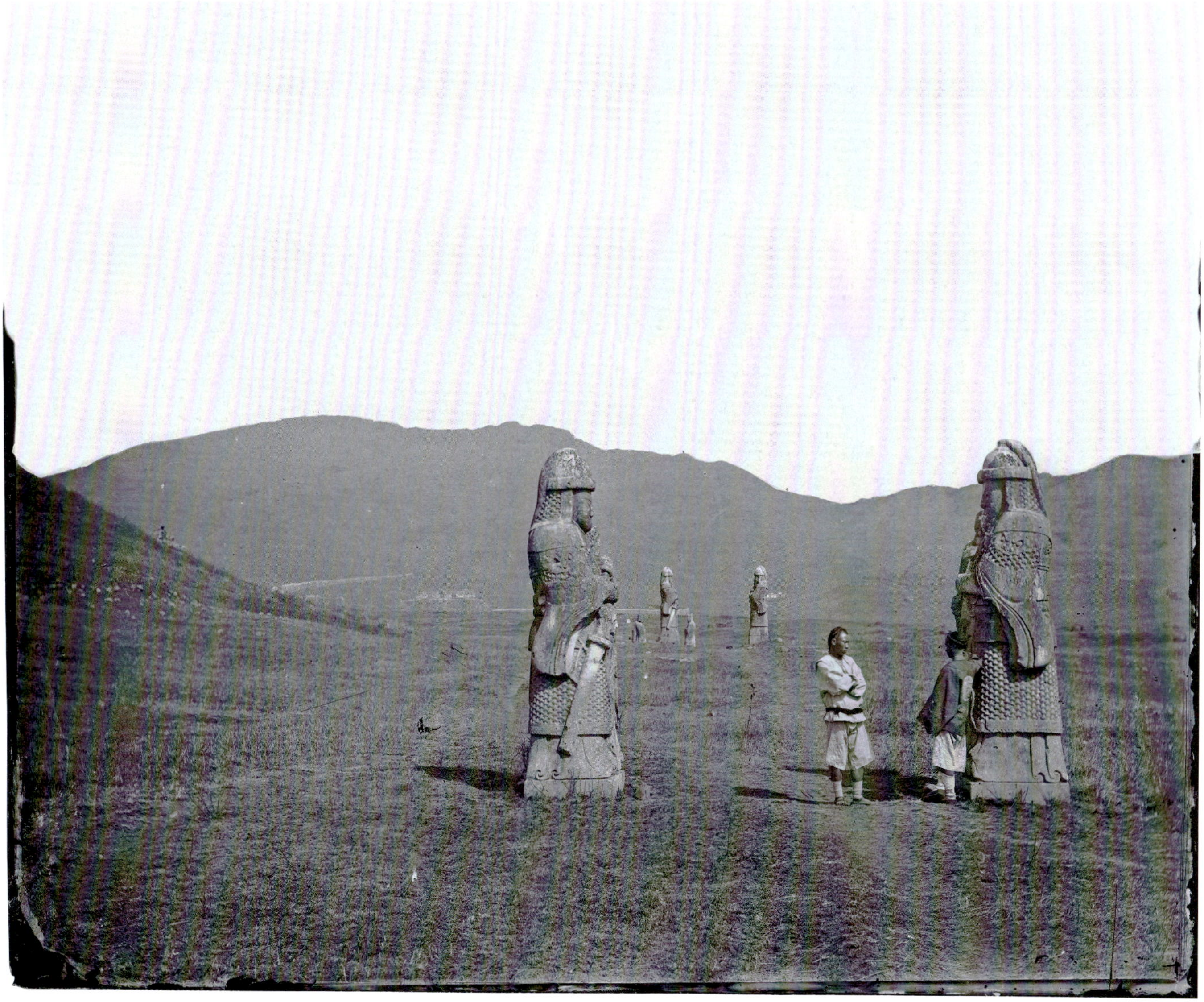

Ming Tomb

Nanjing

The tomb of Zhu Yuanzhang, the first Ming emperor, was for Thomson one of the few traces of Nanjing's former glory. Situated on the Zhongshan hill near to the city's eastern wall, it was one of the largest mausoleums in imperial China. What seemed to impress Thomson most was the giant stone statues of warriors guarding this splendid monument: '*the calm, majestic repose and benign expression of these stone warriors, who seem pleased with the task of guarding the ashes of the dead*'. The two men in the picture were most likely labourers that Thomson had hired to carry his photographic equipment. Their presence demonstrates the enormous size of the stone warriors.

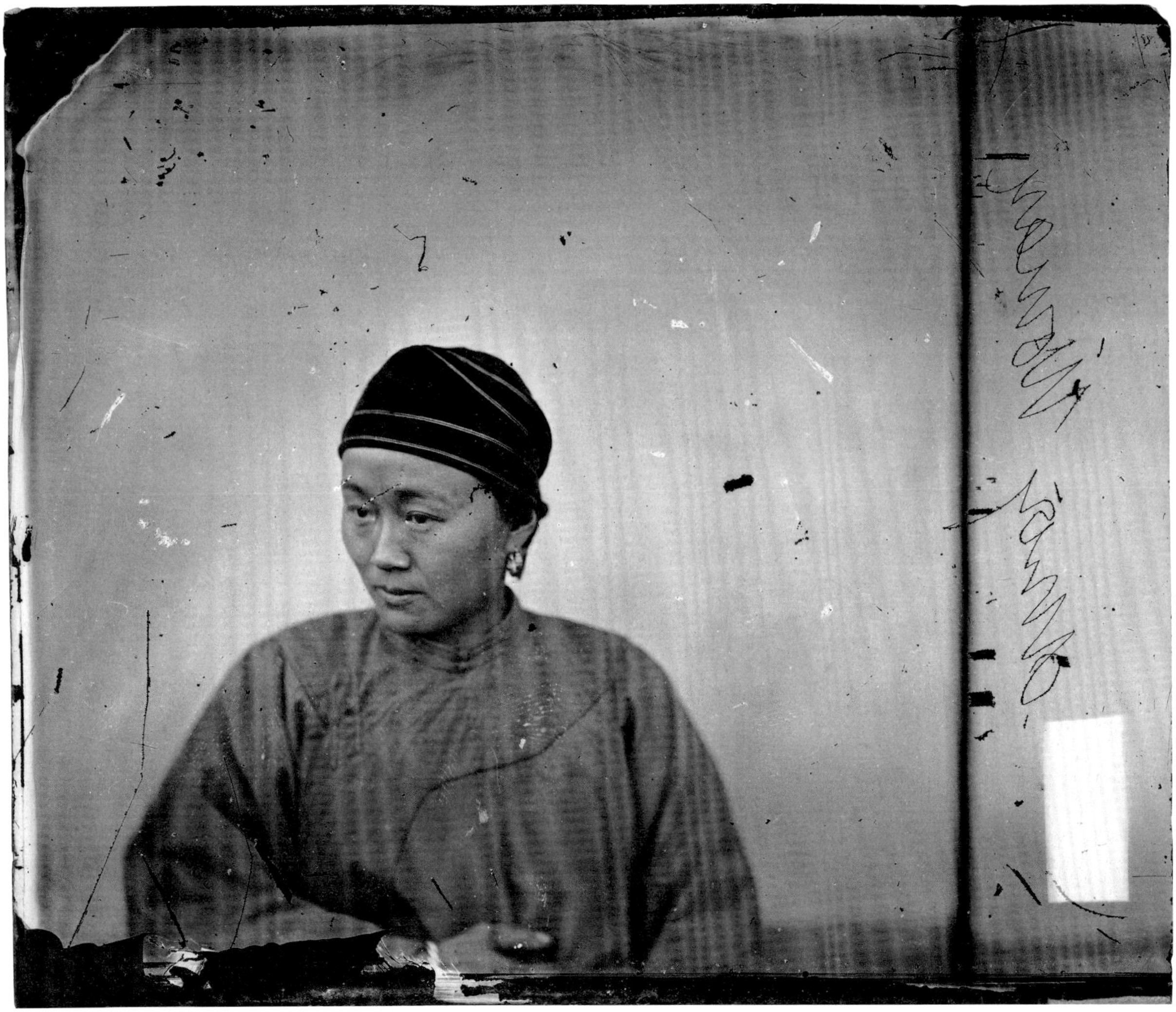

A Shanghainese Woman Wearing a Snood

Shanghai

This photograph shows a woman with a black velvet snood completely covering her hair. Thomson noted this way of wearing hair was very fashionable among women in Shanghai. For him this simple style was '*quaint*' and '*remarkable*', yet he was perhaps unaware of its symbolic value for the fashionable Shanghainese. Velvet was a relatively modern fabric, one probably first brought into China from Central Asia. In the second half of the 19th century, it was regarded as a foreign luxury. During the time of Thomson's visit, Shanghai was beginning to emerge as a modern cosmopolitan city. Many of its population, mostly migrants from nearby regions, aspired to everything foreign, which was a synonym for 'modern' and 'superior'. It was not surprising that this simple-looking snood was then so much in vogue in Shanghai.

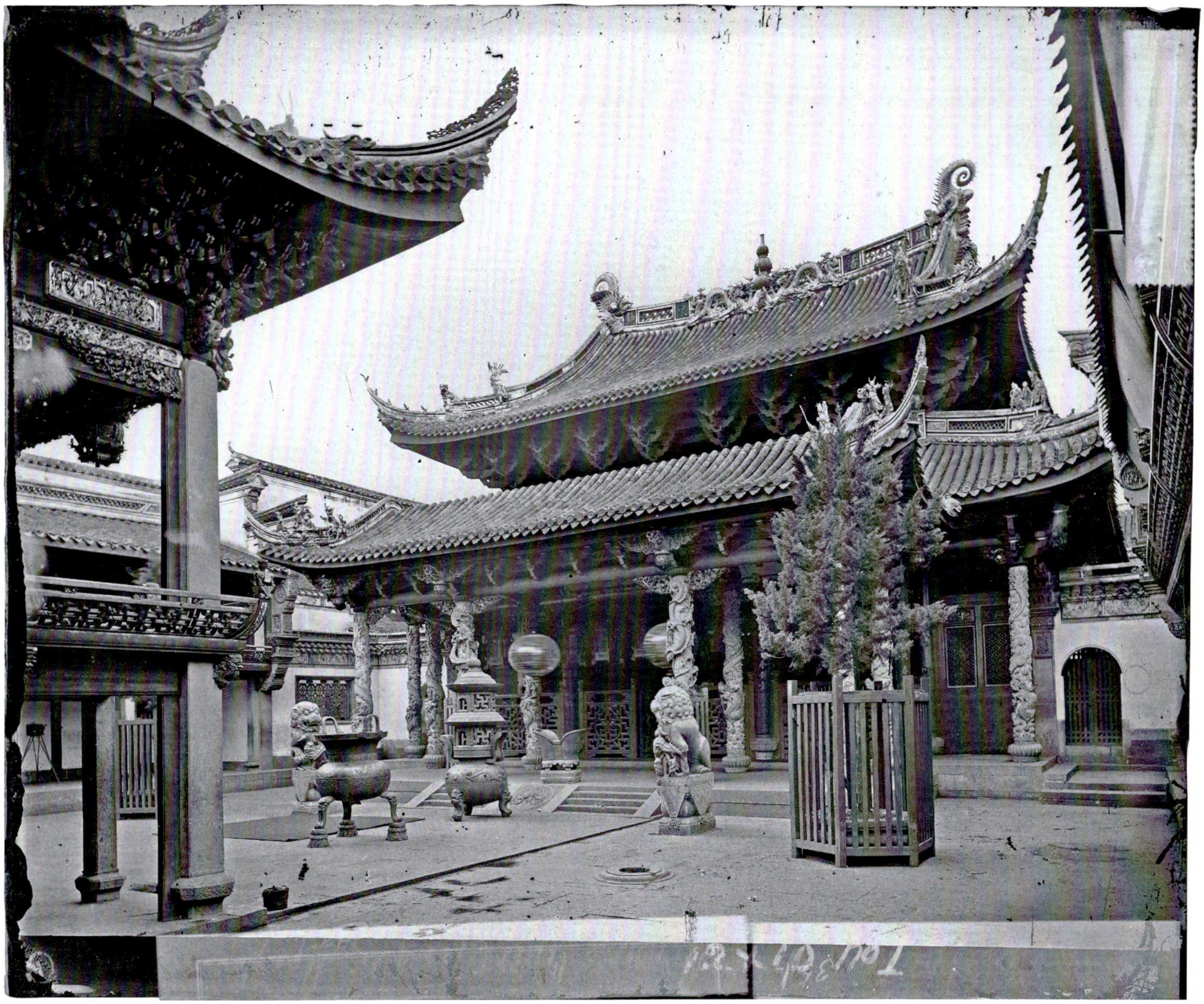

NINGBO TIANHOU TEMPLE OR QINGAN GUILDHALL

Ningbo, Zhejiang

Ningbo Tianhou Temple was a late Qing reconstruction in 1850 of the Song period Tianhou Temple with donations from overseas Chinese shipping merchants; parts of the complex also functioned as a guildhall for those merchants. Because the original temple was built by a native of Fujian and Tianhou was a Fujianese goddess, the temple was also referred to as the Fujian Temple. After the reconstruction it was renamed Qingan Guildhall, in order to celebrate the goddess responsible for pacifying the raging sea. It is the most magnificent building in Ningbo, and for Thomson the finest example of temple architecture in China. Huiguan or Guildhall was an important institution during the Ming and Qing periods, a place where people from the same profession or region could meet. In the imperial capital, Beijing, some of the guildhalls also provided accommodation for those who had travelled to the capital for imperial examinations.

Buddhist Priests at Yongquan Monastery, Drum Mountain

Fuzhou, Fujian

Yongquan monastery is situated seven miles from Fuzhou, halfway up Drum Mountain. It was thought to have been built in the 9th century and then rebuilt several times during the Ming and Qing era. One of the most magnificent religious buildings in Fujian, it was an important centre for studying Mahayana Buddhism. At the time of Thomson's visit, about 200 monks lived there and he was intrigued by their robes which he thought bore a close resemblance to the monastic robes of medieval Europe.

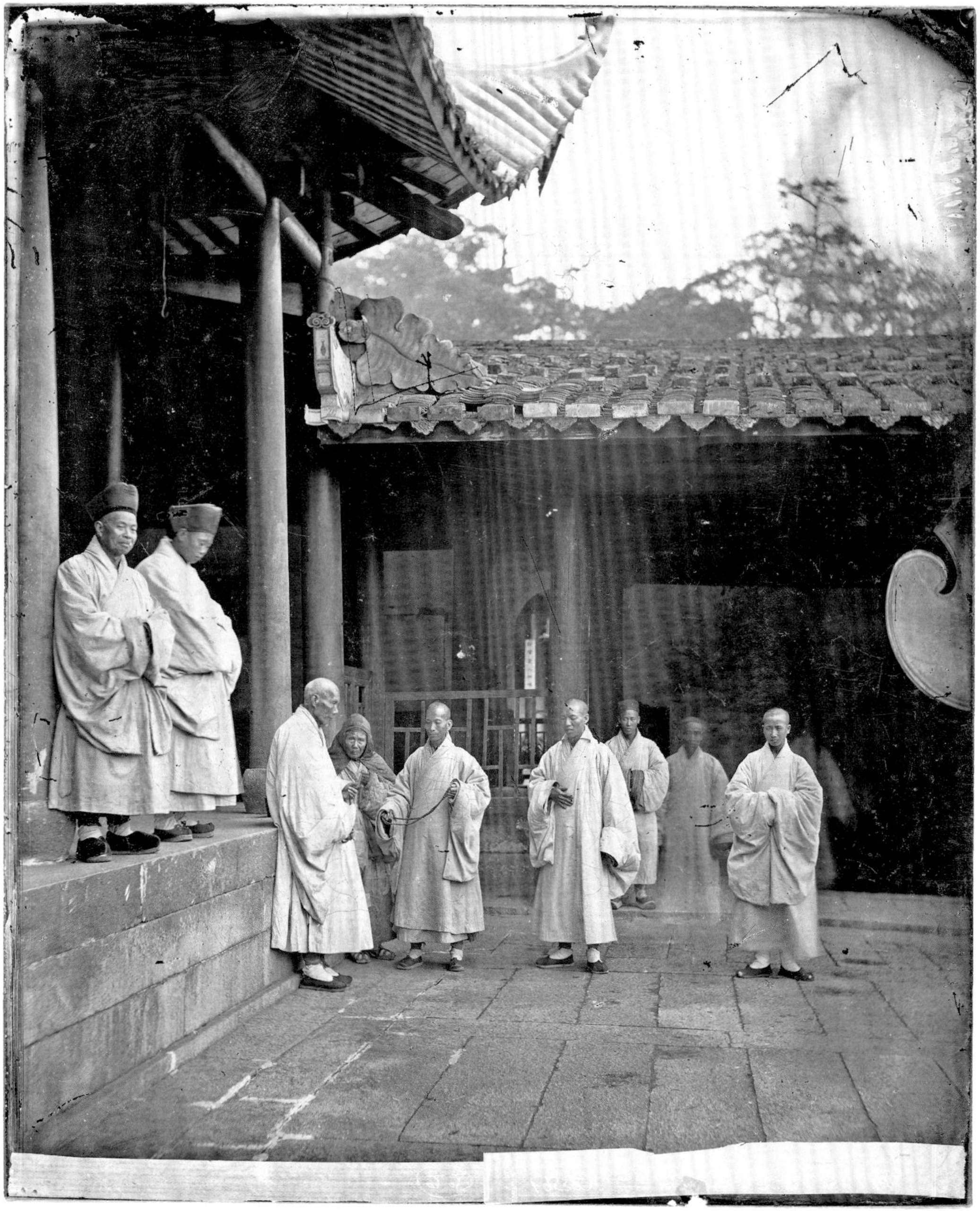

SOUTHERN PUTUO MONASTERY

Xiamen, Fujian

Southern Putuo Monastery is one of the most important Buddhist sanctuaries in Fujian. It was first built in the early 15th century though its history can be traced back to the Tang Dynasty (618-907). It is dedicated to Guanyin, the goddess of Mercy, as is the monastery at Putuo Mountain in Zhejiang. As a result it was given the name Southern Putuo Monastery. Over the years the site has continued to expand and has become a large complex today. It is one of the most important Buddhist teaching institutions in present-day China.

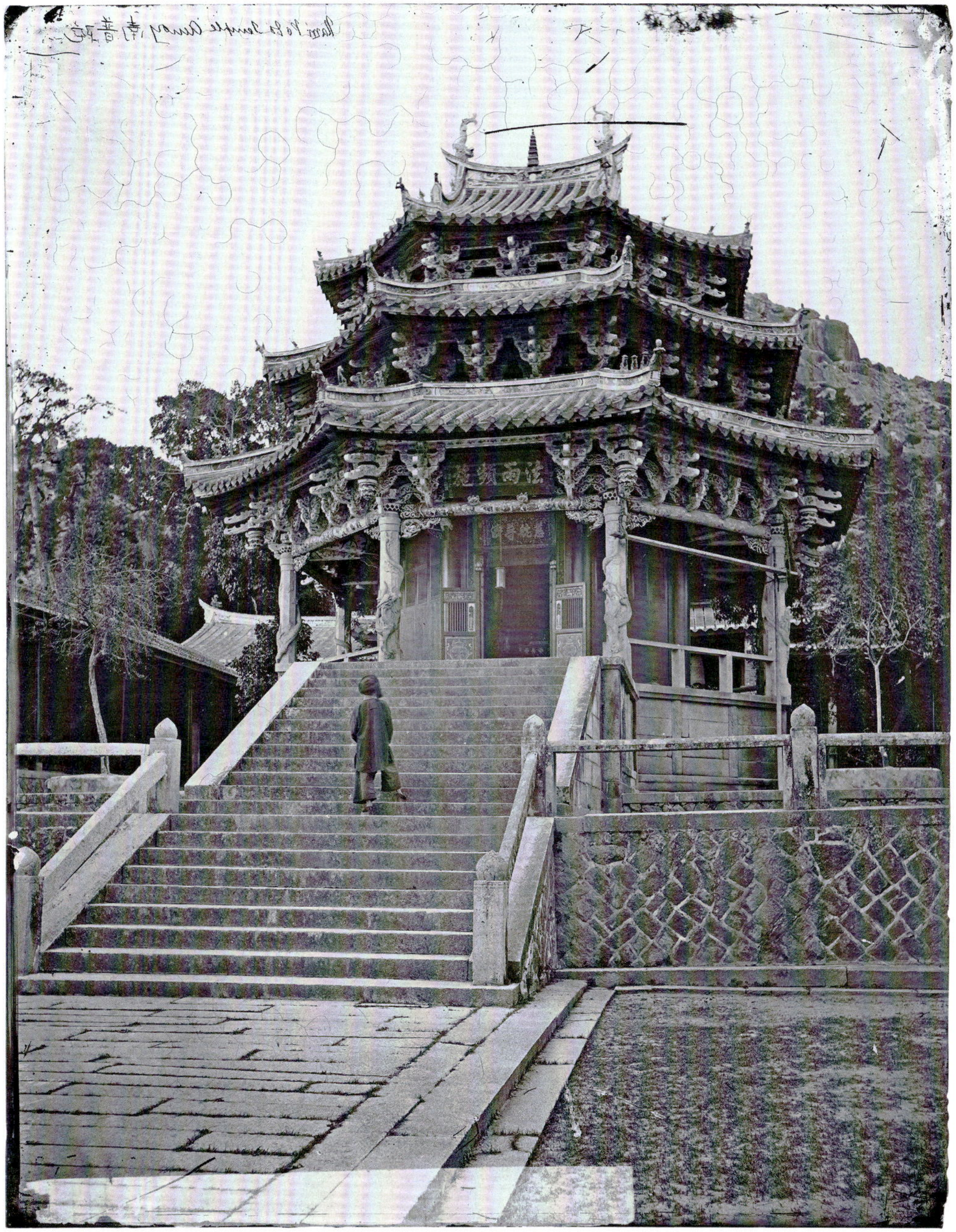

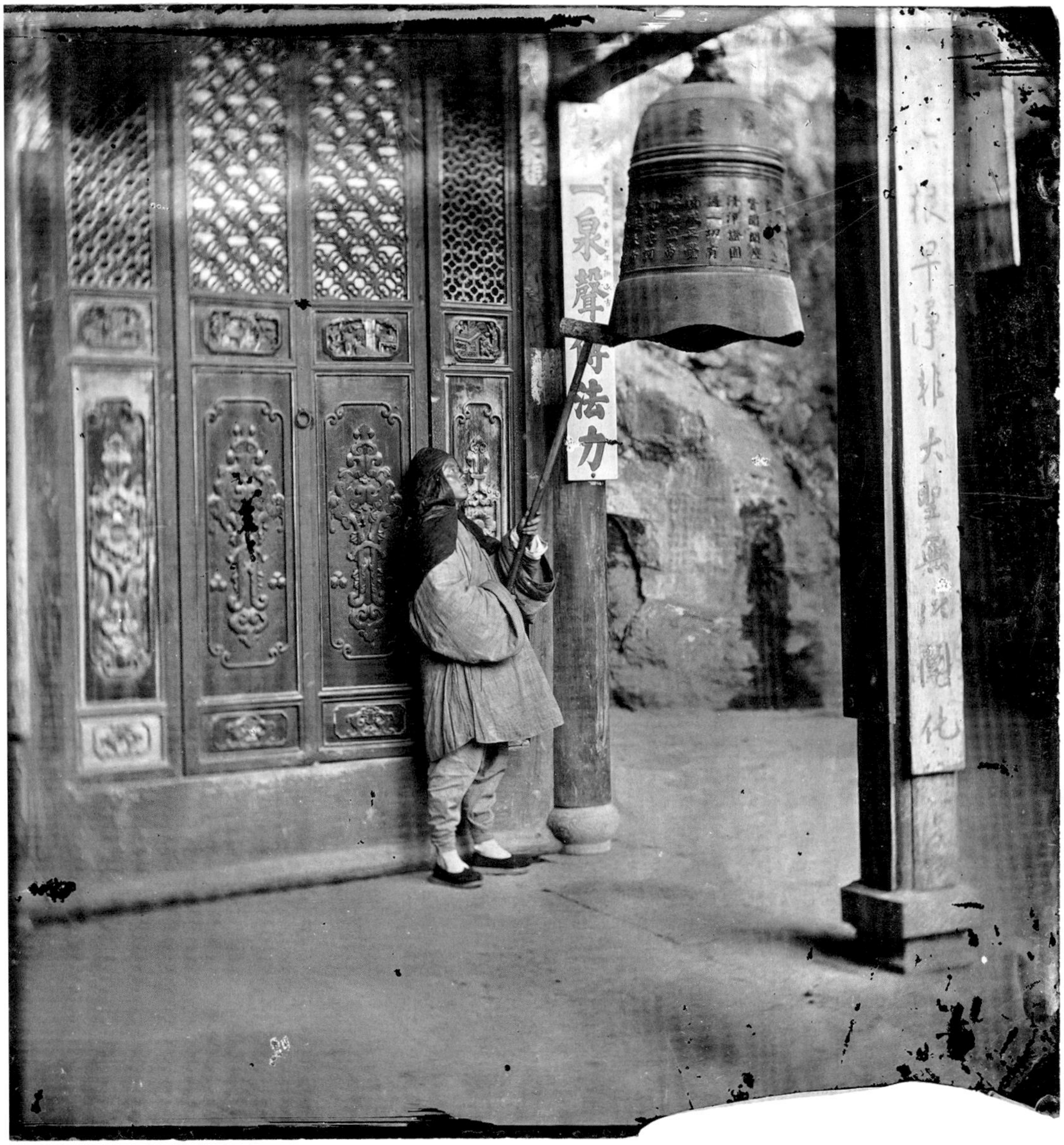

Bell ringing at Fang-guang-yan Monastery

Fujian

Thomson's trip to Fang-Guang-Yan monastery is regarded by some as the most artistically accomplished of all his photographic journeys. Situated at the summit of a high mountain, the monastery is almost as difficult to reach as it is to enter the 'Heavenly door'. In addition to the location, Thomson was deeply impressed by the architecture: '*It looks like nothing I have ever seen or dreamed of seeing, with its broad eaves, carved roofs and ornamented railing painted in the brightest hues.*' Of his stay there, he recalled that each morning he was awoken by the monks chanting or by the ringing of the bell, as seen here.

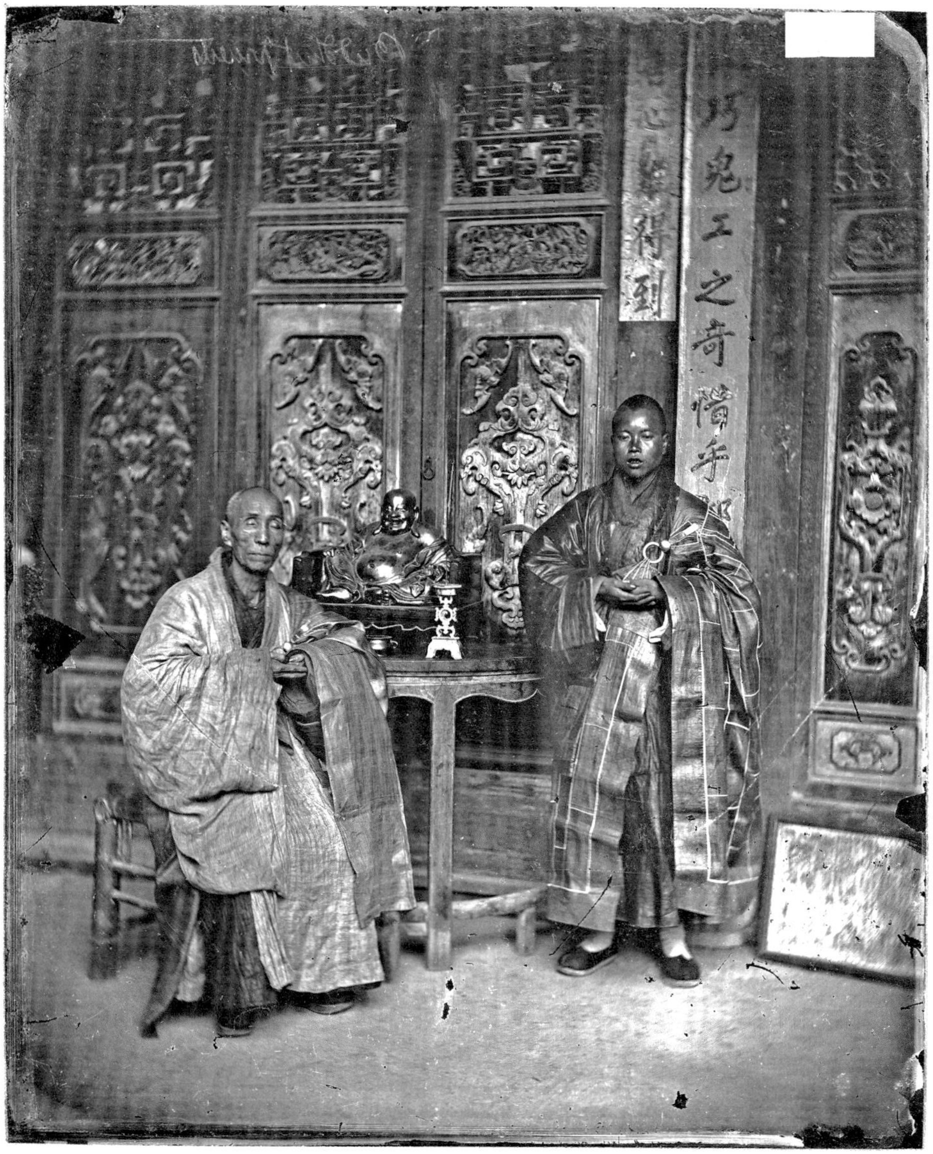

Two Buddhist Priests at Fang-guang-yan Monastery

Fujian

Fang-Guang-Yan monastery is in Yongtai county about 30 kilometres from Fuzhou, on the upper reach of the Min River. It was for Thomson the most interesting of all the sites near Fuzhou. During his visit, he befriended three monks there. The old priest shown in this photograph was blind and, according to Thomson, quite infirm. The younger one however was an '*able bodied, good natured youth*'. Thomson also noted how these monks would keep to their strict daily rituals.

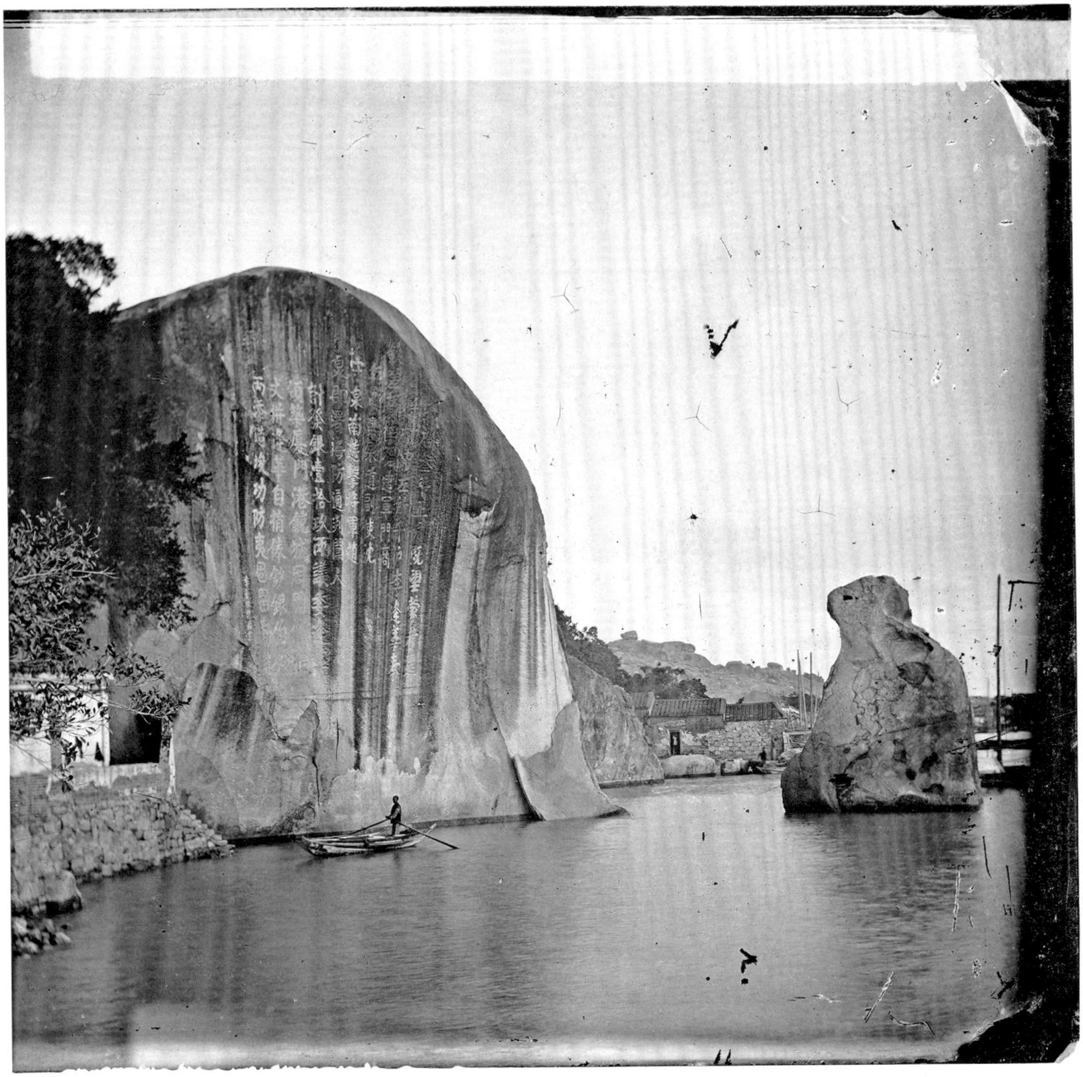

Riguang Rock

Xiamen, Fujian

Riguang Rock or 'Sunshine Rock' was allegedly given its name by a local hero, the anti-Qing Zheng Chenggong. It is the most prominent rock in a series of rocks that crown the hills by the harbour of Xiamen, on the island of Gulangyu. It is engraved with text passages connected with the area's history. Many believed the rocks were closely linked to local feng-shui, so were greatly revered, in the hope that they would bring good fortune to the port.

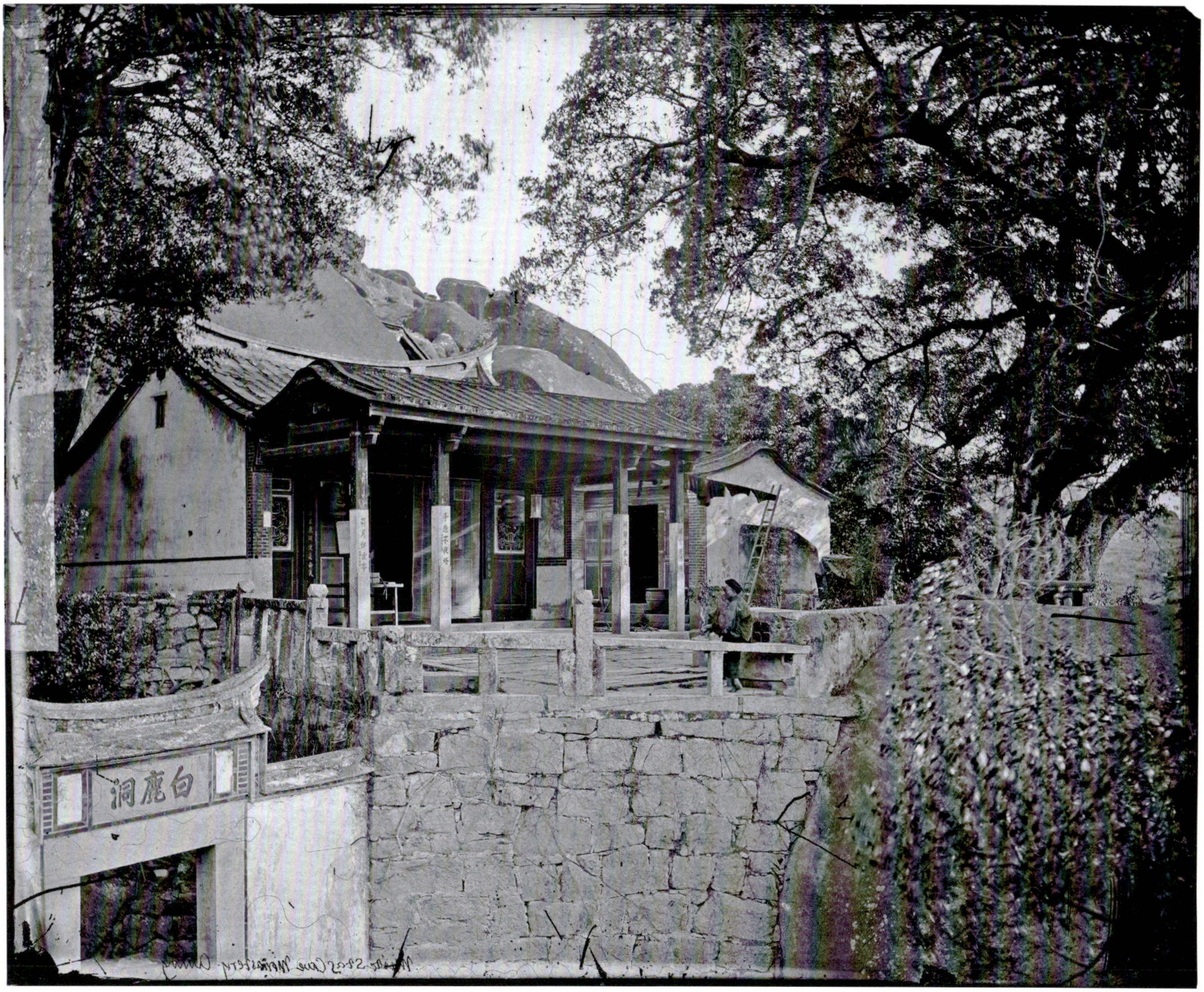

WHITE DEER GROTTO

Xiamen, Fujian

Situated on the Yueping Hill in Xiamen, White Deer Grotto was thought to have once been the home of the celebrated Neo-Confucian scholar Zhu Xi. Zhu Xi was closely connected to the famous White Deer Academy in Jiangxi, which gave its name to the building. Just as White Deer Academy was established as a place for scholarly retreat, White Deer Grotto has long been a favourite place for a summer retreat. According to Thomson, the site enjoyed a commanding view of Xiamen.

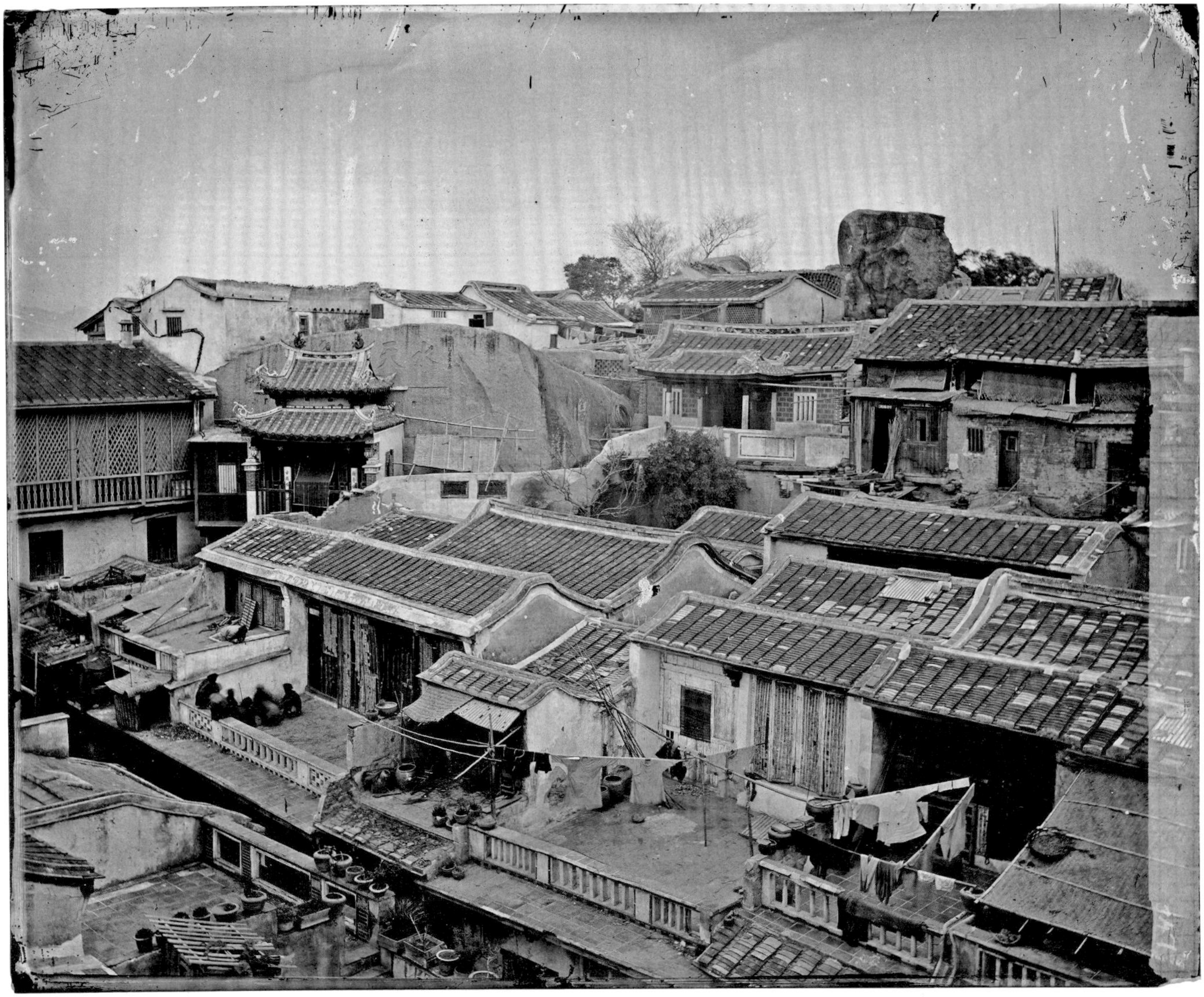

RESIDENTIAL QUARTER

Xiamen, Fujian

Although modern day Xiamen is regarded as a historic and romantic coastal city, in the second half of the 19th century it was seriously dilapidated. Houses in the city itself were crowded and ramshackle, with many in a terrible state of decay. Thomson wrote that the long, dark and narrow streets, paved with cobblestones, were so worn and loose that '*they rest for the most part in treacherous pits of mud . . . if a foot be placed hastily on the rocking flag, a shower of most offensive dirt is splashed up over one's clothes*'. Wealthy merchants and Europeans owned a few handsome houses which were situated either on the top of the hill away from the city or on the island of Gulangyu.

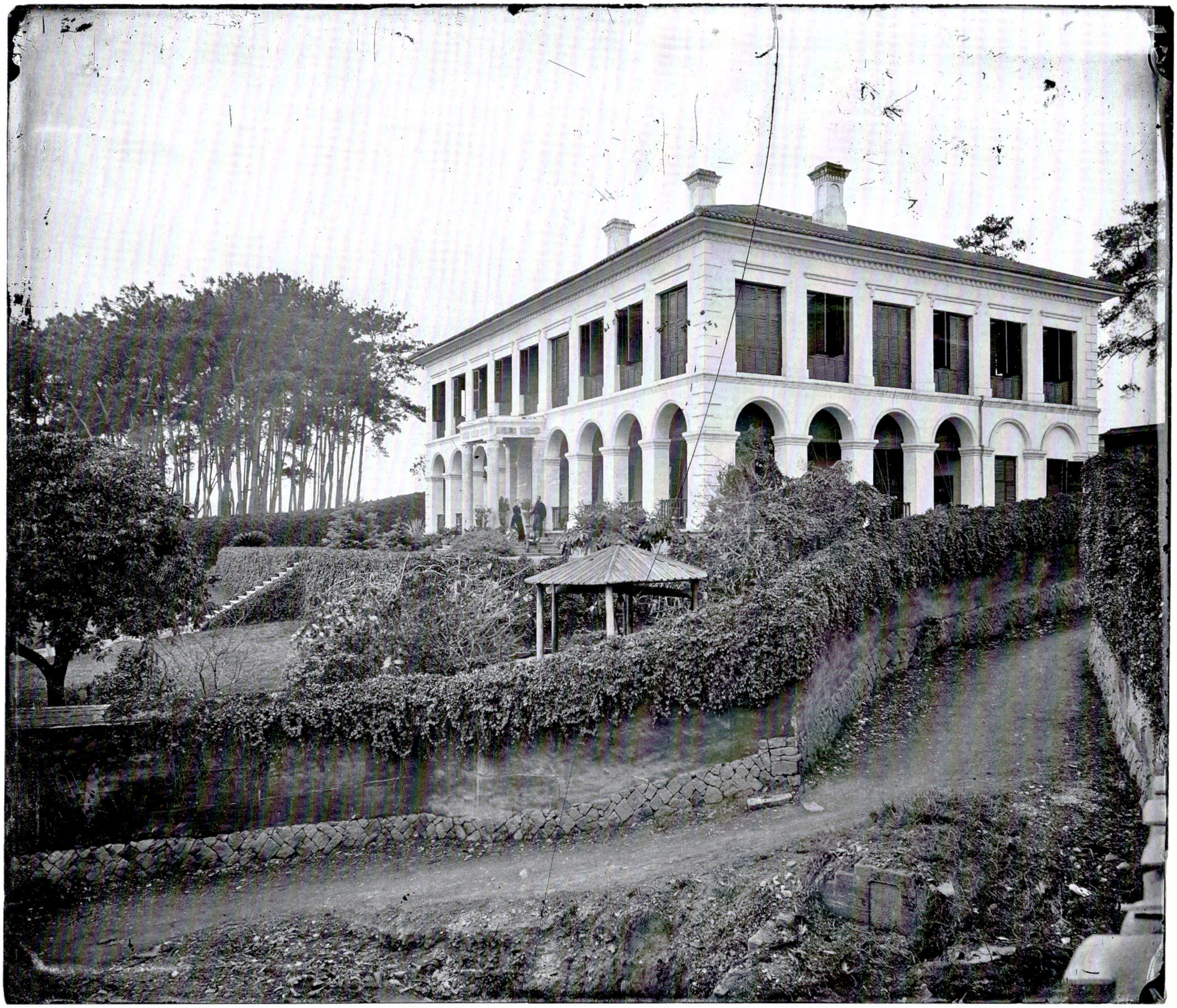

A Colonial-Style House

Fuzhou, Fujian

By the time of Thomson's visit, Fuzhou had a well-established foreign settlement. Thomson wrote that Fuzhou was '*picturesquely situated on eminences which command extensive views of the country around . . . Many varieties of European flowers and vegetables are grown here to great perfection by the Chinese gardeners. It is altogether a sort of place where foreigners may well be content to reside.*' This photograph shows the owners of the house standing by the imposing entrance.

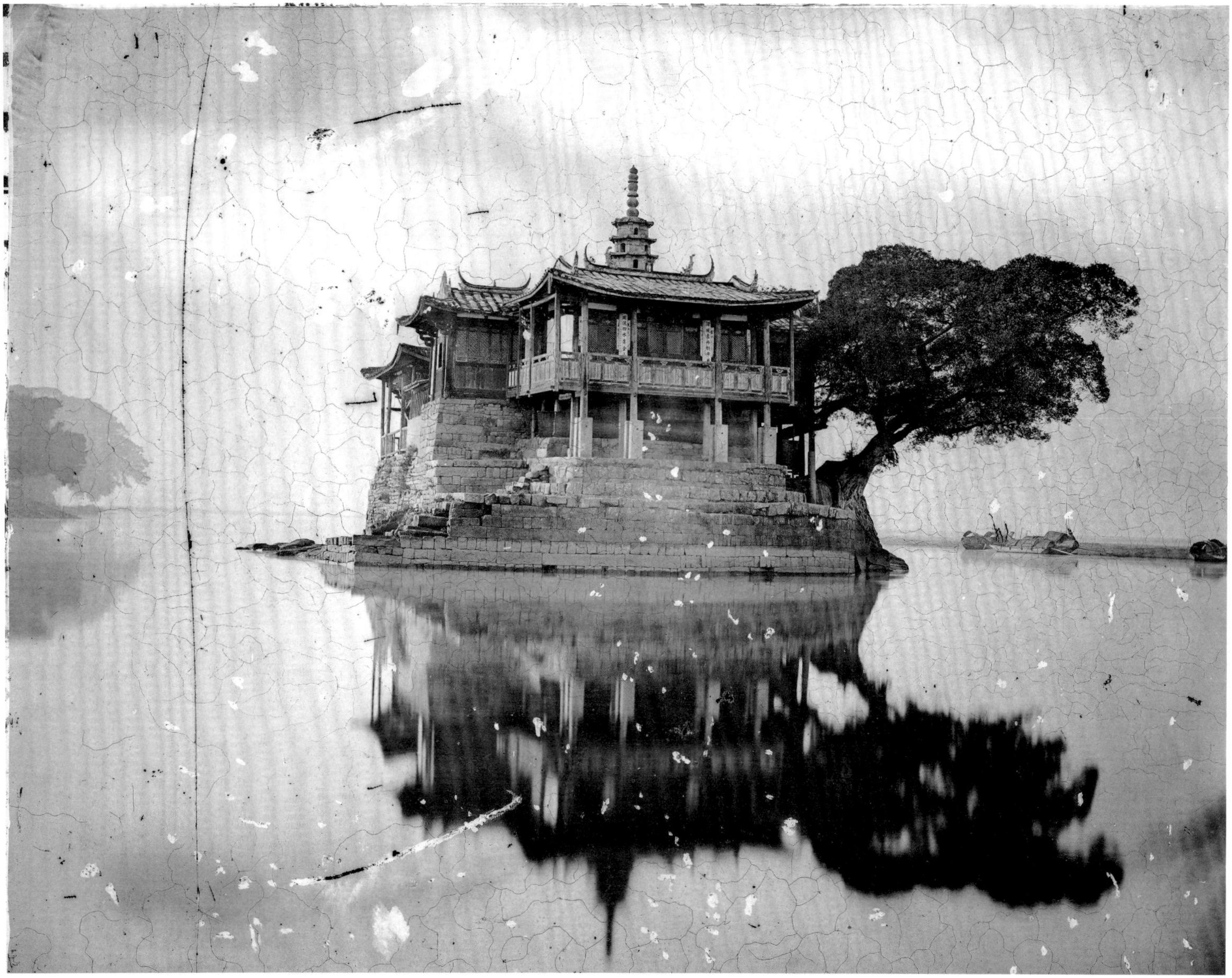

JINSHAN TEMPLE, RIVER MIN

Fuzhou, Fujian

Jinshan Temple, or the 'Pagoda Anchorage', as Thomson called it, is situated on the River Min, just west of Fuzhou. This is the only temple in Fujian to sit on water and has become a tourist attraction today. Thomson, perhaps inspired by Taoist and Buddhist landscape art, framed the island so that it appears to exist in isolation and captured the stillness of the water which contributes to the effect of near-perfect serenity.

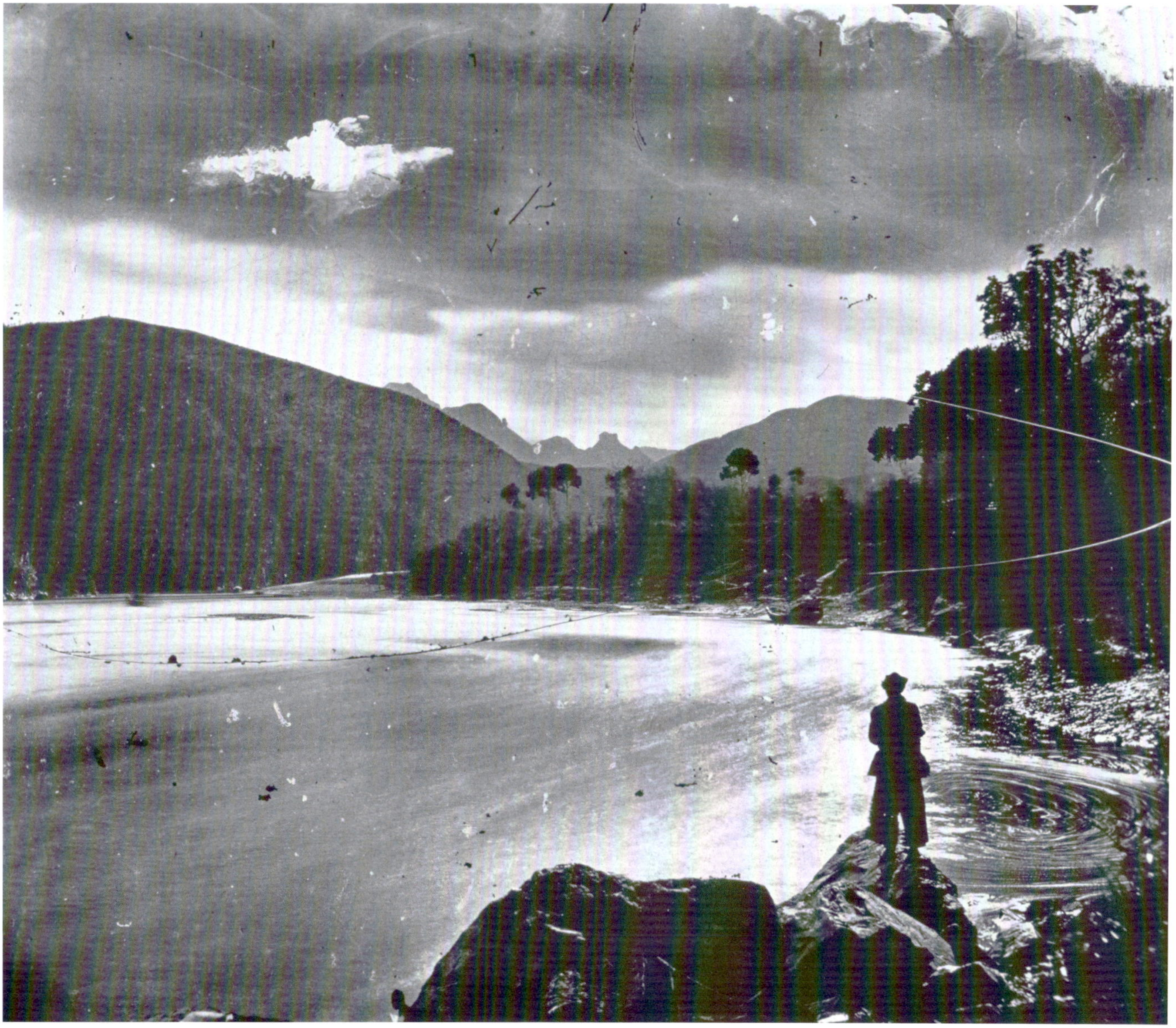

RIVER MIN

Fujian

During his visit to Fujian, Thomson was captivated by the beauty of the River Min. This is a photograph of the Yuen Fu Rapid with a solitary figure in silhouette and the Wuhu or 'Five Tiger' Mountains in the background. It is here that the river widens into a basin with narrow openings at either end.

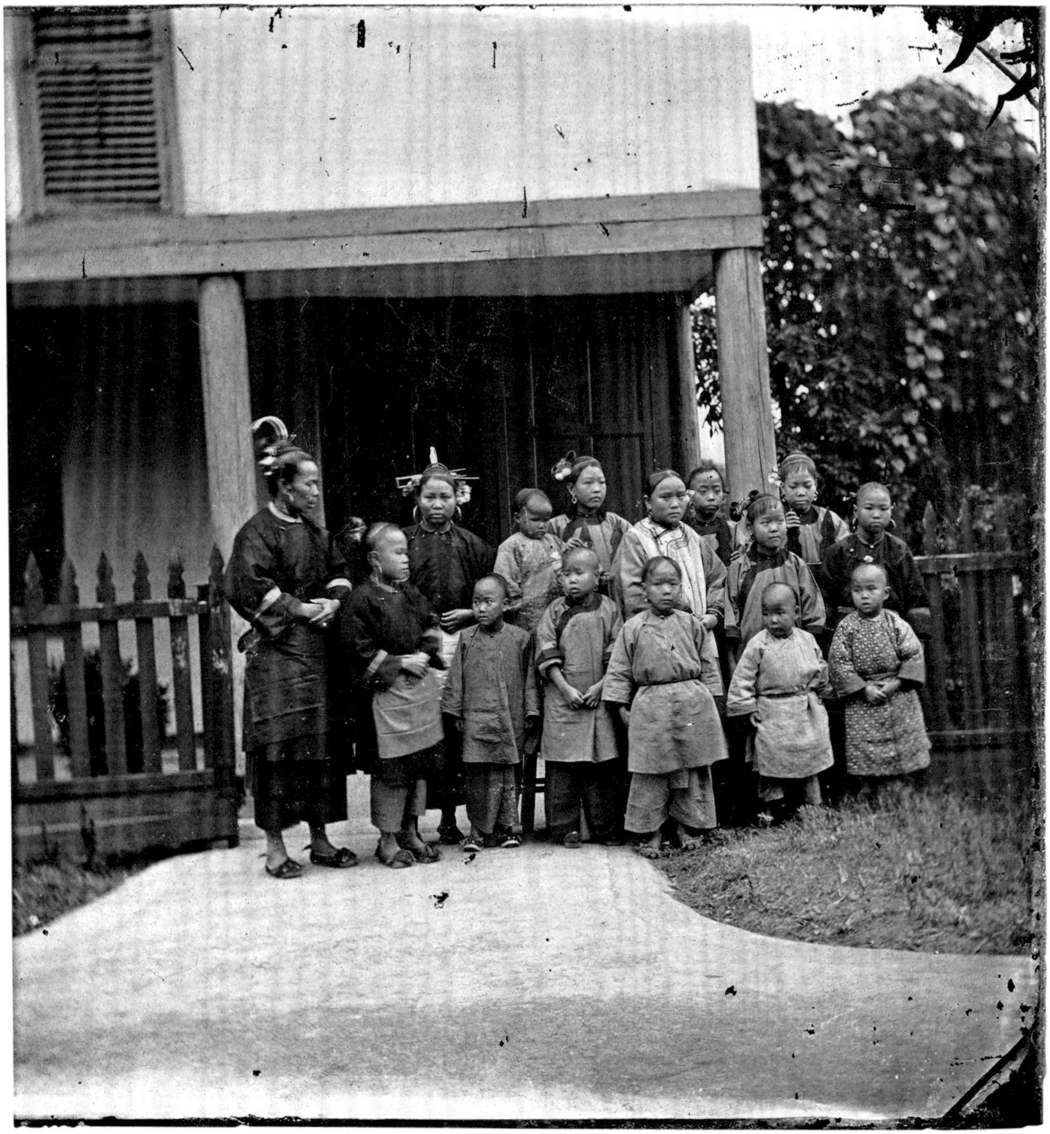

Women and Children from a Tea Plantation

Fuzhou, Fujian

Fuzhou was the main centre for tea production and export, the countryside dotted with plantations. Thomson visited one with terraced hills about 15 miles north of Fuzhou. There the farms were usually only a few acres. The plots were leased to the poor, with the landlords paying the land tax. Tenants had to sell their crops to the landowners at stipulated prices. The fields could yield three crops a year and many locals grew tea because it was the most valued cash crop. The industry employed thousands of poor women and children like those shown here.

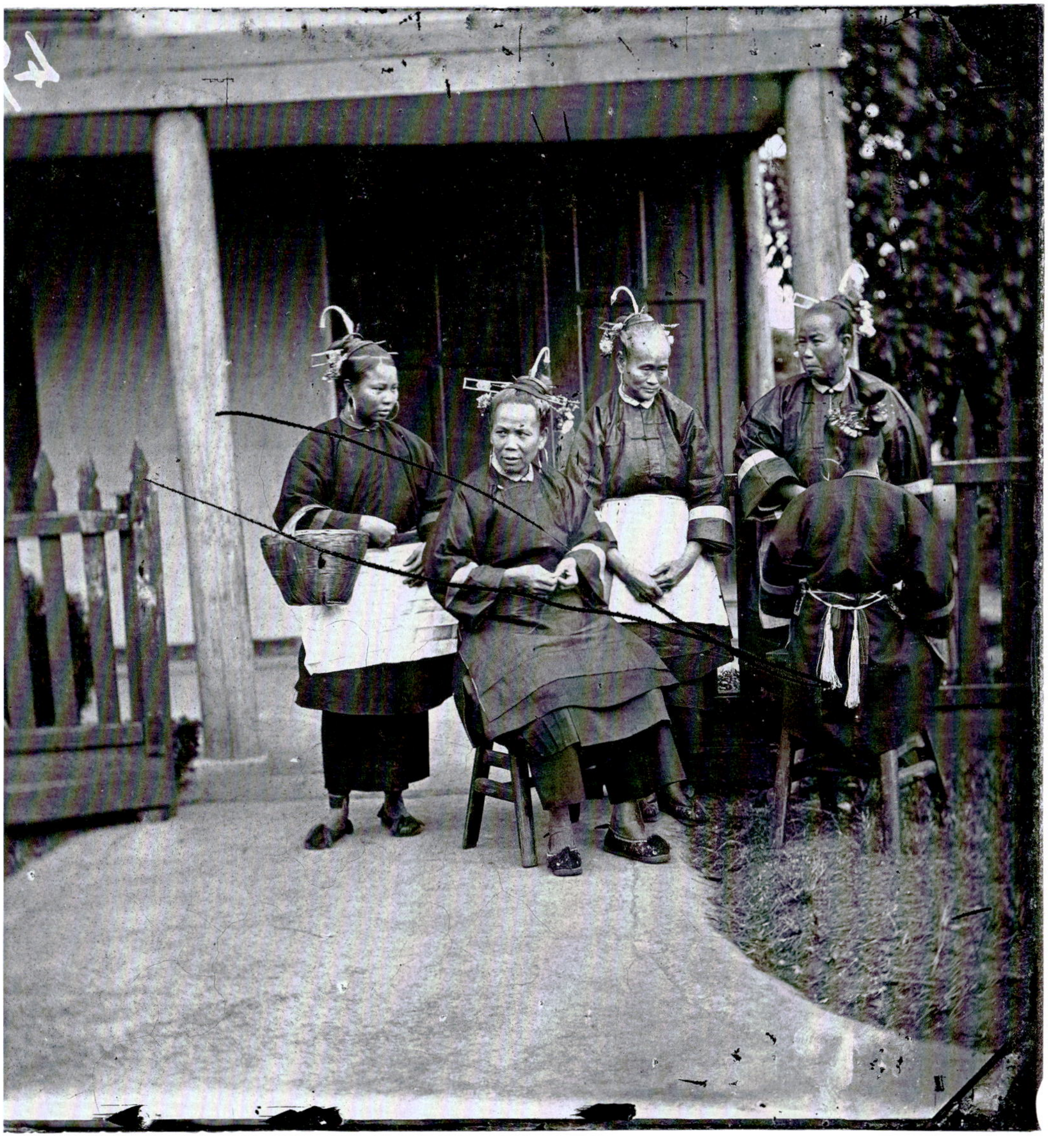

Indigenous Women from Fujian at a Tea Plantation

Fuzhou, Fujian

This group of women were employed by a local tea plantation to work on farms just outside Fuzhou. Thomson admired their appearance, which was strong and healthy. He found them attractive: '*their glossy black hair is decked with silver ornaments and fresh flowers. Their dress is simple and remarkable for its bright cleanliness. They never bound their feet, but rather draw the eye to their natural smallness by wearing prettily embroidered shoes.*'

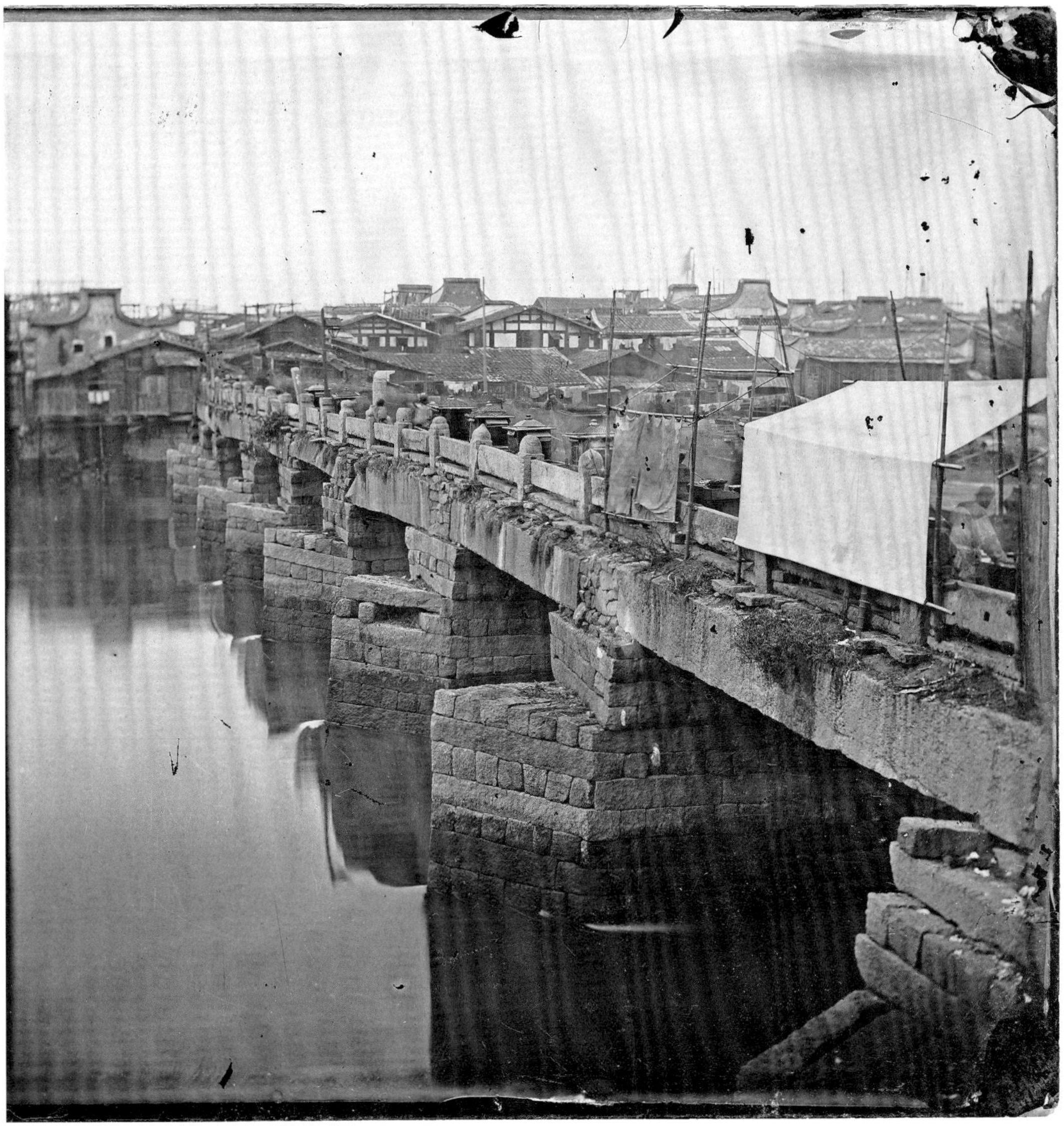

Long View of Wanshou Bridge

Fuzhou, Fujian

This photograph shows the immense size of the bridge, a remarkable technical achievement. At around one quarter of a mile long it featured nearly forty solid stone buttresses. Some of the stones are almost 3 feet square, and 45 feet in length extending from buttress to buttress and acting as sleepers. Above these stone sleepers is a granite platform. Strong stone railings on the sides of the bridge are fastened to stone pillars.

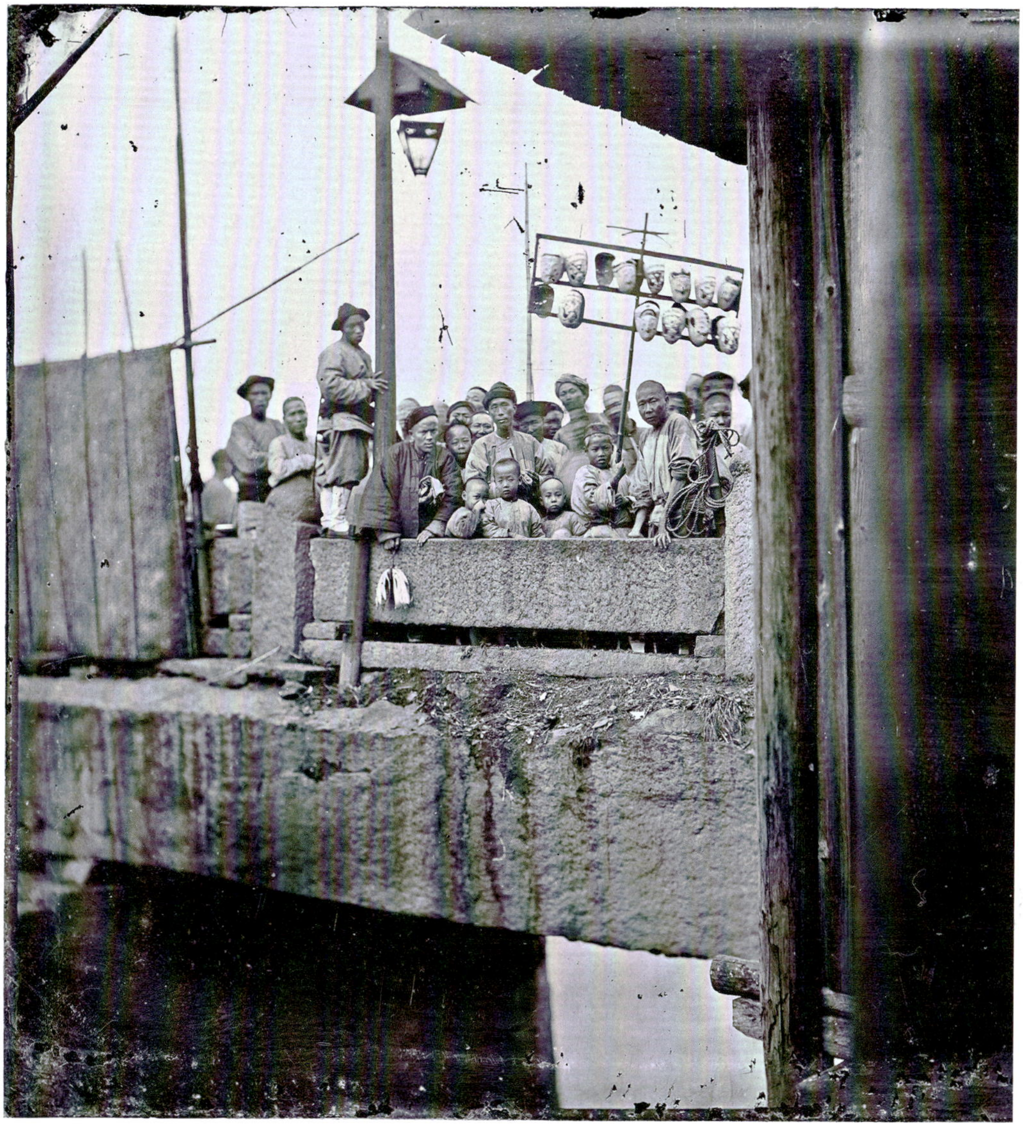

View of Wanshou Bridge

Fuzhou, Fujian

Wanshou Bridge, the bridge of 'Ten Thousand Ages', was thought to have been built in the 9th century. Originally there were shops on this bridge, but by the time of Thomson's visit, it was used solely by pedestrians and for transporting goods. Here we see a large crowd of curious onlookers, including a young boy holding a frame selling colourful face masks, watching Thomson taking his photograph. Thomson perhaps was trying to show the ingenuity of ancient China, whose people were able to build such a colossal structure, one that brought great convenience to local life.

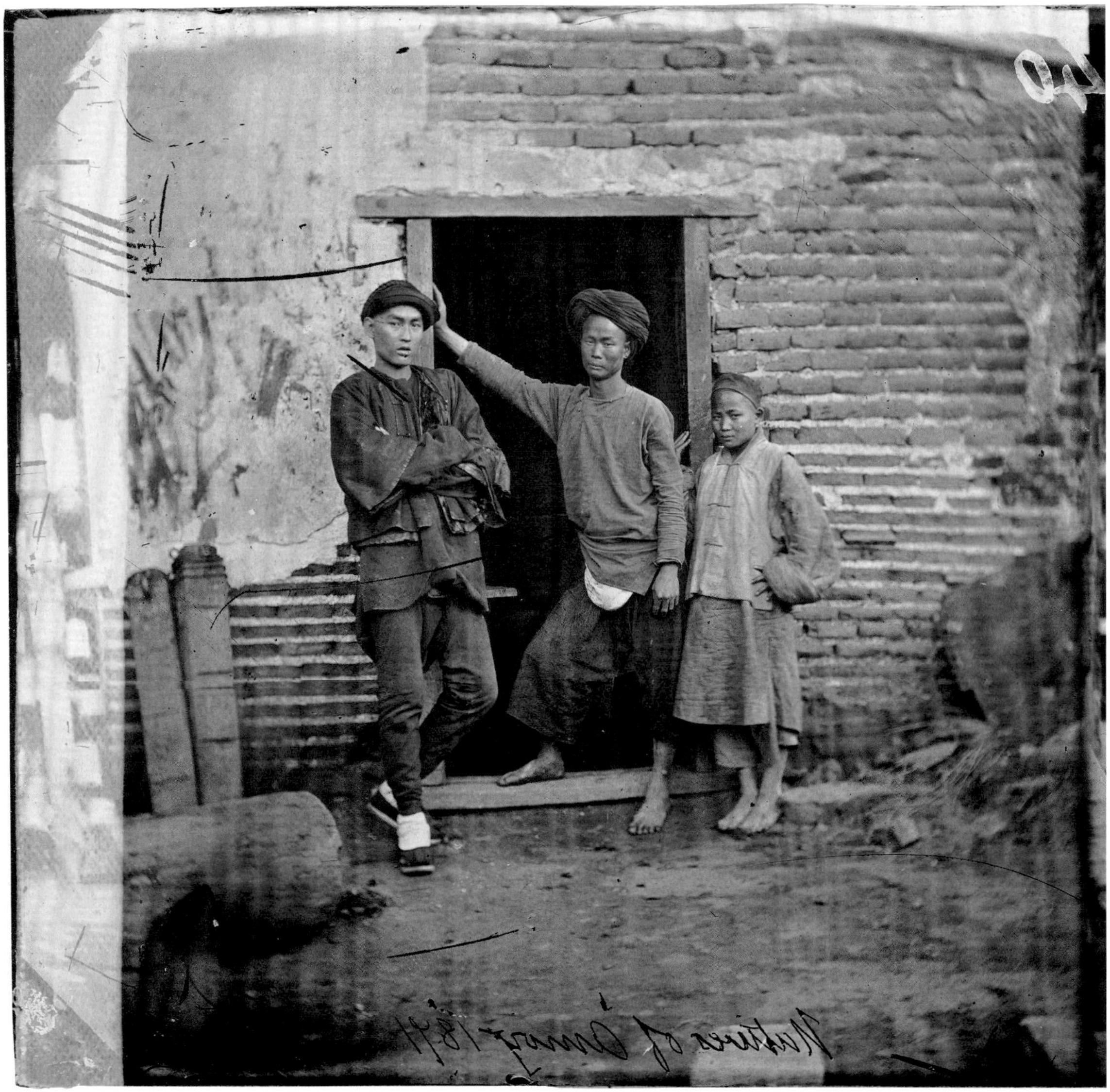

Amoy People

Xiamen, Fujian

Within the Qing empire, Amoy men were known to be rebels or 'southern rascals', who frequently caused problems for the authorities. Although the Manchu had finally conquered the region, many local people continued to maintain a separate identity. Not only did they speak a different dialect, but they also dressed in a different style. Here two men wear turbans to hide the 'queues' (plaited hair) imposed on them by the Manchu. According to Thomson, both men were local '*coolies*' (labourers).

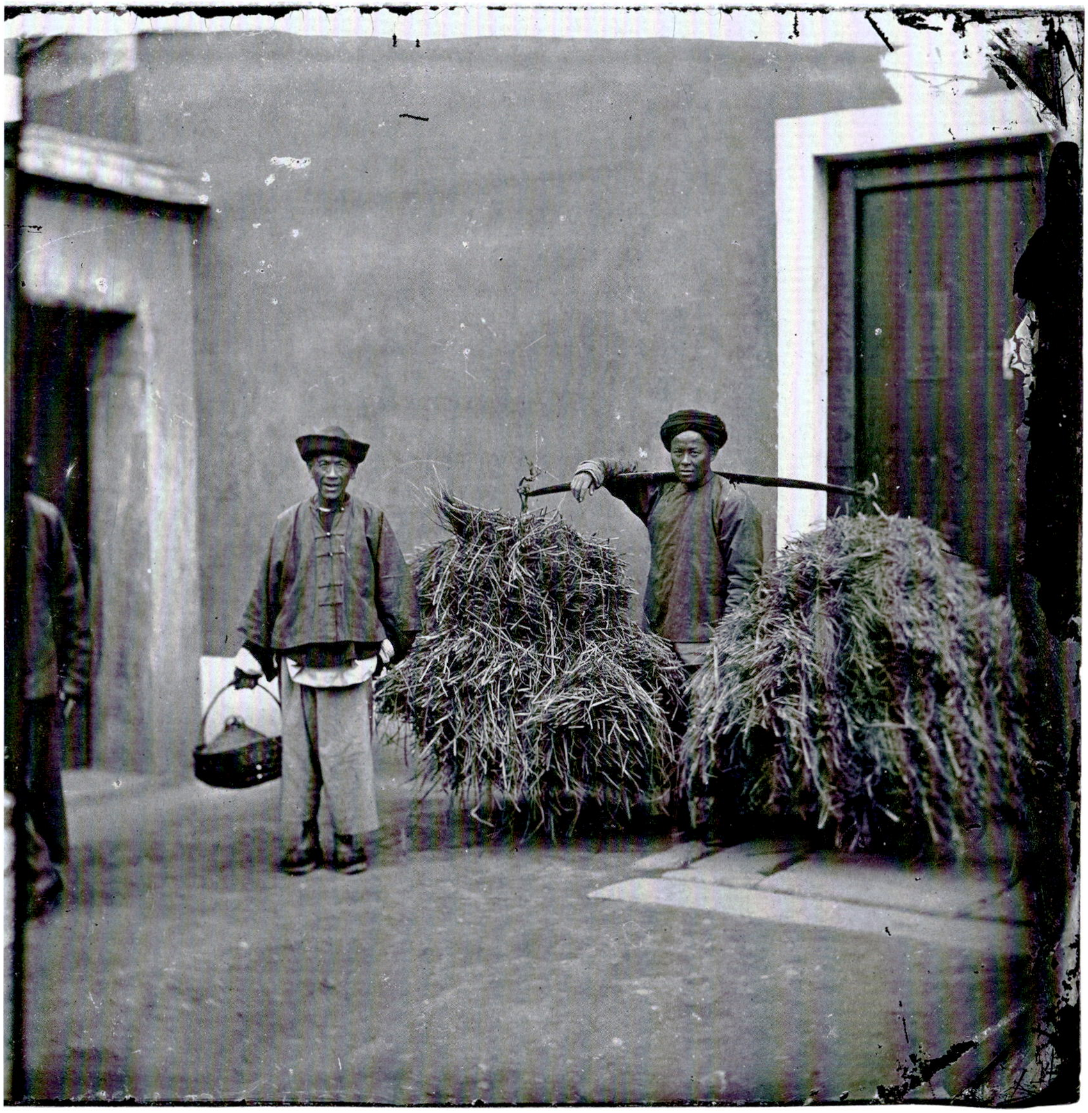

TWO FIELD LABOURERS IN AMOY

Xiamen, Fujian

Two field labourers pose for the camera, one carrying bales of straw on his shoulder, the other with a food container. According to Thomson, people in the Amoy area were very poor: '*an able-bodied man earned five pence a day, while skilled workmen were only paid about eight pence*'. Poverty, famine, anger at official corruption and a strong dislike of the Qing rulers forced many to seek work abroad. From the mid-19th century there was a growing demand for labour from the Americas, Southeast Asia and Australia. Chinese labourers were highly prized for agriculture, construction, and mining work.

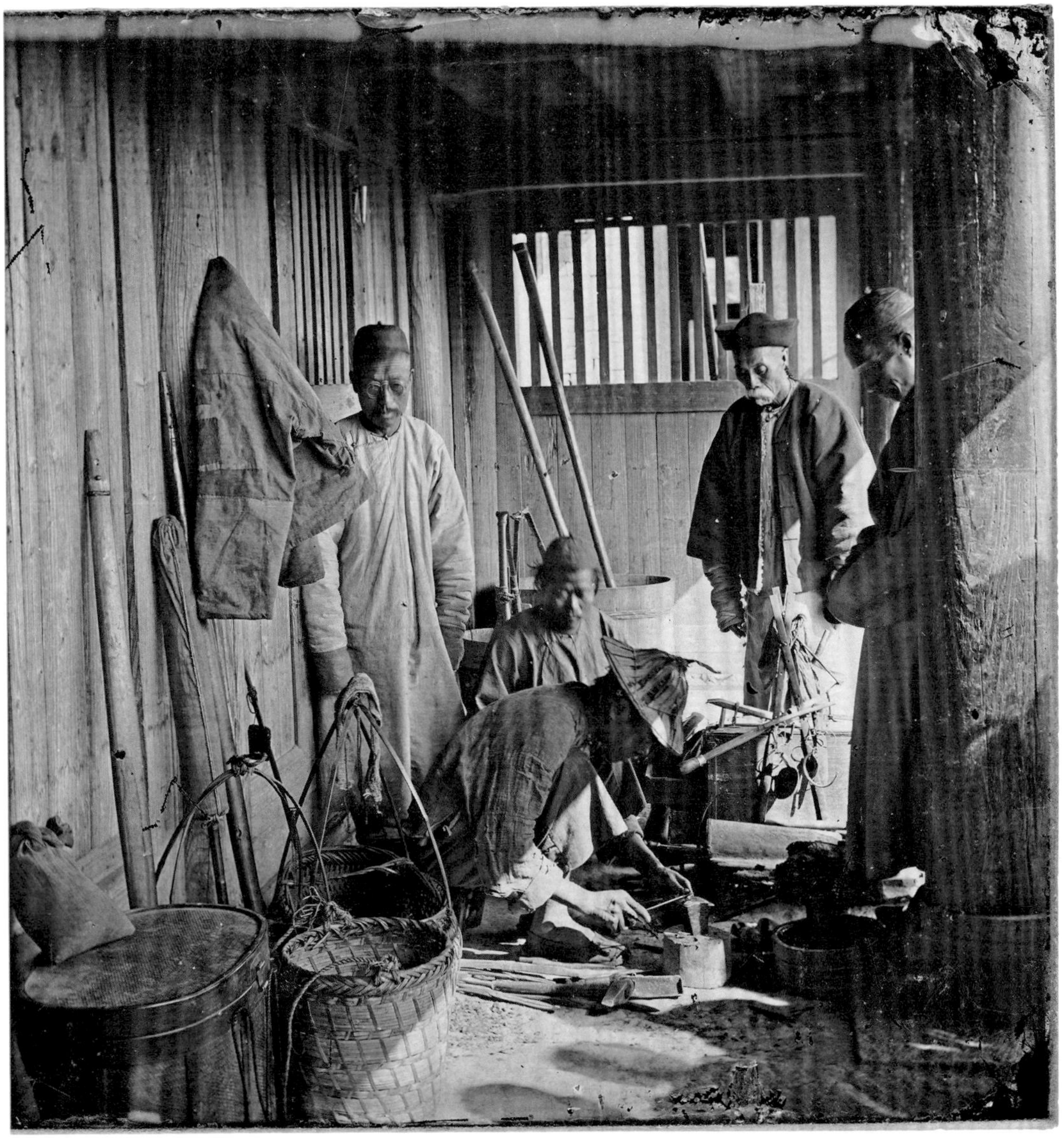

A CHINESE COPPERSMITH AT WORK IN HIS SHOP

Fuzhou, Fujian

Throughout his journeys in China, Thomson was always impressed by the ingenious feats of workmanship he encountered, and the fact that so many craftsmen could produce wonders in front of their humble doorways. He praised the artisan as highly respectable and indispensable, 'never ashamed of his craft or the music that rings from his anvil'. One such is this coppersmith he visited in Fuzhou, who was able to 'take full advantage of the ductility of the metal . . . by beating it from flat sheets into the most varied and complex forms'.

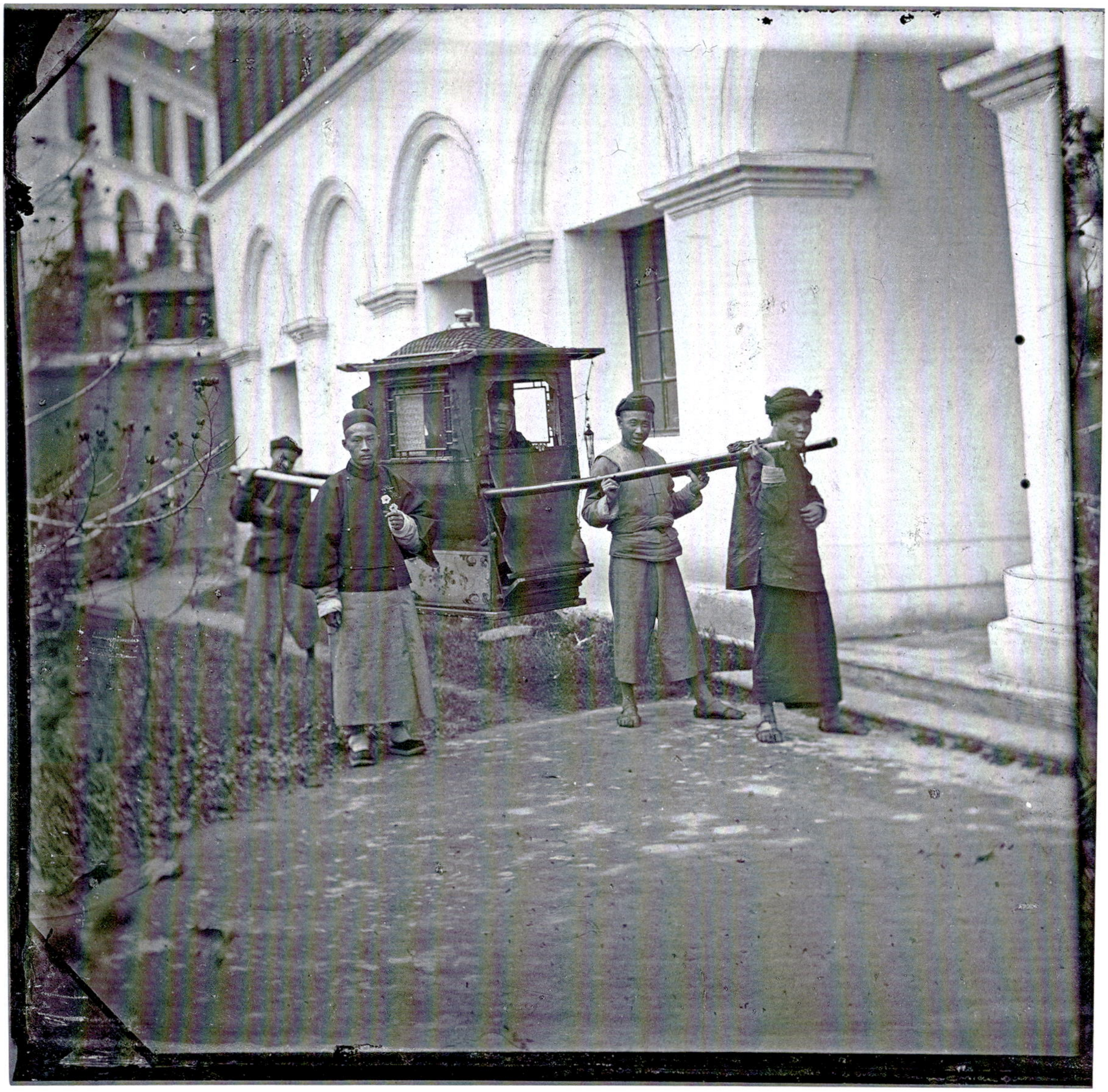

A Sedan Chair

Fujian

Until the advent of modern motorized vehicles, the sedan chair was one of the main means of transport in China, with Mandarin officials and people of wealth and rank keeping their own private sedans. Mandarin officials would indicate their rank by placing certain marks on the frame and cover of the sedan. The number of bearers and footmen in attendance were also indicators of rank. Sedan chairs could be hired, just as taxis are today.

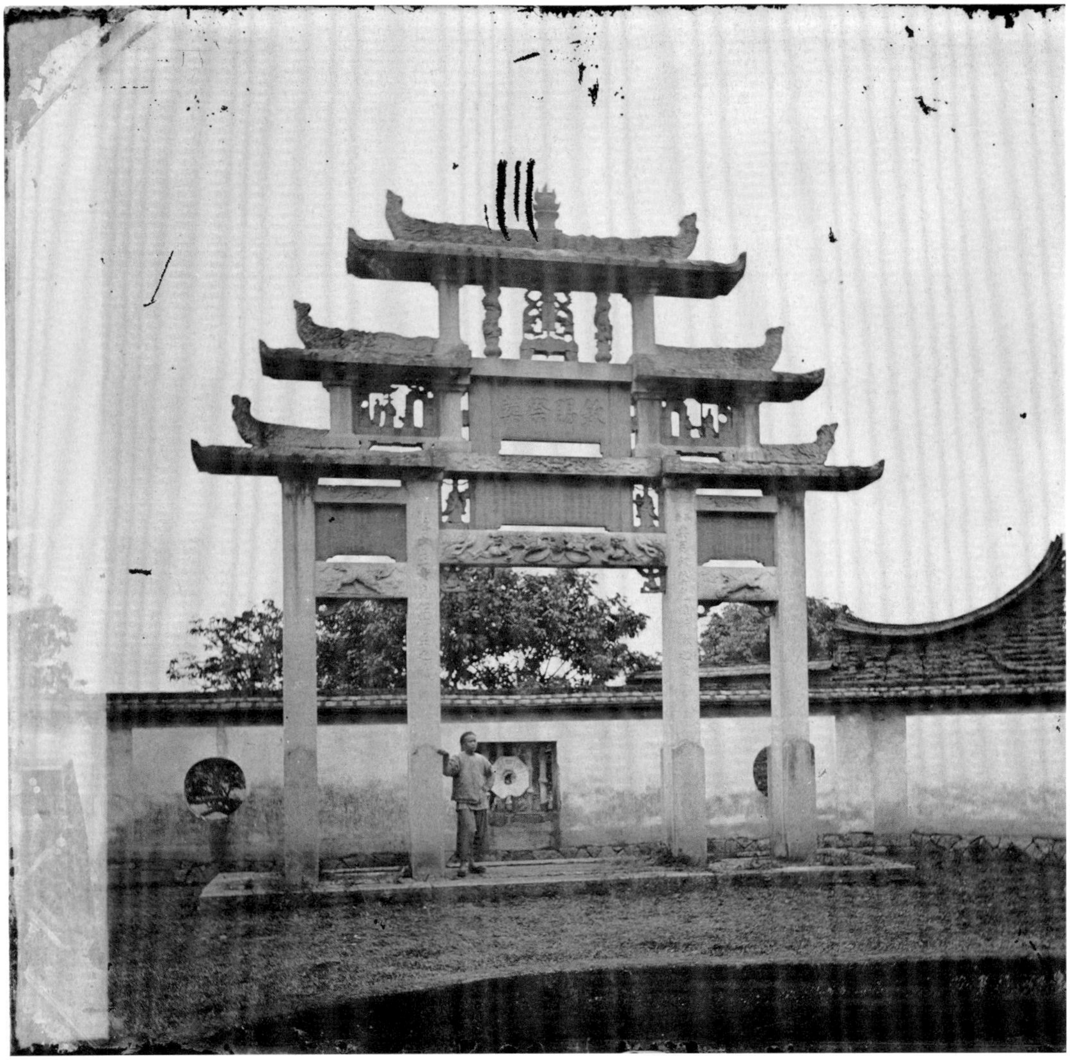

A *Pailou* Dedicated to a Virtuous Widow

Fujian

A *pailou* is an ornamental memorial arch set up in memory of the noble deeds or virtues of the deceased. In imperial China it could only be erected with special permission from the emperor. If a wealthy man had done something remarkable, he might during his lifetime erect a *pailou* for himself at his own expense. A virtuous widow, however, who had reached the age of 50 without remarrying might be permitted to erect an arch to commemorate her life, and the imperial treasury would provide a small sum. This type of *pailou* can commonly be seen in rural China, in particular the areas between Fujian, Zhejiang and Jiangxi. This practice is thought to have begun in the 11th century with the emergence of neo-Confucianism. According to Cheng Yi (1033–1107), a renowned Neo-Confucian scholar, it was better for a widow to starve to death than to remarry.

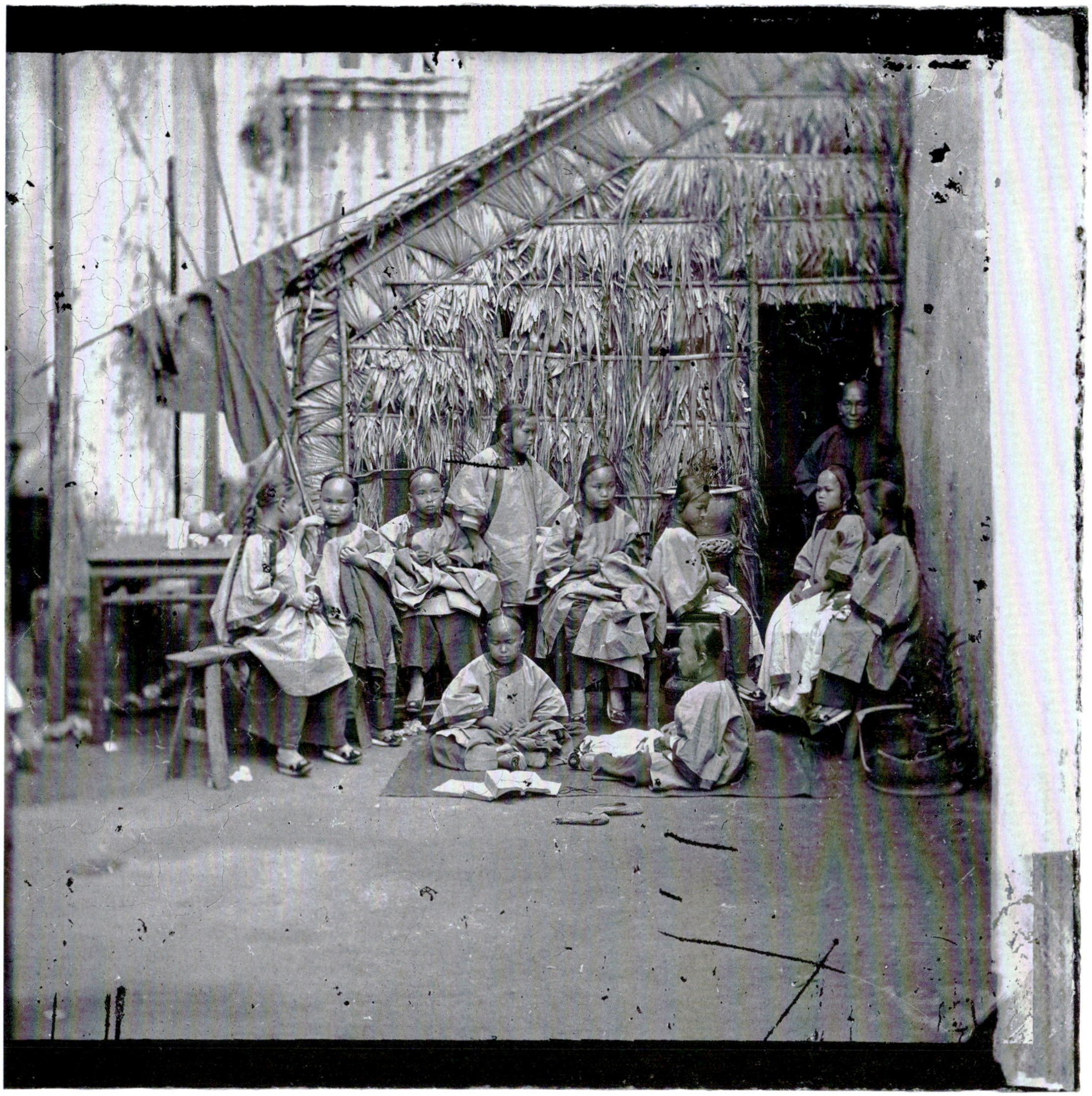

A Foundling Hospital

Xiamen, Fujian

In the 19th century as result of extreme poverty and war, parents who were unable to care for their children would send them to orphanages. Female infanticide was particularly high in Xiamen. A local merchant set up a foundling hospital to care for unwanted children. Often the locals sold their girls to the hospital for as little as five pence, whereas a boy might fetch as much as three pounds. Anyone wishing to adopt could go to the hospital and be given a child free of charge, provided they could prove their '*respectability*'.

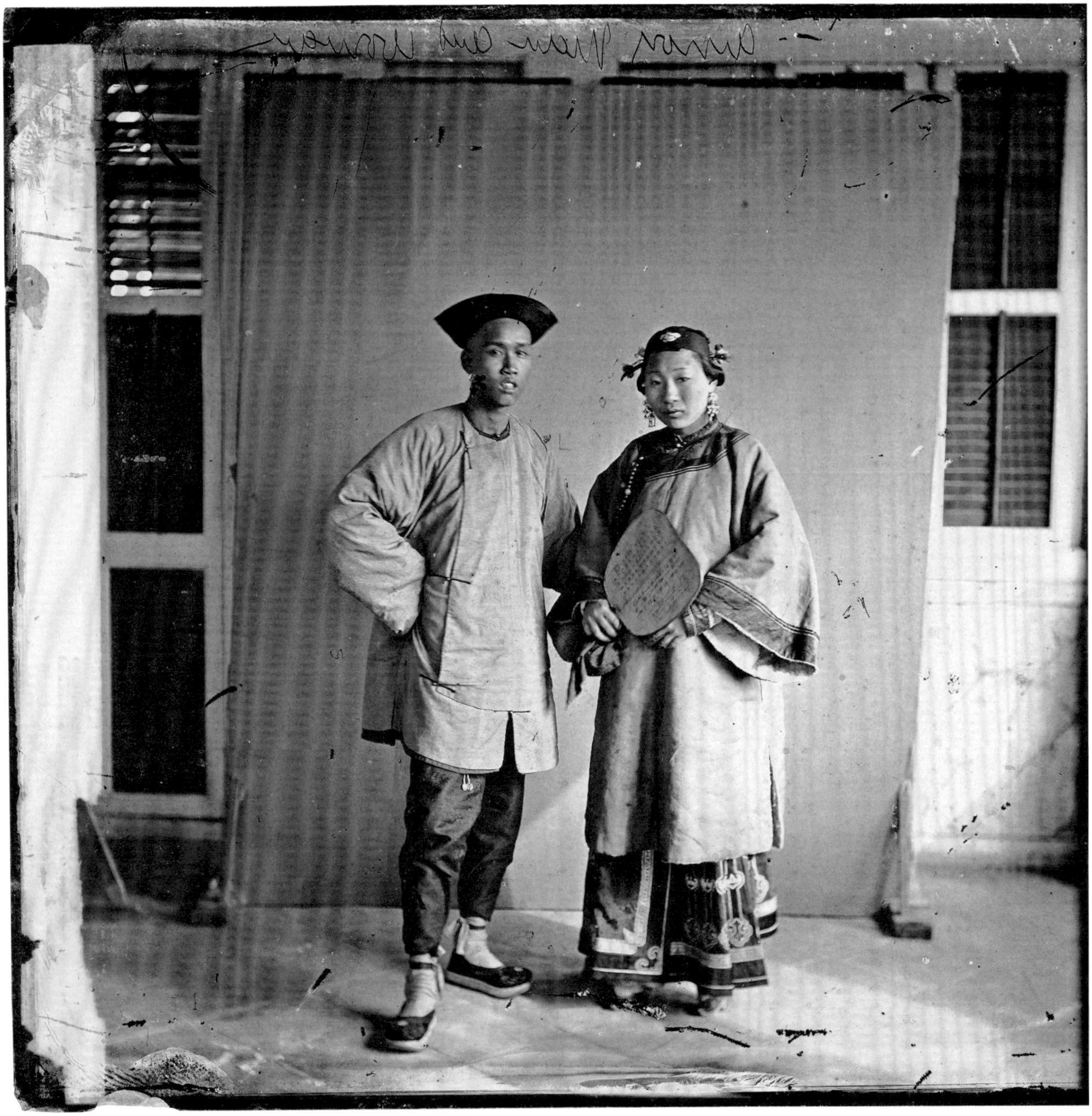

An Amoy Couple

Xiamen, Fujian

The couple from Amoy (Xiamen) stand in front of a European-style house. Thomson was interested in the dress and appearance of local people. This couple is well dressed as the woman wears a beautifully embroidered silk robe suggesting they are from a wealthy family. Thomson noted that quite a few wealthy Chinese merchants lived in beautiful and expensive houses in Amoy.

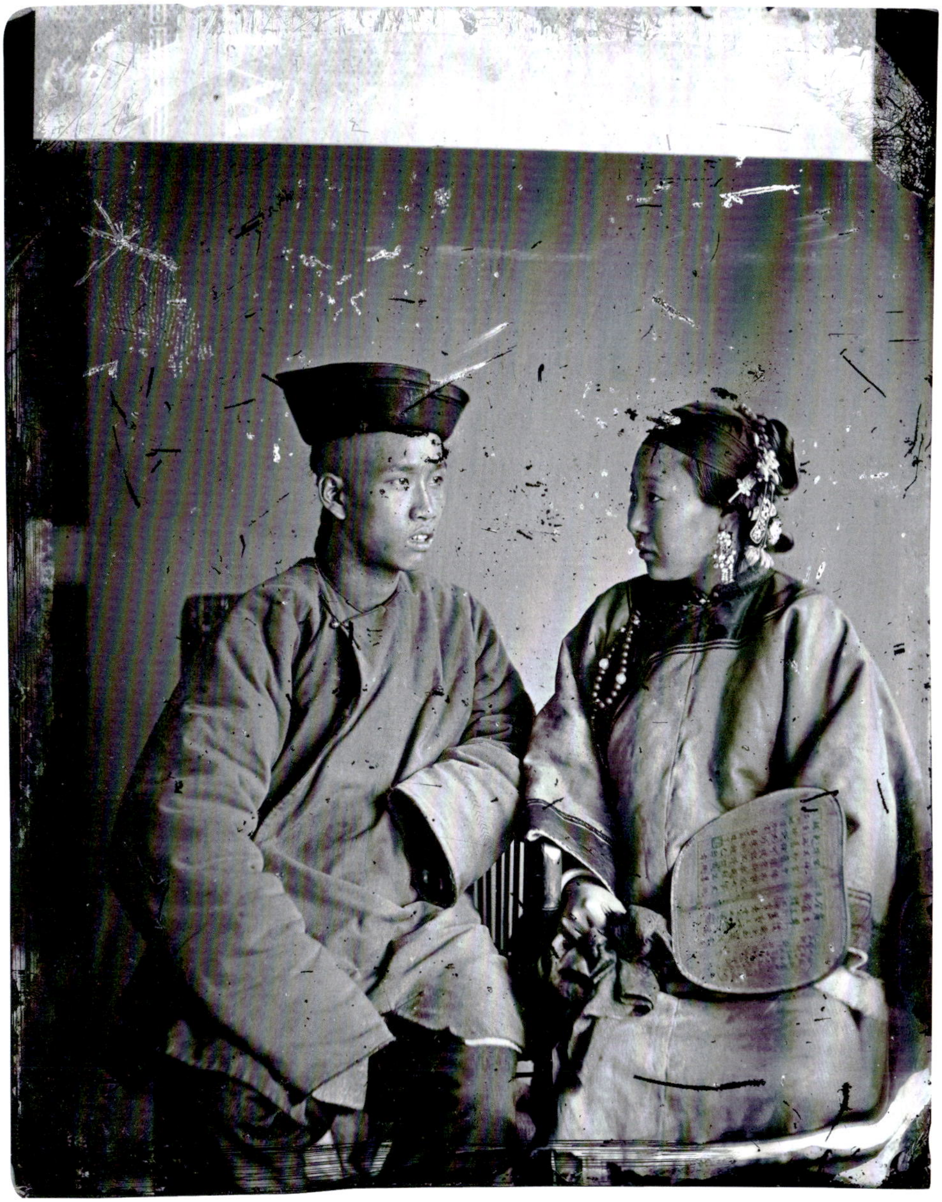

An Amoy Couple

Xiamen, Fujian

The couple here looks awkward. Perhaps Thomson posed them together in a 'western' way unaware that in traditional Chinese society it was considered improper for a couple, in public, to be seated so closely together and facing each other.

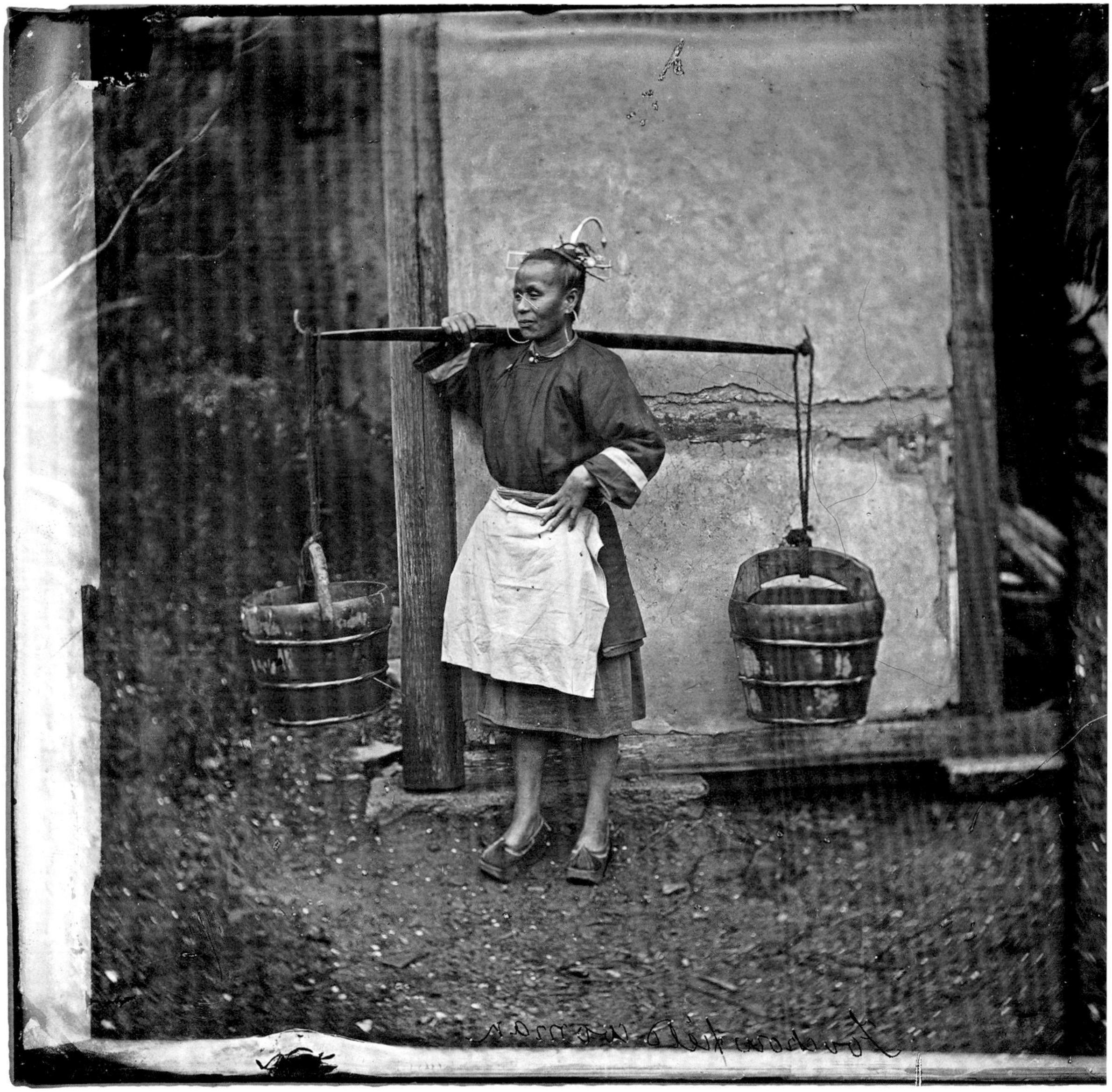

An Indigenous Woman Carrying Buckets

Fuzhou, Fujian

This photograph was taken near a tea plantation on the terraced hills just outside Fuzhou. Terraced fields were common in the Fujian countryside. To fertilize the fields local women had to transport human manure from the city of Fuzhou. They did not bind their feet and carried the same heavy loads as the men. Thomson admired these women as hard work rendered them strong and healthy.

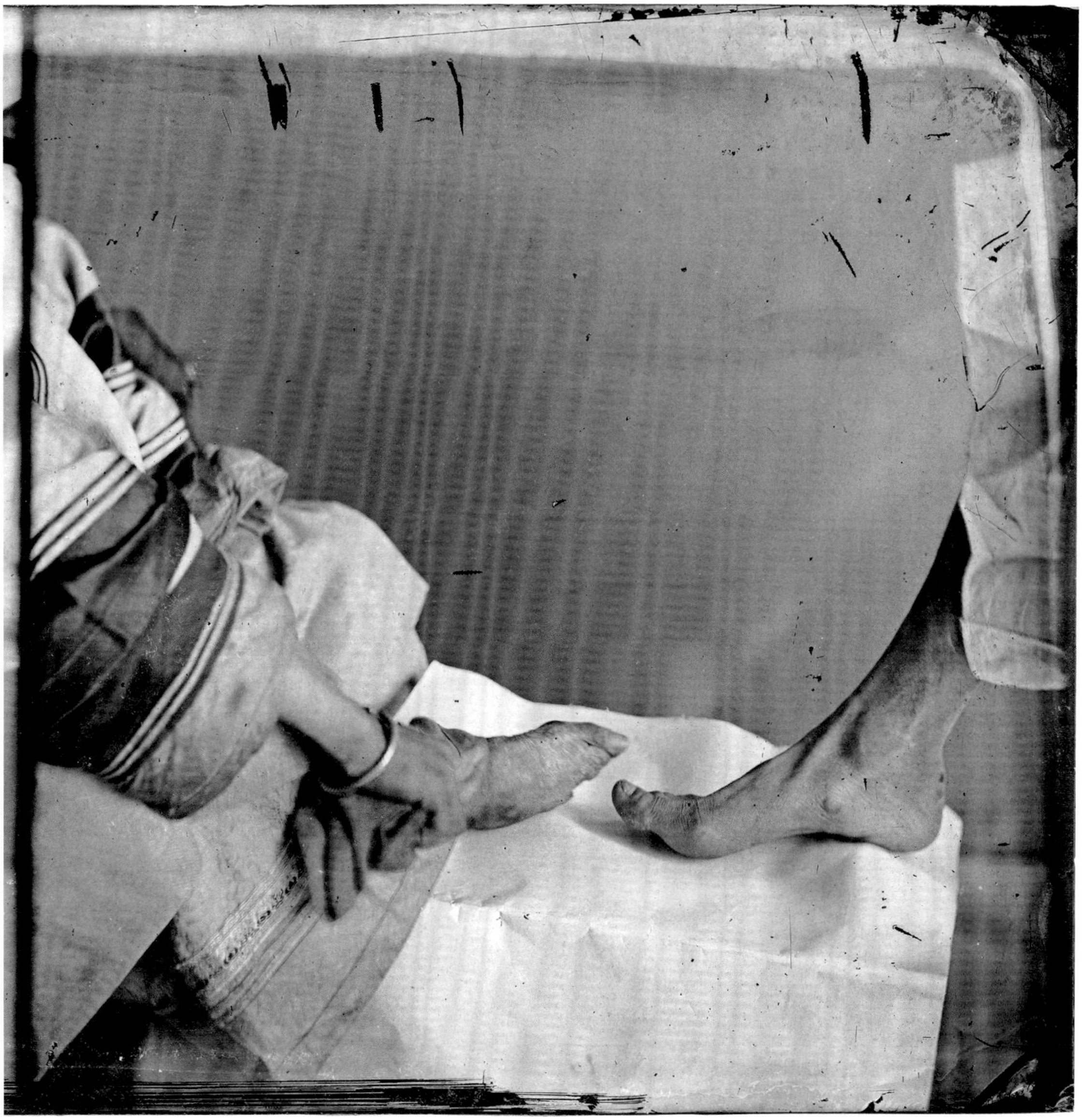

Bound and Unbound Feet of Two Amoy Women

Xiamen, Fujian

The bound feet of Chinese women have always fascinated Westerners. Time and again during his travels in China Thomson tried to get a woman to let him photograph her bound feet, but he failed to do so until he reached Amoy. This photograph contrasts a bound foot with a natural one. According to Thomson, he had to pay both women handsomely to get this shot.

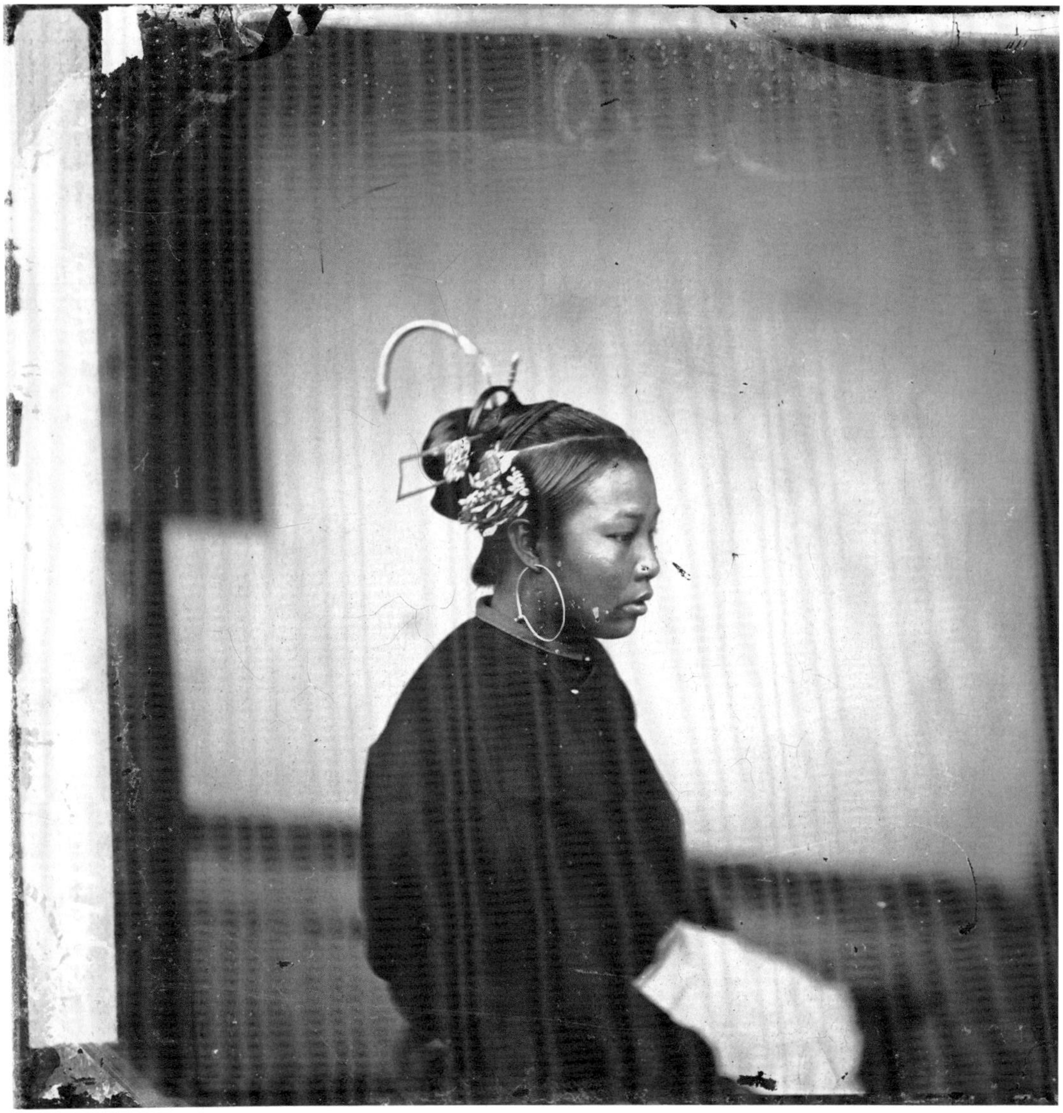

An Indigenous Woman

Fujian

This is a half-length profile portrait of a local woman from the hills near the city of Fuzhou. Seated, she wears large earrings and a coiffure with elaborate silver decorations and fresh flowers. Sun and hard work outdoors have rendered her skin quite dark, or as Thomson described it '*olive in colour with a warm glow*'.

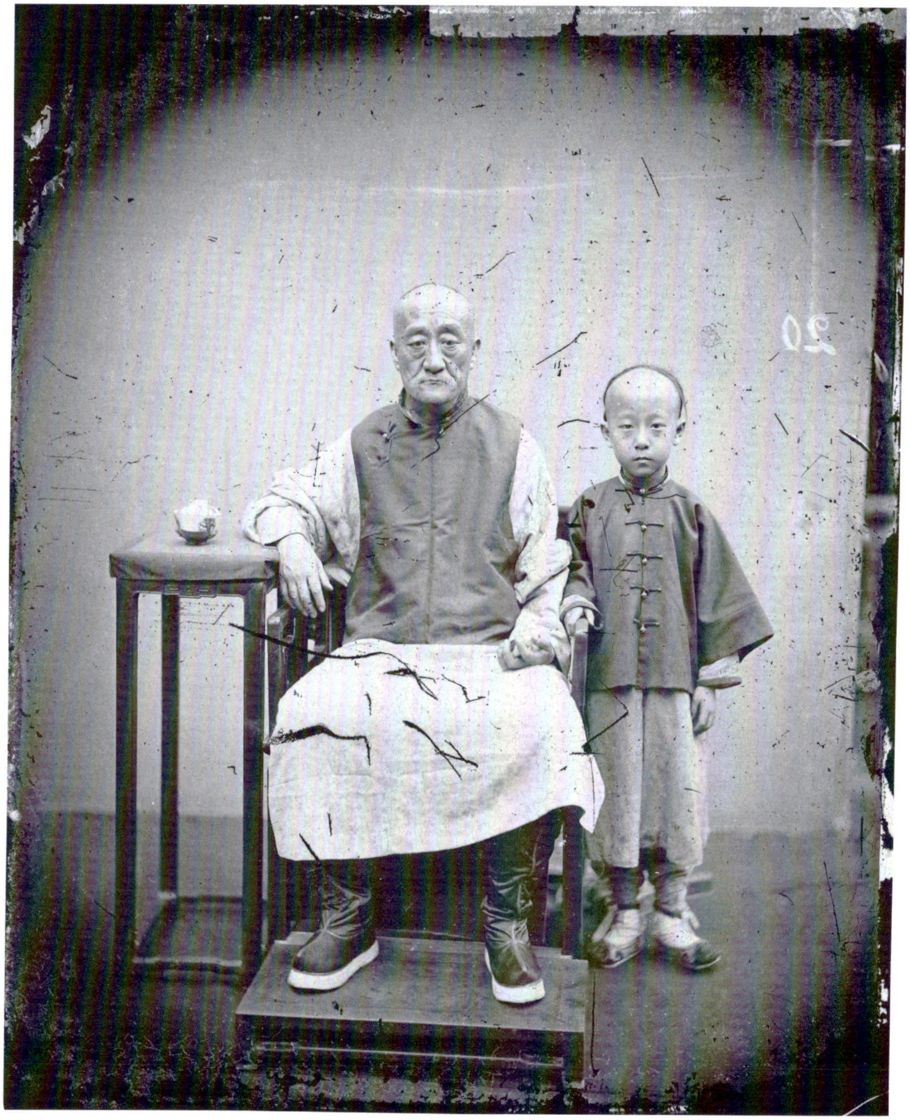

An Old Cantonese Man and a Young Boy

Guangzhou, Guangdong

This photograph shows Thomson having to conform to the established rules of Chinese portraiture. The sitter is posed in the centre, facing the camera, with a child on one side and a tea-table with a teacup on the other. Their faces remain expressionless. In the Chinese tradition, the photograph is a record of the person rather than that of the personality. Such a rigid method was quite contrary to Thomson's own portraiture style with the subject often appearing more human and vivid, and with a more interesting backdrop.

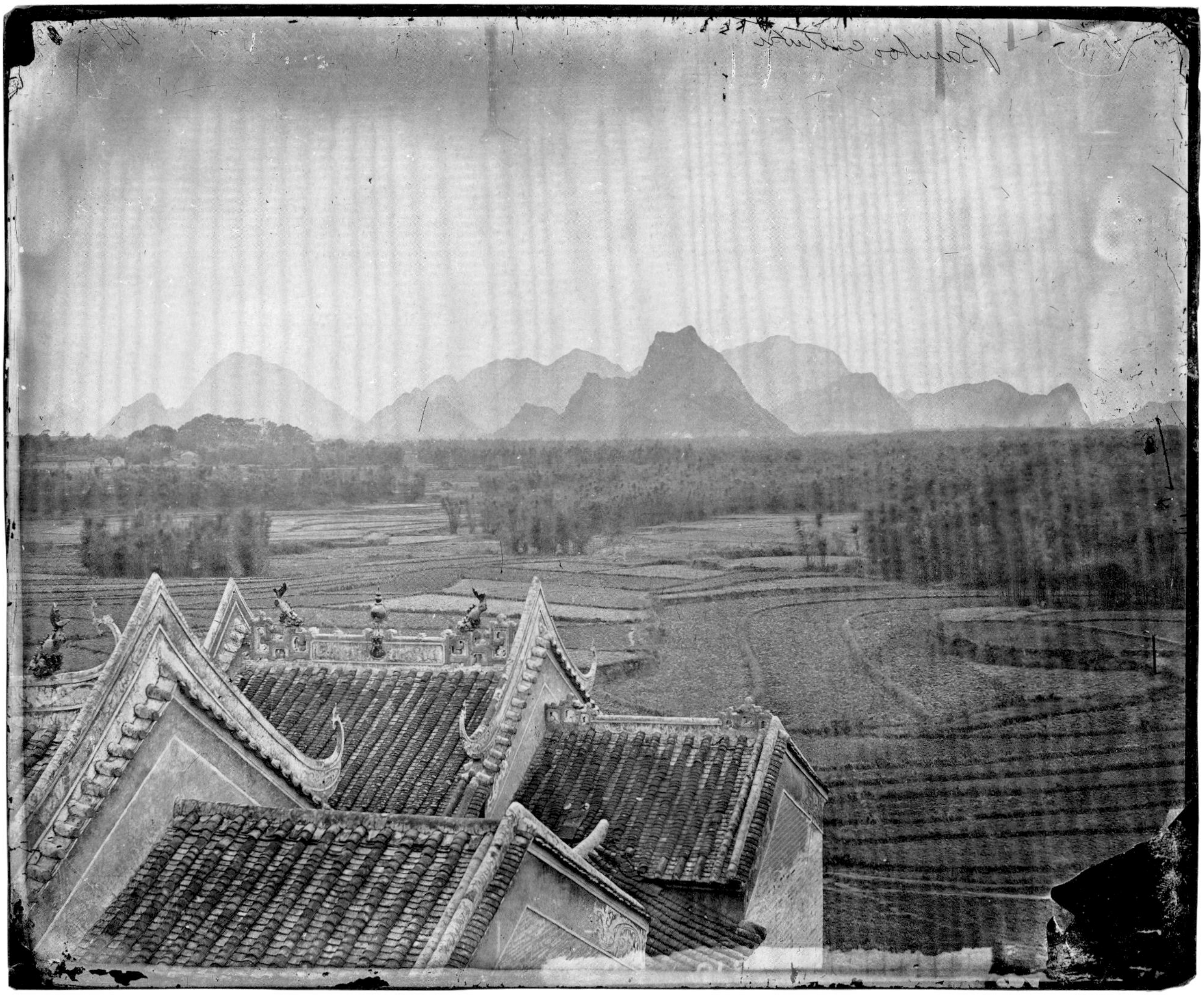

A Bamboo Grove on the North River

Guangdong

This photograph was taken during Thomson's trip on the North River, a branch of the Pearl River. He was completely struck by what he saw: '*The cultivation hereabouts was of a kind I had never seen before; in the foreground were a multitude of fields, banked off for the purposes of irrigation, but already shorn of their crop. Here and there were mounds covered with temples and trees, and beyond, reaching to the base of the distant mountains, were groves of green bamboo, rocking their plumage to and fro in the wind, like the waves of an emerald sea.*' Thomson was inspired by the landscapes he saw, and he endeavoured to capture with his camera some of '*the grandeur of the inland scenery. The vast plain covered with graceful bamboo or the luxurious green of the paddy fields, contrast abruptly with the background . . .*'

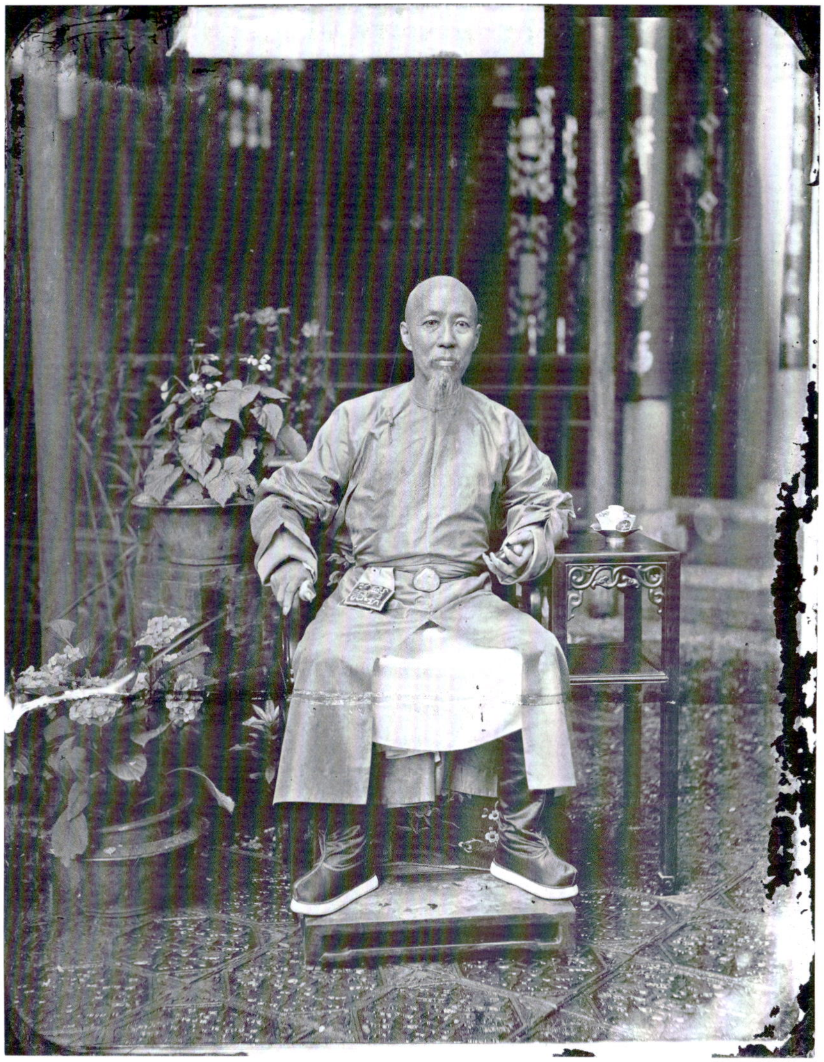

RUILIN, GOVERNOR OF GUANGDONG AND GUANGXI

Guangzhou, Guangdong

For the Europeans, Ruilin was one of the better-known Chinese officials of the late 19th century. Born a Manchu, Ruilin entered public service at an early age but only rose to high government position at the age of 45. In 1865 he was appointed the governor general of Guangdong and Guangxi, where he dealt extensively with the British. He was often praised for his courtesy and for his skill in cultivating a friendly relationship with the British. Under his administration Guangdong prospered and he brought a certain degree of stability to the region.

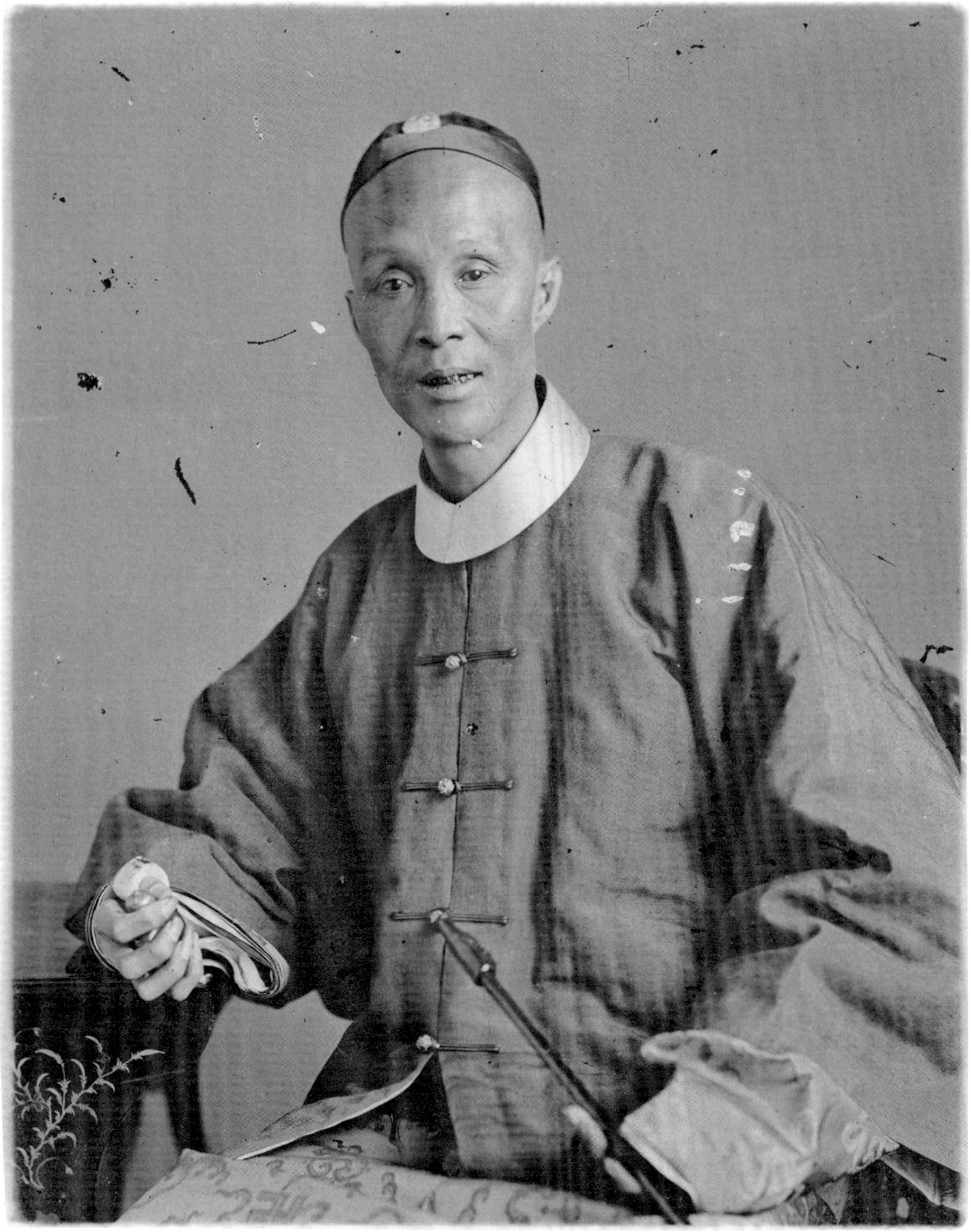

Chinese Merchants

Guangzhou, Guangdong

This example of Thomson's formal Chinese-style portraiture reflects the hierarchy within traditional Chinese society. One or more of these men were possibly compradors, local Chinese employed by foreign companies to manage their businesses. The rise of the comprador was a unique feature of mercantile life in Chinese open ports in the second half of the 19th century and into the 20th century. Although many compradors were successful and wealthy, their social position and contribution to the success of trade in the treaty ports were only recognised recently. The man on the left wears a fur coat, a fashionable luxury in 19th-centry China and a clear indicator of wealth As such they were greatly desired by the rising professional classes in the coastal cities.

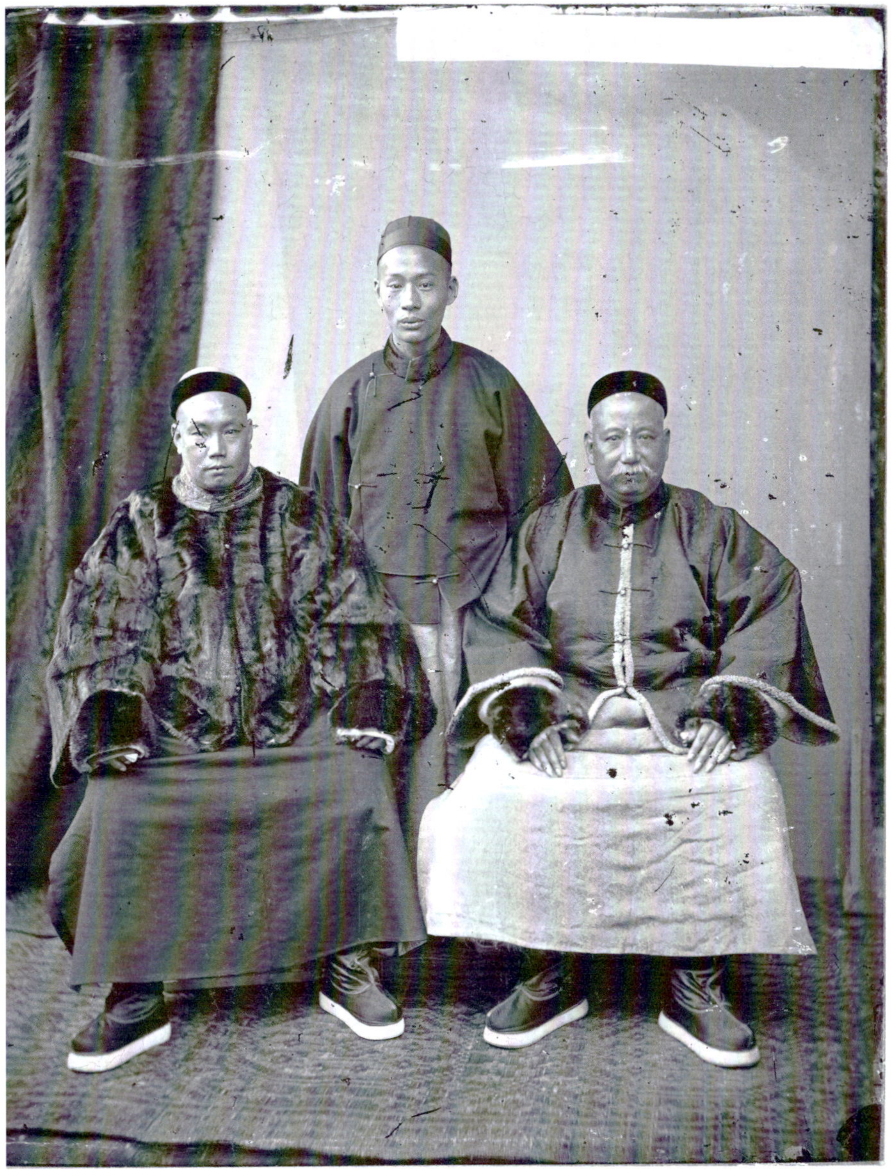

Left: A Cantonese Mandarin Official

Guangzhou, Guangdong

This is a fine example of Thomson's skill as a portrait photographer. The man looks directly into the camera lens, a pose in which 'men of taste' of China wanted to be photographed. According to Thomson this man was a sixth-grade mandarin official and a man of letters who possessed two degrees in imperial examinations.

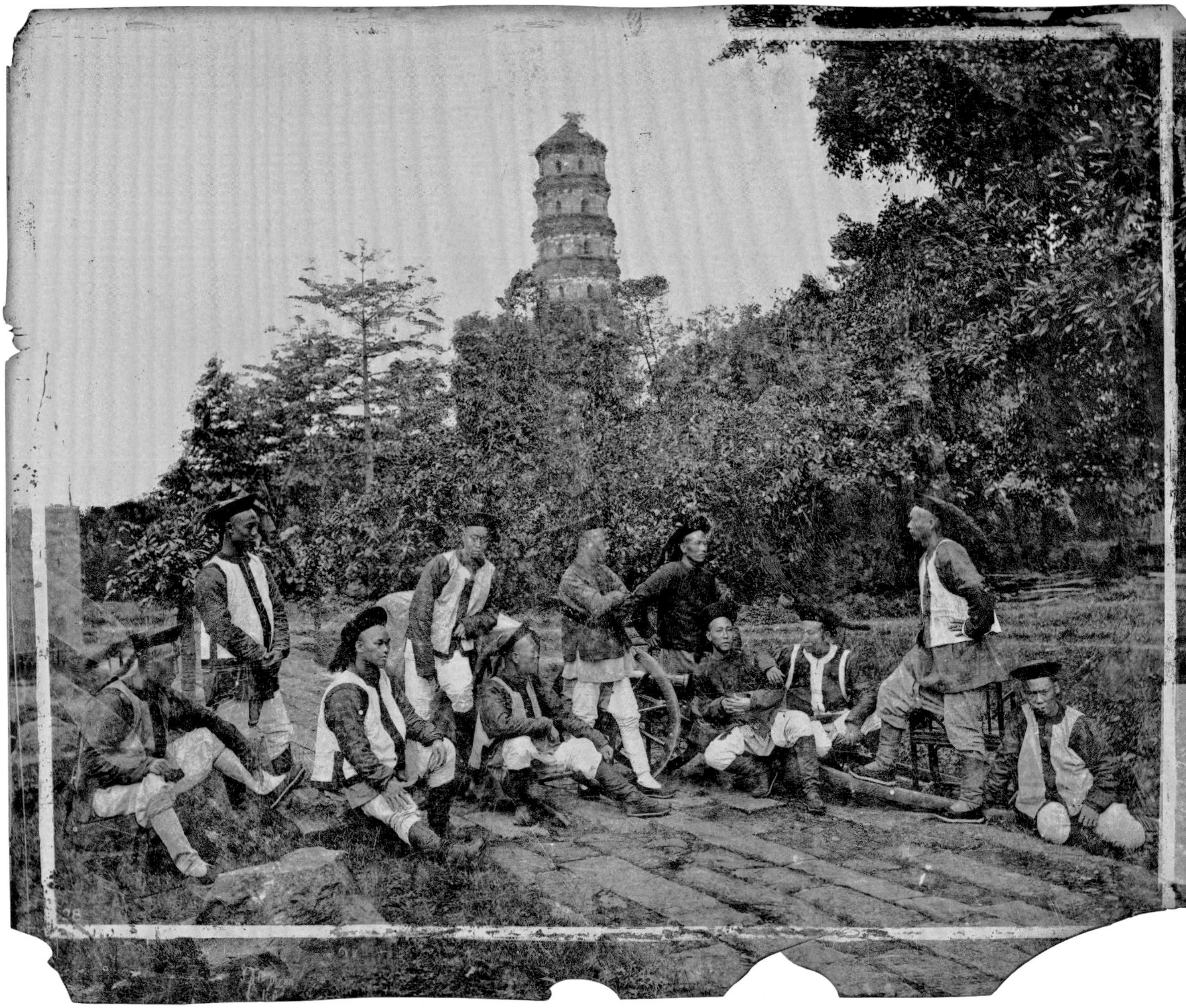

A Group of Manchu Soldiers

Guangzhou, Guangdong

These Manchu soldiers were employed as guards for Sir D. B. Robertson, the British consul at Guangzhou during Thomson's visit. According to Thomson there were 1,800 Manchu soldiers stationed in Guangzhou, forming part of the government's permanent garrison. He remarked that many of them, although extremely poor, were physically strong and fit and that '*they would still make good soldiers*'. These soldiers were trained in the European manner and drilled in the use of foreign arms.

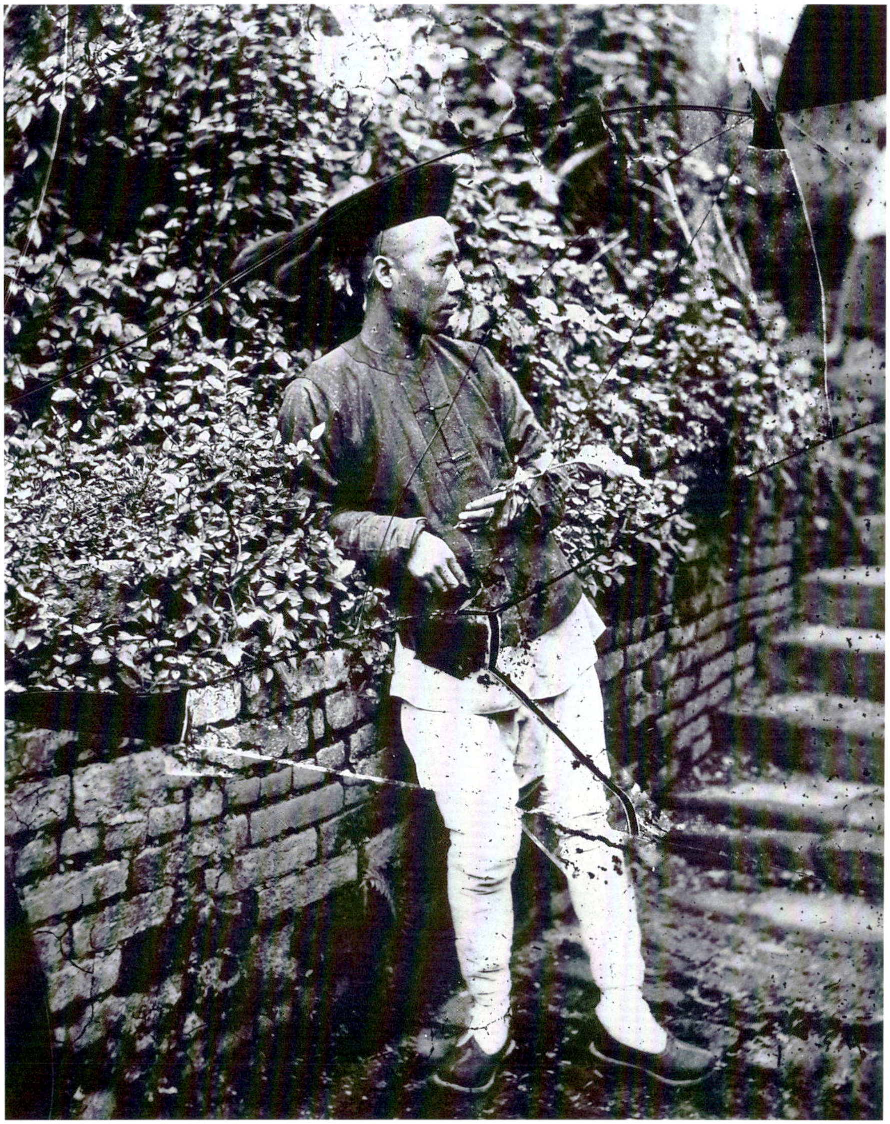

A Manchu Soldier

Guangzhou, Guangdong

Thomson wrote that many Manchu soldiers were of a '*fine manly build and soldierly appearance*'. Thomson was able to build up a rapport and make many of his subjects feel at ease in front of the camera, even though it was a new and strange apparatus not seen by many Chinese before. This is in evidence in this photograph, a useful ability when long exposures required people to stay still for some time.

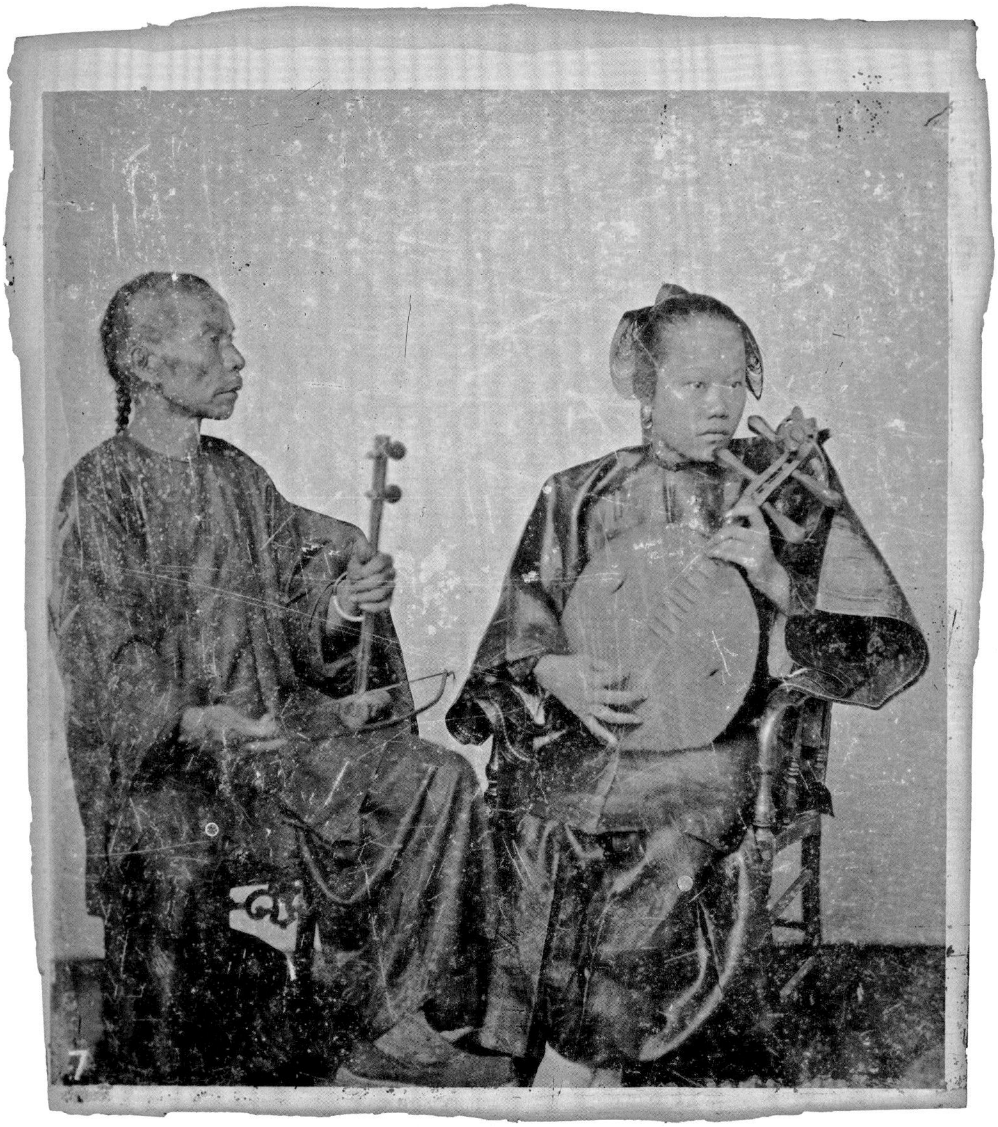

Blind Cantonese Musicians

Guangzhou, Guangdong

Thomson observed that wandering musicians were a Chinese institution. Often blind, music was one of the few professions open to them. Typically, the woman was the singer and the man served as her accompanist, often they would travel as a married couple. The woman in this photo appears to be playing the *yueqin* or 'moon lute', while the man plays a small two-stringed fiddle which most closely resembles the contemporary '*jinghu*' used in the northern genre of Beijing Opera. This combination of lute and fiddle was commonly used to accompany popular local song and opera traditions throughout southern China, especially in Guangdong and Hong Kong. Such performances were seen in a wide range of venues, from brothels to teahouses to homes of the elite. In addition to ballads based on the classic romances and historical dramas, the musicians sometimes incorporated improvised songs about current affairs and local life.

Right: Street Gamblers

Guangzhou, Guangdong

Gambling was common in 19th-century China, especially in the south. Government legislation banning it did not contain the problem but forced gamblers to go underground. Gambling was not confined to gambling houses but took place in clubs and private homes. For the poor labouring class the streets were a common gambling venue.

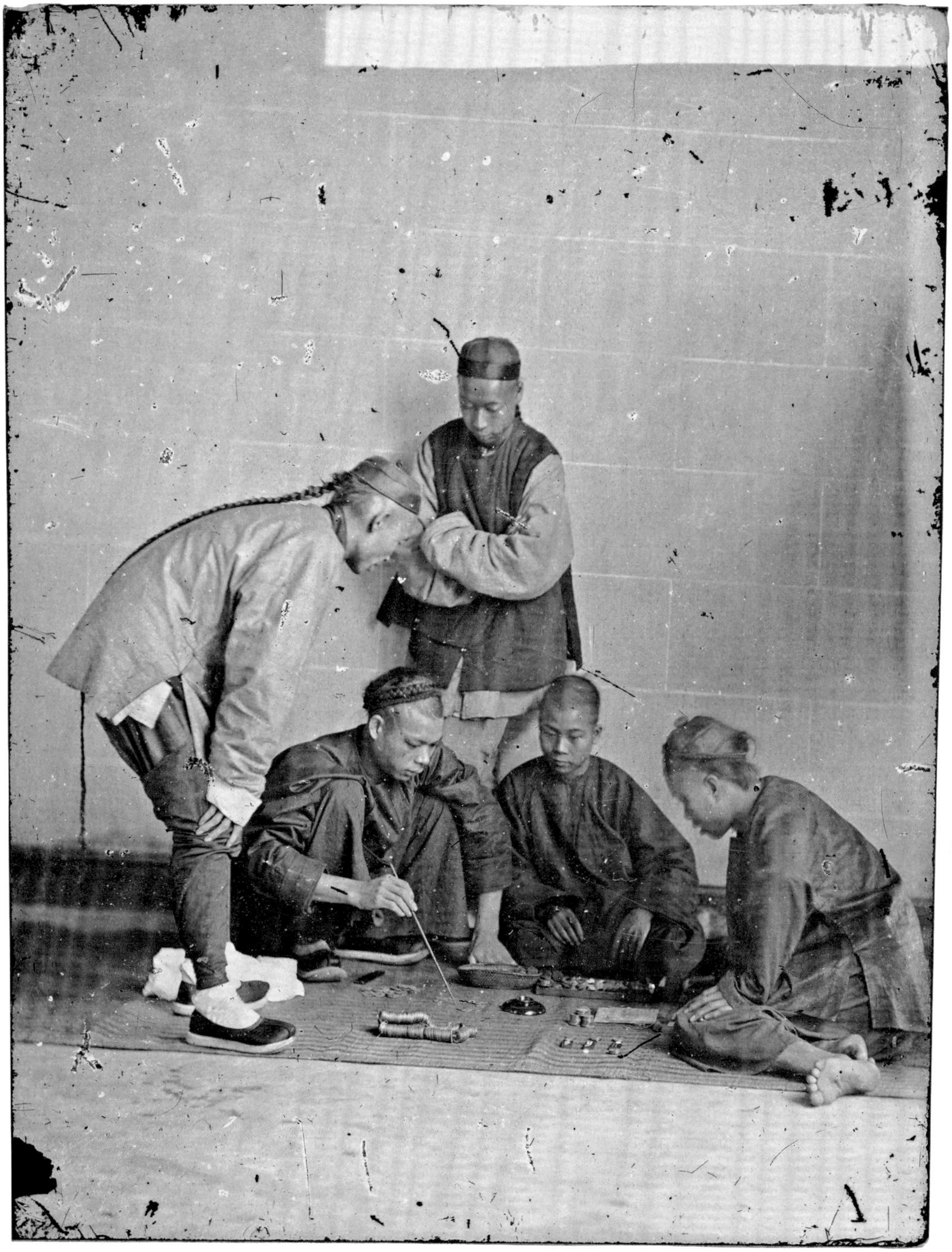

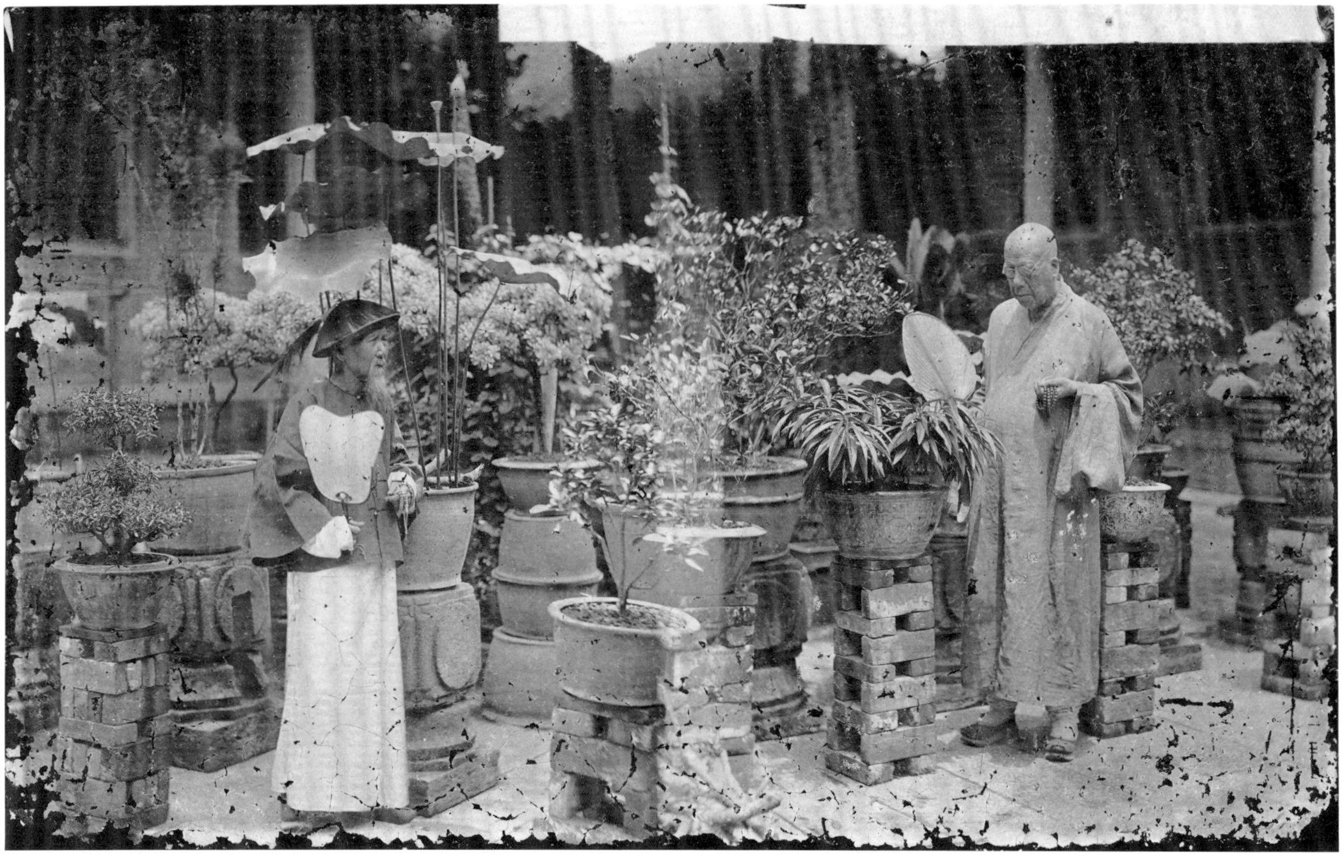

The Abbot at the Temple of Five Hundred Gods

Guangzhou, Guangdong

This is the private courtyard of the 'Temple of Five Hundred Gods' or the 'Magnificent Forest Temple' in Guangzhou. Situated in the western suburbs of the city, it was thought to have been founded by Bodhidharama, a 6th-century Buddhist missionary from India. As the guest of an official of the local Customs Office, Thomson was well received at the Temple and shown to the Abbot's private quarters. This courtyard, according to Thomson, was adorned with a variety of rare and beautiful flowers, including a splendid specimen of the Sacred Lotus. Thomson remarked that the Abbot was devoted to the plants and was pleased to share his love of flowers with him.

Right: Two Buddhist Priests

Guangdong

Thomson was not only fascinated by sacred structures and monuments, but he also by the lives of religious men. Yet as a 19th-century man he could not resist categorising his portrayals. For him there were two types of Buddhist priests in China, those of the south and those of the north. The two men here are Thomson's '*typical Buddhist priests of southern China*'. Both men wear long robes with very wide sleeves. '*To keep a daily reckoning with Heaven*', the older priest wears a rosary around his neck, while the younger holds one in his hand. For Thomson, their features were '*those expressive of weakness of character*', thus '*no foreigner would care to trust him out of sight with a coin, far less with the future welfare of his soul.*'

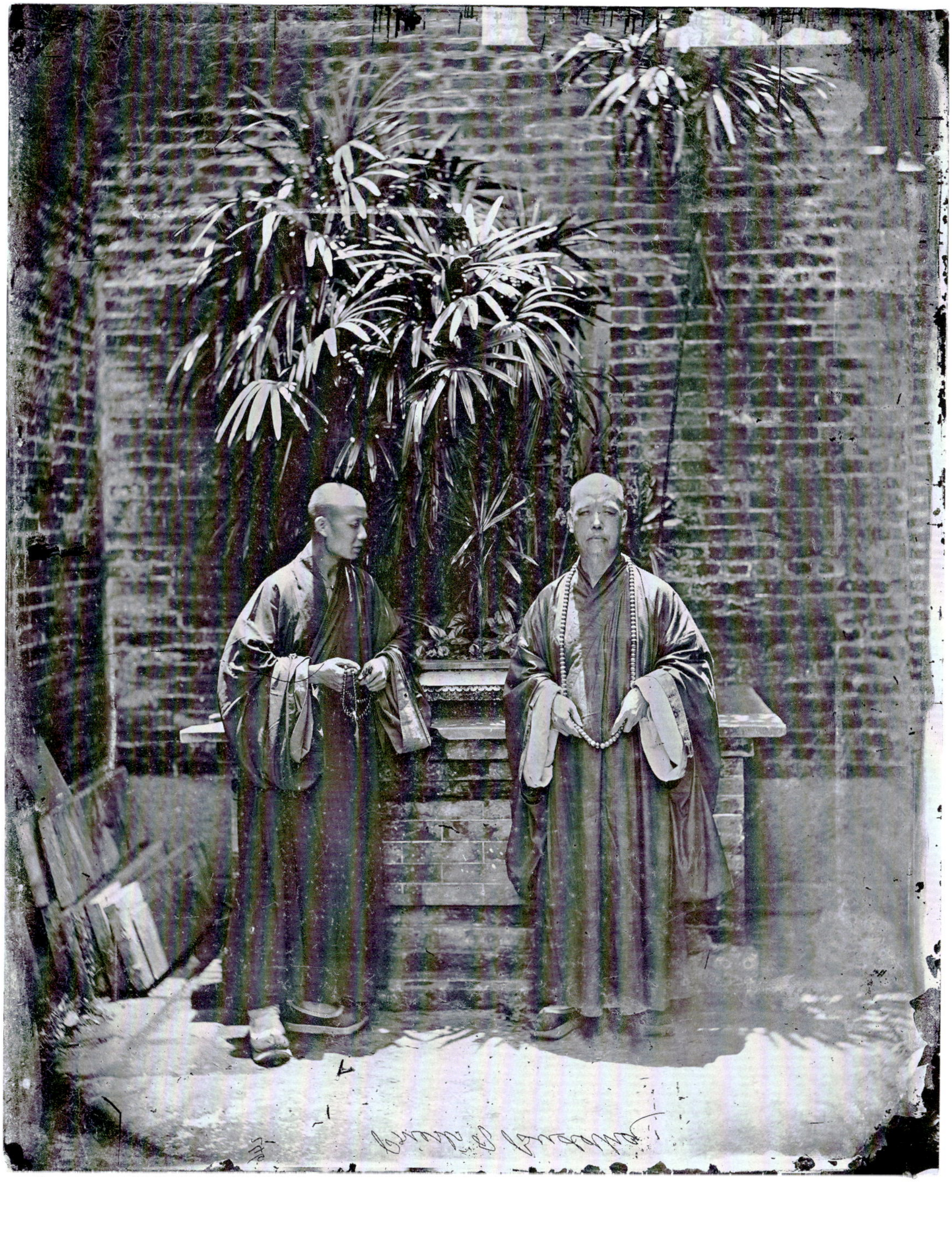

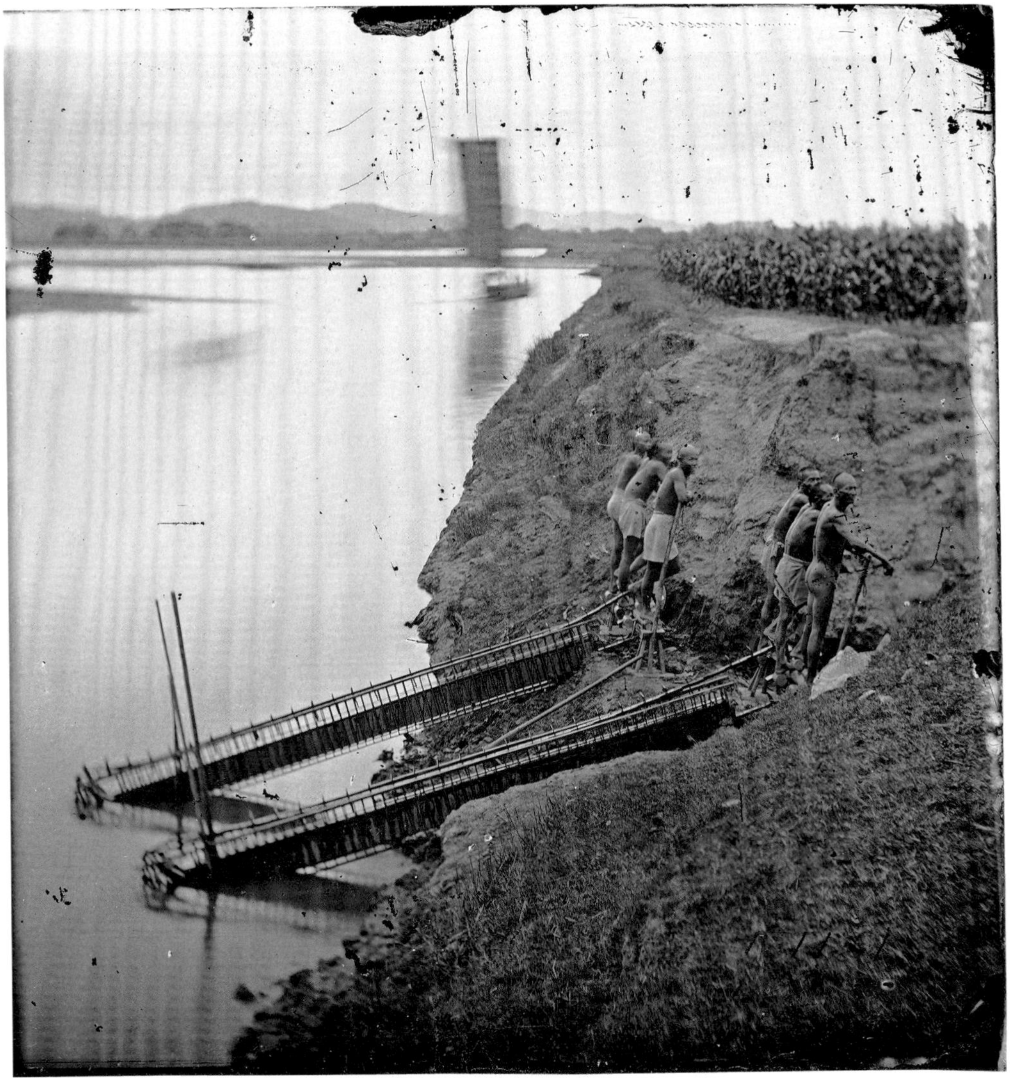

IRRIGATION ON THE HAN RIVER

Shantou, Guangdong

This is the left bank of the Han River near Shantou. During the dry season local people often employed chain pumps for irrigation. The pump consisted of a long square wooden tube into which an endless chain was fitted, carrying a series of wooden diaphragms separated from each other by about six inches. The diaphragms descended over guiding rods above the tube and returned at great speed to raise the water in a continuous flow. At its upper end the chain traversed a wheel having a series of spokes. The chain outside was rotate by pedal power.

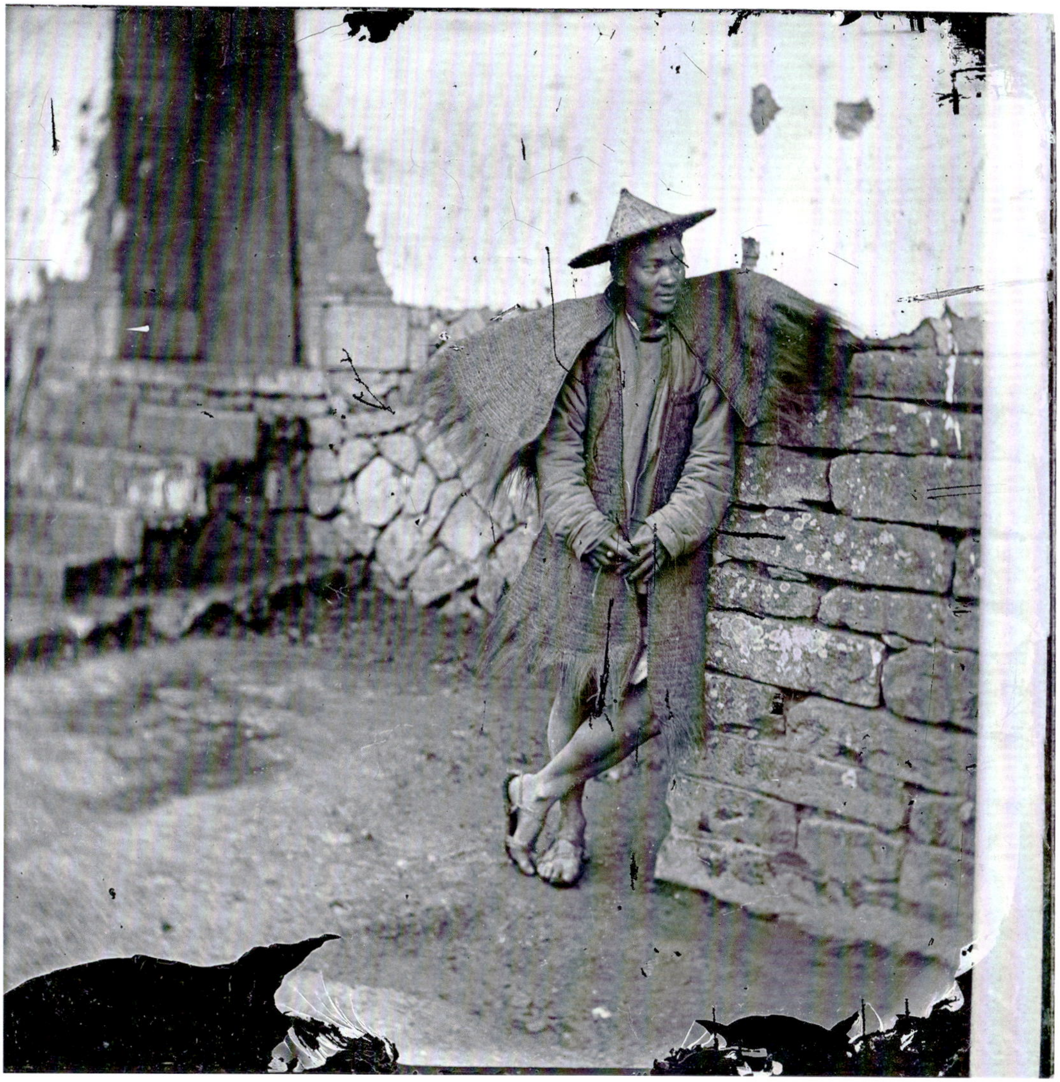

A Cantonese Boatman

Guangzhou, Guangdong

The boatman wears a brimmed hat, a woven cape, and a jerkin with tufted hems. According to Thomson, the boating population in southern China was extremely poor: '*Millions of these hardy sons of toil live from hand to mouth, and are only kept from starving, from piracy, and from rebellion by the cheapness of their staple food, and by the constant demand for their labour.*' He also wrote that because of their simple diet they spent any spare cash they might have on alcohol so that they could keep themselves warm in the winter.

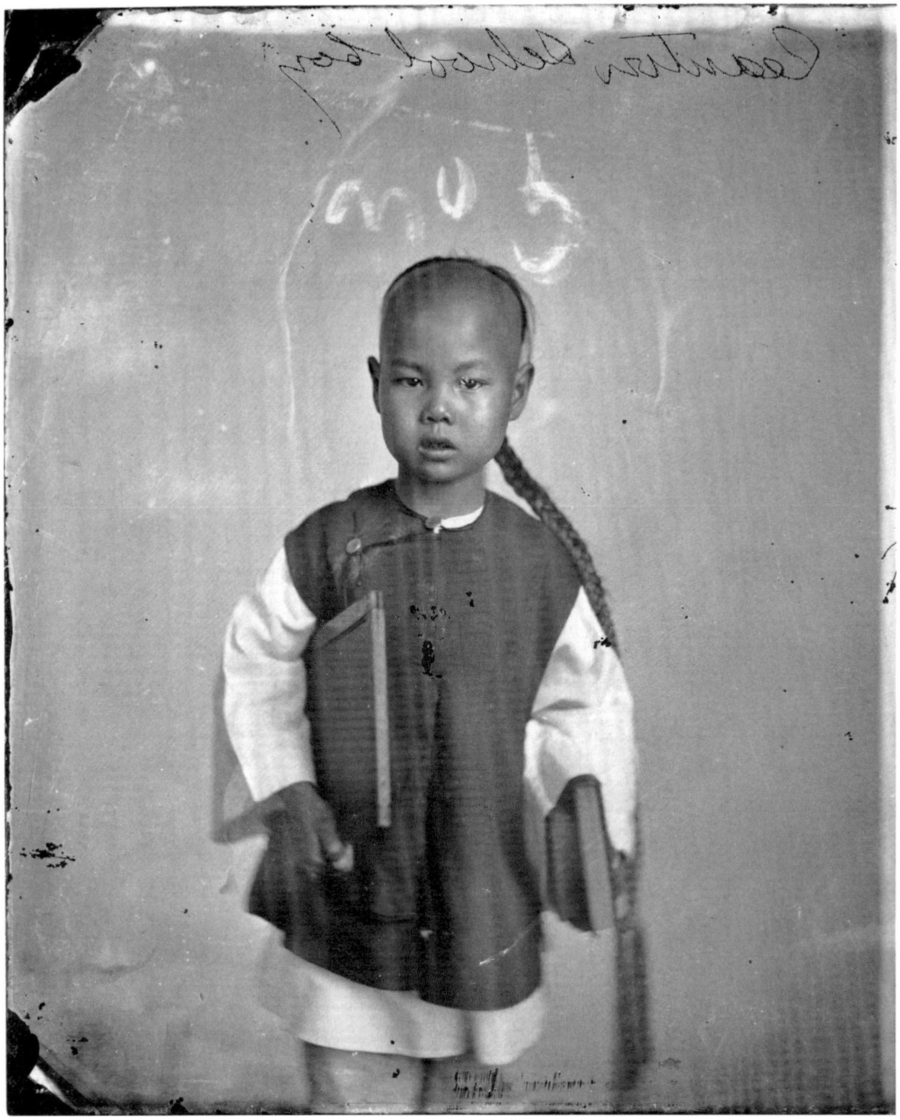

A Cantonese Schoolboy

Guangzhou, Guangdong

Although Thomson often quibbled about the antiquated education system in China, he was greatly impressed by the diligence and aptitude of Chinese schoolboys and their capacity in acquiring knowledge. He wrote of attempts to modernise the education system in different parts of the country, where some schools had adopted western learning. This boy is wearing a queue (plaited hair) and holding a book in one hand and a wooden board in the other. This could be a glass-negative carrying case which Thomson gave him to use as a prop.

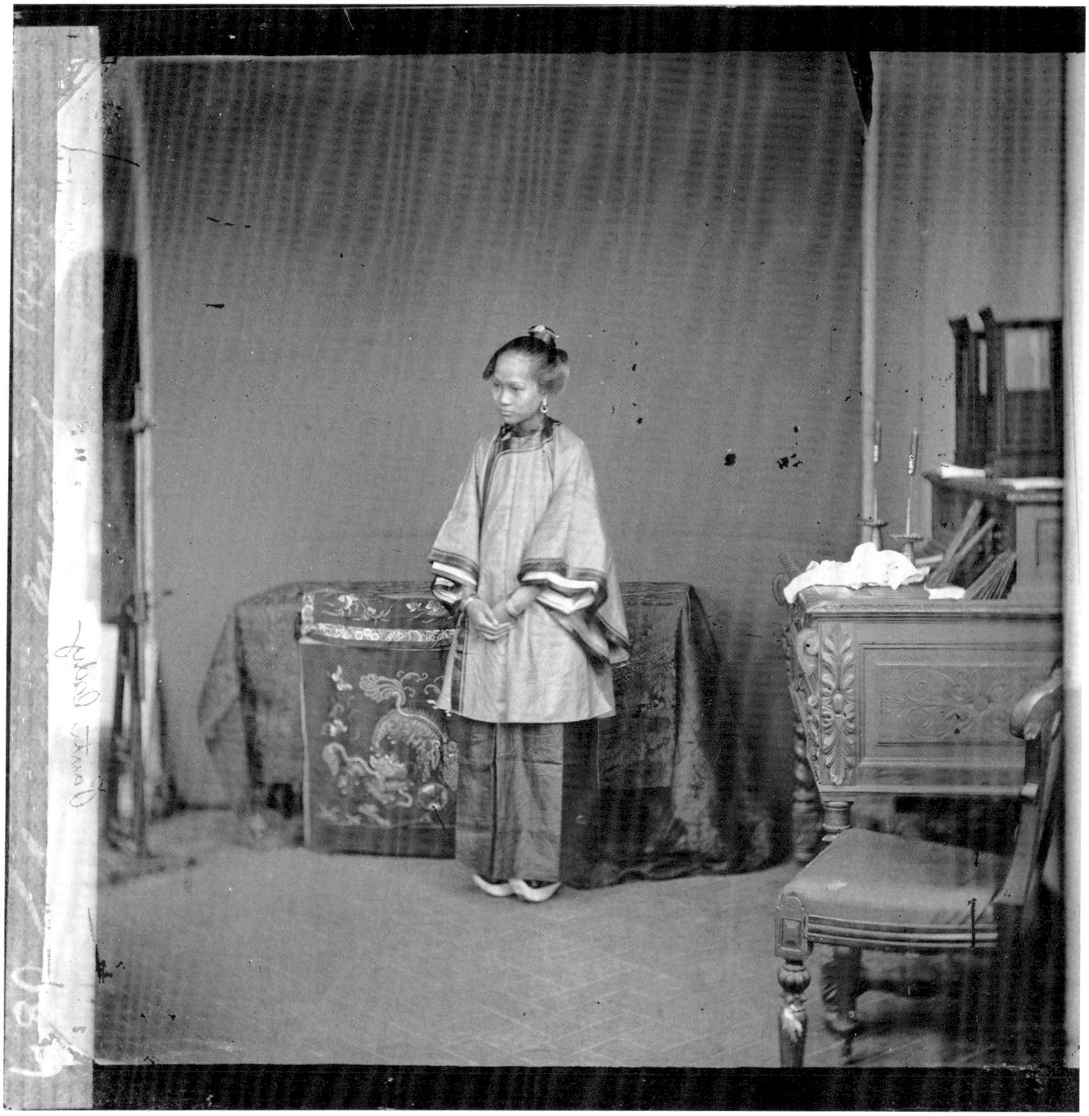

A Cantonese Lady

Guangzhou, Guangdong

This was likely taken in Thomson's studio and shows some of the props that were used in his commissioned portraiture. Behind the Cantonese lady is a simple backdrop with a table covered with embroidered Chinese silk cloth. The side table and chair to the right has twisted 'barley' legs, typical of European furniture design. Canton workshops had been producing export furniture from the 17th century onwards. Many workshops specialised in making furniture based on European prototype designs.

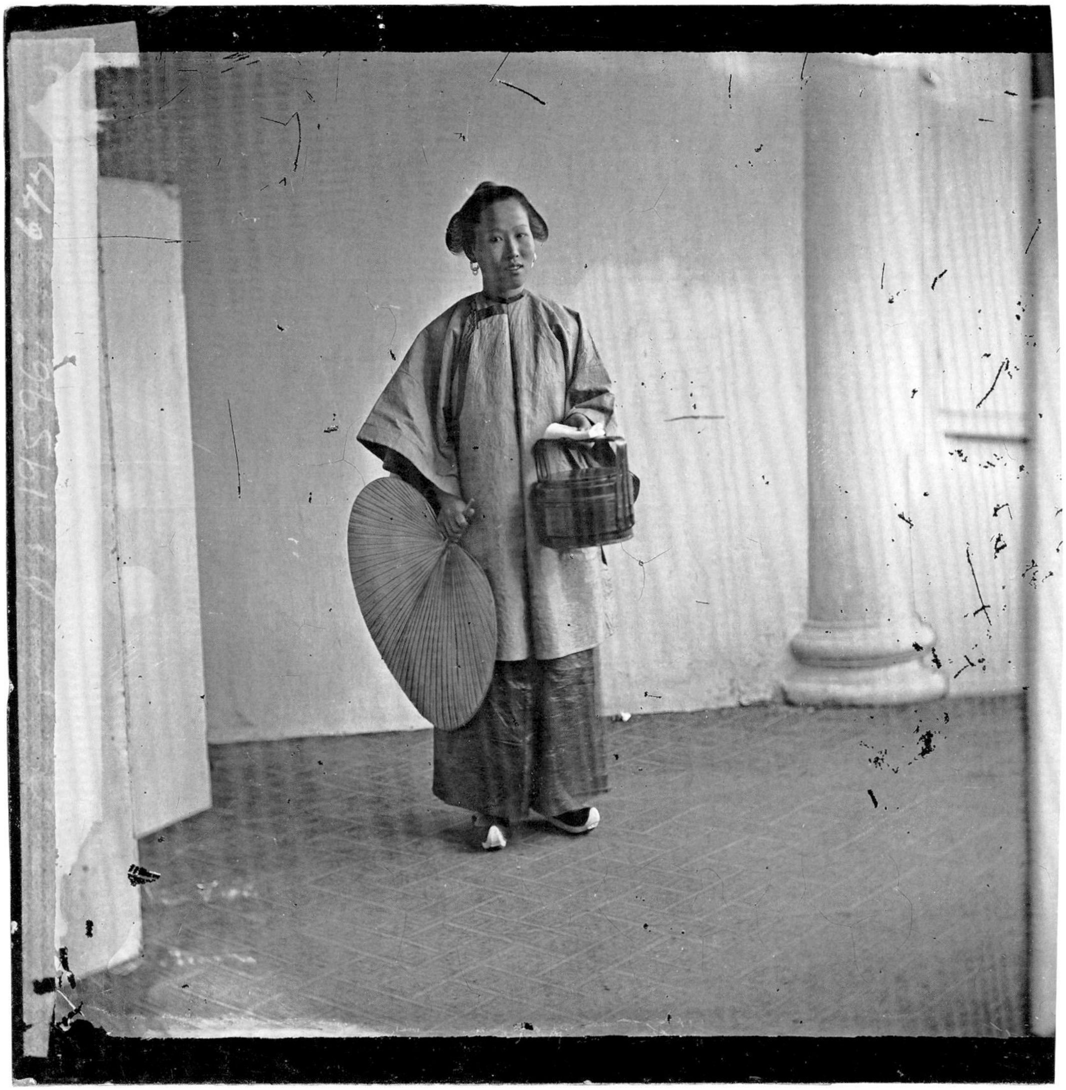

A Cantonese Maid

Guangdong

Photographs of ordinary people remained a central focus of Thomson's work and he often portrayed the lower classes in a very sympathetic light. According to Thomson, this maid's '*slave*' status in fact gave her more freedom than her mistress enjoyed. The maid holds a huge fan to protect her from the sun. The fan was an object of fascination for Thomson as it symbolized another '*Chinese contradiction*'. He reported that the Chinese generally disliked shadows on their faces when they have their photographs taken, '*yet all of them carry fans in order to secure that very shade so essential to existence in the south of China*'.

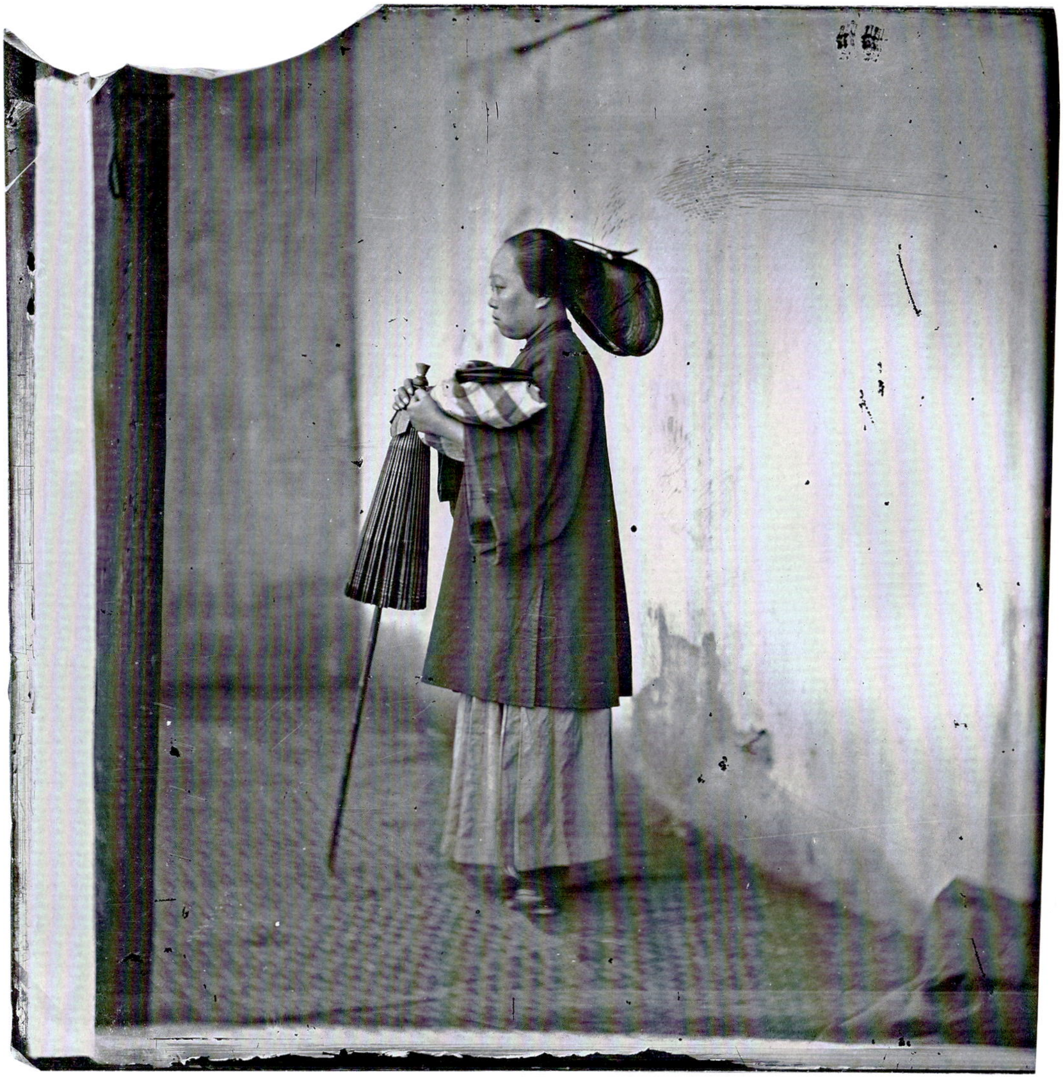

A Chinese Lady Holding a Parasol

Guangdong

Thomson was fascinated by women's hairstyles. Although he noted that Chinese hair was uniformly black and straight, there was great diversity of styles throughout the different regions of China, and these varied according to the prevailing local fashion. This image shows a lady with an elaborate hairstyle, which Thomson described as '*chignon par excellence*'. The chignon was made by a professional hairdresser and wearing one meant that the woman had to sacrifice her comfort when sleeping. This photograph shows a woman holding a closed parasol, further proof of Thomson's statement that shade was essential to the life of southern Chinese.

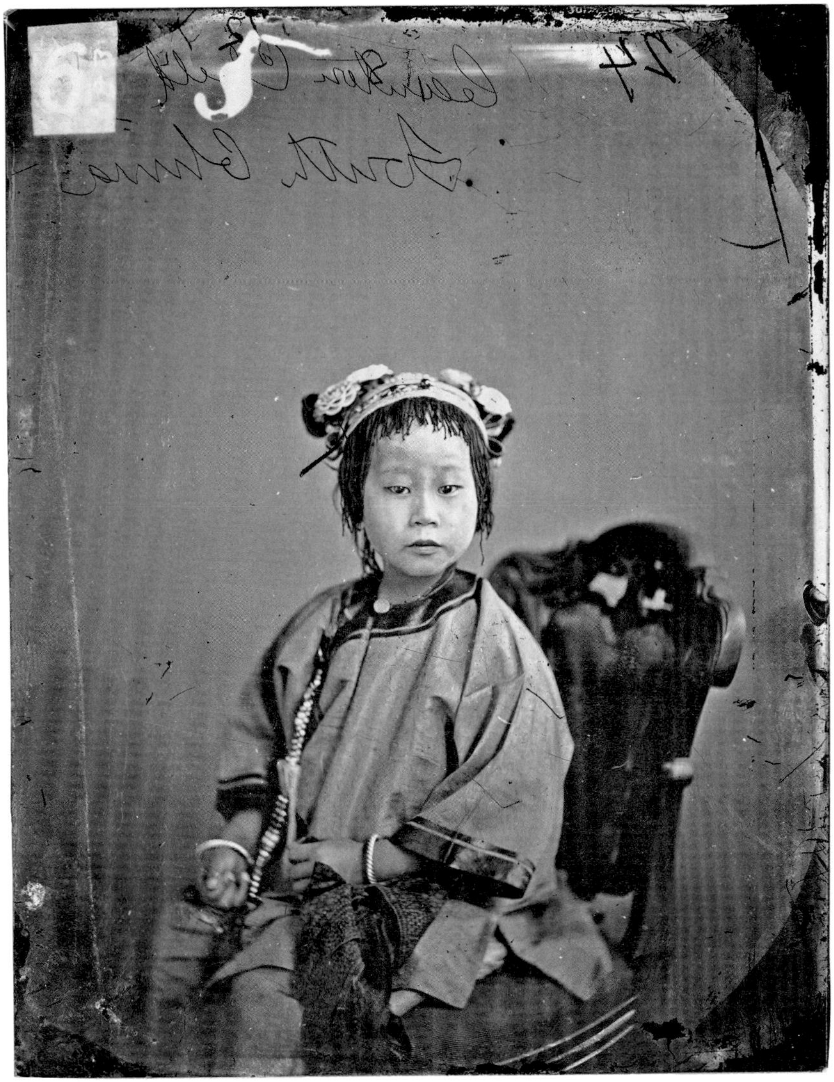

A CHINESE GIRL

Guangdong

The girl's headdress and her outfit suggest she was from a wealthy family. Thomson wrote that the girl's future was bleak since, as a female in 19th-century China, her natural sparkle would soon be diminished as she would have no opportunity to go to school and her face would soon be covered with thick makeup. Thomson found that portraits of children were very difficult to obtain. Most Chinese were suspicious of foreigners, and they were also wary of the camera, which they regarded as a mysterious and dangerous instrument from which children ought to be protected.

A Cantonese Beauty

Guangzhou, Guangdong

Photographed in the southern city of Guangzhou (Canton) famed as a centre of the Chinese export trade to the West, the young lady is dressed in traditional Chinese fashion, although she does not appear wholly Chinese. Her silk coat covers the usual Chinese-embroidered silk jacket of a well-off family, which contrasts with her outspread fan, which is typical of the lacquered and painted fans exported to Europe and America throughout the 19th century. So too, was the painted screen behind her, decorated with trees and flowers and the wood and rattan European-style chair at her side. The thriving export trade brought many nationalities to Canton to fill their ships with goods made there. However the foreign and Chinese populations were kept well apart, the traders only allowed to buy through strictly controlled middlemen.

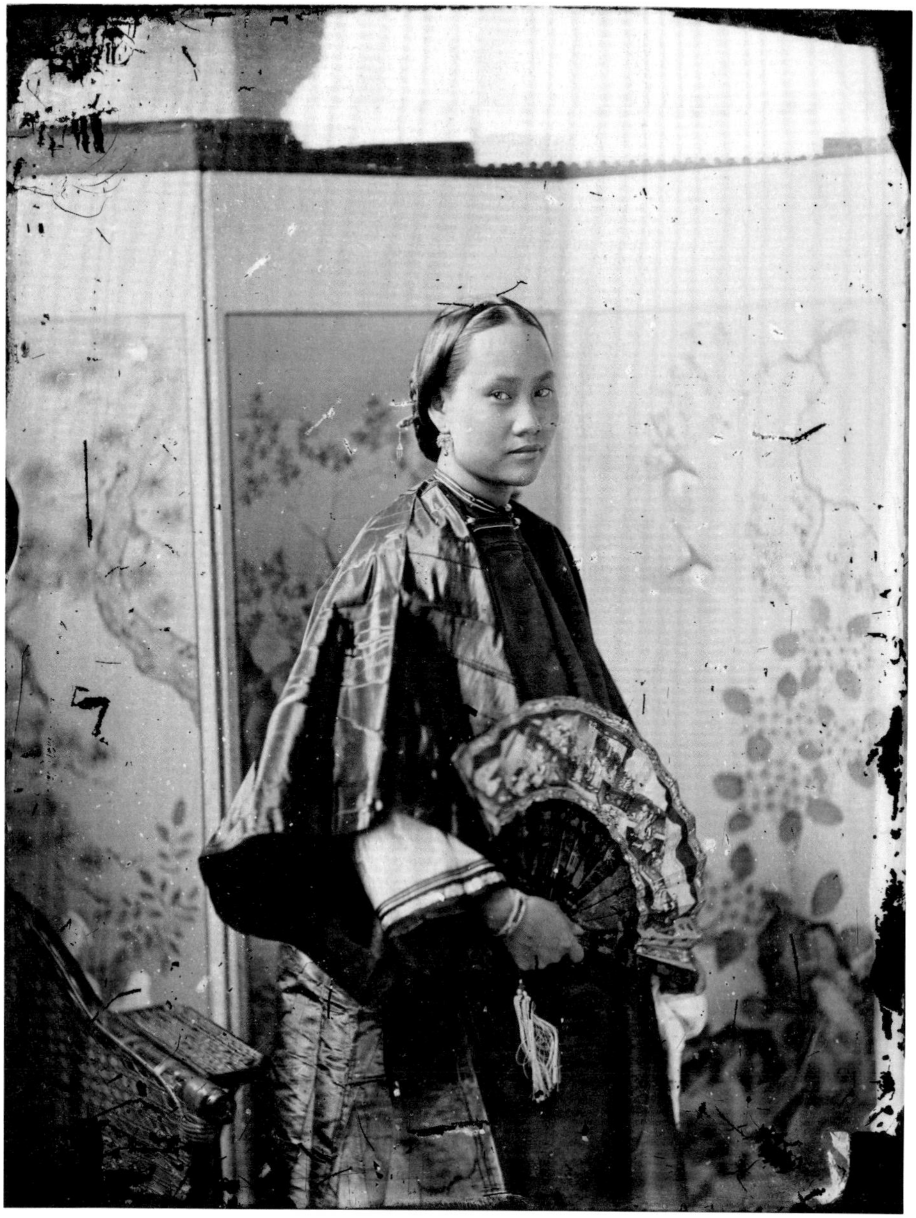

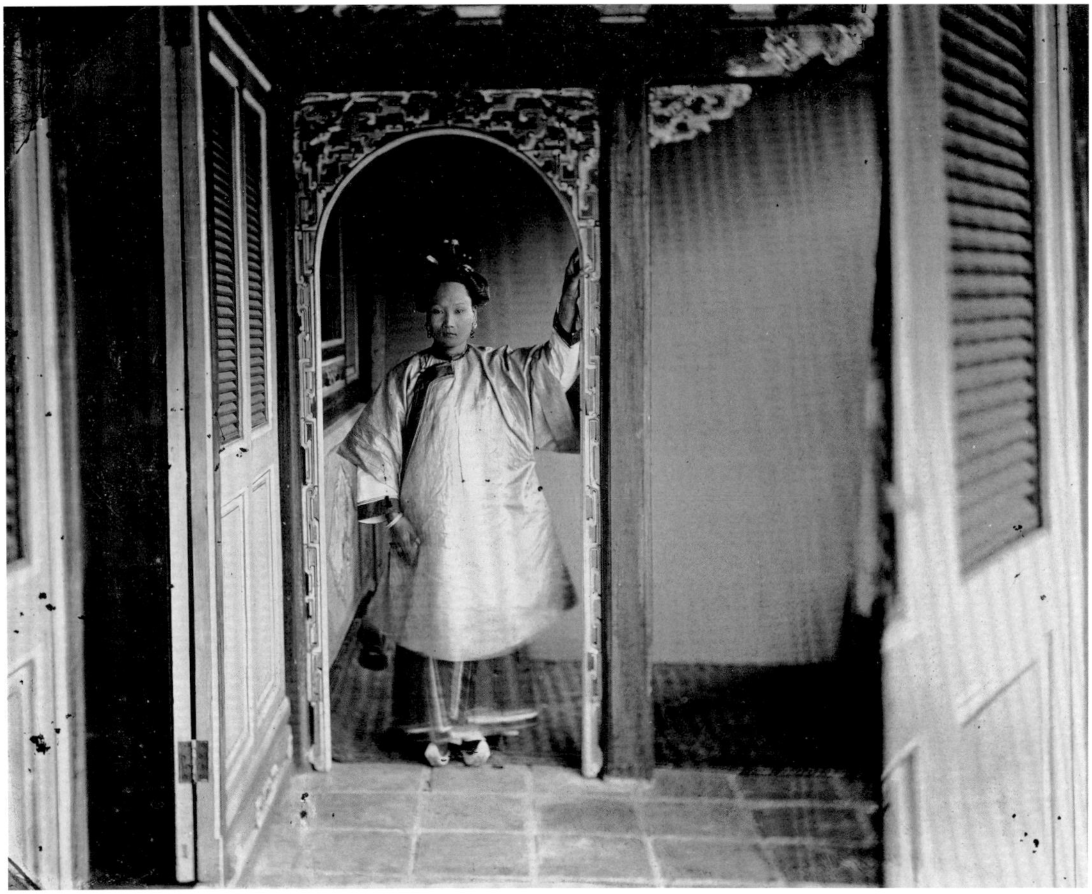

A Cantonese Woman

Guangzhou, Guangdong

Portraits were a vital aspect of Thomson's photographic work and a regular source of income. Throughout his photographic journeys in China, portraiture remained a key feature. While adapting to the local taste for picturing the subject straight on, Thomson also tried to portray as wide a range of Chinese society and life as possible. He was particularly interested in portraying women of varied social backgrounds, from affluent Cantonese ladies to their maids, or from ordinary peasant women in Fujian to Manchu brides. This Cantonese lady is wearing a silk robe and a stylish hair ornament. The backdrop is an elaborately carved doorway on a veranda.

Right: An Old Cantonese Woman

Guangzhou, Guangdong

Thomson wanted this profile portrait of an elderly woman to show not only the hardship and toil she had endured, but also her resilience: '*Her hair has grown thin and white, but she still dresses it with neatness and care*'; she '*still busies herself in the lighter domestic duties; she is skilful with the needle, and invaluable as a nurse in time of sickness.*'

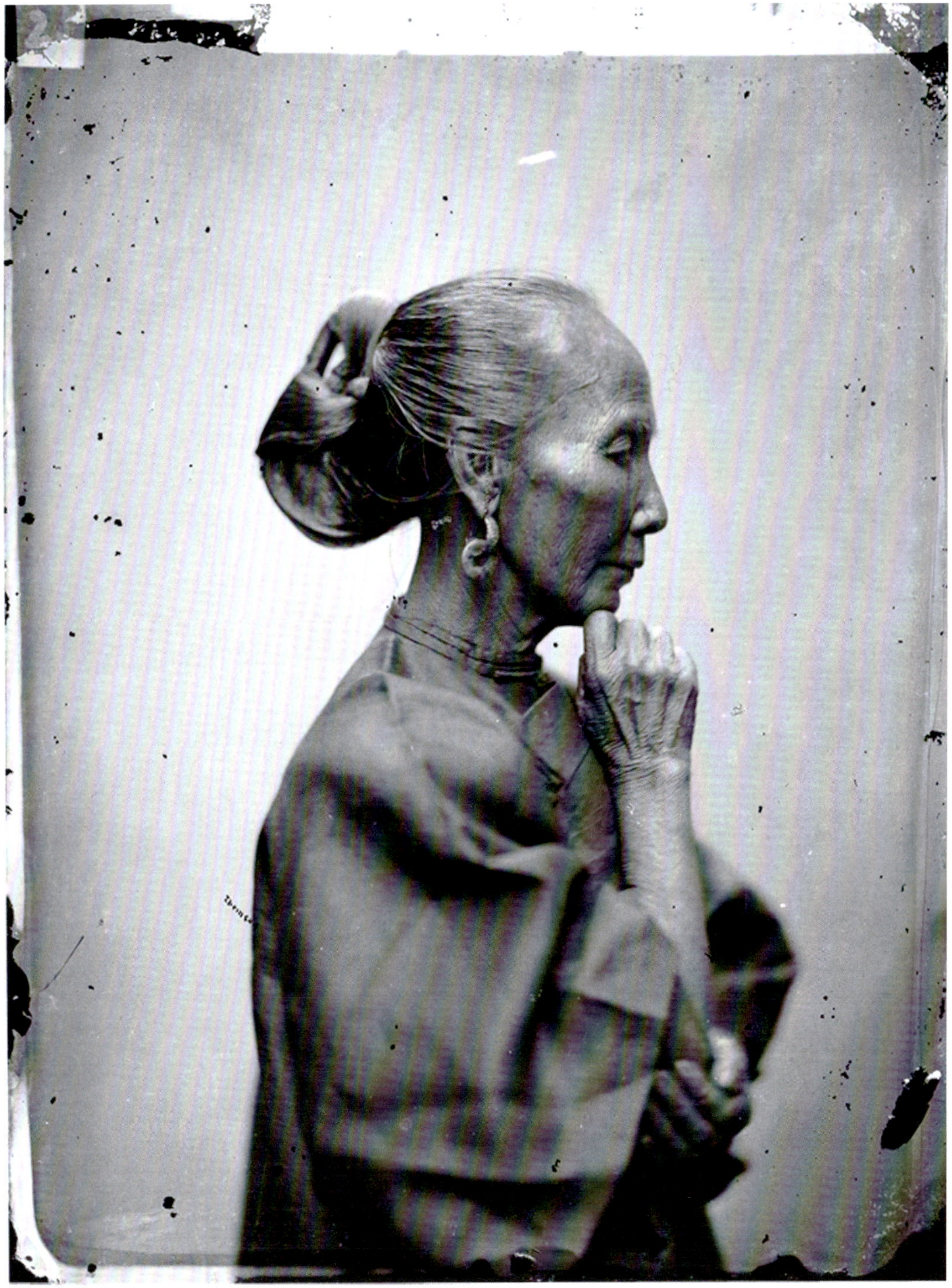

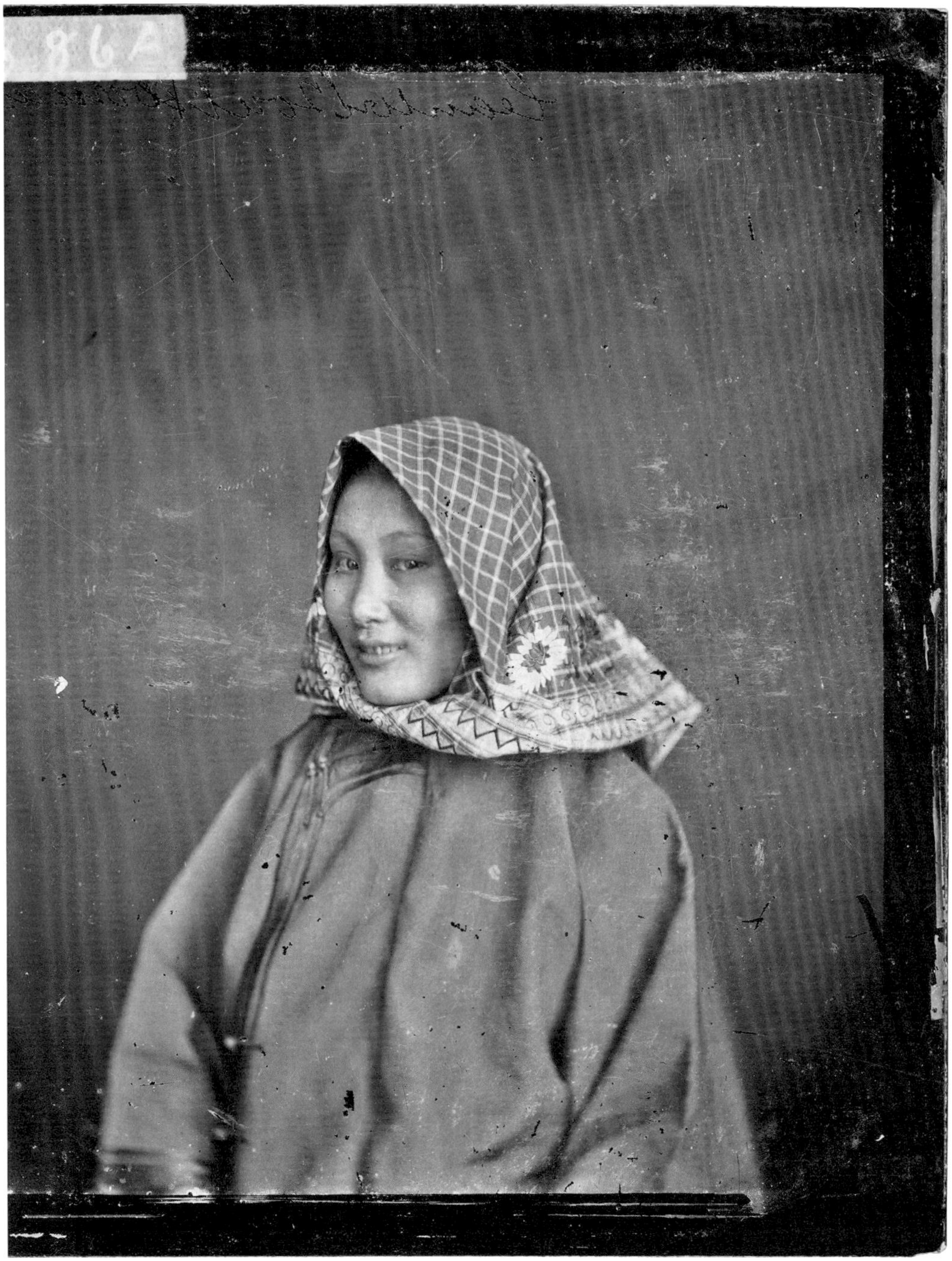
86A

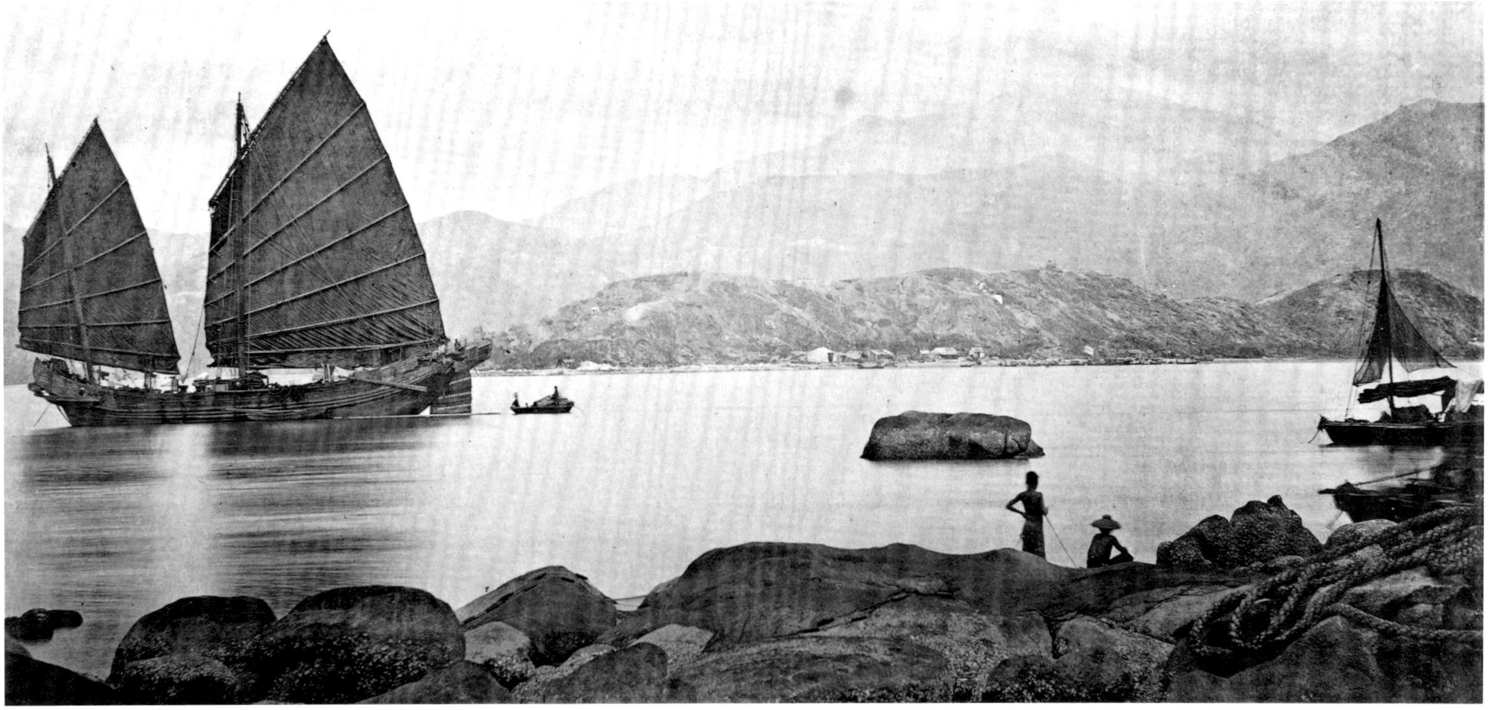

LEFT: A BOATWOMAN

Guangzhou, Guangdong

The Tankas or boat people are an ethnic group in coastal parts of Southern China. They live all their lives on boats or junks and fish for a living. Thomson was greatly attracted by their natural beauty since, as he noted, they never used makeup and were always dressed simply. He further remarked that they were the prettiest and most attractive-looking women he had come across in southern China. This photograph captures the cheeky smile of this confident Tanka woman.

A JUNK

Guangzhou, Guangdong

'Junk' is a European term for a Chinese sailing vessel, which comes from the Javanese word 'jong', meaning a large vessel. Thomson wrote that the one shown here '*is a fine type of its class and has in her model something of the foreign ship, though retaining quite enough of the old Chinese build to soothe the prejudices of the nation.*' In the 19th century this type of junk was popular with traders, and they were often '*well-armed, carrying . . . half-a-dozen smoothbore guns of foreign make for six or eight-pound shot, a number of matchlocks, and a quantity of ammunition.*' This image is an iconic late 19th-century representation of the South China Sea. Similar scenes are to be found in many western paintings of the same period.

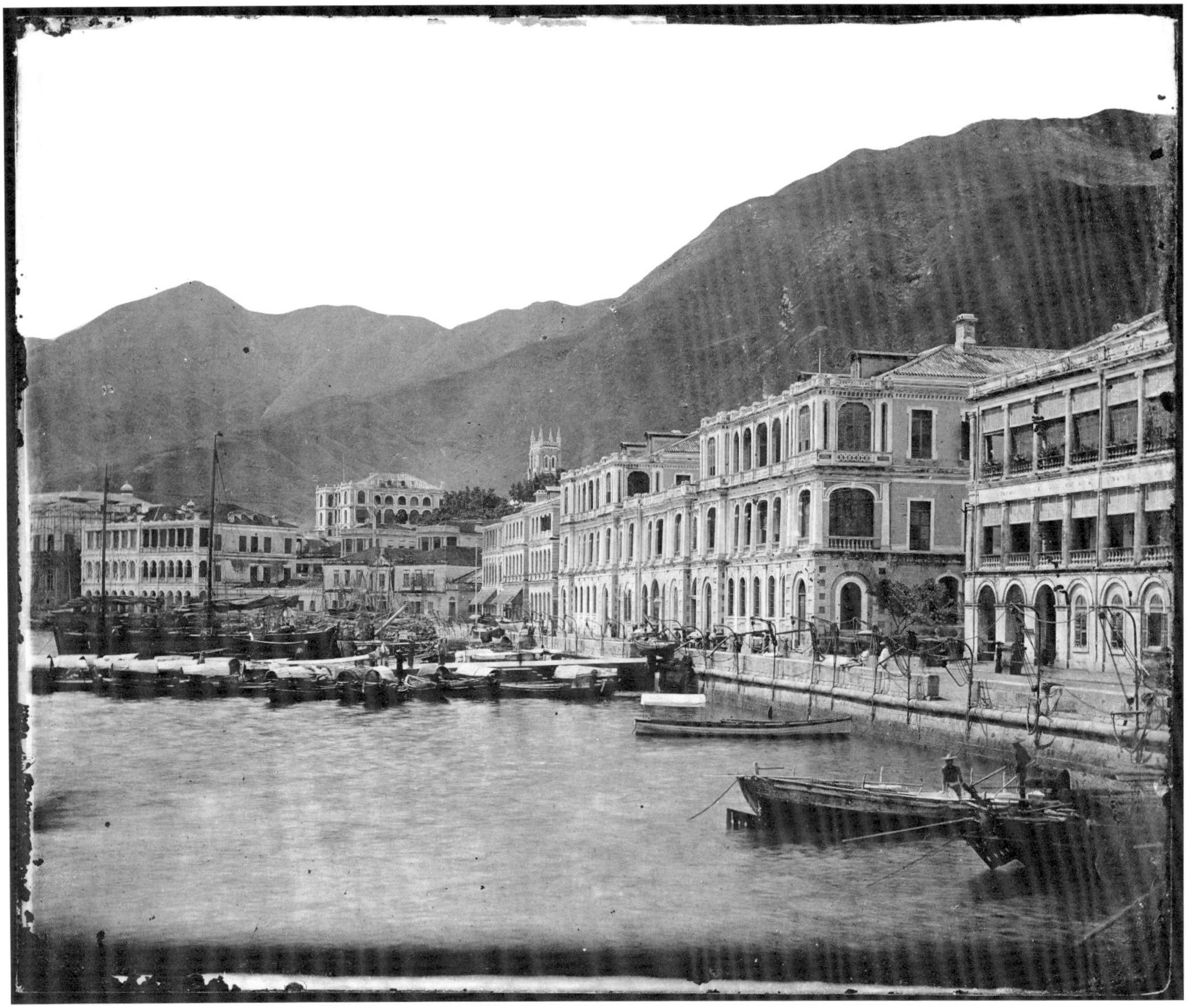

Praya or Des Voeux Road

Hong Kong

Standing on the harbour praya, or today just south of the eastern end of Chater Road, Thomson photographed the imposing façade of the City Hall, completed in 1869, midway during his time in Hong Kong. The attractive northern curve of the praya allowed him to take his view from some distance back. Even so, the bulk of the City Hall hid the buildings higher up: St John's Cathedral and the Government Offices. Due to major land reclamation projects from the late 19th century to the 20th century, today the Des Voeux Road tramline is several streets away from the shoreline.

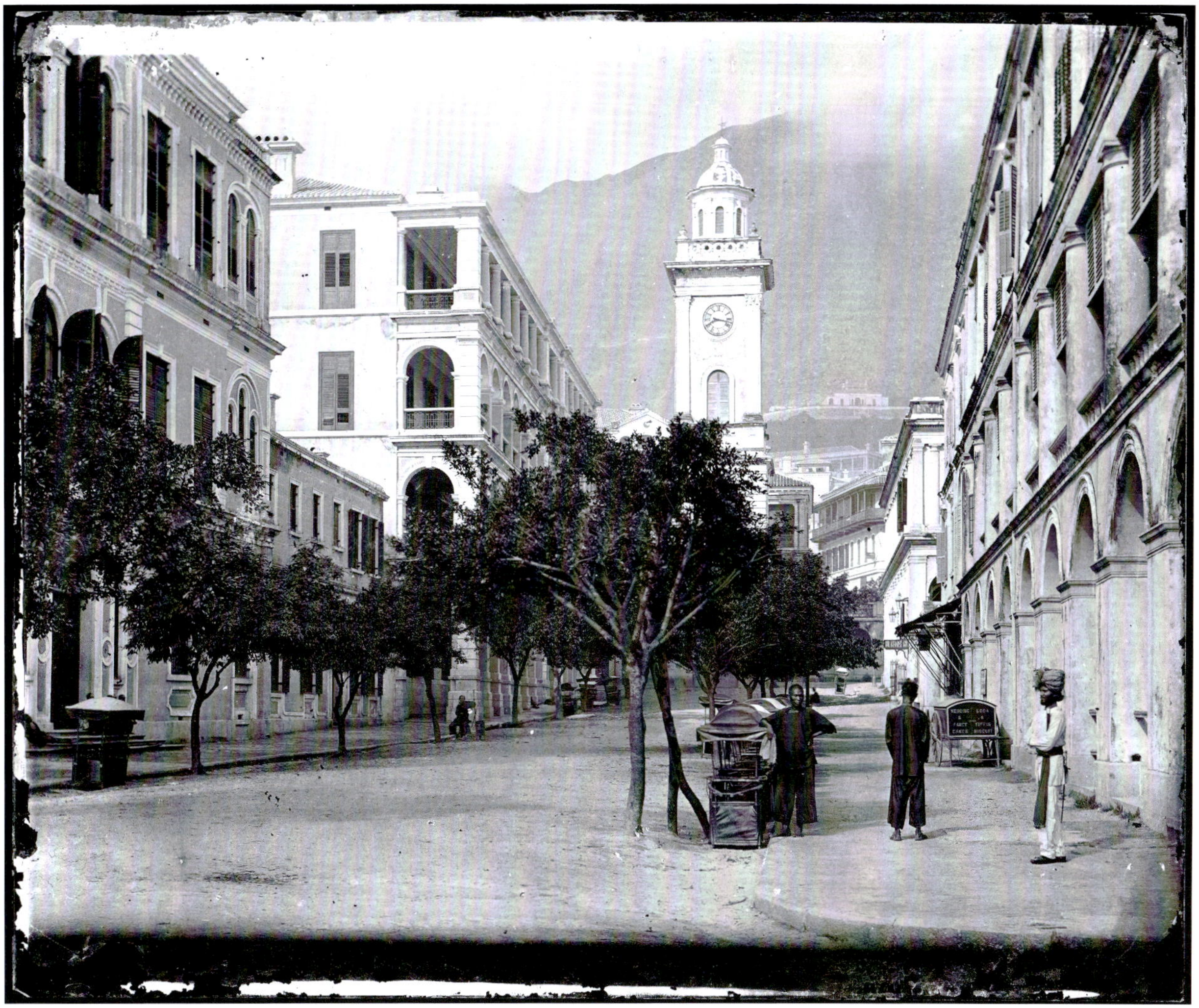

Pedder Street

Hong Kong

One of John Thomson's best-known photograph of Hong Kong, this streetscape looks inland along Pedder Street towards its clock tower. Sited at the northern side of the intersection of Pedder Street and Queen's Road (today's Queen's Road Central) the clock tower was completed in 1862 and demolished in 1913.

In John Thomson's time Pedder Street was a good location for sedan chair bearers to ply their trade, while today it is one of Central district's busiest taxi ranks.

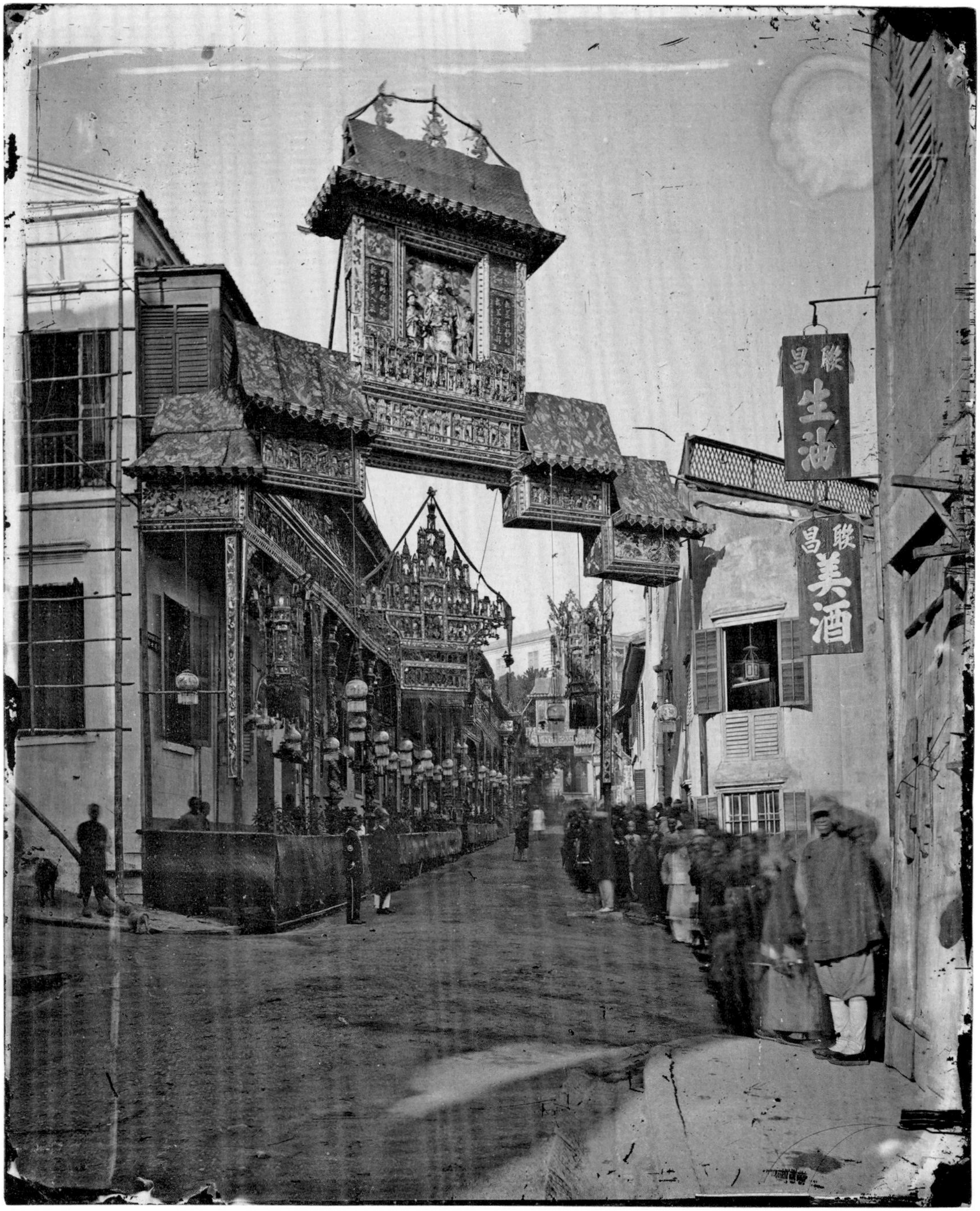
駿昌
生油
駿昌
美酒

LEFT: LYNDHURST TERRACE

Hong Kong

Lyndhurst Terrace is in the Central District of Hong Kong and the photograph was taken during H.R.H. the Duke of Edinburgh's brief visit in 1869. Alfred, Duke of Saxe-Coburg and Gotha, was the second son of Queen Victoria and the first member of the British royal family to visit the Crown Colony. To celebrate the Duke's short stopover on his way to India, great efforts were made to decorate the colony and the streets were full of festivities. Here Lyndhurst Terrace is festooned with lanterns, banners, and a Chinese triumphal arch. John Thomson, only recently settled in Hong Kong, was commissioned to provide the photographs for a commemorative book of the visit.

COCHRANE STREET

Hong Kong

Cochrane Street is a steep hilly street between Queen's Road Central and Lyndhurst Terrace. Wellington Street crosses half way down and there is a pawn shop on the northeast corner. On the far left of the photograph set onto the brick wall, a sign names Cochrane Street. The view was probably taken from above Wellington Street.

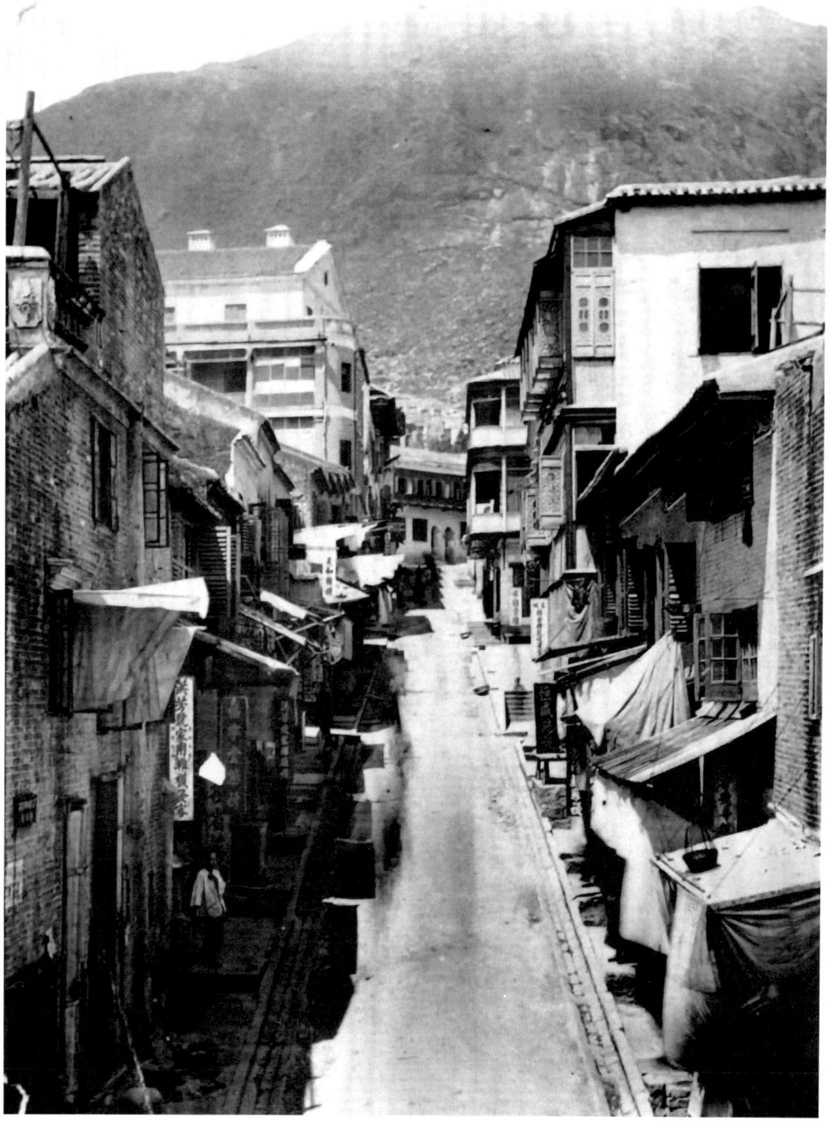

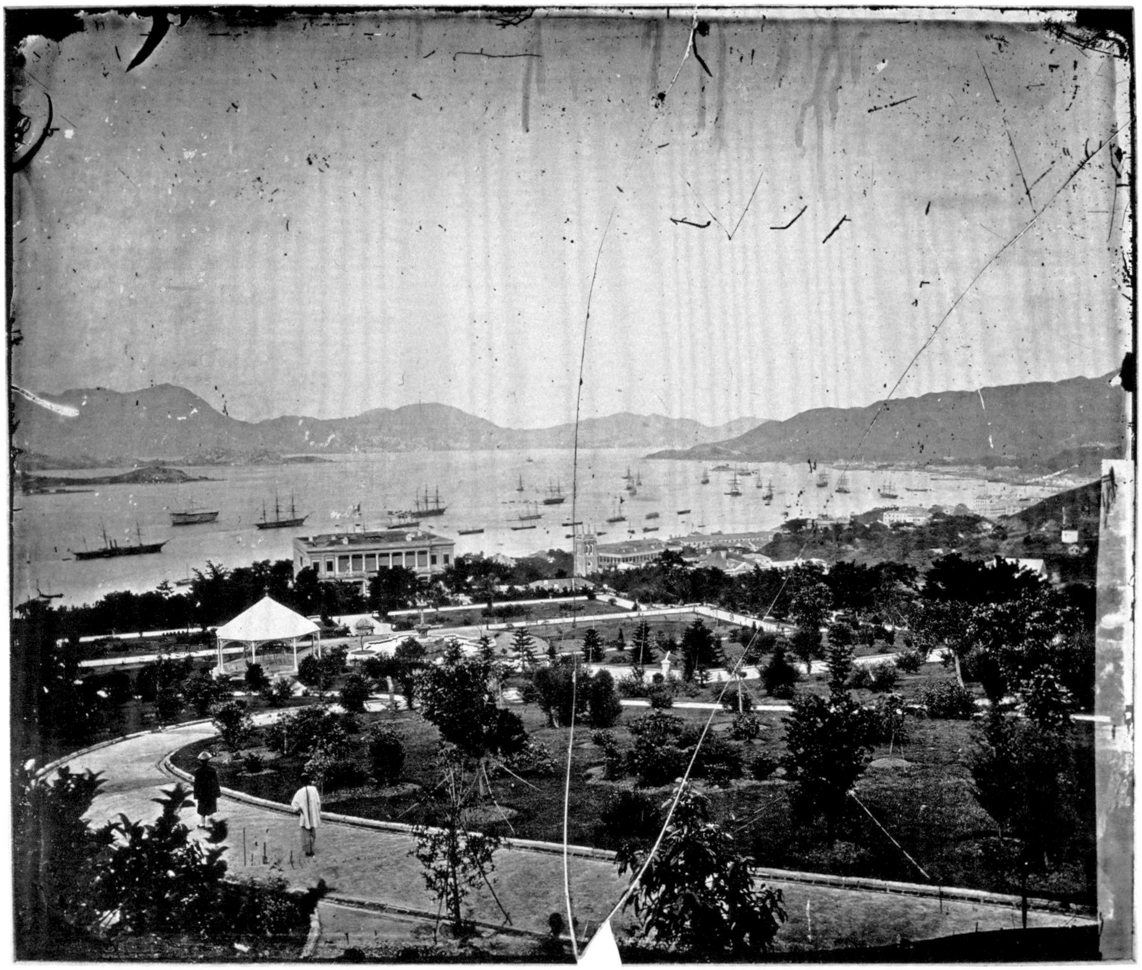

Hong Kong Botanic Gardens from Albany

Hong Kong

The Victorians were obsessed with cultivating exotic plants from distant lands. In the newly found Crown Colony, the idea of a public botanic garden emerged as early as 1848, but it was only in 1871 that the Hong Kong Botanic Gardens opened its doors to the public. The garden was located at mid-levels on the northern slope of Victoria Peak and was built on the site of Ping Tao Garden, which served as a temporary home for the former Governor Sir Henry Pottinger in 1841-2.

In the early 1970s the Botanic Gardens underwent a significant expansion, and it began to house rare or endangered species of animals and birds for conservation and educational purposes. It was renamed the Zoological and Botanical Gardens in 1975. The photo shows a view of Victoria Harbour at the time when the Garden was first opened. In the distance in front of the harbour stood St John's Cathedral and Headquarters House, now known as Flagstaff House.

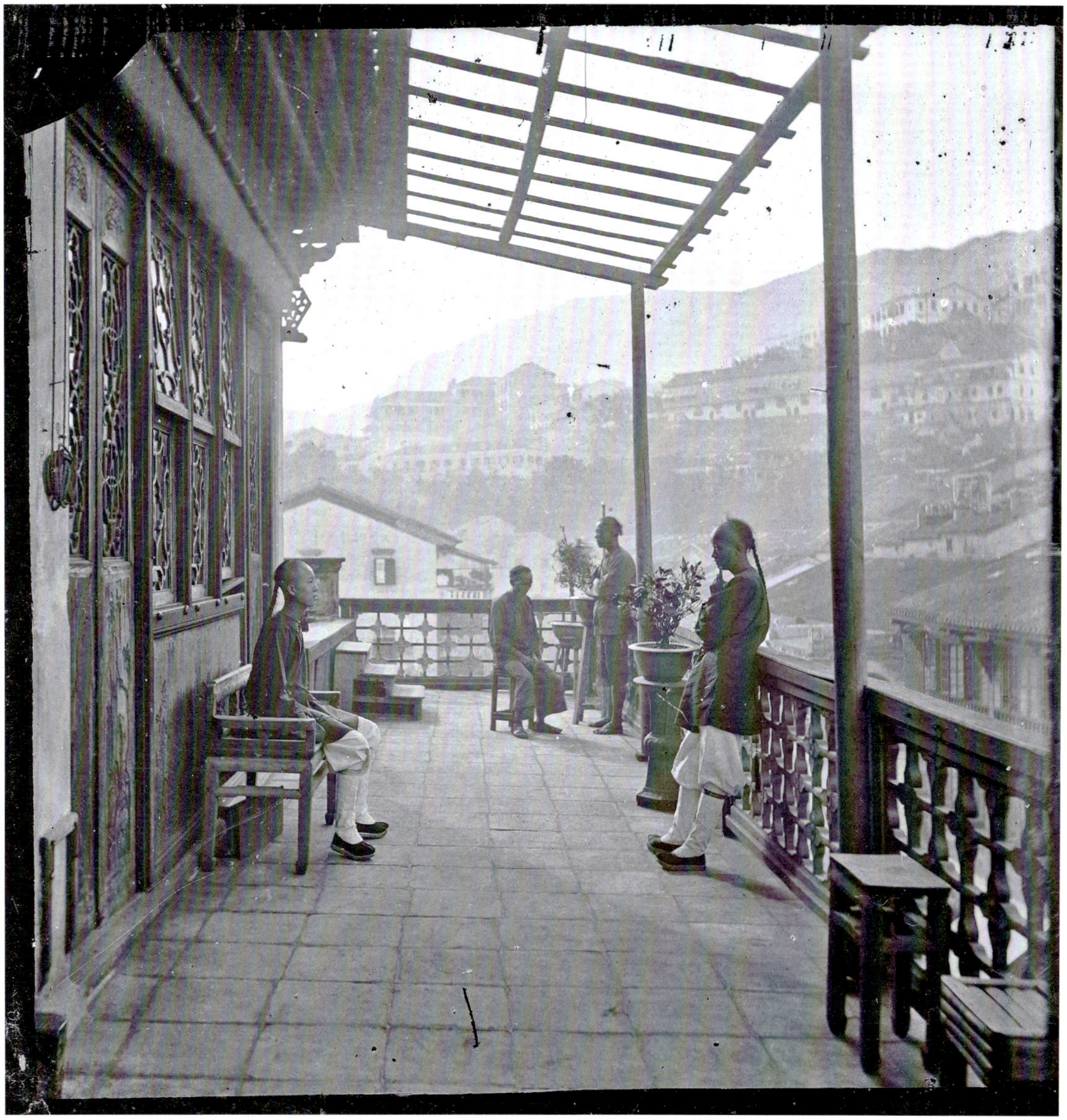

THE VERANDA OF A CHINESE TEAHOUSE

Hong Kong

Tea drinking has been an important feature in southern China for centuries. In the second half of the 19th century, commercial teahouses flourished in response to the influx of Chinese merchants and labourers moving to Hong Kong. There were various types of teahouses catering for different classes. Some of them not only served tea and snacks but also offered opium, as well as female attendants. This photograph shows a typical middle-range teahouse with an open veranda.

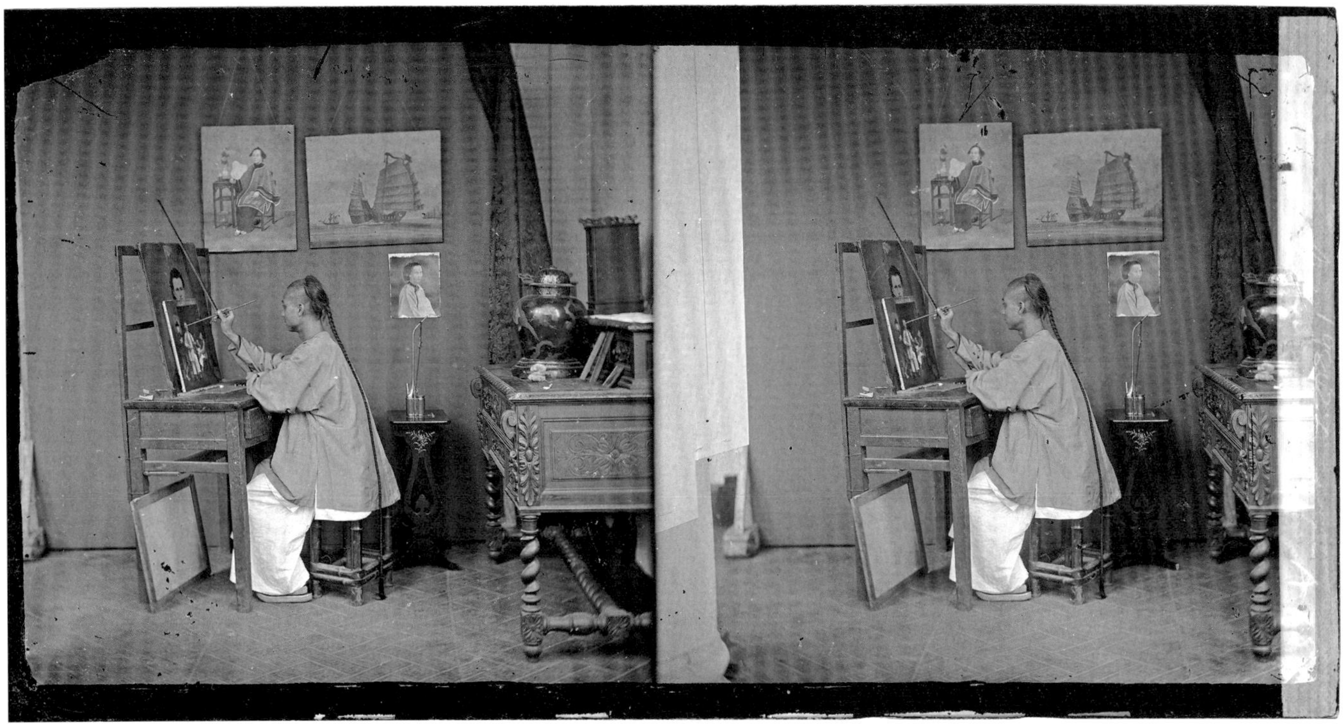

A Chinese Portrait Artist

Hong Kong

Despite the introduction of photography to China, many Chinese still preferred a painted portrait. This was due in part to the fact that photographs of the time were small and in black and white and to have them enlarged was expensive. For those Chinese who embraced photography, it was usually because they did not have the patience to sit through a long portrait-painting session. Instead, they would have a photograph taken, then the portrait painter would make a bigger reproduction of it in colour. At the time the Chinese term "xiezhen" to 'transcribe the real' referred to both photography and portrait painting, suggesting there was little conceptual differentiation between the two in China.

Thomson photographed many subjects using a stereographic camera. Stereographic cameras produced two images which, when placed side by side and viewed through a specially designed viewer, would produce a three-dimensional visual effect. Stereoscopic cameras consisted of either two lenses mounted side by side, or a single lens that was moved to replicate the distance between human eyes. There were many such Stereoscope glass negatives in the Thomson collection.

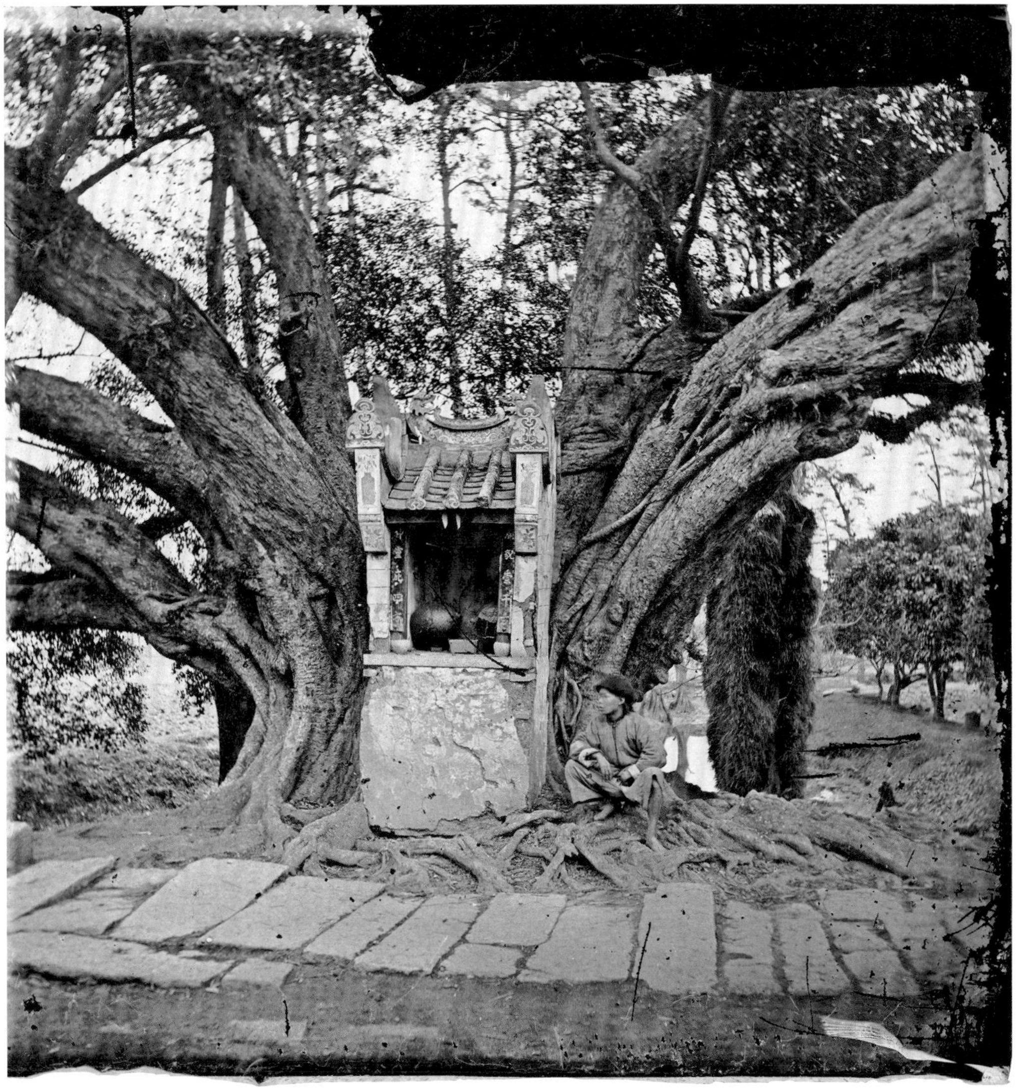

A Roadside Shrine

Taiwan

In Victorian times, Europeans developed a taste for exotic 'scenes' from faraway places, encompassing landscapes as well as portraits. Thomson was not interested in producing what he called '*lifeless charts of the mechanical proportions of nature*' but instead tried to capture the human and spiritual dimensions within scenes. Here Thomson shows a small shrine, which represented the spiritual centre of the village since it connected with the root of the large old tree. It was said that local people, through their offerings at the altar in the centre of the shrine, found a connection with mother earth.

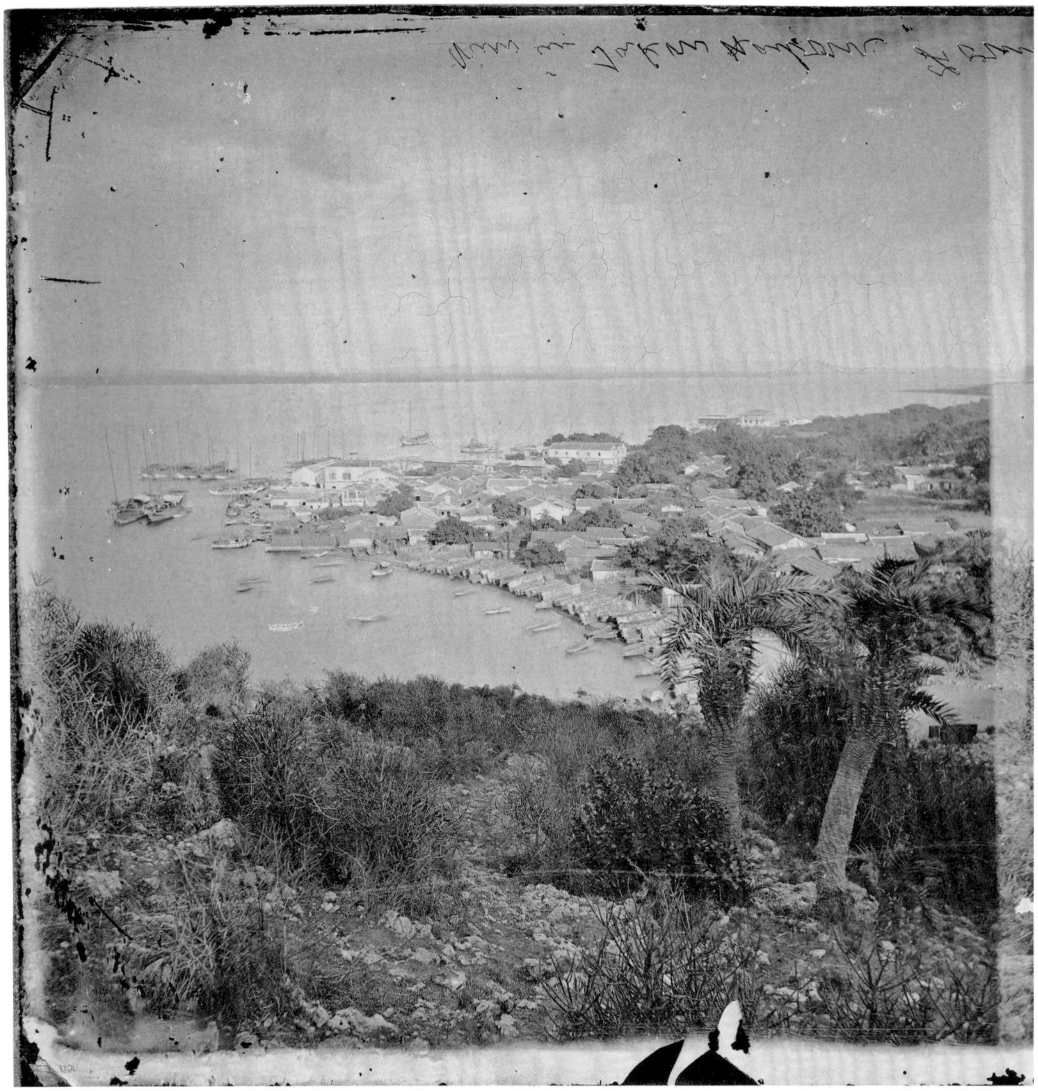

TAKAO HARBOUR

Kaohsiung, Taiwan

Takao, literally meaning 'bamboo forest', was an ancient name for Kaohsiung. For centuries, it was a haven for lawless pirates and rebels. Under the Dutch, and later the Chinese, it became a prosperous fishing port. The rest of the land, landscape and coast remained unspoiled, with a great coral reef and 'luxuriant tropical trees'. With the Treaty of Peking (Beijing) in 1860, the Qing government was forced to open Takao as a port for foreign trade. A British consul was posted there, and a few houses and companies were set up by foreigners. However social unrest continued in Takao, robberies aimed at the privileged British and other Europeans living there were common. This view of the harbour was taken from Takao Mountain, also known as Apes' Hill. The image shows the contrast between the already developed harbour and the uninhabited hill beyond.

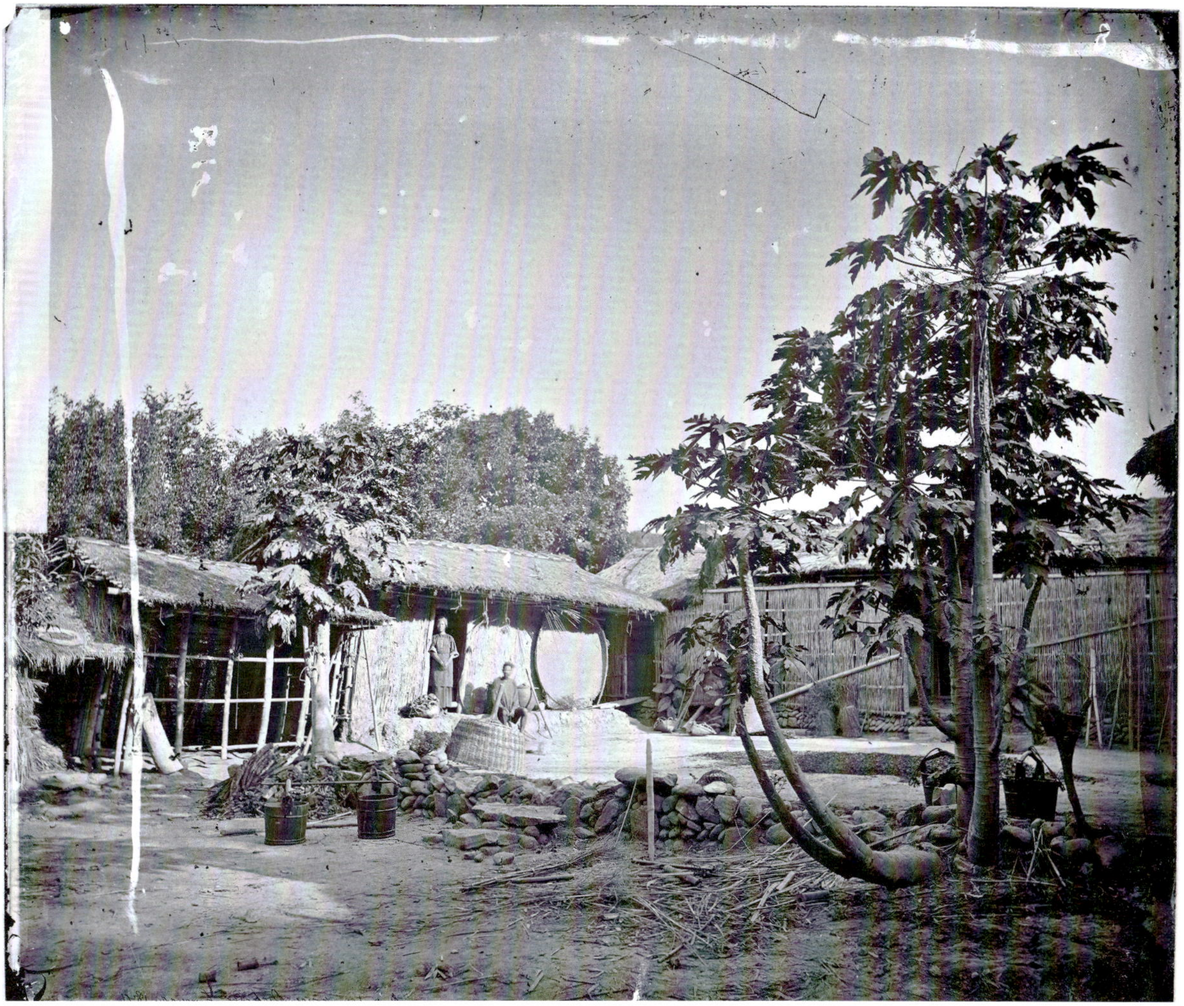

PEPO DWELLINGS IN ZUOJHEN (ZUOZHEN)

Tainan, Taiwan

'Pepo' is a generic term for the aborigines of Taiwan. There are at least 11 groups of aborigines whom Chinese call Pepohoan ('hoan' or 'fan' in Chinese means savages), with each group having its own distinct culture and tradition. The one Thomson came across near Tainan is generally thought to have been the Siraiya, which is the biggest group, and many of them intermarried with the local Chinese. This photograph shows a typical Pepo dwelling in the late 19th century. According to Thomson, it was '*tolerably clean, well-arranged, and comfortable, and presents a striking uniformity of design in the different settlements throughout the island*'. The structure of the dwelling was mainly made from bamboo. It is interesting to note that while the Chinese regarded the Siraiya as 'savages', Thomson found their dwellings were '*superior to those of the Chinese squatters, and the people themselves were better dressed.*'

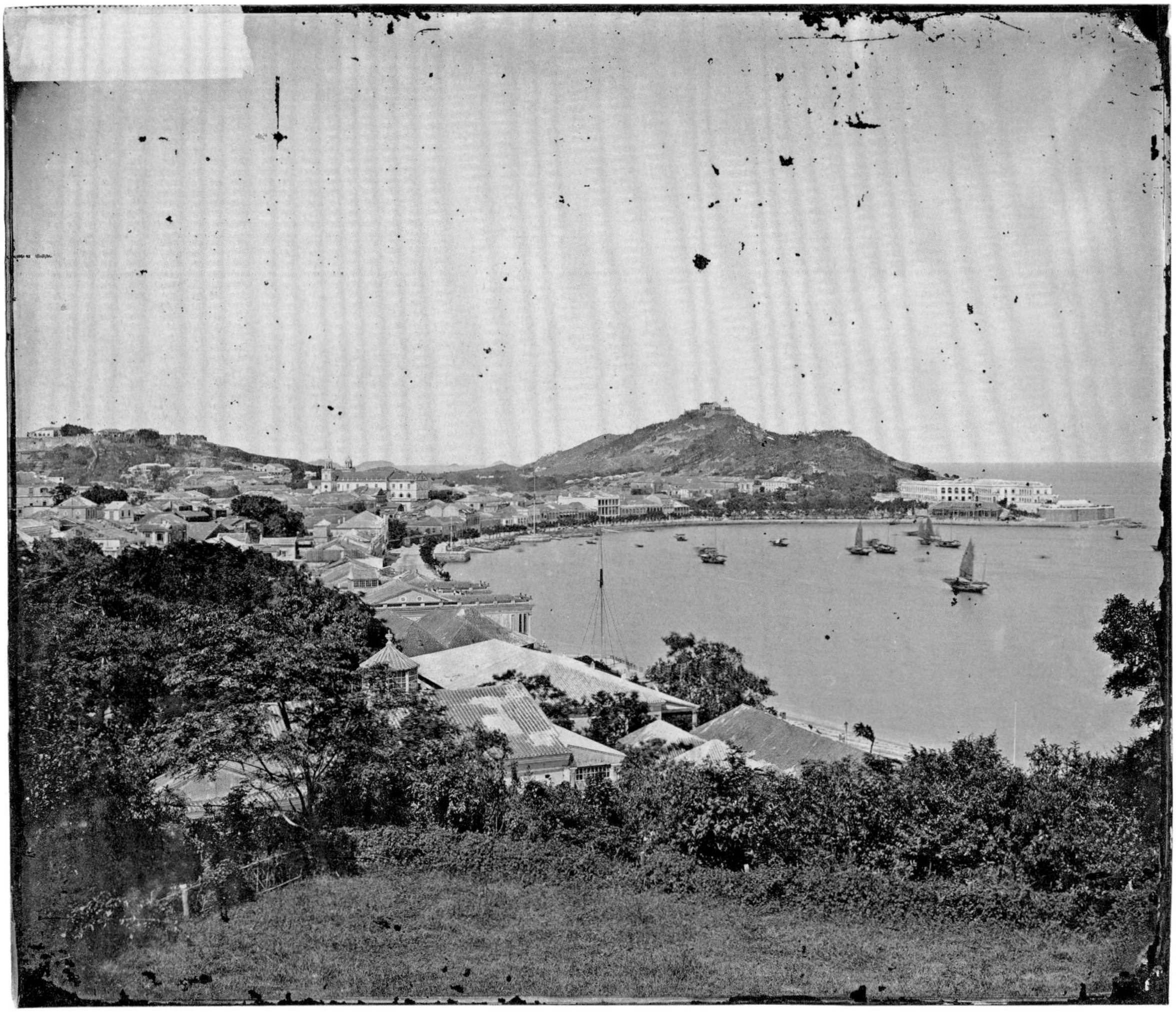

VIEW OF THE PRAIA GRANDE, NAM VAN

Macau

Throughout the 19th century Praia Grande was the most fashionable address in Macau, capturing the imagination of artists and photographers. From the 1820s onwards, a view of the Praia Grande was the must-have souvenir of Macau. Painters such as Chinnery and Lamqua were residents of Macau at the time, and the view of the Praia Grande was a favourite subject. In 1844 Jules Itier, the head of the French Trade Commission in China, made the first photograph of this famous view in the form of a daguerreotype. In 1870, when Thomson took this photograph, he selected a view looking down on the Praia Grande from Penha Hill above Bishop's Bay. Due to extensive 20th century redevelopment, this view now only survives in old paintings, photographs, and postcards.

The Ruins of St. Paul's

Macau

The dilapidated remains of the church of St. Paul, stands adjacent to the Mount Fortress. It was constructed in 1580 by the Jesuit mission and then rebuilt in 1602. The Baroque-style stone façade was completed in the 1620s by a group of exiled Japanese Christians.The church was burned down in 1835.The surviving façade, with its four tiers of colonnades, is covered with carvings and statues that are regarded by some as embodying the perfect fusion of western and eastern cultures. There are statues of the Virgin and saints, symbols of the Garden of Eden and the crucifixion, angels and the devil, a Chinese dragon and a Japanese chrysanthemum, a Portuguese sailing ship and pious warnings inscribed in Chinese.This is an early example of Christian Church architecture in Asia.

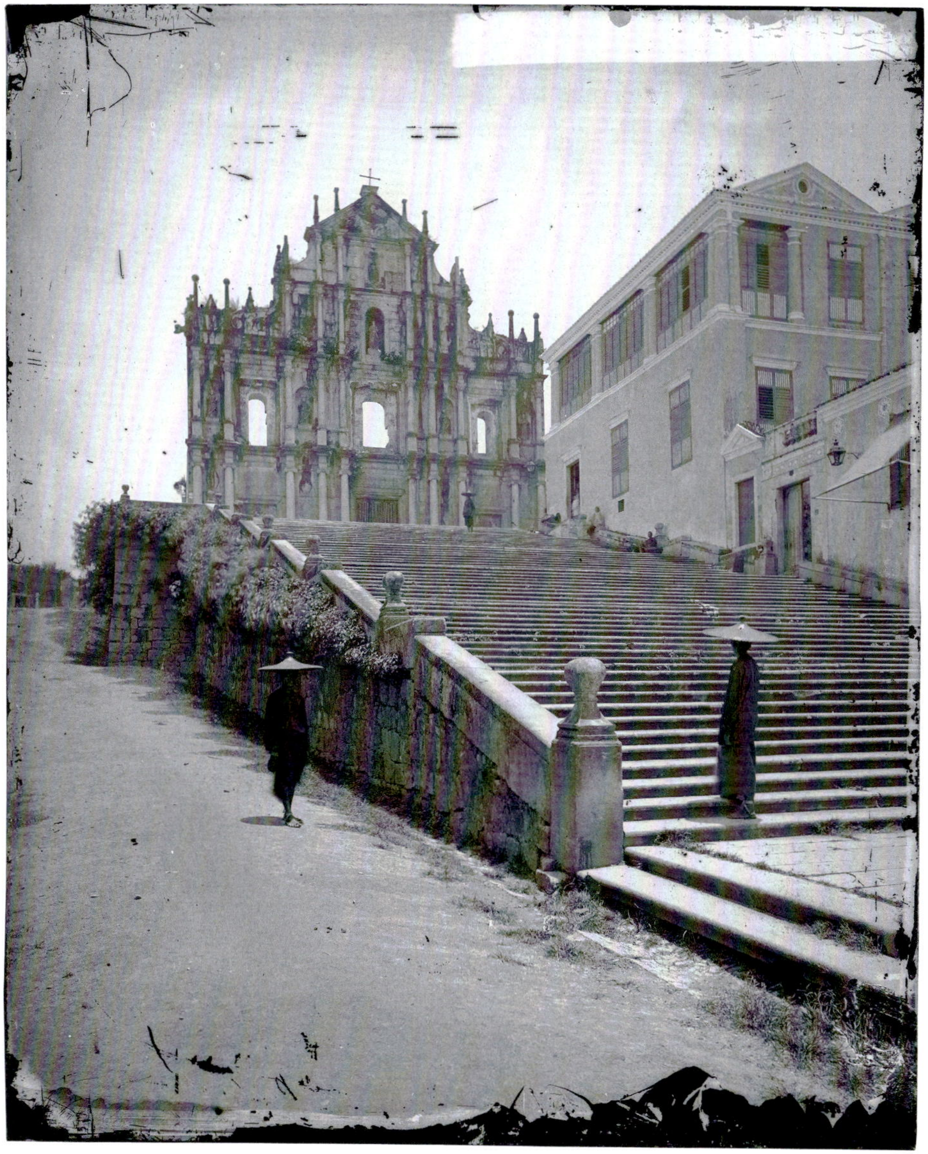

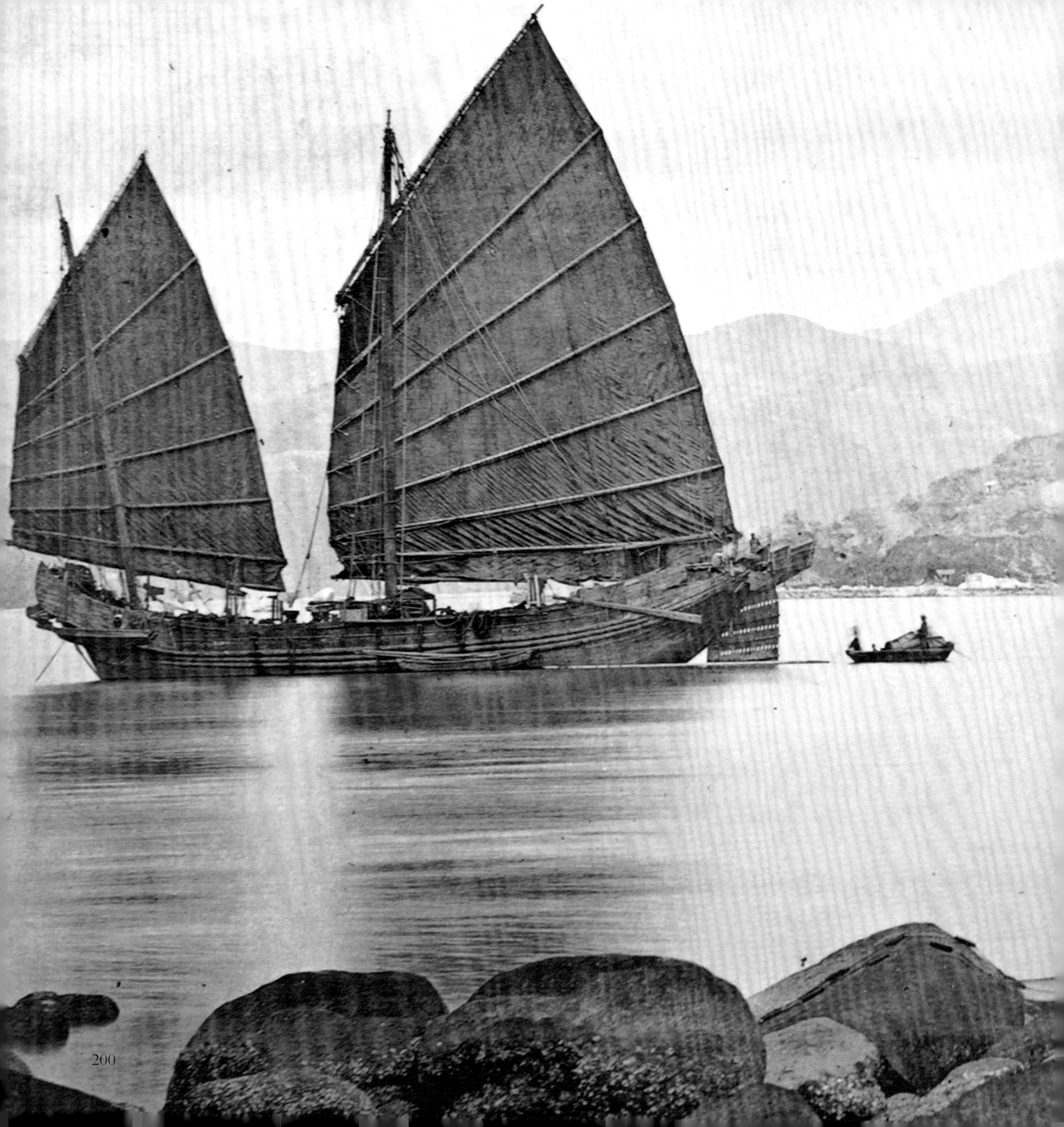

ACKNOWLEDGEMENTS AND FURTHER READING

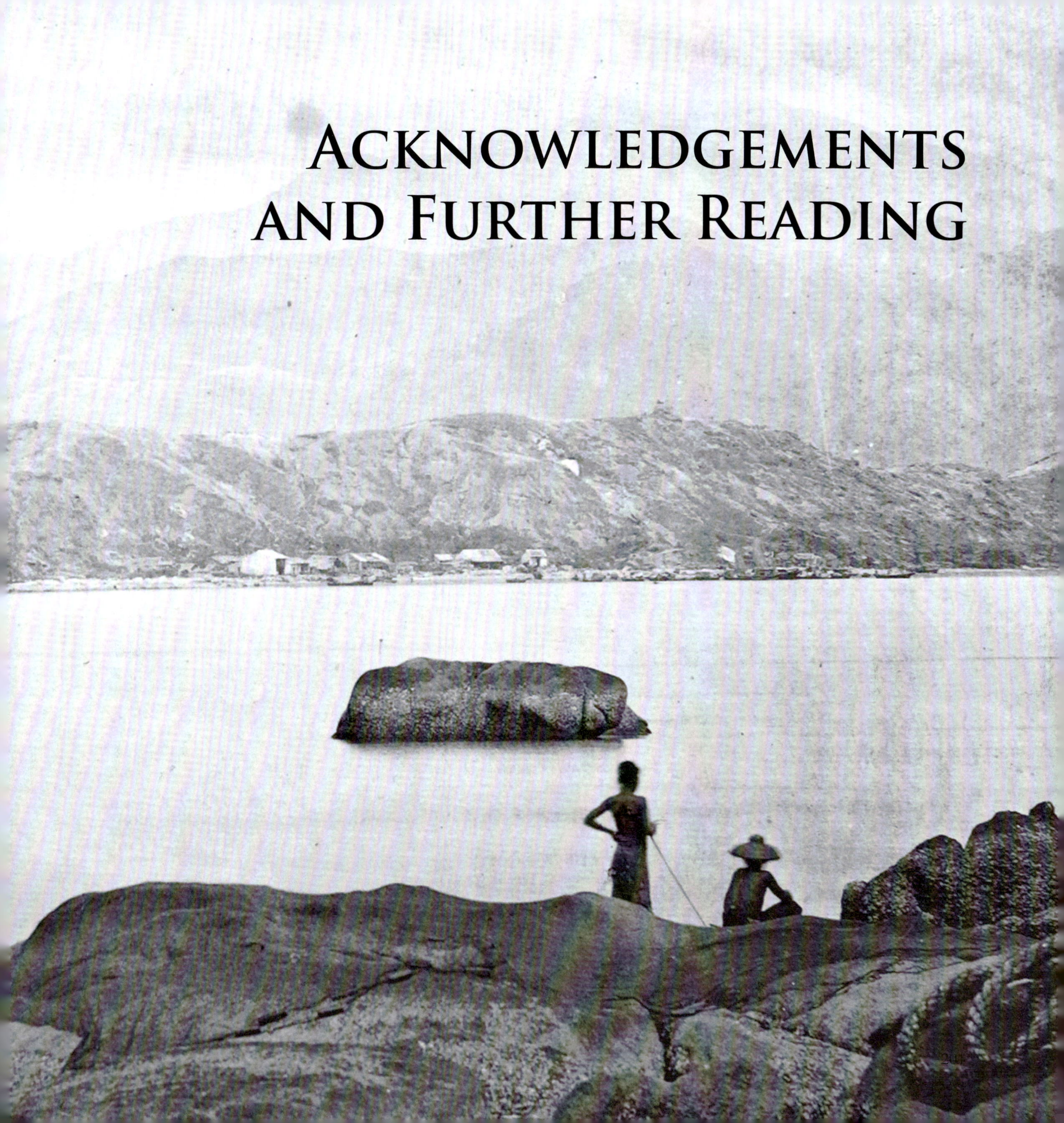

FURTHER READING

Bautze, Joachim K. *Unseen Siam: Early Photography 1860–1910*, Bangkok: River Books, 2017.

Belknap, Geoffrey. 'Through the Looking Glass: Photography, Science and Imperial Motivations in John Thomson's Photographic Expeditions', *History of Science*, vol.52(1), 2014.

Bennett, Terry. *History of Photography in China: Western Photographers 1861-1879*. London: Bernard Quaritch Ltd., 2010.

Cody, Jeffrey W and Terpak, Frances, eds. *Brush & Shutter: Early Photography in China*. Los Angeles: Getty Research Institute, 2011.

Hillemann, Ulrike. *Asian Empire and British knowledge: China and the networks of British imperial expansion*. New York: Palgrave Macmillan, 2009.

Hight, Eleanor M. and Gary D. Sampson, eds. *Colonialist photography: Imagining Race and place*. London: Routledge, 2002.

Lau, Grace. *Picturing the Chinese: Early Western photographs and postcards of China*. San Francisco: Long River Press, 2008.

Ovenden, Richard. *John Thomson (1837-1921): Photographer*. Edinburgh: The Stationery Office, 1997.

Parker, Elliot S. 'John Thomson, 1837-1921 RGS Instructor in Photography', *The Geographical Journal*, vol. 144, no. 3 (Nov., 1978).

Roberts, Claire. *Photography and China*, London: Reaktion Books, 2013.

Ryan, James. "Imperial landscapes: photography, geography and British overseas exploration, 1858-1872," in *Geography and Imperialism*, 1995.

Schwartz, Joan M. and James R. Ryan. *Picturing Place: Photography and the Geographical Imagination*, London: I.B.Tauris, 2003.

Thomson, John. *Illustrations of China and Its People: A Series of Two Hundred Photograph with Letterpress Descriptive of the Places and People Represented*. London: Sampson Low, Marston, Low, and Searle, [1873 to 1874].

------------------. *The Straits of Malacca, Indo-China, and China; or ten years of travels, adventures, and residence abroad*. New York: Harper & Bros., 1875.

-------------------. *Through China with a Camera*. London: Westminster and Constable Co. 1989.

-------------------. "Photography and Exploration," *Proceedings of the Royal Geographical Society*, N.S. 13, 1891.

Wue, Roberta. "Essentially Chinese: The Chinese Portrait Subject in Nineteenth-Century Photography" in *Body and Face in Chinese Visual Culture*, eds. by Wu Hung and Katherine R. Tsiang, Harvard University Press, 2005.

ACKNOWLEDGEMENTS

William Schupbach, Wellcome Collection, London

Professor Nick Pearce, Richmond Chair of Fine Arts, University of Glasgow

Maj. Gen. M.R. Suphawat Kasemsri

Rachanee Supvichit

Dr. Xun Zhou, Reader in History, University of Essex

Following pages:

Opposite
Detail from the group of musicians and dancers shown on page 52.

Page 204-205
Fuzhou was one of five ports opened to foreign residents by the Treaty of Nanjing in 1842, although another decade passed before the city finally entered into trade with foreign countries, its chief export being tea. By the time of Thomson's visit, Fuzhou's foreign settlement, built on the south bank of the Min River, was well established with a mixture of Chinese and European-style houses.

Page 206-207
In front of the former Ananta Samakom Throne Hall within the Grand Palace, the Crown Prince, Prince Chulalongkorn, sits in the centre with his full brother, Prince Bhanurangsi Savangwongse, at his side. Their half-brother Prince Kasemsan Sophak stands slightly apart. In front of them on the carpet are items of regalia. Royal pages crouch down in the foreground.

Page 208
Detail of the stereographic photograph of a portrait painter shown on page 194.

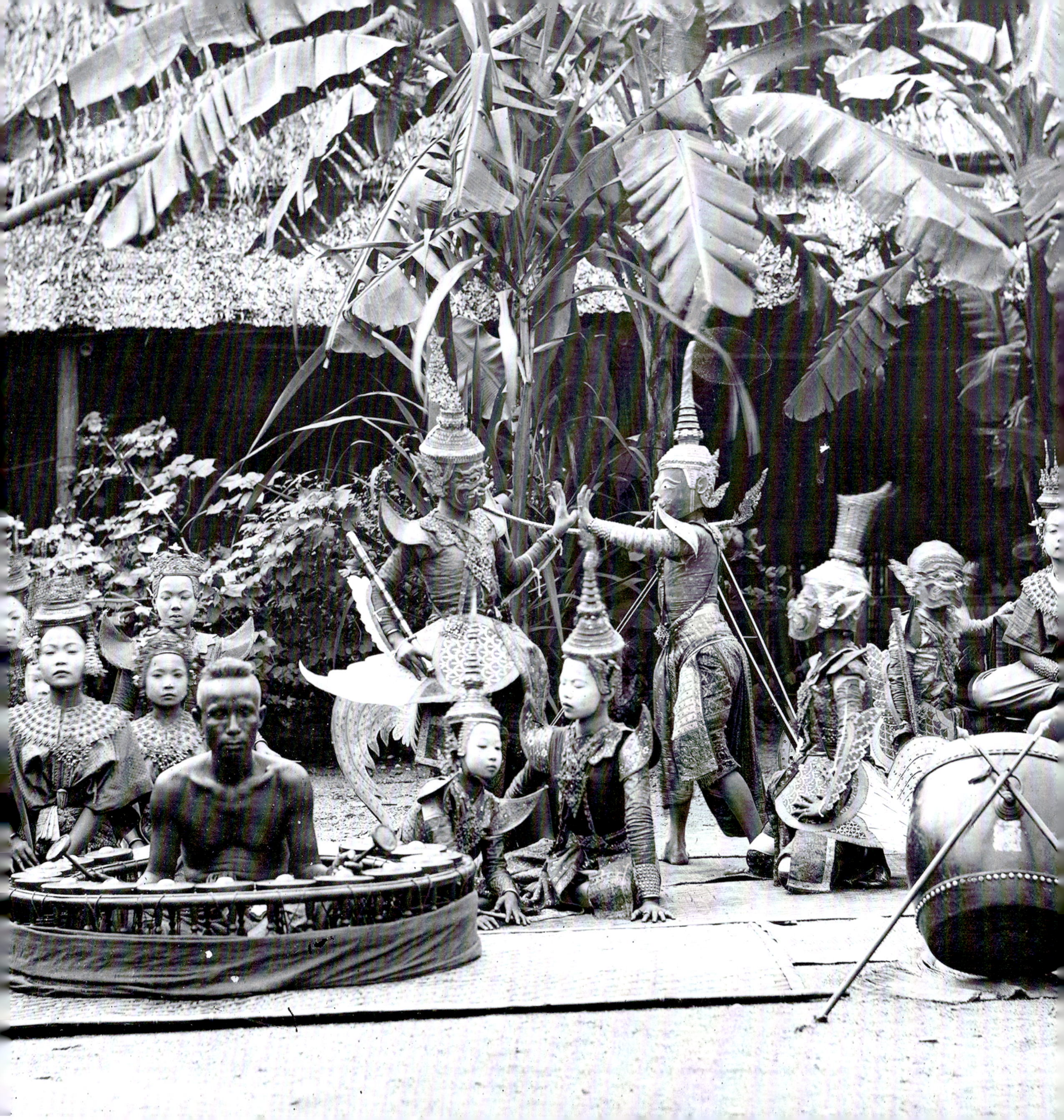

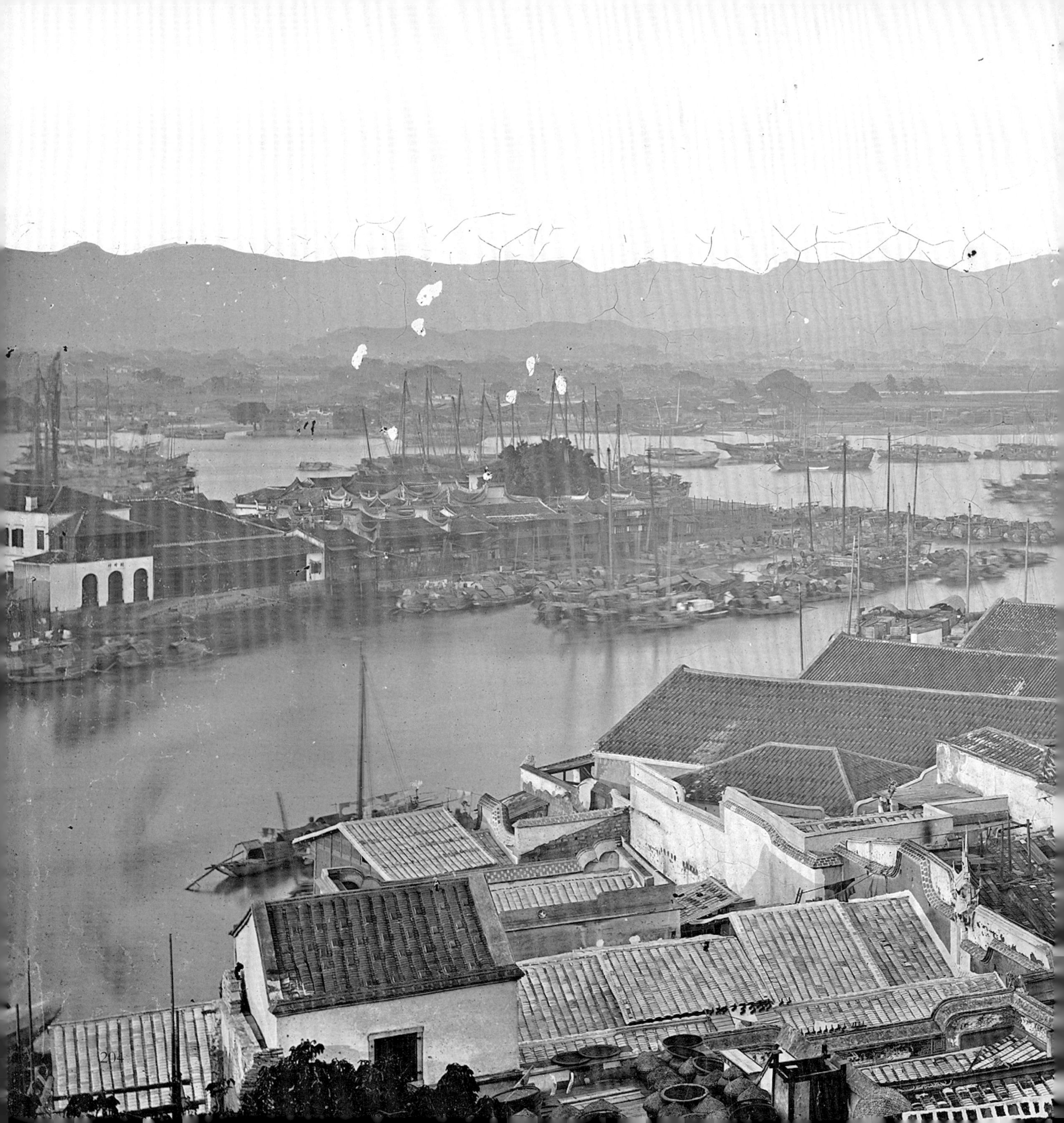

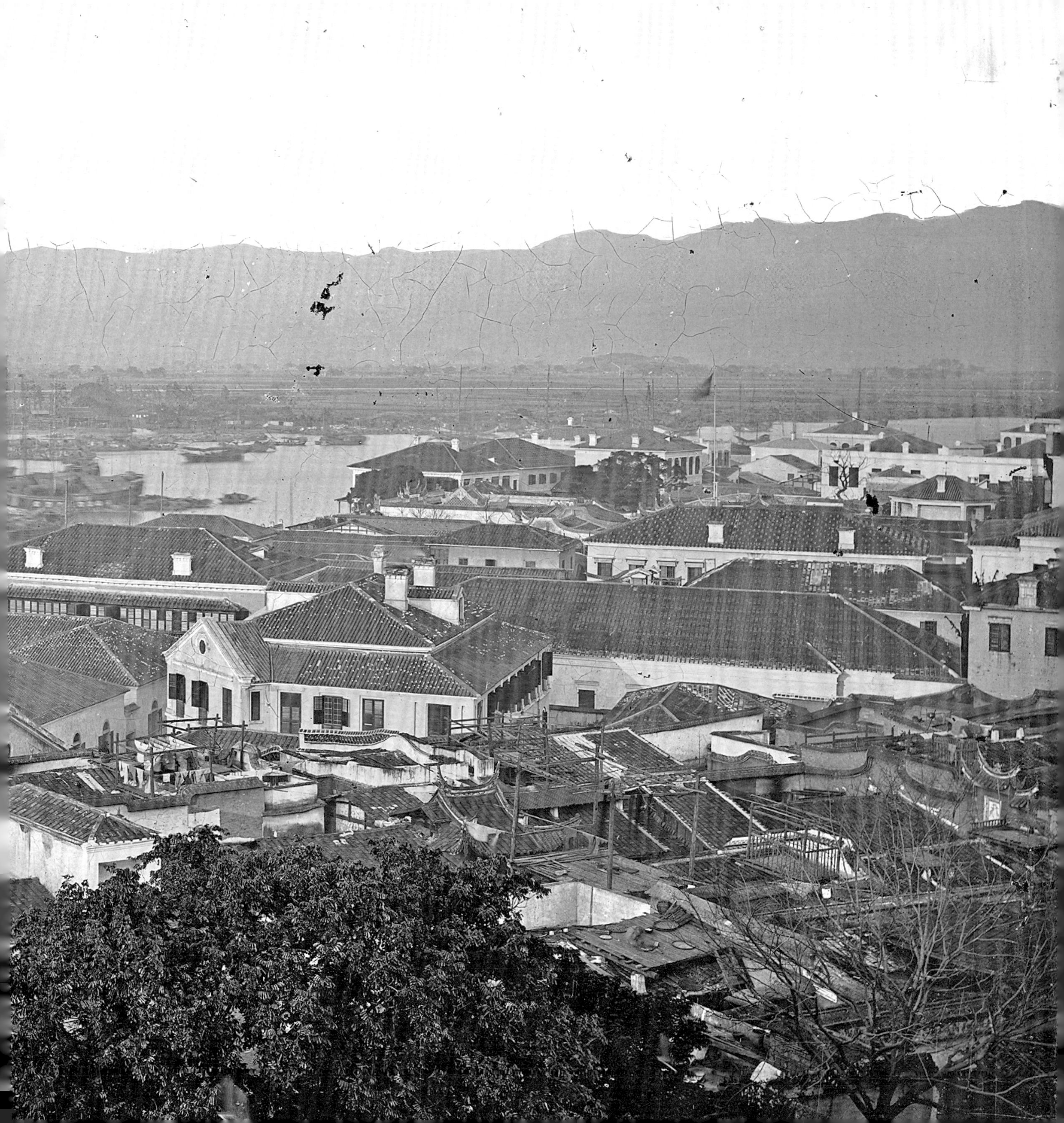

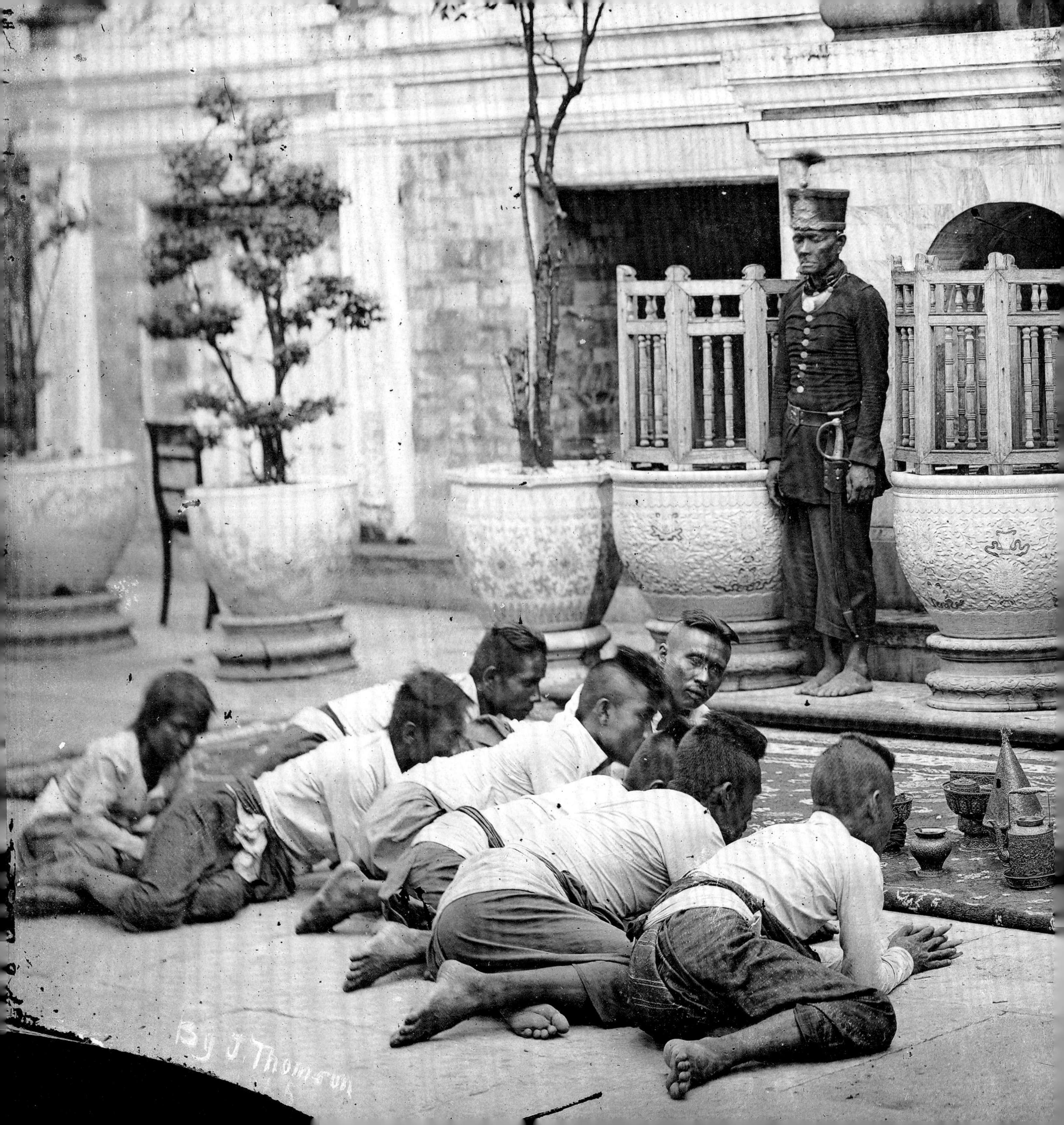
By J. Thomson

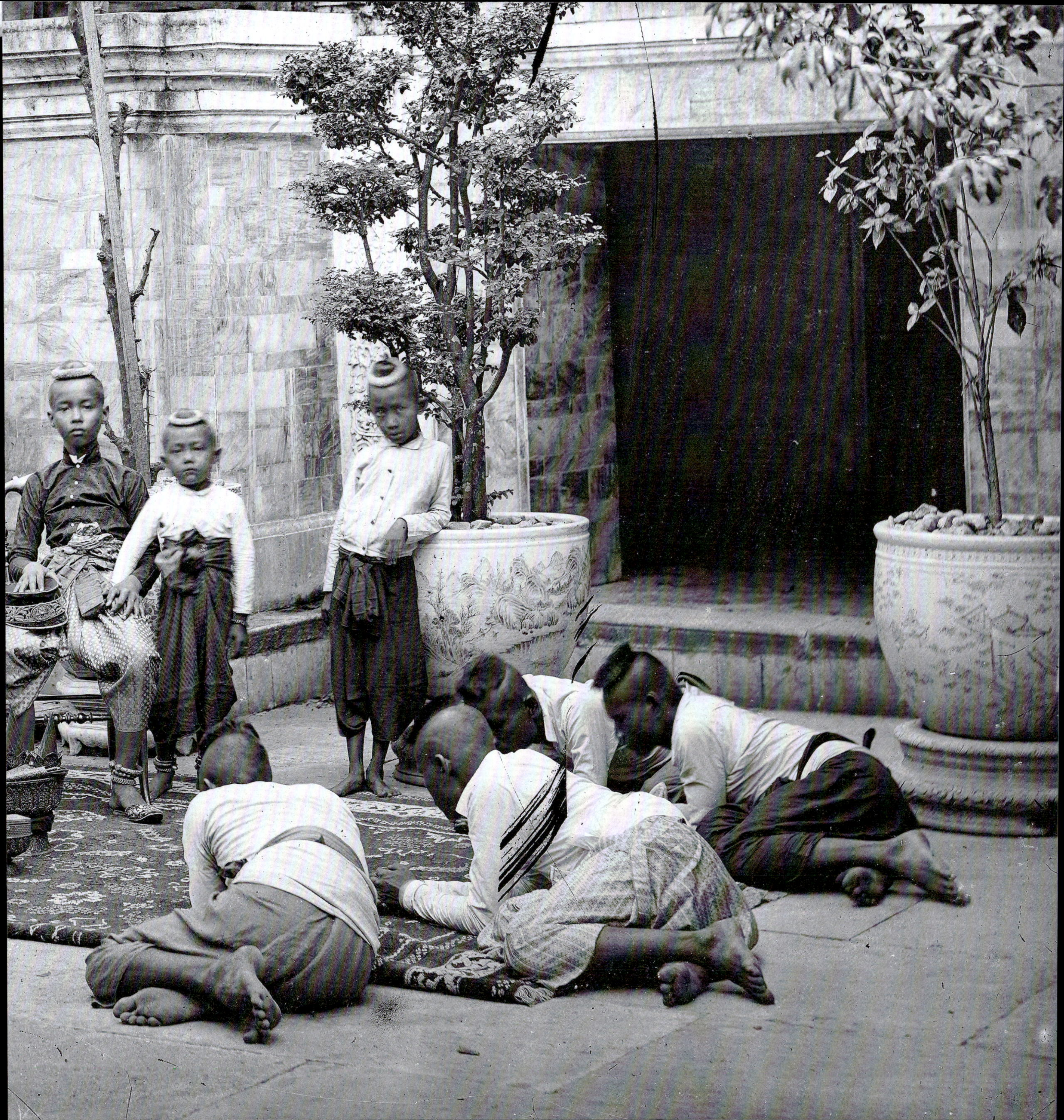

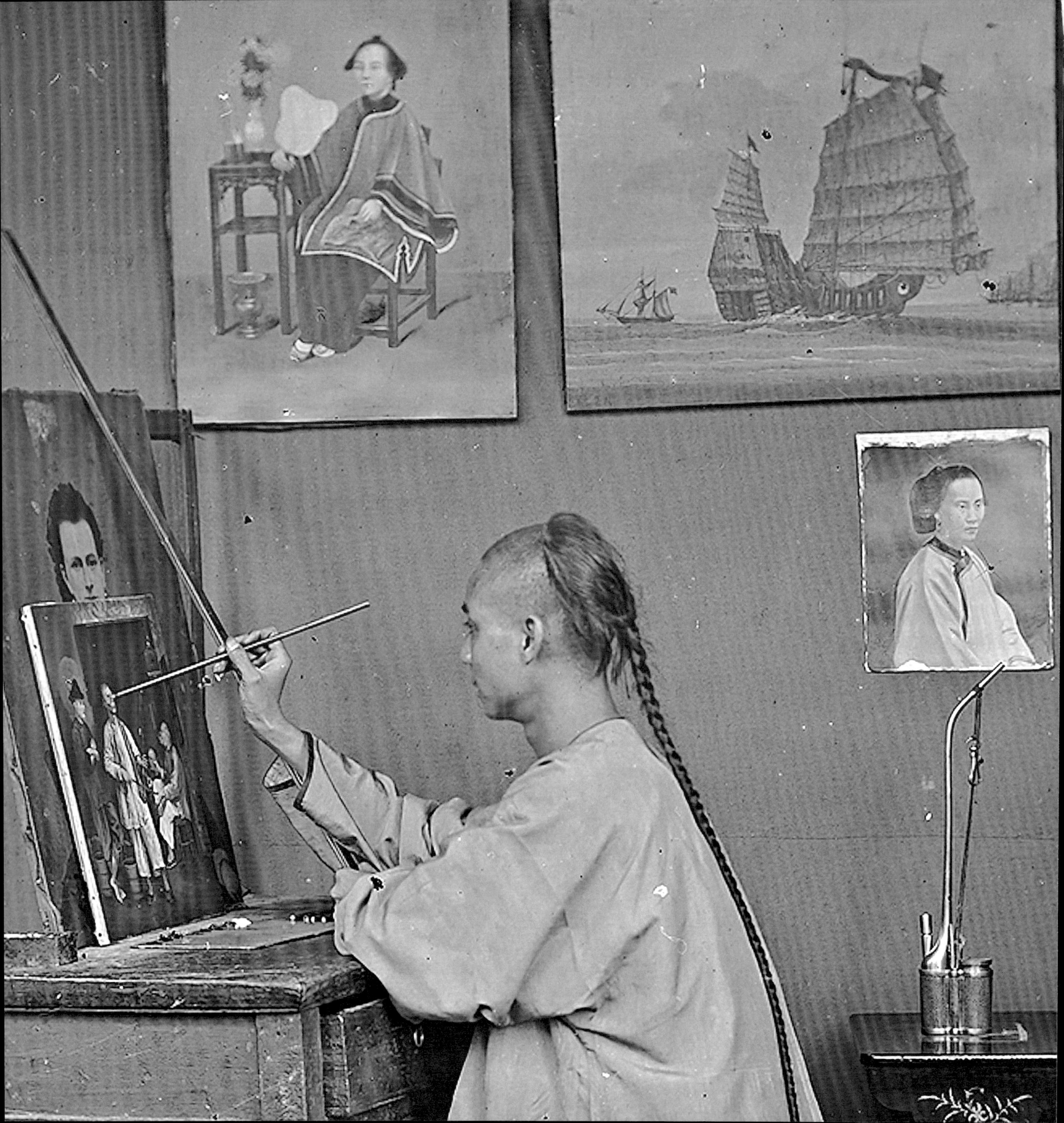